PERFORMING TRAUMA
IN CENTRAL AFRICA

AFRICAN EXPRESSIVE CULTURES
Patrick McNaughton, *editor*

Associate editors
Catherine M. Cole
Barbara G. Hoffman
Eileen Julien
Kassim Koné
D. A. Masolo
Elisha Renne
Z. S. Strother

PERFORMING TRAUMA IN CENTRAL AFRICA

Shadows of Empire

Laura Edmondson

INDIANA UNIVERSITY PRESS

This book is a publication of

Indiana University Press
Office of Scholarly Publishing
Herman B Wells Library 350
1320 East 10th Street
Bloomington, Indiana 47405 USA

iupress.indiana.edu

© 2018 by Laura Edmondson

All rights reserved

No part of this book may be reproduced or utilized in any form or by any means, electronic or mechanical, including photocopying and recording, or by any information storage and retrieval system, without permission in writing from the publisher. The Association of American University Presses' Resolution on Permissions constitutes the only exception to this prohibition.

The paper used in this publication meets the minimum requirements of the American National Standard for Information Sciences—Permanence of Paper for Printed Library Materials, ANSI Z39.48-1992.

Manufactured in the United States of America

Library of Congress Cataloging-in-Publication Data

Names: Edmondson, Laura, 1970– author.
Title: Performing trauma in Central Africa : shadows of empire / Laura Edmondson.
Description: Bloomington : Indiana University Press, 2018. | Series: African expressive cultures | Includes bibliographical references and index.
Identifiers: LCCN 2017050084 (print) | LCCN 2017050627 (ebook) | ISBN 9780253032461 (Ebook) | ISBN 9780253032454 (hardback : alk. paper) | ISBN 9780253032478 (pbk. : alk. paper)
Subjects: LCSH: War and theater—Great Lakes Region (Africa) | Performing Arts—Social aspects—Great Lakes Region (Africa) | Atrocities—Social Aspects—Great Lakes Region (Africa)
Classification: LCC PN2041.W37 (ebook) | LCC PN2041.W37 E36 2018 (print) | DDC 306.4840967—dc23
LC record available at https://lccn.loc.gov/2017050084

1 2 3 4 5   23 22 21 20 19 18

To Johari and Amina

Contents

	Acknowledgments	*ix*
	List of Abbreviations	*xiii*
	Introduction	*1*
1	Competitive Memory in the Great Lakes: Touring Genocide	*35*
2	Marketing Trauma and the Theatre of War in Northern Uganda	*79*
3	Trauma, Inc. in Postgenocide Rwanda	*111*
4	Repetition, Rupture, and *Ruined*: Narratives from the Congo	*161*
5	Gifted by Trauma: The Branding of Postconflict Northern Uganda	*217*
6	Confessions of a Failed Theatre Activist	*269*
	Afterword: Faustin Linyekula and the Labors of Hope	*297*
	References	*309*
	Index	*339*
	About the Author	*349*

Acknowledgments

To write these acknowledgments is to fail. I cannot possibly thank all the countless people who have encouraged and assisted me in the writing of this book, given that it has been in the making for over a decade and spans research in Uganda, Rwanda, the United Kingdom, and the United States. What makes this inability harder to bear is that these encounters are at the core of why I do this research; the making of meaning within and among artistic and academic communities is one of life's gifts. I have turned to the work of J. Halberstam for alternative understandings of failure as a source of political creativity and challenge only to realize that in this case, theory would serve as a shield for my shortcomings. Here the failure of omission speaks of erasure rather than transgression. And so I open with an apology and the hope that I might later remember and restore.

The hospitality I received in Uganda makes this task especially daunting. I acknowledge my colleagues and students at the Department of Literature in Makerere University, whose work serves as a keen reminder of why the humanities in African studies matter. I owe special thanks to the tireless Susan Kiguli for her efforts to help me feel welcome and settled. Nelson Abiti, Deborah Asiimwe GKashugi, Sunday Komakech, Laurence Ocen, and Okweny George Ongom have been instrumental in shaping my thinking about the performance of trauma; I am especially grateful to Laurence and Nelson for their invaluable feedback on chapter 5. Okello Kelo Sam has been a presence in my research from the beginning; his creative and intellectual energy infuses this project. A heartfelt *apwoyo matek* for everything he has done for me and for my family. Thanks to the Ambersoli International School community for providing a place for Johari and Amina to thrive, and my gratitude to the families who welcomed them into their homes. To Anneke Fermont and Nicci Martin, I look forward to the day when we might return at least some of the extraordinary generosity that you have shown us. Thanks to Ismene Zarifis (and Shaka, of course) for being fantastic neighbors and to Janet and Ed Black for their support. My gratitude to the staff at the US embassy, particularly Dorothy Ngalombi, for facilitating the logistics of our stay. *Webale nyo.*

Several Rwandans are key members of the transnational village that informs this book. Our visits to Kigali were consistently rewarding thanks to the unfailing generosity of Hope Azeda; Hope, you and your family are a bright spot in our lives. I am only sorry that I was not able to give your artistic work the attention it fully deserves, but I hope to rectify this in the next book. The same to Odile "Kiki" Gatese, whose Book of Life project serves as a beacon for Great Lakes performance; thanks for your willingness and openness to discuss and share your work and ideas. *Murakoze* to Simon Rwema and Angel Uwamahoro for their invaluable assistance during a fast and furious research visit in 2015, to Jean-Pierre Karegeye and the hard-working Interdisciplinary Genocide Studies Centre staff for facilitating a transformative glimpse into postgenocide Rwanda through the "More Life" initiative in which I participated in 2007 and 2011, and, of course, to Erik Ehn for living the praxis of radical hospitality.

Shifting briefly to the United Kingdom, thanks to Thea Armfield for showing Johari and Amina the sights of Oxford while I buried myself in slides at the Bodleian Library. The fabulous librarians at Oxford, Anti-Slavery International, and Lambeth Palace were unfailingly patient and cheerful, and my understanding of the iconography of the Congo Free State benefited greatly from their help.

Generous financial support was provided by the Fulbright Program, the Leslie Center for the Humanities at Dartmouth College, the Arts and Humanities Program Enhancement Program at Florida State University, and the Joan Sloane Dickey Center for International Understanding at Dartmouth College. Thanks also to the Dickey Center for sponsoring my manuscript review, and to Francine A'ness, Catherine Cole, Nelson Kasfir, Eng-Beng Lim, Irma Mayorga, Catharine Newbury, Naaborko Sackeyfio, and Chris Wohlforth for their incisive yet encouraging feedback. A heartfelt thanks to David Newbury for his razor-sharp attention to chapter 1, although the usual caveat that any mistakes are my own cannot be emphasized enough in this instance. Thanks also to my dean, Barbara Will, for financial support regarding publication costs, as well as her warm encouragement as I made the transition to department chair. I wish to acknowledge the American Society for Theatre Research, which not only provided funding through the Targeted Areas Research Support Grant and the Brooks McNamara Publishing Subvention Grant but also a sense of intellectual community; I am thinking particularly of the participants in the Performance Studies in/from the Global South sessions, who remind me that transnationalism is not only a methodology but also an ethical way of seeing the world. I have also benefited from the thoughtful feedback and encouragement of John Fletcher, Loren Kruger, Sonja Kuftinec, Ana Puga, and Analola Santana; special thanks to Patrick Anderson and Ananda Breed for pushing me to greater clarity and depth. My sincere gratitude to Dee Mortensen and Paige Rasmussen at Indiana University Press; their gentle guidance and ready feedback as I slogged my way through various versions of the manuscript were instrumental to its completion. Charles Eberline's meticulous copyediting helped to bring the writing process to a satisfying finish; thanks also to Martin Lubikowski for contributing such an elegant and informative map.

Earlier versions of chapter 2 and chapter 6 have been previously published. "Marketing Trauma and the Theatre of War in Northern Uganda" appeared in *Theatre Journal* 57 (3): 2005, 451–474; "Confessions of a Failed Theatre Activist" was included in *Avant-Garde Performance and Material Exchange: Vectors of the Radical*, edited by Mike Sell, 41–59 (Houndmills, UK: Palgrave Macmillan, 2011).

Here in New Hampshire, I am blessed with the opportunity to work in a top-notch theatre department with faculty and staff who are gifted, dedicated, and wonderfully supportive; I can't imagine a better place to teach. Beyond the department, I benefit from a cohort of scholars across the humanities and social sciences whom I am proud to consider colleagues; a special mention to those in African and African-American Studies for providing a sense of intellectual community. To my students over the years who have taken Human Rights and Performance, and to all my theatre students who resist the pressures of convention to do what you love: you serve as an essential reminder of the creative power of the performing arts—more so than ever as I write this, in the aftermath of the 2016 election. Thanks to Nana Adjeiwaa-Manu and Haley Gordon for checking and standardizing an endless number of citations and footnotes. You were ideal research assistants thanks to your eagle eye for detail, and I appreciated your independence and initiative.

Friends keep my world in motion. In addition to several others previously named, Mary Coffey, Patricia Herrera, Carrie Sandahl, and Victoria Somoff deserve mention as emotional lifelines. To Jim Igoe and Gladness Msumanje: I continue to miss you. Hanover seems less like home, ever since you left. Jean and Brian Graham-Jones have served as consummate theatre-going companions during my various sojourns in New York City, offering incisive commentary on everything ranging from Eve Ensler to Faustin Linyekula. I also wish to acknowledge Jean's role in encouraging and guiding the original version of the essay "Marketing Trauma" that would serve to galvanize this book; her belief in its potential kept me going during a difficult period in my professional life, and I continue to be grateful.

Thanks to Robert Ajwang for so much, despite what happened. Jane, Evance, Anna, Sunday, Johnson, Samwel: *erokamano*. Your support has meant more than you can imagine.

Saying "thank you" in all the languages of East Africa cannot begin to address the depth of my gratitude to my family. To my parents, Barbara and Ben Edmondson, who have always, always, supported me: your love sustains me and keeps me strong. JB, Melissa, JR, and Caroline: thanks for the love, laughter, and gag gifts. You enrich my definition of home.

Johari and Amina have logged far more hours of fieldwork with me than any of us care to remember; they bore it, for the most part, with good humor. Over the years, they have endured exhausting travel, the most forgetful tooth fairy on the planet, and more than their fair share of loss. I think of you playing in the Gisozi memorial garden at the ages of four and seven, preparing imaginary meals on banana leaves while I ducked in and out of the museum, seeking to shield you from the terrible things that happen in this world. I have failed you, too often. My failure and my love are intertwined. It is my offering to you.

Abbreviations

ADF   Allied Democratic Forces. An insurgency movement against the Ugandan government that is currently based in North Kivu Province of the DRC.

AFDL   French initialism for the Alliance of Democratic Forces for the Liberation of Congo-Zaire, a rebellion against Mobutu Sese Seko's government that was headed by Laurent Kabila and orchestrated and supported by Uganda and Rwanda. It was instrumental in inciting the First Congo War.

CAR   Central African Republic.

CNDP   French initialism for the National Congress for the Defense of the People. Insurgency that began in 2006 against the DRC government; a forerunner of M23.

CWB   Clowns Without Borders.

DRC   Democratic Republic of the Congo (formerly Zaire, the Belgian Congo, and the Congo Free State).

FAR   Forces Armeés Rwandaises (the Rwandan armed forces before 1994).

FARDC   French initialism for the Armed Forces for the Democratic Republic of the Congo, the government army of the DRC.

FDLR   French initialism for the Democratic Forces for the Liberation of Rwanda, a rebel group against the Rwandan government that is primarily active in the eastern DRC.

ICC	International Criminal Court, based in The Hague.
IDP	Internally displaced people.
LRA	Lord's Resistance Army. An insurgency movement against Yoweri Museveni's government that emerged in the late 1980s. Previously based in northern Uganda and the former southern Sudan; remnants of the LRA are now believed to operate in the northeastern DRC, the southwestern CAR, and South Sudan.
M23	An insurgency formed in 2012 against the DRC government and based in the eastern DRC. Named after March 23, 2009, when the CNDP (a forerunner of M23) signed a peace agreement with the DRC government. M23 surrendered in late 2013.
MDD	Music, dance, and drama. Commonly used in Uganda to refer to the performing arts.
NGO	Nongovernmental organization. A broad term that includes both local, grassroots organizations and powerful international ones, all of which seek to provide a range of social and humanitarian services.
NRM/A	National Resistance Movement/Army. Museveni's guerrilla movement that fought against Milton Obote's second regime during the "Bush War" of 1981–1986. Currently the ruling political party of Uganda. NRA refers to the military wing of the NRM (see also UNLA and UPDF).
RCD	Rally for Congolese Democracy. A rebellion group formed in 1998 to fight against Kabila's government; orchestrated by Rwanda and Uganda. Its formation triggered the Second Congo War.
RPF	Rwandan Patriotic Front. Originally an insurgency group that invaded Rwanda from Uganda in 1990; currently the ruling political party of Rwanda under President Paul Kagame.
UNAMIR	The United Nations Assistance Mission for Rwanda, established in 1993 as a peacekeeping force in Rwanda, commanded by General Roméo Dallaire.
UNLA	Uganda National Liberation Army. Obote's government army that fought against Museveni's NRA in the Bush War of 1981–1986.

| UPDA | Uganda People's Democratic Army, an insurgency formed in 1986 from remnants of Obote's army, the UNLA. |
| UPDF | Uganda People's Defence Force, formerly the NRA. The Ugandan military since 1995. |

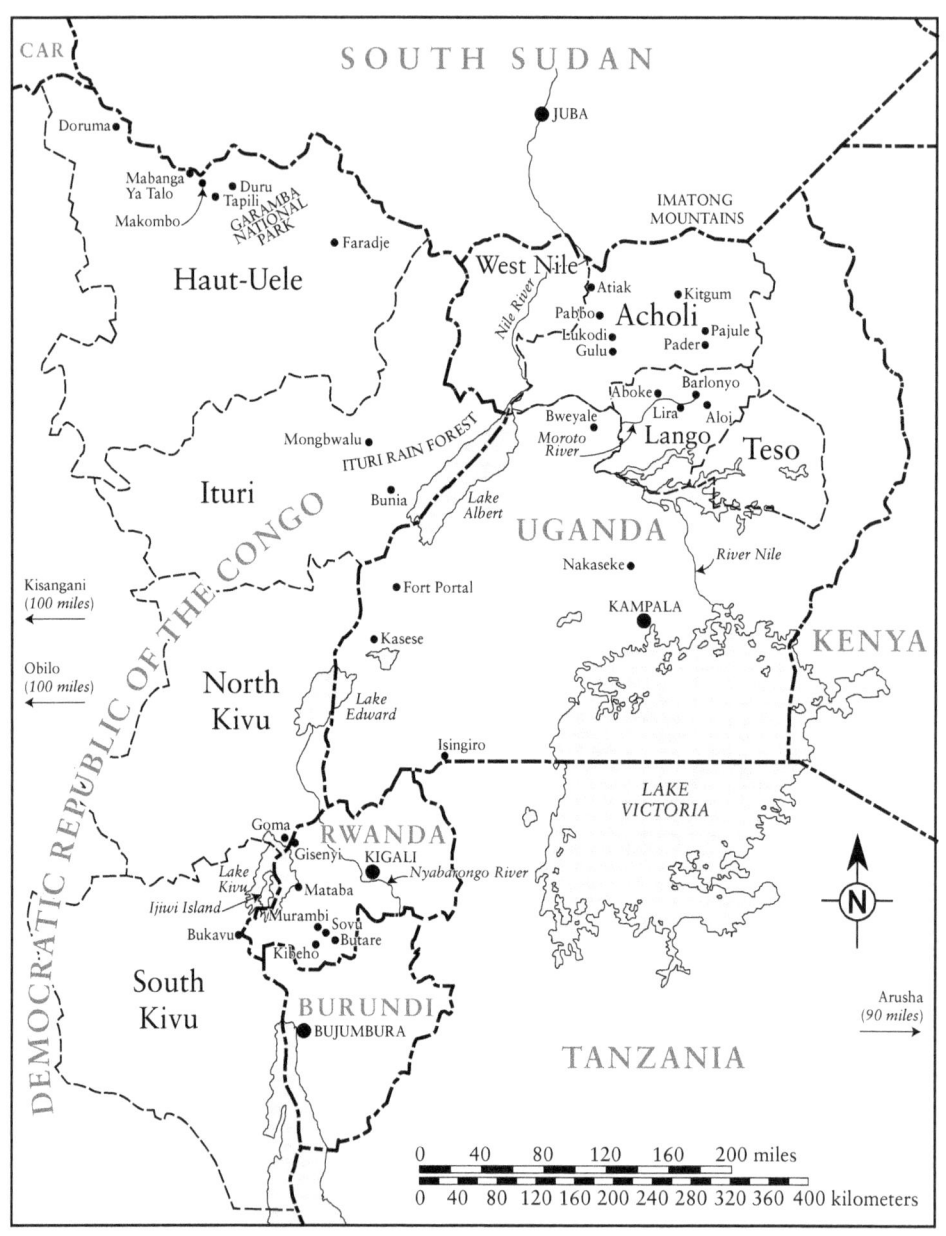

Map. The terrain of *Performing Trauma in Central Africa*.

PERFORMING TRAUMA
IN CENTRAL AFRICA

INTRODUCTION

"How do you measure loss, or pain or trauma? Can you quantify pain? Can you quantify a crisis?" This question appears in *Forgotten World*, a play by Ugandan writer Deborah Asiimwe that explores a surreal world populated with the ghosts of child soldiers.[1] Although this experimental play often transcends geographic context, its primary setting is northern Uganda, where the Lord's Resistance Army (LRA) conscripted several thousand children during a twenty-year conflict.[2] Beyond the painful question of how we convey to others the experience of mass violence, Asiimwe's play explores the complicity of the international community in the commodification of trauma. At the heart of the play is the Photographer, who auctions photographs of traumatized children across the globe to various media conglomerates ranging from Al Jazeera to Fox News. The spirits of six former child soldiers increasingly haunt the Photographer, shattering her complacency as they insist on enacting their experiences of violence through a series of twisted games. She becomes fascinated by their games and narratives to the extent that they colonize her thoughts. She confides to the audience, "The real exhibition is always inside my head.... That is where they play their games."[3] Despite the emotional and cognitive impact of the children, she ultimately fails to overcome her impulse to document their suffering and holds an auction of the photographs: "Four ... five ... six hundred thousand.... I will sit with you at dinner.... This is great.... Two minutes left and we are out of here!"[4] The cynical denouement underscores the relentless cycle of commodification, objectification, and the othering of pain.

2 | Performing Trauma in Central Africa

Fig. 1. Production of *Forgotten World* by Deborah Asiimwe, 2009. Photo by Steven A. Gunther. Courtesy of CalArts.

Forgotten World confronts the economies of war that feed on trauma. "Chaos and crisis are to some their daily bread," the Photographer is cautioned in a reminder of the profitability of war, a business in which she is thoroughly complicit insofar as her livelihood depends on the sale of her photographs.[5] A slide show of images with the "hottest sales" clarifies these dynamics as the Photographer presents her series of portraits of notorious recruiters of child soldiers across the African continent: Charles Taylor of Sierra Leone, Jonas Savimbi of Angola, and, of course, Joseph Kony, the founder and leader of the LRA.[6] With each slide, she enumerates their violent acts, such as physical mutilation of civilians and the abduction of children, with the implication that the scale of violence increases the auction value of these images on the trauma market. The enterprise of humanitarianism also comes under fire when the Photographer mixes up the orderly narrative through which the children are expected to progress: "Lives will be transformed ... rehabilitated ... reintegrated! That's not the order.... Rehabilitated, Transformed, Reintegrated! That is right!"[7] The simplistic slogans of these organizations, which foretell the triumph of humanitarian intervention through the production of newly functioning members of society, adds another layer of complicity in the marketing of war. To return to the original question, pain and suffering can indeed be quantified by the market's peculiar wisdom.

Forgotten World focuses less on the actual event of mass trauma than on its commodification. Marx's expansive definition of commodity as "a thing which through its qualities satisfies human needs of whatever kind" accommodates the recasting of trauma as a thing to be appropriated and consumed.[8] The auctioning of the photographs in *Forgotten World* literalizes and thus demystifies the process in which the multifaceted impact of sustained violence on Ugandan bodies is objectified and bartered in the affect economies of the present media-saturated age. The commodification of African trauma entails a brutal domestication of unspeakable acts into reassuring stereotypes of distant suffering, in which the consumer's precious fiction of safety and security is affirmed. As the Photographer muses, "These tragic stories . . . these photographs. Very sad and very . . . very . . . hm . . . *appealing*."[9] In the world of the play, both narratives and images are used in the marketability of pain. Death becomes circumscribed and contained in an urge to satisfy one of the more peculiar human needs of whatever kind.

Forgotten World asks pointed questions about these acts of consumption. The play opens and concludes with a cocktail party in which the audience is invited onto the stage to view photographs of the children. Spectators are served drinks as they peruse images of African suffering; meanwhile, a recorded voice reminds them that the "exits are well marked" in case of an emergency.[10] Should the veneer of what Susan Sontag calls the "luxury of patronizing reality" begin to crack and the ordinariness of crisis be exposed, the spectators can blithely resume their lives of carefully cultivated and forcefully maintained ignorance.[11] This staging device not only gestures to the predictability of commodification but also unmasks the geopolitical privilege of western desiring subjects.

Ugandan child soldiers step in as the thing to be desired. These children occupy a starring role on the trauma stage in the United States, in no small part because of the efforts of the organization Invisible Children, whose 2004 documentary *Invisible Children: Rough Cut* brought the LRA crisis to the attention of high-school and university students. Invisible Children's sensational footage of the atrocities committed by the LRA, coupled with soothing affirmations of how US privileged youth can help bring the LRA leaders to justice, galvanized and sustained what Teju Cole has termed the "white savior industrial complex."[12] Even as the LRA retreated from northern Uganda in 2006 and the region stabilized, Ugandan child soldiers increasingly appeared in a range of mass-media forms, ranging from a music video for Fall Out Boy's 2007 hit single "I'm like a Lawyer" to a 2009 episode of *Law and Order: Special Victims Unit*.[13] Fascination with the LRA peaked with Invisible Children's release of *Kony 2012*, which raised US$5 million within forty-eight hours. Very, hm, appealing.

I was also susceptible to this appeal. In the mid-1990s, I read about the LRA's abductions in northern Uganda while I was conducting fieldwork in Tanzania. Even though I was shocked by the alarming statistics of mass killing and abductions reported in the Swahili press, I also recall how distant I felt from these events despite Uganda's geographic and political proximity. Tanzanians with whom I discussed the LRA, generally speaking, were able to fold these stories into an affirmation of Tanzania's much-vaunted national stability that stood in contrast to Uganda's fractured and violent postcolonial past. These sensational narratives—as well as their appropriation—stayed with me when I returned to the United States, and in 2004 I visited Gulu to learn how the arts served as a tool for healing and forgiveness in the context of rehabilitation. As I prepared for this visit, I came across Carolyn Nordstrom's stirring call in her landmark study of the Mozambican civil war, *A Different Kind of War Story*, in which she writes, "It is in creativity, in the fashioning of self and world, that people find their most potent weapon against war."[14] Even though I was well schooled in the dynamics of appropriation and counterappropriation in the context of Tanzanian performance, I vividly recall my eagerness to learn how theatre in northern Uganda served as a forum for the articulation of human rights and the rebuilding of self and world. For some mysterious reason—perhaps I had succumbed to the western tendency to romanticize violence as a spark for creativity—I anticipated a rich variety of case studies in which aesthetic experimentation served as a gateway for processing the trauma of war. I explain this background in order to emphasize that I am susceptible to the very forces I have chosen to study. The processes of commodification and the othering of pain are too pervasive, I suspect, for any of us—and I do mean a capacious us—to be immune.

My experiences in Gulu served as the springboard for this book. Although I encountered vivid demonstrations of creativity and resilience in northern Uganda, I also came to realize the stakes of artistic expression in a time of war and the eagerness of humanitarian nongovernmental organizations (NGOs) and the state to appropriate and manipulate these expressions. The year in which I visited Gulu marked the ten-year anniversary of the 1994 Rwandan genocide, an occasion commemorated with an explosion of performance texts and films. Three years later, in 2007, US playwright and activist Eve Ensler launched a mass humanitarian campaign against the "femicide" in the eastern Democratic Republic of the Congo (DRC). As my research expanded, I found that I could more fully understand images and narratives related to these events in Uganda, Rwanda, and the DRC through exploring their connective tissue. Although governments and humanitarian NGOs use these horrors to compete with one another for international attention, the events themselves are linked through a dense regional history of colonial and postcolonial violence, transnational technologies of war, and the praxis of global humanitarianism. In focusing on cultural productions that respond to the LRA conflict, the Rwandan genocide, and the continuing violence in the DRC, I can explore not only the commodification of violence but also why certain kinds of violence are commodified—that is, which ones are deemed to satisfy human needs.

But instead of human needs, I write of empire. I repeatedly encountered a stubborn, homogenizing force that I have come to think of as an "empire of trauma," a global shadow that has infiltrated creative capacities and the interior of memory.[15] A curious predictability insistently cuts across representations of violence in and from the Great Lakes region.[16] The Congolese crisis is perceived through the lens of sexual violence, Rwanda is equated with the 1994 genocide, and northern Uganda is understood in terms of abducted children. One might argue that these singular emphases speak to certain realities and statistics: the 66,000 children abducted by the LRA, the 800,000 Rwandans killed in less than three months in 1994, and the forty-eight Congolese women raped every hour in the DRC.[17] But as I will explain in the following chapters, these statistics are regularly invoked as evidence for master narratives and thus tend to cloud more than they clarify. Rey Chow uses the term "repeatable visibilities" to describe the artificiality and potency of representations as commodities; I found that the tropes coming out of East and Central Africa were repeatable to the point of banality.[18] Empire insists on consistent and simplistic narratives with clear-cut definitions of victim and perpetrator, sweeping aside nuance and complexity in its single-minded quest for spectacles and narratives of suffering. Empire hungers for suffering northern Ugandans, Tutsi victims, and raped Congolese women. These repeatable visibilities are the sustenance on which it feeds.

I borrow the phrase "empire of trauma" from Didier Fassin and Richard Rechtman's *The Empire of Trauma: An Inquiry into the Condition of Victimhood*. Fassin and Rechtman trace how trauma was granted legitimate and moral status in which being defined as a victim entails access to rights and compensation. They explain, "Trauma is not simply the cause of the suffering that is being treated, it is also a resource that can be used to support a right."[19] In the second half of the twentieth century, as international humanitarian organizations sought to heal traumatized populations in the aftermath of catastrophe and war, the gathering of testimony—that is, the narration of trauma—served as a useful justification for these organizations in light of their limited ability to provide material aid. Although Fassin and Rechtman do not theorize their use of the term empire as a rubric for the processes of legitimation and politicization of trauma that occurred during the twentieth century, they acknowledge the ways in which "trauma contributes to constructing new forms of political subjectification and new relations with the contemporary world," thus opening the door for a closer analysis of these dynamics.[20] In coining the phrase "empire of trauma," they hint at the ways in which trauma, humanitarianism, and sovereignty intersect.

Performing Trauma in Central Africa explores performance in the Great Lakes region through the lens of an empire of trauma. This lens speaks powerfully to the politics of representation in Uganda, Rwanda, and the DRC, where victim narratives are often perceived as a point of access to international recognition, as well as the material resources of humanitarian aid. To theorize an empire of trauma is to attend to the ways in which cultural workers maintain and manipulate these narratives as a means of attracting the gaze of empire, and how empire consumes and appropriates these narratives. Fassin and Rechtman write that trauma "excites sympathy and merits compensation," a phrase that speaks to the intersection of emotional appeal and economic incentives.[21] For Central Africans located on the margins of global economies, trauma is not only a cause of suffering but is also perceived as a ticket to access empire's wealth. As John and Jean Comaroff might put it, trauma serves as a useful commodity "for those with no work and little to sell."[22] The processes of commodification ensure that cultural expressions perpetuate the quantification of pain.

The lens of empire also sheds light on the shifting terrain of sovereignty in Central Africa. In theorizing the contours of a humanitarian empire that permeates and even supersedes the state, scholars have coined various terms including "post-postcolonialism," "therapeutic sovereignty," "the global morality market," "traumatic citizenship," "a colonialism of compassion" and "charitable imperialism."[23] These studies underscore the arbitrariness of how humanitarian administrations define victimhood and how these definitions overlap with determinations of citizenship in their quest to alleviate suffering.[24] In her studies of humanitarian interventions in the Balkans, Mariella Pandolfi often invokes Arjun Appadurai's notion of "mobile sovereignty" to describe the transnational reach of humanitarian NGOs and military interventions that exists alongside local structures of governance.[25] Even celebrities such as Bono and Angelina Jolie are implicated in these networks of transnational dominance. In their scathing indictment of celebrity activism in Africa, Lisa Ann Richey and Stefano Ponte describe these activists as "emotional sovereigns" and the "lubricant" for a political-economic formation in which "consumption becomes the mechanism for compassion."[26] The concept of an empire of trauma highlights the role of humanitarian affect in the processes of imperial sovereignty. Empire does not only want to rule the world—it wants to experience warm fuzzies while doing so.[27]

Empire cries. A lot. This book is, in part, a response to the many crying foreigners I saw during my travels in Uganda and Rwanda. They sobbed while visiting memorial sites of the 1994 Rwandan genocide; they wept when listening to testimonies of former child soldiers of the LRA in northern Uganda. They cried in response to the warm welcomes and the bright smiles of Rwandan orphans; they wailed about the extreme poverty in northern Uganda. Although young white women predominated in this public, overt shedding of tears in response to East African structural and episodic violence, these displays often transcended the boundaries of race, sex, and age. What these foreigners held in common was economic and geopolitical privilege, signified by their ability to travel to far corners of the globe out of curiosity and interest rather than flight from limited economic opportunities or political upheaval. They were united in a collective sense of earnestness that brought them to Central Africa in the first place. They were open, naïve, and painfully eager to help. They were playwrights, filmmakers, students, professors. They were minions of empire.

Sentimentality has long been marshaled in the cause of empire. In the early 1700s, a new dramatic genre called sentimental comedy emerged in England, in which praise of virtue was emphasized over ridicule of vice. Open sobbing over the plight of these virtuous characters was perceived as a mark of morality and good character; this new kind of drama was often called "weeping comedy," as if to underscore the performative nature of audience reception.[28] Analogously, one's tears in response to genocide and mass trauma in Central Africa could be a reassuring gesture that one's sense of moral outrage is alive and kicking; that is, the sobbing self is a good self. But as Lynn Festa persuasively argues, eighteenth-century sentimental literature dovetailed with the expansion of a European empire; these texts, which helped "to define who will be acknowledged as human" in the course of imperial expansion, worked to convert the violence of conquest into expressions of benevolence.[29] Festa's analysis invites comparison with twenty-first century trauma tourism. These visitors' willingness to seek out memorials and listen to victim testimonies operates in what Jennifer Hyndman calls "the colonialism of compassion," that is, a kind of affect that ultimately sugarcoats the violence of neoliberalism and neocolonialism.[30] The sobbing self is also an imperial self.

Sovereignty and humanitarianism intersect in an empire of trauma. These weeping foreigners serve as an omnipresent audience for cultural production and creative expression throughout postconflict and conflict regions in Uganda, Rwanda, and the DRC. Ponte and Richey's concept of emotional sovereignty helps clarify my approach to trauma, which I interpret less as a tool of empire than as a lubricant for the cogs of global sovereignty. Certainly the role of trauma in the machinery of global capital has been theorized elsewhere; Naomi Klein, for example, has famously argued that neoliberal systems appropriate or even provoke catastrophic events in order to implement market reform among vulnerable populations and thus encroach on their resources.[31] Although I (and, I dare say, many of the Central Africans mentioned in this book) would agree that state and world orders are keenly aware of the usefulness of episodic violence as a means of keeping populations of the global south in check, this book takes a different slant.[32] It focuses on the summoning of African trauma as a means to satiate and soothe the appetites of empire. Empire demands spectacles of trauma to assuage its fear regarding its own precarity and fragility in an increasingly unstable world order. During a time when "the north appears to be 'evolving' southward," leaving many western citizens to "face the insecurities and instabilities, even the forced mobility and disposability, characteristic of life in much of the non-West," Uganda, Rwanda, and the DRC serve as the ultimate others against which the west can collectively define itself and be reassured of internal solvency.[33] In theorizing the lure of violence, Slavoj Žižek suggests that "there is something inherently mystifying in a direct confrontation with [violence]: the overpowering horror of violent acts and empathy with the victims inexorably function as a lure which prevents us from thinking."[34] Drawing on Žižek, we might interpret the emotional outpouring over the plight of northern Ugandan children or eastern Congolese women as useful distractions from pointed questions and deeper understandings of global politics.[35] African trauma is packaged to obscure rather than to illuminate empire's complicity in a world order that sustains mass death and systemic violence.

My emphasis on the summoning and narrating of trauma makes me wary of defining it. The "thing" that is commodified might bear only a passing resemblance to the actual psychic or physical wound that triggered immediate and long-term suffering on individual and collective levels. Fassin and Rechtman again prove helpful by describing trauma as a signifier to help explain its capaciousness: "Today we talk of rape and genocide, of torture and slavery, of terrorist attacks and natural disasters in the same language, both clinical and metaphorical, of trauma: one signifier for a plurality of ills signified."[36] The reduction of heterogeneity facilitates the erasure of cultural specificities regarding the perception, processing, and narration of trauma. Although this book does periodically address Central African perceptions of trauma, as in chapter 2, when I touch on the investment in realism in northern Uganda that exceeds the imperial gaze, the cultural nuances of trauma are not my focus.[37] Instead, I emphasize the dynamics of consumption and the packaging of suffering that the trauma limelight has deemed appropriate for international visibility and attention. The signifier trumps specificity and nuance.

This is not the book I wanted to write. Empire insinuates itself into a range of public forums discussed in this book, from global forms such as NGO media campaigns to grassroots expressions such as indigenous dance. Like the children's macabre games in *Forgotten World*, these cultural productions might be understood as attempts to attract empire's attention rather than as manifestations of cultural resilience. This book sidesteps conventional understandings of African performance, which is often viewed as a kind of "fun space" or as "flights of imagination" operating outside the constraints of global capitalism; alternatively, it is theorized as a site of resilience or resistance that maintains a sense of cultural autonomy despite economic and political oppression.[38] Theatre, which looms large in this book as a form of creative expression, often receives special mention in African studies because of its potential to script emancipatory or critical narratives in a public forum.³⁹ Although I remain deeply invested in theatre's creative and imaginative capacity, particularly in light of the brilliance and dedication of many Central African artists, the case studies explored in this book insist upon a multilayered understanding of performance.⁴⁰ Although optimistic interpretations periodically surface—see, for example, my analysis of dance in northern Uganda in chapter 2, as well as my discussion of Faustin Linyekula in the afterword—these alternative readings operate alongside rather than in tension with articulations of empire. Performance is widely seized on as a means of accessing the empire of trauma and thus highlights the "ambiguities, opacities and uncertainties of postcolonial visibilities."⁴¹ In his well-known critique of globalization theory, James Ferguson argues that "as the contemporary African material shows so vividly, the 'global' does not 'flow,' thereby connecting . . . contiguous spaces; it hops instead, efficiently connecting the enclaved points in the network while excluding (with equal efficiency) the spaces that lie between the points."⁴² The vast majority of Ugandan, Rwandan, and Congolese people inhabit the in-between spaces; to perform the "right" kind of trauma in the "right" kind of way might open up access to the enclaved points themselves.

In tracking these points, this book does considerable hopping. Although the creative expressions of Central Africans take center stage in this analysis, I also address interventionist and activist efforts of westerners in order to clarify the investment and reach of empire. This analysis draws on fieldwork and textual analysis, as well as my participation in a series of intercultural encounters and collaborations with theatre artists from these countries who have sought an ethical response to war and genocide. Through a careful contextualization of these texts and encounters in the fraught political landscape of the Great Lakes region, this book calls for new understandings of the role of creative expression, cultural agency, and activism in a landscape of conflict, post-conflict, and structural violence. Emotional sovereigns are not limited to megastars like Bono but also include the earnest college student making her way to Uganda and Rwanda to try to make a difference. And the US-based theatre scholar is not necessarily impervious to empire's charms. I cried, too.

Slouching toward Empire

Theorizing empire in a postcolonial African context raises academic hackles, not least because the term calls to mind Michael Hardt and Antonio Negri's controversial manifesto *Empire*. Hardt and Negri posit a new world order in which diffuse multinational and supranational institutions have effaced previously cohesive and legitimized states.[43] They argue that unlike traditional imperial forms that relied on classical notions of territorial sovereignty, as in the instance of the European colonization of Africa in the late nineteenth century, Empire with a capital E "is a *decentered* and *deterritorializing* apparatus of rule that progressively incorporates the entire global realm within its open, expanding frontiers."[44] Borrowing extensively from Giles Deleuze and Félix Guattari's concepts of horizontal and rhizomatic modes of power, Hardt and Negri characterize millennial forms of power as lines of flight, that is, as a deterritorializing rather than a stratifying force.[45] Instead of manifesting itself through boundaries and binaries, global hegemony exerts itself through permeation and infiltration, breaking down distinctions between inside and outside, public and private.

Hardt and Negri's concept of Empire has minimal relevance in a continent where state sovereignty has often been cobbled together through a complex system of neopatrimony, foreign aid, and authoritarian tactics. Central African contexts include a variety of state survival strategies that make a mockery of Hardt and Negri's notion of a smooth global space with all-encompassing reach. President Yoweri Museveni of Uganda, for example, generally tolerates a relatively robust Ugandan press but is quick to crack down on protests and rallies organized by the political opposition. President Paul Kagame of Rwanda has sharply curtailed press freedom and opposition politics but has embraced neoliberalization tactics, such as the privatization of the public sector and large-scale conglomerate investment.[46] Although Uganda, Rwanda, and the DRC are linked by shared political, ethnic, and regional affiliations, categorizing them under the rubric "empire" erases vastly different political structures and approaches to democratization, militarization, and social welfare.

Hardt and Negri's grand rhetoric also fails to account for the acute marginalization of Africa in global capital. Although Uganda and Rwanda do not quite match the DRC's notoriety for ranking near the bottom in various indexes of infant mortality, life expectancy, and literacy, substantial numbers of the populations in all three countries eke out lives of economic desperation.[47] Hardt and Negri acknowledge Africa's exceptionalism when they write that "most subordinated regions, such as areas of sub-Saharan Africa, are effectively secluded from capital flows and new technologies, and they thus find themselves on the verge of starvation."[48] But despite these attempts to account for Africa's intractable alterity, the book's broad scope sits uneasily with Africanists. As Kevin Dunn points out, Hardt and Negri demonstrate a contradictory reasoning that leaves "Africa occupying an ambiguous relationship with Empire—simultaneously incorporated and excised."[49] Not surprisingly, the field of African studies has responded to Hardt and Negri's "epochal claim" with pointed silence.[50]

In place of empire, neoliberalism beckons as a more obvious platform that accounts for a marketplace of trauma in which the logic of capital deems testimonies and other performative expressions of suffering "useful" and productive. Erica Caple James, for example, describes how Haitian suffering became "productive" as a tool of NGO governance, noting that "a professional transformation of suffering . . . fed a growing humanitarian market."[51] Similarly, Hardt and Negri often resort to neoliberal terminology to describe the permeations and permutations of empire.[52] Throughout this book, I also borrow from neoliberal theory to trace the marketing of trauma. In chapter 4, for example, I discuss how an empire of trauma participates in techniques of neoliberal governance with its emphasis on apolitical and compliant subjectivity. Representations of trauma in the eastern DRC cannot be fully understood without referencing the international campaign against the violent excesses of King Leopold's Congo Free State (1885–1906), which serves as one of the most spectacular and forceful antecedents of modern humanitarianism. But what is decidedly new (read: neoliberal) about present-day discourse concerning the eastern region as the "rape capital of the world" is that the female victims are interpreted as docile subjects submissive to modes of Western ideals of neoliberalism and governance, and thus their experiences of trauma are invoked to legitimize their participation. In a similar vein, the title of chapter 3, which pays tribute to the Comaroffs' *Ethnicity, Inc.*, underscores the processes through which trauma is compartmentalized and incorporated into the machinery of late capitalism in the example of postgenocide Rwanda.[53] The fleeting and arbitrary nature of the resources of humanitarianism raises the stakes of competition.

Despite these caveats, I hold fast to empire as a framework. Hardt and Negri's Empire repeatedly and insistently blurs the dichotomies of private/public, fact/fiction, and reality/spectacle—a dynamic that clarifies the transformation of personal experiences of trauma into public expression. The reified status of victim testimony, long privileged as a source of truth-knowing about suffering individuals or groups, has facilitated what James calls its "global saturation." James notes that "the performance of trauma narratives has become a necessary transaction in order for sufferers to participate in local, national, and international compassion economies."[54] Trauma is translated into testimony in hopes of gaining access to the economies of empire. Drawing on Guy Debord's *The Society and the Spectacle* in their discussion of mass media in the age of empire, Hardt and Negri heighten the stakes of trauma economies in their argument that "in the society of the spectacle only what appears exists."[55] This logic calls for postcolonial subjects to seize the workings of spectacle in order to lay claim to existence, which serves as a gateway to the politics of rights, recognition, and material gain. In this context, commodification might be understood as a desirable alternative to abandonment.[56]

In the humanitarian market, testimony serves as currency. Didier Fassin explains that "suffering beings" become complicit in the process of "essentializ[ing] the victim" insofar as "these persons often willingly submit to the category assigned to them: they understand the logic of this construction, and they anticipate its potential benefits."[57] He then takes this argument a step further—not only are trauma narratives exchanged in order to gain access to humanitarian capital, but also these narratives might be actively shaped in response to empire's appetites. As he writes, "The individuals in question tend to conform to this portrait [of suffering], knowing that it will have an impact on public opinion, and thus offer to the humanitarian agents the part of their experience that feeds the construction of them as human beings crushed by fate."[58] If trauma functions as a commodity, nuggets of pain will be used as raw material to manufacture full-blown tales of woe. Fact and fiction might be blurred to such a degree that the possibility of counterfeit currency looms.[59]

In theorizing an empire of trauma, it would be easy to leap onto the critical bandwagon and lambast international NGOs for their active and enthusiastic participation in these narratives of victimization. During the *Kony 2012* controversy, critics attacked Invisible Children for implying that the conflict was still decimating northern Uganda despite the LRA's departure from Uganda in 2006.[60] In suggesting that the conflict was still alive and well in northern Uganda, Invisible Children negated local efforts to sustain a hard-won semblance of stability. Although I acknowledge and unpack the damage wrought by top-down forces, this exercise is reminiscent of shooting fish in a barrel. A more complicated and fraught task is to consider local complicities of organizations and individuals in an empire of trauma. For example, I often refer to Hope North, which was founded in 1998 as an alternative resettlement community for war-affected Acholi and currently serves as a secondary school and vocational program. Hope North was founded by Okello Kelo Sam, himself an Acholi whose brother was abducted by the LRA in 1996. Until November 2012—about six years after hostilities on Ugandan soil had ended—the Hope North website continued to perpetuate the notion of a northern Uganda at war, proclaiming, for example, that "the civil war in northern Uganda has raged now for 22 years, making it one of the world's most neglected humanitarian crises."[61] This outdated piece of information could be chalked up to a simple labor shortage; the internet abounds with out-of-date websites that do not necessarily speak of the perniciousness of empire. The website was, however, often updated with other events and news about Hope North and its students over this six-year period, whereas the master narrative of the LRA war was left untouched. An alternative reading is that it serves as a classic example of how Fassin's "suffering beings" are complicit in the perpetuation of northern Uganda's image as a war zone.[62] But even more complicated is the way in which Sam's personal involvement in the war takes on various forms depending on the humanitarian context in which he shares details of his complicated life history, as well as how this history is perceived by outsiders (see chapter 5). My findings suggest that even the interior of memory is vulnerable to empire's reach.

Social scientists caution that notions of truth and testimony become destabilized in conflict and postconflict zones. Interviewing a survivor involves not only gleaning data but also negotiating humanitarian expectations. As Alex Argenti-Pillen puts it, how these survivors "talk about violence can … no longer be studied in isolation from the ways they have learned to present themselves to humanitarian agencies."[63] In their research on former LRA abductees, for example, Christopher Blattman and Jeannie Annan verified the identities of their informants because of widespread eagerness to claim the status of abductee in hopes of accessing material assistance.[64] A project such as mine could be said to be stating the obvious since these dynamics proliferate in resource-poor contexts. My aim, though, is not to footnote them but to place them center stage; I argue that these dynamics exceed the relationship between researcher and informant and spill into the realm of creative expression. This approach builds on James Thompson's work on humanitarian performance, in which he explores how humanitarian agencies perpetuate a "troubling mix of iconic images, compassion economics, celebrity concern, and the staging of misery," but it also considers how a humanitarian aesthetic has become internalized by local actors.[65] As described in chapter 6, when the students of Hope North developed a play in 2007 that put forward a critique of foreign intervention, they were quick to rein themselves in and suppressed the play of their own accord once they began to realize the implications of their lively and humorous performance. In its place, they offered a drastically scaled-down performance that provided a far more palatable and conventional humanitarian narrative. Creativity was not only circumscribed but actively self-censored before the gaze of empire.

Twenty-first-century manifestations of empire and late capitalism are inextricable. But in contrast to the nimbleness of neoliberalism, characterized by "extreme dynamism, mobility of practice, responsiveness to contingencies and strategic entanglements with politics," the empire of trauma is a ponderous beast that relies on the overtly paternalistic stance of humanitarianism and blatant dependence on top-down structures and clear divisions between victims and benefactors.[66] Its tastes run to contained versions of trauma that emphasize exceptionalism and disruption; it rejects evidence of its ordinariness for much of the world's population and the violence of the everyday. Instead of the dynamism of neoliberal strategies and techniques, an empire of trauma demands blunt humanitarian narratives and simplified images of spectacularized suffering. In addition, its insistence on "finding" traumatized victims in the face of contradictory evidence can be breathtakingly obtuse. Ugandan child soldiers, Rwandan genocide survivors, and Congolese rape victims were found on slender or even nonexistent evidence, as if they were invoked at will. This predictability and homogeneity speak of the blatant nature of conquest—"I name you as traumatized, and therefore you exist"—rather than the subtleties of neoliberalism. Although the tactics of marketing, branding, and commodification are used to draw empire's mercurial attention, neoliberalism makes up only part of the story.

Empire might be voracious, but it is also gullible. Reappropriations and rejections proliferate under the very eyes of empire, which becomes vulnerable in its ponderousness and predictability. I observed numerous instances in which foreigners were quite willing to be duped as long as they believed that they were encountering "authentic" notions of trauma that adhered to their preconceived notions of African victimization. In such cases, trauma must be served regardless of its context.[67] This ponderousness and banality feed into my understanding of empire and help explain my earlier reference to empire as a beast. Speaking of empire as a beast recalls numerous *Punch* cartoons from the colonial era that depicted colonialism and imperialism in animal form. An octopus, a lion, an eagle, and a python were variously used as metaphorical images of empire's grasping reach, domination, and hold.[68] But the kind of beast I am thinking of is more predictable and less cunning than these images suggest. It is akin to what Heidegger called a "benumbed" beast, a term he used in his 1929–1930 lecture course to describe "the way in which the animal is absorbed in itself" and its sense of captivation.[69] To further differentiate the benumbedness of an animal from the selfhood of the human being, he writes that "the animal *behaves within an environment but never within a world*"; that is, an animal is confined to perceiving the parts of the world that are of immediate relevance to its survival.[70] I borrow from Heidegger to underscore the self-absorbed, driven, captivated behavior of empire. Certainly, this notion of the benumbed beast moves far afield from Hardt and Negri's concept of empire, which they describe as vampiric, as if to underscore its seemingly supernatural ability to survive "by sucking off the blood of the living."[71] But the uncanny abilities of Hardt and Negri's empire do not apply to an empire of trauma, which is predictable in its appetites to the point that it can be fooled. My point here is not to underestimate empire's ability to colonize even the creative capacities of East and Central African cultural workers who tailor their expressions to satisfy its tastes. I am intrigued, though, by the possibility that beasts—unlike, say, vampires—fall prey to their own benumbment.

STATE ATTACHMENTS

This book considers the staging of mass trauma in Central Africa through a transnational lens. As studies such as René Lemarchand's *The Dynamics of Violence in Central Africa* and Gérard Prunier's *Africa's World War* make relentlessly clear, it is untenable to isolate the armed conflicts and mass killings of Central Africa in a national frame.[72] *Africa's World War* refers to a deadly conflagration that engulfed the DRC starting in 1998, which can be roughly traced to the 1994 genocide in Rwanda and the flight of genocidaires to refugee camps in the eastern DRC, which was then called Zaire. (This unfolding of events, which also includes a war fought in the former Zaire from 1996 to 1997, is discussed in much greater detail in chapter 1.) Although the war ultimately involved seven African countries on both sides of the conflict, Rwanda and Uganda assumed a leading role in their combined efforts to topple the

Kinshasa government. The war formally ended with the signing of a peace agreement in 2003; however, Rwanda and Uganda continued to back new insurgencies in the eastern region, most notably the M23 rebellion, which lasted from 2012 to 2013. Meanwhile, the LRA has come to epitomize the havoc of transnational violence. Since its departure from Uganda in 2006, the group has committed massacres and abductions in the northeastern DRC and the southeastern Central African Republic; attempts at military intervention have only exacerbated regional violence. The conflict in eastern Zaire and the movements of the LRA are just two of the most obvious examples of how violence exceeds and confounds national borders, giving rise to what David Newbury calls "convergent catastrophes."[73]

The complexity of these convergent catastrophes has failed to intimidate playwrights. Given the status of the 1994 Rwandan genocide as a defining event of the late twentieth century, it is not surprising that most of these creative efforts have been devoted to this episode of horrific violence. Several US and UK playwrights have addressed the genocide, including Erik Ehn (*Maria Kizito*), J. T. Rogers (*The Overwhelming*), Sonja Linden (*I Have a Remarkable Document Given to Me by a Young Lady from Rwanda*), and most recently Katori Hall (*Our Lady of Kibeho*).[74] Rwandan playwright and director Hope Azeda created *Rwanda My Hope* in collaboration with the Mashirika Theatre Company for the ten-year commemoration of the genocide held in Amahoro Stadium in Kigali; then, for the twentieth commemoration ceremony, also held at the stadium, she created another powerful dance/drama titled *Shadows of Memory*.[75] Both productions employed hundreds of actors in a spectacular gesture toward the "mass noun" of genocide.[76] The thousands of child soldiers conscripted by the LRA in northern Uganda have also caught the imagination and attention of several playwrights, as indicated by Asiimwe's previously discussed *Forgotten World*, *Time of Fire* by Ugandan playwright Charles Mulekwa, *dogsbody* by Ehn, and *Butterflies of Uganda* by US playwrights Darin Dahms and Soenke Weiss.[77] Northern Ugandan playwrights who have addressed the LRA conflict include Okello Kelo Sam, mentioned earlier as the founder of Hope North, and Lucy Judith Adong.[78] Plays about the conflict in the eastern DRC are dominated by *Ruined* by US playwright Lynn Nottage, which won the Pulitzer Prize for Drama in 2009 and went on to become one of the most produced plays in the United States in the 2010–2011 season; it received its French-language premiere in Kinshasa in 2011.[79] These scripts run the gamut of aesthetic genres—from theatre of testimony to realism, absurdism, surrealism, or some combination thereof—in their translations of mass trauma to the stage.

Many of these plays emerged in a transnational context. Several playwrights have close artistic and personal connections; for example, Mulekwa, Azeda, Sam, and Asiimwe are all graduates of the Music, Dance, and Drama (MDD) program at Makerere University in Kampala and serve as a testament to Uganda's vibrant tradition of playwriting.[80] Azeda's background as a Rwandan Tutsi who grew up in exile in Uganda speaks to the transnational intersections of Uganda and Rwanda that will be explored in more detail in chapter 1. Moreover, these playwrights are eager to take advantage of a growing regional identity, similar to what Evan Mwangi calls the "transnational ethos" that prevails in the contemporary East African music scene.[81] Several, for example, have participated in a series of transnational encounters that seek an ethical response to violence and conflict. Ehn's writing of *Maria Kizito* sparked an annual program called More Life in which he partnered with Jean-Pierre Karegeye of the Kigali-based Interdisciplinary Genocide Studies Center for a series of cultural exchanges. Asiimwe, Azeda, Hall, Mulekwa, Nottage, and Sam have all participated in More Life, and Asiimwe's *Forgotten World*, Nottage's *Ruined*, and Hall's *Our Lady of Kibeho* drew on their experiences and observations in the exchanges. These encounters have generated a kind of transnational elbow-rubbing that creates part of the context for this book; indeed, my experiences in Ehn's initiatives inform three of these chapters.[82] The momentum of these creative alliances and coalitions resonates with concepts of minor transnationalism and critical regionalism and thus serves as a powerful counterpoint to the border-crossing paths of violence.[83] The enthusiasm of East and Central African performing artists in forging a creative minor-to-minor network and an artistic regionalism could pave the way toward a recognition of the seriality of genocide—not to homogenize specific experiences of violence but to recognize how they overlap and intersect in a globalizing world order.

Before indulging in romanticized ideas of regional identity as a means of superseding empire, I should acknowledge that I was hard pressed to find these ideas in the performance texts themselves. Given the extent of the transnational journeys, backgrounds, borrowings, and energy that serve as the context for the plays, it is striking that the texts are resoundingly silent on the transnational nature of the endemic violence of the Great Lakes. This silence is most readily discerned in the plays; Nottage's *Ruined*, for example, contains a few passing references to Uganda, but Rwanda is never mentioned, even though its aggression against eastern Congo and its exploitation of the region's famed mineral resources are instrumental to a basic understanding of the conflict. Similarly, none of the existing plays about Rwanda venture beyond the country's borders to delve into the quagmire of the Great Lakes region, which has been plagued with a series of massacres of both Tutsi and Hutu. Granted, a certain amount of simplification and reduction is inevitable in any dramatic representation of mass atrocity. Even to begin to delve into these complexities would usually entail a thick, carefully footnoted monograph instead of a two-, three-, or even six-hour play, such as the 1999 multimedia performance text *Rwanda 94* created by the Belgian theatre collective Groupov. Furthermore, as Paul Rae points out, one of theatre's strengths is its ability to distill complexities and resonate across geographic boundaries and historical eras.[84] The plays might serve as gateways to deeper understanding, and thus their silences and simplifications are perhaps justified.

But I argue that these specific silences reveal not only the domestication of empire but also the looming presence of the African state. In this sense, my work responds to critiques of Hardt and Negri for their dismissal of the role of the nation-state in contemporary politics.[85] In Central Africa, the state's role is intrusive and vigorous. The Rwandan postgenocide government has cultivated a strong centralized apparatus through a strategic combination of totalitarianism and poverty-alleviation initiatives. Kagame, who became president of Rwanda in 2000, might be hailed as a savior for his work toward stabilizing the volatility of ethnic relations in Rwanda, but he is also criticized for his repression of civil freedoms and opposition politics. Although the specter of "failed state" or even "nonstate" status has dogged the heels of Uganda and the DRC, these governments are also ruled by classic prototypes of African strongmen—Museveni, who has served as president of Uganda since 1986, and Joseph Kabila, who became president of the DRC in 2001 after the assassination of his father, Laurent-Désiré Kabila.[86] All three states can be classified as semiauthoritarian regimes in which heads of state rule with a firm and occasionally threatening hand.[87]

Narrative serves as a tool in their cultivation of control. Sergei Guriev and Daniel Treisman argue that totalitarian governments of the early twenty-first century have mostly transitioned from the tactics of outright mass violence to a "less carnivorous" form of government, that is, a "soft autocracy" that seeks to maintain control through the manipulation of popular belief through censorship and propaganda.[88] Although the state in Central Africa continues to use tactics of calculated violence, Guriev and Treisman's ideas help clarify how narratives of trauma contribute to the workings of soft autocracy. As will be discussed further in chapter 3, Kagame is arguably the cleverest in jerking empire's strings; it is a far more fraught enterprise to criticize his regime than it is to criticize Museveni's or Kabila's. As a result, a tacit agreement reigns among a wide range of international witnesses—particularly, in my experience, theatre artists and playwrights—to look the other way regarding Rwanda's controversial track record regarding war crimes and political repression. This silence cannot be chalked up to a lack of understanding; one needs only to scratch the surface of the conflict through the most basic internet search to come across these critical counternarratives. Empire works in tandem with the state to circumscribe creativity and complexity. Their combined reach is formidable; the silence encompasses plays created within Central Africa and those beyond.

This shared reluctance in the region and abroad clarifies the limitations of theatre in the realm of human rights. Theatre artists are often complicit in the sanitization and simplification of violence through fashioning clear-cut narratives of good and evil; here, though, I speak of a more insidious aesthetic that helps sustain a public secret—what Michael Taussig defines as "that which is generally known, but cannot be articulated"—and thus avoids challenging or even complicating official state narratives.[89] Scholars of mass violence commonly invoke the term "unspeakable" to describe violence of such magnitude that it defies description and confounds the imagination. I have come to prefer the term "nonspeakable violence," in which the prefix suggests a deliberate force of negation as opposed to "unspeakable," which implies a reversal or the opposite. This term helps underscore the machinations of the state and expose the kinds of violence that delegitimize its moral claim to power.

The role of nonspeakable violence complicates the project of literary analysis. Analyzing a play usually means unpacking subtle meanings that complicate or challenge the main dramatic action or dominant narrative. I use this kind of analysis, for example, in my discussion of Nottage's *Ruined* in chapter 4, which demonstrates how the play not only affirms mainstream US narratives of the eastern Congolese conflict but also supplements these narratives through a sly critique of neoliberal economies of violence. This approach can be likened to what Žižek calls "sideways glances" at violence since it helps illuminate layers of structural and systemic suffering concealed by mesmerizing scenes of direct, event-centered violence.[90] Because of the fraught political conditions in which some of these artists and playwrights operate, however, this approach is not always advisable. Indeed, identifying alternative narratives could make some of the authors and artists vulnerable to surveillance and censorship. In many cases, the creators of these performance texts cannot be cloaked as anonymous sources; as a result, I have chosen not to write about certain plays and performance texts even though they are worthy of multiple and sustained sideways glances. In other words, my work maintains its own kind of public secrecy. Many of the texts discussed in this book are caught between an authoritarian state and an imperial empire and thus are limited in their ability to offer subversion, contestation, and resistance. The point is not to excoriate these works for their complicity in state-centric narratives of violence but instead to heed Walter Benjamin's call to do justice to the secret rather than expose it.[91] In this instance, to do justice to the secret is to identify the stakeholders of empire.

Resilience and Its Discontents

Agency occupies a vexed role in this discussion. To discount the role of agency in an empire of trauma is to perpetuate, as Graham Huggan puts it, the notion of "some vast imperial conspiracy sucking in its unwary victims."[92] My focus on the seepage of empire runs the danger of reaffirming clichéd neocolonial narratives that position Central Africans as passive and uniformly subservient, thus paving the way for yet another intrusion of the white savior industrial complex. One obvious solution is to focus not only on how these actors cater to these narratives but also how they take advantage of them. They might make a reassuring show of drinking the humanitarian Kool-Aid in order to enter the empire of trauma, but they are decidedly capable of diluting and remixing it to suit their own purposes.

But emphasizing the agency of African subjects might sugarcoat the pernicious effects of empire. As Adam Branch has observed, humanitarian and human rights organizations appropriate the concepts of agency and resilience in order to justify their intervention in African contexts: "It is the celebrated 'resilience' of Africans that provides the substrate for these empowering interventions.... Once responsible order is re-established in the political, social, cultural domains, it is argued, Africa can manage itself."[93] How can one discuss agency and cultural resilience—concepts of which the humanities are perhaps too fond—in a way that does not simplify these dynamics? Gullibility does not supersede perniciousness. Even if victims of trauma disengage from traditional narratives of suffering, empire might insist on scripting it for them. Even if said victims do not participate in the business of marketing trauma, international audiences still demand customer satisfaction.

Performance theory might offer a way out of this conundrum. "Both subversion and legitimation can emerge in the same utterance or act," writes Margaret Drewal in her analysis of African performance, speaking of the ability of performance to imagine new worlds but also to reaffirm hierarchical social orders.[94] Therein lies the academic rub because to pursue this reasoning leads the scholar of African performance through a Möbius strip of resistance and reaffirmation, leaving larger questions untouched while upholding academic clichés. Although I explore how victims and survivors use master narratives of trauma for their own purposes and ends, I am also apprehensive that this line of reasoning perpetuates a time-worn academic approach to cultural and artistic expressions. It is commonplace in the humanities to adhere to the "affirm/subvert" narrative—that is, how the social order is affirmed on the one hand and subverted on the other—and certainly this book offers up this chestnut at regular intervals. See how the empire of trauma consumes and overpowers, but also see how the empire of trauma is manipulated and tricked. Consider how representations of trauma titillate and dehumanize, but then observe how these representations are appropriated and transformed. Discuss how humanitarian narratives not only bolster but also destabilize the status quo. Obviously, this approach is useful in examining the forces of structural and direct violence, as well as foregrounding the agency of local actors in negotiating and overcoming these forces. But this kind of academic narrative evades disturbing implications about the role of performance in postconflict settings. Alternative narratives exist, but to what effect?

The unpacking of texts and contexts helps shed light on the dynamics of empire, the nonspeakability of violence, and the capacity of creativity on the margins of capital. Chapter 1 focuses on the transnational and historical context of mass violence in the Great Lakes. Although this historical overview is meant primarily for readers who lack familiarity with the region's colonial and postcolonial history, it also addresses rhetorical competition over suffering to clarify how even trauma has been deemed a scarce resource.

Chapter 2 focuses on the intersection of empire and creative expression on the terrain of northern Uganda during the LRA conflict. Specifically, it examines the subtleties of performance in a rehabilitation center for former child soldiers sponsored by the international NGO World Vision. I draw on my observations and personal experiences at the center in 2004 to suggest that drama is valued primarily as a marketing tool to reach international and national audiences rather than as a forum of creative expression. I go on, however, to suggest that the framework of marketing does not satisfactorily explain the fierce investment in a linear story and the trappings of realism; indeed, a local investment in orderly narrative coexists with the forces of empire. The final section argues that former LRA captives use indigenous dances to carve out a space in which cultural memories and empire intersect.

Chapter 3 shifts to Rwanda, focusing on the performative strategies of the postgenocide state. I expand on Filip Reyntjens's frequently cited notion of the "genocide credit" to suggest that the concept of a "genocide attachment" might help capture the complexities of Rwanda's relationship with the west.[95] I also suggest that the state's theme song is less the manipulation of international guilt than a nuanced understanding of the politics of shame. I then turn to the work of Immaculée Ilibagiza, arguably the best-known Rwandan genocide survivor in the world because of her best-selling memoir *Left to Tell: How I Found God amidst the Rwandan Holocaust*.[96] In contrast to the guilt- and shame-wielding state, Ilibagiza offers love and forgiveness as a balm of redemption to her western followers. The combination of pain and pleasure work together to satisfy empire's contradictory appetites.

Chapter 4 historicizes the commodification of trauma through an exploration of repetitions and discontinuities in two humanitarian campaigns: the crusade against King Leopold's Congo Free State in the early twentieth century and the movement to associate "blood minerals" with sexual violence in the eastern Congo that began about a decade ago. I respond to the sensational images of suffering Congolese that permeate the humanitarian literature of both campaigns by following Žižek's suggestion to look "sideways" at violence, a glance that reveals the troubling politics of labor and gender. Who is allowed to work—that is, which Congolese are considered productive—and why? I then consider Nottage's play *Ruined*, which rejects the legacies of colonialism and humanitarianism to embrace a neoliberal world in which trauma serves as a means of livelihood.

In chapter 5, I return to northern Uganda for an exploration of empire's ferocity in the postconflict era. I examine how northern Uganda seeks to brand itself as traumatized, and how that brand is hijacked by a variety of celebrities who are eager to "help." The final section considers the processes of rebranding in the context of memorial ceremonies of the LRA conflict, which sidestep the politics of memory in order to make a sustained demand on the Ugandan state.

Chapter 6 takes a distinctly theoretical turn. It moves between Rwanda and Uganda in its consideration of theatre activism in a transnational frame. This chapter draws on my experiences as a participant in Ehn's More Life cultural exchange program in the summer of 2007 to argue for a productive failure of activism as practiced by US theatre artists in the Great Lakes region. The program introduced me to an alternative model of theatre activism, one that troubles the hierarchies that pervade an empire of trauma and articulates a space of what I call, borrowing from Emmanuel Lévinas, "radical passivity." In an age in which foreign intervention too often functions as a foil for imperial expansion, radical passivity serves as a useful starting point for an ethical approach to intercultural performance that might evade the machinery of empire. In an afterword, I draw on the work of Congolese choreographer Faustin Linyekula to theorize a laboring of hope that refuses to convey a positive narrative spin on African suffering.

My first visit to northern Uganda in 2004 marked what Alain Badiou might call a "truth event" in that any romanticized ideas I possessed concerning the role of theatre and performance in a war zone splintered under the weight of an empire of trauma.[97] In addition to visits to Rwanda and Uganda during the summers of 2007 and 2011 as part of Ehn's More Life program, I also taught at Makerere University in Kampala for ten months from 2012 to 2013, during which I conducted additional research in northern Uganda and Rwanda. A visit in the summer of 2015 was used to share drafts of my chapters with key informants in order to review quotations and other information. My ideas have also been informed by my encounters with East and Central African artists in the United States through artistic residencies and creative collaborations. Finally, I attended a wide range of theatre productions in the United States that addressed Central African trauma, as well as alternative forms of cultural production, such as a gala fund-raiser for Hope North in Manhattan and a Catholic retreat led by Immaculée Ilibagiza in central Pennsylvania. In sum, my methodology ranged from observing memorial ceremonies in northern Uganda to collaborating on a play with Okello Sam about the LRA conflict, from attending the off-Broadway production of *Our Lady of Kibeho* to visiting Kibeho itself in order to understand the intersection of international tourism and memorialization, and from analyzing the text of *Ru-*

ined to examining archival photographs of the Congo Reform Association from the early twentieth century. This approach might take George Marcus's model of multisitedness to an unwieldy extreme, but it also clarifies the vagaries, technologies, and pervasiveness of empire.⁹⁸ With sincere apologies to the performance artist Guillermo Gómez-Peña, who poetically mused that "I carry the border with me, and I find new borders wherever I go," I believe that as a US national of western European descent, I carried empire with me, and I found new empires wherever I went.⁹⁹

Asiimwe's question that opened this introduction—"Can you quantify a crisis?"—haunts this analysis as it moves among the genocide in Rwanda, the decimation of northern Uganda, and the ongoing crisis in the eastern region of the DRC. How can one discuss conflicts of such magnitude and complexity without participating in a kind of academic cocktail party? Scholarly texts are hardly immune to an empire of trauma. Indeed, this book's focus on episodic (as opposed to structural) violence means that it participates in the kind of direct glance at violence Žižek critiques, or what Scott Straus calls a "trade in horror."¹⁰⁰ One might argue that this book is a testament to empire's insidious power, and that my work would be more productively spent on the subtleties of structural violence as opposed to a mesmerized gaze at genocide and mass death.

But in the realm of performance, a direct glance can become fragmented. In an especially powerful scene in Asiimwe's play, the ghost of a child soldier relives her memories of making soup with her young sister (whom, it is suggested, she has killed by LRA orders). She begins chanting a recipe for chicken soup in a grotesque example of how truth and illusion, the quotidian and the extreme, mutually implode:

> This is the recipe on how to make chicken soup rocks measure half a cup of sand a full plate of chicken feathers remember the feathers have to be black don't add onions or tomatoes that will spoil the test pour the sand and the black chicken feathers into the pot and stir for five minutes on medium heat add two cups of water and heat to boil remove from heat and add salt and sugar stir while the substance cools now [it's] time to turn the substance into small balls of rocks don't wear gloves while making the balls of rocks just [bare] hands what you have prepared should be able to feed thirteen people a whole platoon place the rocks and soup on a tray if you have one and do not worry about the strings they will grow by themselves beneath your tongue now you are ready to serve hm delicious ugh ugh (*She begins pulling at her tongue compulsively*).¹⁰¹

The most carefully crafted and sustained narrative—a recipe for trauma, if you will—can collapse under the weight of memory, and the most ordinary objects will generate pain. Her attempt to pull out her tongue can be interpreted as a refusal to produce the victim testimony so eagerly consumed by the west, even as the character of the Photographer observes and records her actions in a vivid reminder of how the forces of marketing and consumption infiltrate the most intimate moments of pain. Michael Taussig writes of "epistemic murk," glossed as the "unstable interplay of truth and illusion" that characterizes cultures of terror.[102] Asiimwe's play experiments with what can be called the aesthetics of epistemic murk in its fusion of memory, terror, and narrative. The Photographer is oblivious: "God! Look at this! You are so photogenic!" she exclaims,[103] snapping the girl's photograph with glee. The obliviousness of empire is showcased and spectacularized.

Forgotten World is hardly alone in its bold exploration of the epistemic murk of violence. Although I look critically at how these plays and cultural texts participate in humanitarian and state-centric narratives of violence, I also recognize those moments in which an aesthetics of murk destabilizes carefully constructed and anxiously managed narratives of war and genocide. Artists and cultural workers pursue a kind of Badiouian fidelity in their efforts to represent to the horror of sustained violence; I seek to learn from as well as question their theorizing of violence through creative expression. I also work to recall the specific context from which this violence emerged; the balls of rocks in Asiimwe's speech, for example, speak directly to their symbolism in the LRA, which endows rocks with the magical power to explode in the presence of the enemy or to obscure the enemy's vision.[104] In order to evade both the panacea of hope and the dismissiveness of despair, this book strives to do justice to texts and contexts alike.

Notes

1. Deborah Asiimwe, *Forgotten World*, 39. *Forgotten World* was produced at the California Institute of the Arts in 2009, when Asiimwe was completing her MFA program in playwriting. The play also received a staged reading at the Public Theatre in New York City in 2010. At the time of this writing, the play has not been published. Page numbers refer to an unpublished manuscript in the author's possession; I am grateful to Asiimwe for providing me with the script.

2. The play seeks to make the point that child soldiers are hardly confined to Uganda or the African continent; for example, the children sing lullabies from Korea and the People's Republic of China as a gesture to the global reach of this practice. However, the names of the children and the Swahili military phrases that occur throughout the script locate the play primarily in Uganda. (Although Swahili is used throughout East and Central Africa, it is often associated primarily with the military in Uganda.) The play was inspired by testimonies of former soldiers of the LRA (see "Making Art in Troubled Times," *Café Libre* blog, February 2, 2010, https://quartierlibre.wordpress.com/2010/02/02/a-tender-embrace-of-the-dark-side/).

3. Asiimwe, *Forgotten World*, 62.
4. Ibid., 62.
5. Ibid., 39.
6. Ibid., 5.
7. Ibid., 62.
8. Marx 1976 [1867], 125.
9. Asiimwe, *Forgotten World*, 11.
10. Ibid., 4, 62.
11. Sontag 2003, 111. The phrase "ordinariness of crisis" is a rephrasing of what Lauren Berlant calls crisis ordinariness (2011, 10).
12. Teju Cole, "The White-Savior Industrial Complex," *Atlantic*, March 21, 2012.
13. The Fall Out Boy video for "I'm like a Lawyer with the Way I'm Always Trying to Get You Off (Me & You)," can be viewed at https://www.youtube.com/watch?v=FAgbZdrWiN4, accessed January 25, 2016. The *Law and Order* episode, titled "Hell," aired on March 31, 2009. Another example of the LRA's circulation in US media is the 2011 film *Machine Gun Preacher*, directed by Marc Forster and starring Gerard Butler as Sam Childers, who has become famous for his humanitarian work in present-day South Sudan.
14. Nordstrom 1997, 4.
15. Fassin and Rechtman 2009. See Ferguson 2006, 15–16, for an explication of how the term "shadow" is used in Africanist discourse to describe a kind of doubling. My subtitle, "shadows of empire," draws from Ferguson to call attention to the doubling of texts and audiences in the context of Central African performance, which is meant not only for those physically present but also an imagined empire. Ferguson notes that a shadow "is not only a dim or empty likeness," but rather "an attached twin," that is, "an inseparable other-who-is-also-oneself to whom one is bound" (17). The shadow of empire has become inextricable from the act of spectatorship and creative expression.
16. The Great Lakes region generally encompasses Uganda, Rwanda, Burundi, and the DRC; however, depending on the context in which the term is used, up to twelve other countries (including, for example, Tanzania, Kenya, Malawi, the Central African Republic, and Mozambique) have been classified as belonging to what Reyntjens has called the "greater Great Lakes" (2009, 4). Omeje and Hepner (2013, 9–10) provide a useful summary of various definitions of the region; see also Lemarchand 2011, 3. Obviously, my focus on Rwanda, northern Uganda, and the eastern DRC is a highly selective interpretation of the Great Lakes label that is influenced primarily by what "sells" in an empire of trauma; for example, the violence of the Burundian civil war from 1993 to 2005 and the upsurge of violence that erupted in 2015 after Pierre Nkurunziza's successful but controversial bid for a third term in office have been largely ignored in favor of the conflict in the eastern DRC, and thus Burundi is rarely mentioned in this book. I occasionally pair the categories "East African" and "Central African" in an attempt to acknowledge that these three countries straddle both regional categorizations.

The relatively recent momentum of the East African Community (EAC), which includes Burundi, Kenya, Rwanda, South Sudan, Tanzania, and Uganda, and which the DRC government has expressed interest in joining, counters the more conventional academic classification of Rwanda, the DRC, and (less often) Uganda as Central African countries.

17. These statistics are frequently repeated in academic literature and journalism. The statistic of 66,000 abducted children can be traced to Blattman and Annan 2010b; the rape statistics in the DRC were originally put forth in Peterman, Palermo, and Bredenkamp 2011. The figure of 800,000 dead from the Rwandan genocide has become the most widely accepted statistic; see Verpoorten 2005 for a useful discussion of the Rwandan death toll in 1994.

18. Chow 2010, 71; see also Chrétien 2003, 22.

19. Fassin and Rechtman 2009, 10.

20. Ibid., 216.

21. Ibid., 5.

22. John Comaroff and Jean Comaroff 2009, 9.

23. These terms appear in, respectively, Piot 2010; Nguyen 2010; Bob 2005; James 2004; Hyndman 2000, xvi; and Ndaliko 2016.

24. See Fassin 2007a, 151, for a definition of humanitarian government. See also Fassin 2010 for a discussion of how humanitarianism serves as a tool of sovereignty.

25. Pandolfi 2008, 2010; Appadurai 1996. Elsewhere, though, Pandolfi uses the term "migrant sovereignty" (2003, 369), which speaks to the arbitrariness and even instability of this kind of sovereignty—here one moment and vanished the next, in search of the next great human catastrophe. Similarly, Erica Bornstein and Peter Redfield explicitly warn against conceptualizing humanitarianism as an empire: "Even as the humanitarian collective remains dwarfed by conventional military expenditure, its loose assemblage of affiliations and associations also lacks the centralized coordination of a modern fighting force, let alone a state or empire" (2011, 20). That said, the concept of a humanitarian empire has considerable traction; see, for example, John Comaroff and Jean Comaroff 2008, 10; Barnett 2011; Büscher and Vlassenroot 2010; and Krause 2014.

26. Richey and Ponte 2011, 12–13.

27. I am drawing here on Koen Stroeken's comment "Rather than just ruling the world, Empire wants to be legitimate" (2013, 242).

28. Sherbo 1957. A similar genre appeared in France called *comédie larmoyante*.

29. Festa 2006, 3.

30. Hyndman 2000, xvi. See also Berlant 2008 for a rich discussion of the role of sentimentality in US contexts.

31. Klein 2007.

32. See, for example, *La République Démocratique du Congo face au complot de balkanisation et d'implosion* (Congolese Institute for Development and Strategic Studies, 2013), a sizable collection of essays by Congolese journalists and academics that subscribes to a widely popular theory that powerful foreign interests are invested in the breakup (or balkanization) of the DRC into smaller polities. See Stearns 2013 for a description of this theory and his response; he suggests that donors have reacted out of "apathy and ignorance, not hegemonic ambitions" (102). See also Autesserre 2010, 17–18.

33. Jean Comaroff and John Comaroff 2011, 14.

34. Žižek 2008, 3.

35. During the media storm unleashed upon the release of Invisible Children's *Kony 2012*, which called for strengthening US military intervention in the pursuit of Joseph Kony, Nige-

rian writer Teju Cole sent an acerbic tweet that illuminates this dynamic: "Feverish worry over that awful African warlord. But close to 1.5 million Iraqis died from an American war of choice. Worry about that" (quoted in "The White-Savior Industrial Complex," *Atlantic*, March 21, 2012). Although Cole's point about how the film distracted the US public from its complicity in Iraqi suffering is well taken, Achille Mbembe cautions against an oversimplification of how empire instrumentalizes trauma and mass death. Mbembe folds the otherness of death into the workings of necropolitics, meaning that sovereignty resides "in the power and the capacity to dictate who may live and who must die" (2003, 11), a form of biopower that exceeds the confines of the nation-state and thus resonates with the framework of empire and humanitarianism. He cites Georges Bataille's statement that "the sovereign is he who is as if death were not" (quoted in Mbembe 2003, 16) and explains that "sovereignty definitely calls for the risk of death" on the part of its subjects (ibid.). Mbembe's ideas suggest that the otherness of trauma and the threat of death exceed strategies of distraction and permeate the very structure of empire.

36. Fassin and Rechtman 2009, xi.

37. Hinton and Hinton 2015, which brings together medical and anthropological considerations of trauma, provides a useful corrective (see, in particular, A. Taylor 2015). Other useful texts include Buckley-Zistel 2006, 2008; Burnet 2005, 2012; and Finnström 2008.

38. Werbner 2002, 3; see also Appiah 1992, 157.

39. See, for example, Barber 2000 and Fabian 1990.

40. Chérie Rivers Ndaliko articulates a similar tension in her compelling study on Yole!Africa, an arts and cultural center in Goma in the eastern DRC, writing of "critical dynamics that require rigorous investigation lest the illusion of artistic empowerment obscure lethal manipulations and manifestations of power" (2016, 252).

41. Chow 2010, 76.

42. Ferguson 2006, 47.

43. *Empire* (2000), the first of a trilogy, was followed by *Multitude: War and Democracy in the Age of Empire* in 2004 and *Commonwealth* in 2009. I found *Empire* especially helpful for conceptualizing the erosion of private expression in the service of global capital.

44. Hardt and Negri 2000, xii. Emphasis in the original.

45. Deleuze and Guattari 1987.

46. See Goodfellow 2013 for a discussion of the "noise" of Kampala versus the "silence" of Kigali, and Sundaram 2016 for a chilling account of Rwanda's suppression of independent journalism. Uganda has consistently ranked above Rwanda in indexes of freedom of the press; in 2016, in the annual Press Freedom index, Reporters without Borders ranked Uganda at 102 and Rwanda at 161 out of 180 countries. The DRC was ranked at 152. See https://rsf.org/en/ranking.

47. For example, the DRC, along with Niger, ranks near the bottom of the 2015 Human Development Index, at 176. See *The 2015 Human Development Report*, available at www.undp.org. As will be discussed in more detail in chapter 3, Rwanda may have earned high international praise for its remarkable economic growth and poverty-reduction plan, but its success story masks a growing inequality that consigns about half the population, particularly urban youth and small-scale farmers, to lives of extreme poverty (Ansoms and Rostagno 2012; see also Huggins 2009). Critics of Rwanda's economic policies point to their negative impact on poor urban youth, many of whom lack access to advanced education, technical training, and land, as well as their marginalization of small-scale farmers in the country's pursuit of monocropping and agribusiness. Similarly, Catharine Newbury's analysis of the disastrous

consequences of the postgenocide state's coercive *imidugudu* (villagization) policy reveals that the policy "reduced economic security and quality of life" and "increased social tensions, particularly along ethnic lines" (2011, 235). Northern Uganda has demonstrated signs of economic growth in recent years, but it still lags behind the rest of the country; a 2014 report partly sponsored by UNICEF, for example, noted that child poverty rates are highest in that region. See "Situation Analysis of Child Poverty and Deprivation," available at http://www.unicef.org/uganda/CPR_-_statistical_analysis%281%29.pdf, accessed August 17, 2017.

48. Hardt and Negri 2000, 288.

49. Dunn 2004, 154.

50. Ong 2007, 4. Exceptions certainly exist; see Hoffman 2011 as an example of Africanist scholarship that engages with Hardt and Negri's ideas of empire.

51. James 2010, 33.

52. See, for example, Hardt and Negri 2000, 332. A comparison of Hardt and Negri's concept of Empire with that of neoliberalism suggests a kind of tomato/tomahto dynamic. As a useful demarcation point between the forces of Empire and neoliberalism, Aihwa Ong points out that Hardt and Negri's concept of empire is more Marxian than Foucauldian in its homogenized formulation (2007, 40), which reinforces my understanding of empire as a largely implacable force. It should also be noted that the lack of nuance and finesse in empire's machinations facilitates my tendency in this book to describe empire's shadow audience with the homogenized term "westerners." Specificity is hardly empire's strong point, as the term itself underscores. It should be acknowledged, however, that to described this imagined audience as "western" erases differences among and between multiple nationalities. Ndaliko, for example, identifies the "dedication to playing the hero" as a specifically US tendency whereas the European stance is one of undifferentiated paternalism (2016, 12). The term also tends to elide the increasingly powerful presence of the People's Republic of China in the region; it's quite possible that the empire of trauma, in its slow and plodding way, will come to tailor its narratives and images to suit this particular demographic.

53. John Comaroff and Jean Comaroff 2009; see also Crisafulli and Redmond 2012 and Slaughter 2007. My intellectual debt to the Comaroffs' book is considerable given that their analysis of the commodification and commercialization of culture and ethnicity intersects and overlaps with my understanding of performing trauma.

54. James 2010, 29.

55. Debord 1995 [1967]; Hardt and Negri 2000, 322.

56. Here I am borrowing from James's point that "traumatic citizenship . . . remains preferable to abandonment in this era of neomodern insecurity" (2009, 158). See also Mbembe's statement that "we might observe that, many people want to become objects, or be treated as such, if only because becoming an object one might end up being treated better than as a human" ("Africa and the Future: An Interview with Achille Mbembe," with Thomas M. Blaser, *Africa's a Country* [blog], November 20, 2013, available at http://africasacountry.com/2013/11/africa-and-the-future-an-interview-with-achille-mbembe/, accessed August 20, 2017).

57. Fassin 2007b, 512.

58. Ibid., 517.

59. A notorious example of this kind of embellishment hit the international press in 2014 when it was revealed that Somaly Mam, a Cambodian activist who founded the Somaly Mam Foundation for victims of sex trafficking, might have falsified her life narrative as a former sex slave. See Pippa Biddle, "We're All Liars: Why Creative Storytelling Is the Non-profit Sector's

Drug of Choice" (*Huffington Post*, May 28, 2014) for an examination of the Mam scandal that is highly pertinent to this discussion. Biddle writes, "Just as professional athletes take steroids, it seems as if embellishing or even fabricating stories has become the stimulant of choice for nonprofit leaders looking to gain a competitive edge. There is a push to show that you've been challenged, and overcome more than anyone else; that you are a shining example of humanity. The pressure to live up to this ideal is, ironically, incentivizing falsehoods."

60. See Edmondson 2012 for more detailed discussion of the criticism of *Kony 2012*.

61. The website is hopenorth.org; this phrase first came to my attention in February 2011 before the website was substantially revised in November 2012, perhaps in response to criticism of *Kony 2012*.

62. Fassin 2007b, 512.

63. Argenti-Pillen 2003, xii. See also Lombard's caveats about her research on military culture in the Central African Republic (2012, 341n18) and Coulter's cautioning tone about the life narratives she gathered from female ex-combatants in Sierra Leone (2009, 23–30).

64. Blattman and Annan 2010b, 134.

65. J. Thompson 2014, 3. Hesford 2011 also provides a critique of representations of human rights violations across a wide swath of documentary film, photography, theatre, and art exhibitions; her aim was to consider how "the visual field of human rights internationalism often functions as a site of power for and normative expression of American nationalisms, cosmopolitanisms, and neoliberal global politics" (3). Although my focus on Central Africa is still vast in scope, my grounding in the politics and history of the region allows for a fuller understanding of the interplay of state, empire, and local forces; further, as a theatre and performance studies scholar, I take the interplay of narrative and spectacle for granted since they are inextricable in the context of performance. In a similar vein, Ana Elena Puga and Víctor Espinosa are developing an excellent study of how a melodramatic imagination infuses representations of migrant suffering. They draw on Fassin to argue that those who advocate for migrants rely on "undignified vehicles for packaging pain, for highlighting its value in an economy in which consumers, or spectators, will 'pay' in a currency of empathy, sympathy, or tolerance."

66. Ong 2007, 3. See also Hilgers 2012.

67. A classic example of this dynamic occurred when I was a participant in Erik Ehn and Jean-Pierre Karegeye's 2011 More Life program, which focused on learning from postconflict areas about the potential of peace building and reconciliation, as well as the contribution of the performing arts to these initiatives. (I write about this initiative in more detail in chapter 6.) I hesitate to provide specific examples since the participants in the group were all well intentioned—almost painfully so. Suffice it to say that a twelve-year-old Rwandan boy encountered in the streets of Kigali could present himself as a survivor of the genocide, even though the genocide had occurred seventeen years ago, and be readily believed. Those participants who encountered the boy were deeply resistant to alternative explanations when other members of the group pointed out the discrepancy in his story.

68. For examples, see "The Devilfish in Egyptian Waters," 1882 (http://www.granger.com/popuppreview.asp?image=0056521), "My Boys!," 1885 (http://punch.photoshelter.com/image/I0000iIP5sxaYbZo), "On the Swoop!," 1890 (http://punch.photoshelter.com/image/I00008B8CQ64LA1k), and "In the Rubber Coils," 1906 (http://punch.photoshelter.com/image/I0000qJnpn6a06wo). This last image is reproduced in chapter 4.

69. Heidegger 1995 [1983].

70. Ibid., 239; emphasis in the original. Heidegger's term is *Benommenheit*, which has been translated as "benumbedness," "benumbement," or "captivation." Heidegger's anthropocentric refusal to recognize the potential of animal selfhood has been thoroughly deconstructed; see, for example, Derrida 2009. With the caveat that a metaphorical lens reduces the complexities of animal subjectivity, I do find the conception of empire as an (abstract) beast useful for thinking through differences between neoliberalism and empire. Also, just to be very clear, my application of the term "beast" to describe an empire of trauma is a rejection of Heidegger's racist conflation of animals with the "Negro" and the colonized, a trope that Mbembe (2001) has forcefully and thoroughly critiqued.

71. Hardt and Negri 2000, 62. Their understanding of empire as vampiric borrows from Marx 1976 [1867].

72. Lemarchand 2009; Prunier 2009. These sources are just two examples from a wealth of literature that attests to the transnational scope of the conflicts; see chapter 1 for additional citations.

73. D. Newbury 1996, 1997. Although the phrase "convergent catastrophes" helps underscore the seepage across national borders, Newbury cautions that they should not be understood "simply as an extension of one another" but as crises that stem from "deep local roots" (1997, 211). Some of the roots of these conflicts are explored in chapter 1.

74. Ehn's *Maria Kizito* premiered in 2004 at 7 Stages in Atlanta; *The Overwhelming* premiered at the Royal National Court in 2006 and received its US premiere at the Roundabout Theatre in New York City in 2007. Linden's two-hander play about a Tutsi refugee in London premiered in 2003 at the Finborough Theatre in London and received its US premiere at Kansas City Rep in 2005. It went on to become the most produced play about the Rwandan genocide in the United States, receiving productions in Washington, D.C., Milwaukee, Chicago, Los Angeles, Indianapolis, Atlanta, Coral Gables, and Boston. Katori Hall's play premiered off-Broadway at the Signature Theatre in October 2014; it will be discussed in more detail in chapter 3. Other noteworthy plays include Ken Urban's *A Sense of an Ending* (unpublished manuscript in author's possession), Tanika Gupta's *Sanctuary* (London: Oberon Books, 2002), Catherine Filloux's *Lemkin's House* (2009), and Steve Waters's *World Music* (2003). (See Edmondson 2009a for a discussion of Ehn's *Maria Kizito* and Edmondson 2009b for an analysis of Linden's, Gupta's, and Waters's plays.) It should also be noted that the outpouring of texts about the Rwandan genocide is not limited to single-author plays. *Rwanda 94* (1999), a multimedia performance text that was generated through a four-year collaboration between the Belgian theatre collective Groupov and Rwandan artists, should be noted here, as well as *Fagaala* (2004), a modern dance interpretation of the Rwandan genocide that was choreographed by Germaine Acogny, the head of the acclaimed Senegalese modern dance company Jant-Bi, in collaboration with Japanese choreographer Kota Yamasaki. The work of Rwandan choreographer and playwright Odile Katese is also noteworthy; for example, she workshopped her play *Ngwino Ubeho (Come and Be Alive)* at the 2009 Sundance Theatre Lab in collaboration with artists from Burkina Faso, Togo, and the United States. Her work *The Book of Life* is discussed briefly in the afterword. For additional discussion of Rwandan approaches to dramatizing the genocide, see Kalisa 2006 and Breed 2014.

75. For more information on *Shadows of Memory*, see Al Jazeera, "Rwanda Marks 20th Anniversary of Genocide," April 8, 2014; and "Rwandans Grieve at Genocide Memorial 20 Years On," *Radio France Internationale*, April 7, 2014. The BBC published several photographs of the performance, available at http://www.bbc.com/news/world-africa-26925763.

76. Patraka 1999, 87.

77. Mulekwa's *Time of Fire*, which presents a composite perspective of Uganda's postcolonial history of war, premiered in 1999 at the Birmingham Repertory Theatre in the United Kingdom and was published by Nick Hern in 2000; *dogsbody* premiered at the Theatre of Yugen in San Francisco in 2009 and is currently unpublished. *Butterflies of Uganda* premiered at the Greenway Court Theatre in Los Angeles in 2007 and was published that same year by Brendow; it was performed at the National Theatre in Kampala in 2008.

78. Sam's play *Forged in Fire* is discussed in more detail in chapter 5; Adong's play *Silent Voices* is discussed briefly in the afterword.

79. See the Theatre Communication Group's lists of most produced plays in 2010–2011 at http://www.tcg.org/publications/at/attopten.cfm. The Kinshasa performance, which was produced and sponsored by the US embassy in Kinshasa, was directed by Alexandre Kalengayi Mwambayi and performed by actors of Centre des Recherches d'Arts du Spectacle Africain on November 14, 2011. The play was translated into French with the title *Détruite*.

80. MDD at Makerere has been officially retitled the Department of Performing Arts and Film; however, it is still often called the MDD Department.

81. Mwangi 2007, 322.

82. Several of these artists (Ehn, Asiimwe, Sam, Azeda, and Mulekwa) were also brought together in the summer of 2008 as part of "Eti! East Africa Speaks!," a residency for East African theatre artists that was held at Dartmouth College and in New York City, which I co-organized with Mulekwa and Roberta Levitow of Theatre without Borders. A related program is Sundance Institute East Africa (SIEA), a branch of the Sundance Theatre Lab, which was spearheaded by Levitow and staffed by Asiimwe; the program is now being folded into the Kampala International Theatre Festival organized by Asiimwe. More information about SIEA can be found at http://www.sundance.org/programs/east-africa/. Azeda and Adong have both participated in SIEA; Asiimwe was also active in an administrative role.

83. Françoise Lionnet and Shu-mei Shih coin the phrase "minor transnationalism" to describe a kind of "minor-to-minor network" that "negotiates with national, ethnic, and cultural boundaries, thus allowing for the emergence of the minor's inherent complexity and multiplicity" (2005, 8). Instead of tired postcolonial models that depend on First World centers and Third World margins, Lionnet and Shih emphasize the affiliations and creative borrowings from within and across those margins. In a similar move, Gayatri Chakravorty Spivak advocates "critical regionalism" as a means of expanding identity politics beyond the isolating apparatus of the nation-state. She asks, "Can these regional cross-hatchings happen in a less random way to produce something other than nation-statism, tied by national sovereignty, to check post–cold war Euro-US's perennial dream of universalism?" (Butler and Spivak 2007, 91–92).

84. Rae 2009, 20.

85. Maurer, for example, argues that their concept of empire is "hollow" because it does not acknowledge how "Empire and nation are intimately entwined." He explains that "we fear that in their rush to herald the arrival of a postmodern sovereignty, Hardt and Negri have missed paying close attention to some of the most salient constitutive practices of imperialisms (both new and old), including, most pointedly for us, the enduring framework of the modern nation-state and its sustaining myth of the rule of law" (2003, 90).

86. A report by the US Central Intelligence Agency listed Uganda fourth on a list of fifteen countries "at high risk of state failure" in 2030. See "Global Trends 2030: Alternative

Worlds," available at http://www.dni.gov/files/documents/GlobalTrends_2030.pdf, accessed October 16, 2017. The reference to "nonstate" is found in Herbst and Mills 2013.

87. At the time of this writing, all three countries are either experiencing debates about the legality of running for additional presidential terms or have already lifted term limits. In 2005, Museveni engineered changes in the constitution to lift term limits so that he could run again in 2006 and 2011; he successfully ran yet again in 2016. In 2017, it was widely expected that Parliament would vote to remove the age restriction for presidential candidates, opening the way for Museveni to run for a sixth term in 2021 at the age of 76. In Rwanda in late 2015, a referendum approved constitutional amendments that would allow Kagame to potentially remain in office until 2034. Subsequently, Kagame won a third term in a landslide during the August 2017 elections. In the DRC, riots broke out in 2015 over fears that Kabila would be changing term limits in the constitution. Security forces fired into the crowds of demonstrators in Kinshasa, killing an estimated twenty-one people; thirty-six people died in total ("DR Congo: Deadly Crackdown on Protests," January 24, 2015, available at hrw.org). In 2016, violence broke out again in Kinshasa in response to the government's decision to postpone the election until 2018. Clashes between security and opposition forces in September of that year are believed to have caused an estimated fifty-three deaths; most of the dead were killed by security forces, according to the United Nations ("Rights Monitors, DRC at Odds over Death Toll in September Protests," *VOA News*, October 21, 2016). In October 2017, it was announced that elections would be held in December 2018.

88. Guriev and Treisman 2015, 2, 3.

89. Taussig 1999, 5.

90. Žižek 2008.

91. Benjamin 1977, 31.

92. Huggan 2001, 12.

93. Branch 2011, 28; see also 131.

94. Drewal 1991, 2.

95. Reyntjens 1996, 2004.

96. Ilibagiza 2006.

97. Badiou 2001.

98. Marcus 1998.

99. Gómez-Peña 1996, 5. Long-term immersive fieldwork in, for example, the town of Atiak in northern Uganda or Kibeho in southern Rwanda might have helped me shed at least some of these trappings of empire; the resulting book would be quite different.

100. Straus 2006, xii.

101. Asiimwe, *Forgotten World*, 47.

102. Taussig 1986, 492.

103. Asiimwe, *Forgotten World*, 55.

104. C. Dolan 2009, 305. My thanks to Nelson Kasfir for pointing out this connection.

1

COMPETITIVE MEMORY IN THE GREAT LAKES

Touring Genocide

According to TripAdvisor, the number one thing to do in Kigali is to visit the Kigali Memorial Centre. The center, which opened in 2004 at a cost of approximately $2.5 million, was designed and curated by the UK-based organization Aegis Trust in partnership with the Kigali City Council.[1] What was originally a cluster of five mass graves has expanded to include historical exhibits, memorial gardens, an amphitheatre, archives, and a café; the graves, which have increased to fourteen, hold the remains of an estimated 250,000 victims.[2] Rwanda's "official house of pain" has become an obligatory stop for foreign diplomats and other VIPs passing through Kigali.[3] "Nobody who comes to this memorial site is ever the same when they leave," US ambassador to the United Nations Samantha Power said tearfully to journalists when she visited the center as part of a delegation in 2013.[4] "Take tissues," advises a TripAdvisor reviewer.[5]

The curators use a range of representational strategies in a determined effort to capture the horror of those three months. From the facticity of videotaped testimonies and photographs to the abstractness of sculpture and stained-glass windows, the museum seeks to capture the immensity of genocide through a variety of techniques. Visitors who move past the mass graves encounter a memorial garden complex, in which a waterfall signifies the country's descent into genocide, and roses invoke the individuality of the victims. Those looking for a more gut-wrenching experience can visit the Children's Room in the museum, which contains a display of enlarged backlit photographs of fourteen children who were killed in the genocide. Viewers learn painfully short snippets of information about each child's favorite food, personality, final words, and means of death; the truncated bullet points underscore the brutal absence of testimony. A subtler gesture to the vastness of mourning can be found in a room lined with hundreds of photographs of victims, all donated by the victims' families. The photographs are clipped onto wire and thus achieve a sense of immediacy and familiarity. More photographs are regularly added to the collection as a reminder of the open-ended nature of loss.

The TripAdvisor reviewers are especially complimentary of the museum's historical exhibit, which provides a detailed explanation of the genocide through a series of panels that intermingle images, video, and text.[6] The exhibit is divided into three broad sections: "Before," "During the Genocide," and "After." The first few panels present precolonial Rwanda as a utopia in which Hutu, Tutsi, and Twa lived together harmoniously under the reign of a Tutsi monarchy. The next section, "The Colonial Period," describes how the colonial powers of Belgium and Germany destroyed this sense of harmony through policies of favoritism toward the Tutsi, whom they perceived as a race superior to that of the Hutu. "We had lived in peace for many centuries," a panel explains, "but now the divide between us had begun." Ethnic tension intensified through a series of events—as in 1959, for example, when the majority Hutu rose up against the monarchy, triggering the flight of several thousand Tutsi to neighboring countries, and in 1990, when the Rwandan Patriotic Front (RPF), formed by Tutsi refugees living in exile in Uganda, invaded northern Rwanda and sparked a civil war. The genocide began almost immediately after President Juvenal Habyarimana's plane was shot down on April 6, 1994: "Rwanda had turned into a nation of brutal, sadistic merciless killers and of innocent victims, overnight." Only the RPF, which had been battling its way through the country while the genocide raged, was able to restore order when it overthrew the genocidal Hutu regime in early July, three months after the genocide had begun. As told in the section "After the Genocide," the RPF's dedication to equal rights and the rule of law ushered in a period of reconciliation; its establishment of the community-based system of justice called *gacaca* "played a significant role in laying the foundations of peace and reconciliation in Rwanda." Other panels contain a scathing exposé of the reprehensible behavior of the international community in its refusal to intervene in the killing, as well as an acknowledgment of General Roméo Dallaire's fruitless attempts to persuade the United Nations to send more troops in support of the UN Assistance Mission in Rwanda (UNAMIR).

As Amy Sodaro observes, the Kigali Memorial Centre is "well-curated, compelling, and sophisticated."[7] She and other commentators have noted, however, that a singular historical narrative imposes order and coherence on the museum's layers of emotional complexity.[8] The tale of precolonial harmony, colonial division, the 1994 genocide, and the reestablishment of harmony is reiterated throughout the memorial. The historical narrative of the museum exhibit—"Before," "During," and "After"—is repeated in more artistically in the memorial garden, in which the "river of time" takes visitors from the garden of unity (symbolized by a circular fountain) to the garden of division, in which the circular structure is broken into a kind of pentagram to signify an explosion. The circle is reestablished at the garden of reconciliation, where an elephant with a cell phone seeks to share the good news of Rwanda's triumph with the world. Even the "room of sculptures," filled with evocative and gorgeous abstract figures created by the artist Laurent Hategekimana, repeats the tale of precolonial harmony, the emergence of violence, the genocide, and the aftermath, as explained through a series of captions and in the audio tour. Throughout the museum, the concept of the genocide as the defining moment of Rwandan identity is repeatedly and insistently driven home.

Kenneth W. Harrow terms this narrative one of exceptionalism. He borrows from Giorgio Agamben's *State of Exception* to argue that the genocide is consistently depicted as an exceptional event, with "an inexorable history, with an inevitable path": "All this reads like Greek tragedy, and is entitled tragedy, unfortunately, time and time again. And it leads, always, inevitably, inexorably, to that moment of anagnorisis, of genocide, that culminating, defining moment, ontologically separate from, albeit explained by, that which went before it."[9] Agamben famously argues that the so-called state of exception serves merely as rhetorical justification for governments to enact increasingly authoritarian legislation, thus regularizing and normalizing the exception. In a similar vein, Harrow suggests that the rhetoric of exceptionalism works to conceal the regularity of mass killing in the Great Lakes region. In addition, Harrow's use of the term "tragedy" to describe the narration of the Rwandan genocide underscores the instrumentalizing of the Rwandan genocide on a global scale. Narrating the events of 1994 as tragedy allows the western spectator to experience a sense of catharsis, a term used by Aristotle to describe the purging of negative emotions that occurs as an effect of tragedy.[10] Through this vicarious experience of Rwandan trauma, the spectator experiences a moment of cleansing that ultimately erases the specificity of the genocide. Genocide is thus appropriated as a means of emotional healing. Take tissues.

The Rwandan genocide of 1994, in which an estimated 800,000 Rwandans, most of whom were Tutsi, were systematically exterminated in approximately three months, plays a crucial role in the region's maelstrom of violence.[11] Those three months serve as a watershed moment in the history, politics, and identity making of East and Central Africa, and the legacy and rhetoric of that genocide infiltrate the region. But scratching the surface of historical context reveals a staggering number of genocides and massacres that cannot be understood in isolation, as suggested by the title of René Lemarchand's essay "Genocide in the Great Lakes: Which Genocide? Whose Genocide?"[12] The violence in the eastern DRC, northern Uganda, and 1994 Rwanda are intricately intertwined. Teasing out these regional intersections works against the simplification and domestication of a linear tragic narrative.

Although I retain a degree of linearity in the interests of coherence, I trace a more expansive narrative in which I emphasize the roots and routes of these multifaceted conflicts. "Roots and routes" is a common catchphrase in discussions of transnationality and transnationalism because it not only calls attention to localized causes and players but also situates them in a globalizing world. In *Violence Performed: Local Roots and Global Routes of Conflict*, for example, Patrick Anderson and Jisha Menon address representations of violence embodied within the nation (the "roots") and the spectacular commodification of violence in the media (the "routes"), as well as the "co-implication" of these two terms.[13] But roots and routes are not just coimplicated in the Great Lakes region—they are fused. Attempts to trace the roots of violence reveal a labyrinth of routes in which colonial histories, political alliances, ethnic and regional affiliations, land disputes, and the flights of refugees converge.

I also track how the rhetoric of genocide punctuates this history. Charges of genocide proliferate in the Great Lakes in order to articulate grievances and attempt to gain political traction. This discourse resonates with what Dylan Rodríguez terms "the institutionalized rhetorics of genocide," which "suggest a discrete but identifiably common historical modality of modern suffering within which an otherwise discrepant totality of human experiences can be rationalized, remediated, and potentially repaired—or at least universally acknowledged."[14] Genocide is positioned as exceptional in order to forestall the understanding that "such devastation is, finally, not exceptional, abnormal, or historically episodic when accounting for the historical continuums of racial and racial-colonial dominance."[15] Genocide scholars and activists who insist on a restrictive use of the term might unwittingly perpetuate the notion of exceptionalism by detaching the act of genocide from "the forms of constitutive dehumanization that precede, constitute, and overwhelm the very thing(s) that *genocide* intends to apprehend and, ultimately, definitively name."[16] With Rodríguez's warning in mind, my aim is to consider how genocide has become what historian W. B. Gallie calls "an essentially contested concept."[17] How is the term used both "aggressively and defensively" in the political and historical discourse of the region, and how is the shadow of Rwanda 1994 extended or dissipated in the process?[18] How might these contestations sustain the dynamics of competitive memory, in which groups, governments, and individuals vie for the status of victimhood? I also revisit Harrow's use of anagnorisis to describe the 1994 genocide as that "culminating, defining moment" in Rwandan tragedy. Given that anagnorisis is an Aristotelian term that refers to the protagonist's moment of discovery and recognition, how might the events of 1994 facilitate a recognition of the mutuality of Ugandan, Congolese, and Rwandan suffering and the unexceptionalism of genocide?

Narratives of Colonial and Postcolonial Violence

The following historical sketch emphasizes the role of colonialism in exacerbating ethnic tensions as a source of regional violence.[19] The very concept of the Great Lakes is a colonial invention; the term was coined by nineteenth-century European (mostly English) explorers obsessed with locating the source of the Nile.[20] In their quest, they "discovered" several centralized kingdoms that dominated the interlacustrine region. German, Belgian, and British colonizers would come to favor the monarchical societies, such as the Buganda and Rwanda kingdoms, as superior to the small-scale political communities typical of northern Uganda; they generally perceived these monarchies as conforming to European models of governance and thus oversimplified subtle and diverse interpretations of centralized authority.[21] Starting in the early eighteenth century, political centralization that cohered around ritual kingship emerged through an intersection of dynamic personal mobility, changing social identities, and forms of ritual power.[22] Court intrigues and civil strife had generated an often turbulent political landscape by the time of European colonization in the late nineteenth century. Local elites were often adroit at using colonial policies and structures to facilitate their extension and consolidation of power.[23]

By the late nineteenth century, the Nyiginya dynasty of Rwanda stood out for its degree of hierarchy, centralization, and highly stratified social structure compared with other regional kingdoms, such as Burundi to the south or the Shi, located west of Lake Kivu in the present-day eastern DRC. In contrast to the Kigali Memorial Centre's exhibit that depicts precolonial Rwanda as a unified, peaceful kingdom in which Hutu, Tutsi, and Twa lived harmoniously under the benevolent rule of a Tutsi king, the Rwandan kingdom was characterized by the "persistence of profound internal conflict."[24] From the mid-eighteenth century to the late nineteenth century, the consolidation of court power in Rwanda was accompanied by intense, if sporadic, conflict at two levels: conflict among competing factions within the court and conflict between court army regiments (*ngabo*) and local populations (especially in the north and west).[25] These recurring conflicts not only created havoc within Rwanda but also sowed the seeds for later strife through a series of refugee movements, some of which reached the mountainous plateaus west of Lake Kivu in areas that would become part of the DRC.[26] Despite their diverse origins, these autonomous layers of Rwanda-speaking migrants and refugees would, by the late twentieth century, be grouped together as "Banyarwanda," or "those who come from Rwanda." An understanding of the local dynamics that generated these multiple and discrete waves of migration complicates and even contradicts the memorial's portrayal of precolonial Rwanda as harmonious and static.

The historical exhibit in the Kigali memorial goes on to explain that the German and Belgian colonial administrations shattered Rwanda's precolonial harmony through the introduction of fixed and hierarchical tribal identities. This narrative adheres to official Rwandan historiography, which traces the beginning of genocide ideology to the imposition of colonial rule. As Kagame phrased it in his speech at the twentieth-anniversary commemoration of the genocide in 2014, "The most devastating legacy of European control of Rwanda was the transformation of social distinctions into so-called 'races.' We were classified and dissected, and whatever differences existed were magnified according to a framework invented elsewhere. . . . This was the beginning of the genocide against the Tutsi."[27] Kagame's comment about "the transformation of social distinctions into so-called 'races'" is a reference to the notorious Hamitic hypothesis conceived and promoted by European anthropologists and explorers. In an attempt to account for the highly centralized political formations found in this region, Europeans, unable to comprehend that this model of governance could emerge from the Africans themselves, developed the theory that a "Hamitic-Semitic" pastoralist people who originated in western Asia had invaded the region from Ethiopia and founded these kingdoms. Colonial administrators in Rwanda and Burundi thus divided dynamic allegiances of kinship, clan, and ethnicity into a stark dichotomy of the "Hamitic" Tutsi pastoralists versus the "indigenous" Hutu farmers. Moreover, the Hamitic hypothesis privileged the Tutsi as a "race of lords" and the Hutu as "the class of serfs," as quoted from a 1948 Belgian account; as Jean-Pierre Chrétien puts it more bluntly, the complexities of Rwandan ethnicity became polarized as "Oriental Masters versus Aunt Jemima Negroes."[28] This notion played out with particular perniciousness among Belgian colonizers in the area of Ruanda-Urundi, which was originally a relatively neglected part of German East Africa before it was handed over to Belgium as part of the spoils of World War I. Belgium's enthusiasm for the Hamitic narrative would earn its colonial practices a particularly harsh assessment among historians. Catharine Newbury, for example, argues that "the Belgian administration in Rwanda, even more than in most colonial systems, sought to structure social order, to rationalize and standardize heterogeneous social relations, and to reinforce the powers of the 'natural rulers.'"[29] Belgian racist ideology translated into administrative practice through the introduction of ethnic identity cards in the 1930s that firmly demarcated Rwandan subjects as Hutu, Tutsi, or Twa—a practice that was not instituted, for example, in British Uganda.[30]

But colonial polarization worked in tandem with local forces. The harsh practices of Kigeri Rwabugiri, who reigned from 1865 to 1895 in what Jan Vansina calls "an unrelenting rise of a tide of terror," were also to blame for the hardening of ethnic identities.[31] One of the king's most divisive practices included a system of forced labor (*ubureetwa*) that was imposed only on the Hutu.[32] As a result, former designations of Hutu and Tutsi as markers of cultural difference became "increasingly stratified and rigidified," and "Hutu identity came to be associated with and eventually defined by inferior status."[33] Empirical historical research indicates that German and Belgian colonialism exacerbated rather than instigated ethnic tensions and stratification. To return to Kagame's statement, the "devastating legacy" of European colonialism is undeniable—as will be discussed, the Hamitic hypothesis was to play out with shocking brutality in a series of massacres starting in 1963. But to focus only on the colonial impact to the exclusion of other historical legacies that preceded European arrival precludes a serious, in-depth contextualization of what would unfold in the postcolonial era.[34]

Similar dynamics played out in British Uganda, where local polities both appropriated and contested colonial structures. The Baganda, a dominant ethnic group by the late nineteenth century as a result of two centuries of expansion, were especially adept at using the British presence to extend their reach. Although British policy did not formalize and standardize ethnic categories to the same degree as Belgian policy, the British still perceived monarchical societies, especially the Buganda kingdom, as superior to the decentralized political formations more typical of the northern region.[35] Ronald Atkinson usefully summarized the reasons for the colonizers' neglect of the north, drawing on the example of British attitudes toward the Acholi people:

> This opinion was due in part to the physical remoteness, sparse population, and limited productive capacity of the land, in part to the Acholi people's supposed "natural" laziness and aversion to work (the initial Acholi response to peasant cash cropping and labor migration was not enthusiastic). Second was the relatively small-scale and decentralized nature of Acholi political organization, which made the Acholi neither an especially feared enemy nor a valued ally. And third was Acholi social and cultural practices—especially the wearing of minimal clothing—which both the British and Baganda elite looked down upon as bizarre and primitive.[36]

Once British neglect gave way to intrusion in the early twentieth century—reflected in British efforts to collect taxes, promote cash crops, and require the registration of firearms—the Acholi responded with fierce resistance.[37] The Langi, another northern group who would play a key role in the political landscape of postcolonial Uganda, were ruled primarily through Ganda proxies until just before World War I—an arrangement that underscored the workings of Ganda subimperialism during British rule.[38] Colonial disdain of northern peoples laid the foundation for modern-day stereotypes regarding "the savage north." Statements such as historian Phares Mutibwa's that "there has always existed more backwardness and perhaps a more disorganized and evil society" in the northern region can be traced in part to British colonial legacies, as well as the readiness of southern elites to bolster ethnic stereotypes that positioned them as superior.[39]

In contrast to the forms of colonial encounter in Uganda and Rwanda, the Congo Free State established by King Leopold II of Belgium constituted a "surrealistic oddity" in the scramble for Africa.[40] As a result of at least ten years of behind-the-scenes machinations, Leopold II was granted trusteeship of almost ten million square acres of central Africa under the name the

"Congo Free State" at the Berlin Conference in 1885–1886. Instead of the area being named a colony under the jurisdiction of the Belgian parliament, Leopold became "the absolute ruler of this new state that was to grow some eighty times larger than its metropolis."[41] The king sank his personal assets into building the state infrastructure, which included the establishment of a standing army called the Force Publique in which indigenous Congolese served under the command of European officers. The wild rubber vines that proliferated in the equatorial rain forest of the Congo Free State promised Leopold a profitable return on his investment, and he called on various companies, among which the most notorious was the Anglo-Belgian India Rubber Company (ABIR), to run large portions of the country. He then proceeded to collect half of the sizable profits. The widespread brutality that was carried out by the rubber companies and the Force Publique, which included whippings, mutilations, hostage takings, and massacres of entire villages, stands out as an especially ruthless chapter in European imperialism. In his well-known account of the Congo Free State, *King Leopold's Ghost*, Adam Hochschild argues that an estimated ten million people, or about half the population, died in what he calls "a death toll of Holocaust dimensions."[42]

But the rhetoric of genocide tends to distract attention from the everyday violence of Belgian imperialism and colonialism. Vansina's research in the Kasai region, for example, considers the structural impact of Leopold's rule on the local population, which included a declining birth rate and widespread disease, as well as outright deaths.[43] Preoccupation with the whippings, mutilations, and massacres of the Congo Free State obscures the long-term violence of Belgian colonialism, which formally began in 1908, when Leopold handed the Congo over to the Belgian parliament, and endured for another fifty-two years until independence was achieved in 1960. Although the overt brutality of the Congo Free State lessened after the parliament annexed the region as the Belgian Congo, the perniciousness of later Belgian colonialism created a paradoxical situation in which one of the most industrialized colonies on the continent had produced only seventeen university graduates out of a population of over twenty million by 1960.[44] Even though the eastern region of the Belgian Congo was relatively ignored until after World War I, Belgian practices of restructuring and engineering ethnicities culminated in what Koen Vlassenroot calls "the territorialization of identity," meaning that identity was clearly defined in relation to territory, "further hardening ethnicity as the main organizing principle of local society."[45] Starting in 1937, for example, the resettlement of approximately 85,000 mostly Hutu migrants from Rwanda to Kivu Province as a cheap labor source facilitated the territorialization of identity in light of the colonial administration's policies that privileged migrant Rwandans over "indigenous" Congolese.[46]

In Rwanda itself, the hardening of ethnic identity proceeded apace among the Hutu and Tutsi elite. During the 1950s, simmering tensions expressed themselves through an appropriation of the Hamitic myth, which leaders of both ethnicities had learned in colonial schools and seminaries. As David Newbury explains, "Tutsi leaders argued that they had earned their superior position by right of conquest and by their supposed 'innate' superiority to rule, a conceit which underlay the infamous 'premise of inequality' in Rwanda."[47] This rhetoric justified the Tutsi nobility's monopolization of power; decades of collusion with the colonial administration had strengthened their access to and control over land, labor, and cattle. In turn, the Hutu elite used the Hamitic myth to justify their opposition to Tutsi rule. In light of what they presumed to be their prior occupation, "they rejected [Tutsi] conquest as legitimizing authority."[48] This interpretation of colonial rhetoric was showcased, for example, in the "Hutu Manifesto" of 1957, a treatise by nine Hutu intellectuals that invoked collective Hutu oppression by the foreign "Hamites" to make their case for majority rule. Newbury stresses, though, that the Hamitic hypothesis lacked traction in many rural areas. "What [the peasants] experienced was a result of colonial oppression, not ultimate origins; for them, it was the simple exercise of power that created and reinforced the hierarchies of social superiority."[49] At this point in Rwandan history, the gap between the haves and the have-nots (which included impoverished Rwandans of all ethnic backgrounds) was perhaps more salient among ordinary Rwandans as a political motivation than colonial theories of ethnic origin.[50] The refusal of the Tutsi ruling class to respond to the concerns of the Hutu elite regarding their systematic exclusion from positions of power further intensified tensions. As the tide of decolonization sweeping the continent approached, political parties were legally allowed to form, many of which subsequently divided along ethnic lines.[51]

These tensions ultimately erupted in the so-called Revolution of 1959. After the sudden death of the Tutsi king, the ensuing power struggle between partisans of the monarchy and those who opposed Tutsi rule generated a series of attacks and counterattacks. Scott Straus categorizes two kinds of violence in 1959: violence carried out by mostly young Hutu men attacking Tutsi and looting their homes, and violence committed by supporters of the Tutsi monarchy targeting political leaders from the main opposition parties, which advocated for majority rule.⁵² In response to the unrest, several thousand Tutsi fled to the neighboring countries of Burundi, the Congo, Tanzania, and Uganda, creating a sizable Tutsi diaspora in the Great Lakes region. The revolution ended in 1961 when the Hutu elite abolished the monarchy and declared a republic. They accomplished this feat with the active support of the Belgian colonial administration, which had turned against the Tutsi elite, the former "darlings of the colonizer," and sided with the Hutu opposition and their calls for majority rule.⁵³ A Hutu-dominated administration was established at the time of independence from Belgium in 1962, with President Grégoire Kayibanda, one of the authors of the "Hutu Manifesto," at the helm. A year later, an estimated ten thousand to twelve thousand Tutsi were massacred, an event that Bertrand Russell termed "the most horrible and systematic massacre . . . since the extermination of the Jews by the Nazis."⁵⁴ The rhetoric of ethnic extremism was increasingly taking hold, and the relatively muted violence of 1959 was giving way to widespread killing.⁵⁵ Sporadic massacres against the Tutsi were to continue during Kayibanda's regime.

The Hutu in neighboring Burundi were to experience massacres as well. Although my historical narrative focuses on Uganda, Rwanda, and the DRC, the maelstrom of Great Lakes violence cannot be fully understood without a significant detour through Burundi, which had been separated from Rwanda at the time of independence. As in Rwanda in the late 1950s, a Tutsi elite controlled Burundi; however, unlike the elite in Rwanda, this elite consolidated its control during the transition to independence and cracked down on signs of Hutu unrest. Peter Uvin notes "the vicious dynamic between the two neighboring countries, with [violent] events in each country presenting to the other, in a kind of distorted mirror, the proof of its worse fears, its worst nightmare."⁵⁶ Gérard Prunier also uses the term "mirror" to describe the relation between the two countries: "Their parallel—and at times common—past histories, their comparable social structures, their constant and almost obsessive mutual scrutiny, fated them to be natural mirrors of each other's hopes, woes, and transformations."⁵⁷ The term "mirror" runs the risk of obscuring deep historical differences between the two regions, including, but not limited to, the structure of royalty, the nature of ethnicity, the dynamics of clientship, and army organization. In sum, the term overstates their similarities and repeats the colonial homogenization that lumped the two areas together as Ruanda-Urundi.⁵⁸ That said, the idea of mirroring carries some traction in the postcolonial era in light of the mutual impact of specific events across the Rwanda/Burundi border. The 1963 massacre of Rwandan Tutsi described earlier was partly triggered by a failed invasion of Rwandan Tutsi exiles who had fled to Burundi in response to the 1959 uprising. In 1972, the Tutsi regime in Burundi responded to a Hutu uprising by killing at least 100,000 to 150,000 Hutu in less than three months, in what has been called "the first clear genocide since the Holocaust."[59] The Hutu who fled to Rwanda became instrumental in the spread of Hutu extremism.[60] Indeed, Lemarchand describes the 1972 massacre of Burundian Hutu as the "historical thread that enables us to make sense of subsequent developments," emphasizing its impact on the unfolding of events in Rwanda two decades later.[61]

Other repercussions of the 1972 genocide in Burundi were more immediate. Anti-Tutsi pogroms broke out in Rwanda in response to the carnage across the border; the resulting unrest created the conditions for Juvenal Habyarimana's 1973 seizure of power from Kayibanda.[62] Although Kayibanda and Habyarimana shared Hutu ethnicity, the coup emerged out of deep-seated schisms and tensions between northern and southern Rwanda and thus serves as a reminder that the overriding ethnic framework of Hutu versus Tutsi often conceals complex tensions that cut across region and clan. In what might seem an eerie parallel with contemporary descriptions of postgenocide Rwanda under President Kagame, which is often celebrated as an exemplary African country because of its working infrastructure and economic progress, Habyarimana's Rwanda was hailed as model of integrated rural development: "A small hard-working honest, moral, God-fearing, and stable country—that was the tirelessly diffused image."[63] Although the post-1973 government was less blatantly extremist than Kayibanda's regime—many Rwandan Tutsi initially welcomed Habyarimana for restoring their sense of safety—Habyarimana's administration continued the systematic disenfranchisement of Rwandan Tutsi through quota systems and ethnic identity cards.[64] Habyarimana also experienced increasing pressure about the "right to return" of the sizable Tutsi diaspora in surrounding countries; rough estimates indicate that by 1990, more than half a million Rwandan Tutsi were living in exile.[65]

The aftermath of the Hutu Revolution was acutely felt in the eastern Congo, where up to sixty thousand Tutsi had fled.[66] The "fifty-niners" were relatively wealthy in comparison with their Hutu and Tutsi predecessors who had migrated during the colonial era. Through a combination of bribery and the machinations of Bisengimana Rwema, a well-placed Congolese Tutsi in the postindependence government, these refugees were able to acquire massive amounts of land, much of which had been expropriated from Belgian landowners.[67] Stark divisions between "indigenous" Congolese and the "foreign" Banyarwanda (some of whose ancestors had migrated as far back as the eighteenth century) were exacerbated by alliances between Congolese Tutsi and national and regional politicians. Conflict came to a head in the so-called Kanyarwanda War (1963–1966), in which both Tutsi and Hutu were massacred. As Lemarchand bluntly puts it, "The tendency among 'native' Congolese was to view all Banyarwanda ['people of Rwanda'] living in eastern Congo as the incarnation of a multifaceted menace."[68] Mobutu Sese Seko, who had seized power in 1965 and renamed the country Zaire in 1971, fanned the flames of resentment against the Banyarwanda through his policies of favoritism.[69] As Séverine Autesserre explains, Mobutu promoted ethnic minorities "because they could help him govern without threatening his regime."[70] Several Banyarwanda, for example, received top political positions in his administration. Although the current conflict in the eastern DRC is often understood through the lens of conflict minerals and sexual violence, Autesserre argues persuasively that the conflict can be fully understood only in the context of colonial and postcolonial land conflicts and political jockeying in the Kivus.[71]

Meanwhile, Uganda, which achieved independence from Great Britain in 1962, was struggling with its own volatility. As a result of British colonial policies, northerners dominated the army at the time of independence; in addition, competing rivalries among the southern kingdoms set the stage for continued northern dominance. The first prime minister, Milton Obote, hailed from Lango in the north; his role existed uneasily alongside the presidency of Ganda king Edward Mutesa. Even though Mutesa's role was largely ceremonial, his kingdom had been granted federal status within Uganda. Tensions over this power-sharing arrangement culminated in Obote's ousting of Mutesa in 1966 and the subsequent abolishment of the kingdoms. In response to deep historical grievances toward the Baganda held by many Ugandans, Obote appointed a disproportionate number of northerners, particularly Acholi and Langi, to positions in the civil service and the military. In this attempt to dismantle the colonial privilege accorded to monarchy-based societies of the south, Obote "introduce[ed] a new north-south cleavage into national politics and a new state-based privilege upon that cleavage—the north over the south."[72] To help contextualize the rise of the RPF in the late 1980s, it is worth noting that Obote also discriminated against the "fifty-niners" from Rwanda, of whom approximately 200,000 had fled to Uganda, partly because of a sense of affiliation with the pastoralist Ankole-Hima people in the southern region.[73] The Rwandan refugees in Uganda were to serve as either a handy scapegoat for popular discontent or an ally in successive regimes.[74]

In part as a response to the increasing unpopularity of Obote's rule, Idi Amin overthrew Obote's government in January 1971. Although Amin was also a northerner, he came from West Nile in far northwestern Uganda, and thus he sought to purge the army of Acholi and Langi and relied instead on troops from his own area. During the years of his regime, Amin's troops killed thousands of Acholi and Langi.[75] After a notorious period of brutality, Amin, in his turn, was overthrown in 1979 with the assistance of Tanzanian troops, and Obote returned to power in 1980 after the short-lived presidencies of Yusuf Lule and Godfrey Binaisa.[76] Obote promptly reappointed Acholi and Langi to military positions, and, as part of a recurring cycle of recrimination, many of these reinstated troops took revenge against those from the West Nile District—citizens as well as soldiers—in the early 1980s. What was widely perceived as Obote's favoritism toward Langi, though, exacerbated tensions between Langi and Acholi soldiers, which eventually culminated in another coup in 1985 by "the two Okellos" (Tito Okello and Bazilio Olara-Okello, both of whom were Acholi army generals).[77] The alliances of earlier periods disintegrated, setting the stage for further distrust and resentment among army factions during the LRA conflict.[78]

Obote's second regime was also marked by civil war. In 1981, a young, energetic leader named Yoweri Museveni, a member of the southern Ankole-Hima ethnic group, established a rebel coalition force, the National Resistance Movement (NRM), to fight against Obote's Uganda National Liberation Army (UNLA), a conflict commonly termed the Bush War.[79] The NRM generated support throughout southern Uganda partly by playing on deep-seated fears of northern domination and thus deepened the historic north/south divide. In his analysis of the violence during Obote's and Amin's regimes, Abdu Kasozi calls the carnage in the Luwero Triangle (an era just north of Kampala, where most of the fighting occurred) a "Ugandan holocaust," referring in particular to the brutal violence of (mostly northern) government soldiers against southern civilians, in which an estimated 200,000 civilians died.[80] The massacres of southerners at the hands of Obote's UNLA troops remain a bitter memory in the south.[81] The 1985 coup that ousted Obote just temporarily stopped the conflict; only when Museveni's army invaded Kampala in 1986 and overthrew the Okello regime did the war come to an official end.

Museveni's success was partly due to his considerable support from the disaffected Rwandan "fifty-niners" and their descendants as NRM fighters. According to Mahmood Mamdani, when the NRM invaded Kampala in 1986, about one-quarter of Museveni's force of sixteen thousand were of Rwandan origin.[82] Kagame, who was among the original group of fighters in Museveni's first attack against Obote's regime in 1981, rose through the ranks and became the chief of military intelligence once Museveni came to power in 1986.[83] Kagame was not unique in this respect; for their loyalty, Museveni rewarded several Rwandans with high positions in the military and government upon his accession to the presidency.[84] Later, this early alliance of the Rwandans with the NRM in the 1980s would exert a powerful influence on the events of post-1994 Rwanda and the DRC.

With the establishment of Museveni's NRM government, a new chapter of violence in the north was about to unfold. Obote's troops had fled north after their defeat, and Museveni's troops pursued them with determination. As Adam Branch puts it, Museveni's troops "launched a counterinsurgency without an insurgency" because the returning UNLA soldiers were often alienated and disenfranchised in their home communities.[85] In August 1986, to respond to the NRM threat, three thousand to four thousand of these former Ugandan troops regrouped as the Uganda People's Democratic Army (UPDA); "at this point, the imagined insurgency became real."[86] The atrocities committed by the NRM troops in the northern region strengthened the currents of anger against Museveni's government, which in turn facilitated the rise of another insurgency, the Holy Spirit Movement, led by Alice Lakwena. In an attempt to reintegrate these demobilized soldiers who were causing havoc among civilians in Acholiland, Lakwena used her spiritual power to mobilize a discourse of healing that allowed her to assert authority over the members of former fighting forces—and Acholi citizens generally—eventually assembling an army of seven thousand to ten thousand troops that famously marched on Kampala in 1987 with the aim of overthrowing Museveni.[87] Although the march ultimately failed, the Holy Spirit Movement provided a powerful rhetoric of spirituality-based rebellion that Joseph Kony would eventually appropriate into the formation of the LRA. In the immediate aftermath of Lakwena's rebellion, the NRM cracked down even more brutally; in

1989, for example, the rape of Acholi men, called *tek gungu*, was an especially notorious army tactic.[88]

Prunier calls attention to an especially complicated (and controversial) transnational route of violence between northern Uganda and Rwanda. As previously mentioned, many Rwandans were appointed to high ranks in Museveni's army as loyal allies. Some of these Rwandan officers were involved in the atrocities committed against the Acholi in Museveni's campaign against Alice Lakwena's insurgency. Prunier claims that these soldiers "committed massacres, to such an extent that President Museveni had to send special military judges to the north to curb his own army." He identifies Kagame as one of these judges and adds that some of the defendants would become his subordinates in the RPF.[89] As Branch notes, writing in 2011, "Even today, the first wave of [Museveni's forces] that entered Acholiland are often referred to as Rwandese, and much is made of the Rwandan origin of the Deputy Army Commander at the time, Fred Rwigyema, and of rumors of Museveni's Rwandan origins."[90] As will be discussed in chapter 5, such sentiments seriously compromise present-day cultural exchanges between Rwandans and northern Ugandans, initiated in the mistaken belief that they would identify with each other's suffering instead of realizing that Rwandans might be perceived as perpetrators.

The emergence of the LRA in 1988 should at least partly be understood as a response to the massive human rights abuses against the Acholi people perpetrated by the troops associated with Museveni's NRM in their determination to "pacify" the area.[91] Former members of the Holy Spirit Movement and the UPDA were included in Joseph Kony's new insurgency; indeed, Kony, who claimed that Alice Lakwena was his aunt, originally called his movement the Holy Spirit Movement.[92] In its early years, the LRA constituted a relatively low-level (if still extremely violent) insurgency. By 1994, however, it began receiving full support from the Sudanese government and established several camps in the southern part of Sudan.[93] From that time, the LRA rapidly increased from about three hundred men to a fighting force of more than three thousand, and the scale of the violence ramped up alarmingly.[94] Although the LRA had ostensibly been formed to overthrow Museveni's government, LRA troops more often came to "punish" their fellow Acholi—whom they believed were sympathizers of the government—with mutilation, abduction, pillaging, rape, and murder.[95] Civilians suffered a horrific toll as a result of being caught between the LRA and the NRM (renamed the Uganda People's Defence Force, or UPDF, in 1995). Government troops resorted to their own versions of punishment—mass detentions, torture, killing, looting, and rape—in their zeal to identify LRA sympathizers. Starting in 1996, the state also forcibly displaced approximately one million northern Ugandans into internally displaced people (IDP) camps; the shocking conditions of the camps, which included malnutrition, disease, and insecurity, are regularly invoked as a defining feature of the LRA conflict.[96]

In addition to the insurgency in the north, Museveni faced a growing "Rwandan problem." The Rwandan refugees in Uganda had become a political liability for Museveni because other Ugandans generally resented what they perceived as the Rwandans' favored status in his administration and military.[97] In 1987, the refugees founded the Rwandan Patriotic Front (RPF) in support of broad themes of democracy, national unity, and the right of return for Rwandan refugees.[98] At the time of its creation, according to Mamdani, members were divided over whether they should pursue an armed return to Rwanda or naturalization in their host country; however, in response to Museveni's reneging on earlier promises of Ugandan citizenship for these refugees, this ambivalence had given way by 1990 to a clear insistence on armed return.[99] In October of that year, a force of a few thousand RPF troops invaded Rwanda from Uganda.[100]

The war triggered by the RPF invasion, the first phase of which ended in 1993 with the signing of a peace agreement with Habyarimana's government, and the 1994 genocide intersect in ways that continue to be extremely controversial to discuss. Lemarchand usefully summarizes the coinciding of these two events: "The Rwanda blood bath came about as a planned, organized, and coordinated response of Hutu extremists to the very real threats posed to the Hutu state by the RPF."[101] As the invasion gained strength and the RPF took control over increasing swaths of territory in northern Rwanda, fear over the return of Tutsi domination seized the Hutu population and contributed significantly to a climate of uncertainty, making them vulnerable to the inflammatory rhetoric of the coalition extremist movement known as Hutu Power. Tensions were exacerbated by the mass displacement (about one-seventh of the population) of Rwandans fleeing the RPF; stories of RPF atrocities committed against northern Rwandans spread like wildfire.[102] Economic uncertainties triggered by a sharp decline in coffee prices and policies of structural adjustment are believed to have heightened the tension.[103] Local massacres of Tutsi were carried out from 1990 to 1993 as "test runs" for the cataclysm of

1994.[104] The 1993 assassination of the Burundian Hutu president Melchior Ndadaye at the hands of his Tutsi-dominated military, which sparked a ten-year civil war in Burundi, provided additional fuel for currents of ethnic extremism in Rwanda; indeed, Alison Des Forges comments that "Hutu Power ... was built upon the corpse of Ndadaye."[105] The signing of the peace agreement between the RPF and the Rwandan government known as the Arusha Accords in 1993 increased rather than dissipated tensions because hard-liners in Habyarimana's government and in the political opposition were alarmed at the concessions being made to the RPF, a contingent of which was installed in the national parliament building in Kigali that same year. To oversee the creation of the transitional government, the United Nations established the UNAMIR force of 1,300 peacekeepers under the supervision of Dallaire. As painstakingly detailed by Des Forges, evidence of genocidal preparations (distribution of assault weapons, training of youth militias, the compilation of lists of prominent Tutsi, and outright killing) became increasingly common starting from November 1993. Local human rights organizations and development NGOs denounced these preparations to no effect.[106]

The cataclysm erupted on the evening of April 6, 1994, when Habyarimana's plane was shot down as he was flying back to Kigali from peace talks in Arusha, Tanzania. Everyone on board, including the new Burundian president, Cyprien Ntaryamira, and Habyarimana himself, was killed. The genocide commenced within hours after the shooting down of the president's plane, leading to speculation that the downing served as a prearranged signal among Hutu hard-liners and extremists; the identity of the assailants, however, continues to be debated.[107] At the beginning, the genocide was carried out primarily by the Presidential Guard and other elite military units, concentrated mostly within Kigali. By April 8, though, "genocide became official government policy," and youth militias, known most commonly as Interahamwe, took up the cause in numerous prefectures.[108] Terrified Rwandans fled to churches, schools, and hospitals, which had offered safety in previous massacres and periods of unrest. Instead of providing refuge, these places of mass gatherings facilitated the killing on an even larger scale. Most of the genocide's most notorious massacres, such as those at the Kibeho parish church and the Murambi technical school (discussed in chapters 3 and 6, respectively), had occurred by the end of April. Des Forges estimates that around one-half of the Tutsi population was exterminated in this first month.[109]

As previously noted, the Kigali Memorial Centre describes this seeming frenzy as a sudden rupture: "Rwanda had turned into a nation of brutal, sadistic merciless killers and of innocent victims, overnight." To explain the singular intensity and scale of the genocide, which exceeds the scope of any other mass killing discussed in this chapter, the curators resort to an ahistorical explanation that erases the multifaceted and deep combination of roots and routes that produced this singular event. But when the "overnight" is situated in its historical context, it stretches back at least to the nineteenth century. The Hamitic hypothesis was carried to its logical and deadly extreme as the hate radio station RTLM urged people to smash the "pretty little nose[s]" of the Tutsi and an extremist politician called for sending the Tutsi "home" to Ethiopia via the Nyabarongo River, which became choked with thousands of bodies in 1994.[110] At roadblocks, the identity cards introduced during the colonial era that categorized Rwandans as either Hutu, Tutsi, or Twa often served as determinations of life or death. The genocidal state capitalized on hardened ethnic categories to persuade Hutu that Tutsi relatives, neighbors, and friends were the "enemy" and that Hutu were the innocent victims of the Tutsi aggressors. Nevertheless, despite the intensity and efficiency of the genocidal apparatus, numerous Rwandans were not persuaded by this rhetoric and attempted to find an uneasy negotiation between survival and ethics as the country went up in flames. The museum's stark dichotomy of "brutal, sadistic merciless killers" and "innocent victims" notwithstanding, the gray area between these two categories was capacious and densely occupied.[111]

The international community chalked up the killing to "tribal warfare" and "racial hatred" and determinedly looked the other way. After the murder of ten Belgian peacekeepers on April 7, Belgium and Bangladesh withdrew their troops, leaving Dallaire with a force of 540 peacekeepers, mostly from Ghana, to cope with the onslaught.[112] The United States and other western powers steadfastly refused to intervene, even to jam the radio waves of RTLM. It was only in late June that a massive influx of French troops sought to establish a humanitarian safe zone in southwestern Rwanda, called Operation Turquoise, but even this attempt has been roundly condemned as a facade to provide a safe escape route for genocidaires to escape into neighboring Zaire. Operation Turquoise might have helped save some Tutsi—Immaculée Ilibagiza, whose story of survival is described in chapter 3, sought and briefly received refuge in one of the French camps—but, as Des Forges comments, Operation

Turquoise was "as much to prevent an RPF conquest of the entire country as to save civilian lives."[113]

Within days after the genocide began, the RPF ended the cease-fire and launched a massive attack aimed at routing the Rwandan state, which was already severely weakened by internal opposition and division.[114] The RPF's seizure of Kigali on July 4 is commonly used to demarcate the end of the genocide; its precise role in ending the genocide is a more complicated question.[115] As the RPF consolidated control, approximately 700,000 former Tutsi exiles returned to Rwanda.[116] The RPF government took several celebrated steps toward establishing a culture of reconciliation, such as abolishing identity cards that designated ethnicity and launching the *gacaca* system to try lesser perpetrators of the genocide. But its authoritative approach to governance became manifest through its sharp curtailing of political space and alternative narratives. The story delineated in the Kigali memorial demonstrates the heavy hand of the state through multiple omissions and elisions, all of which shore up notions of collective Tutsi victimhood and, alternatively, RPF heroism. Its romanticized portrayal of precolonial Rwanda, for example, elides the system of forced labor that increasingly targeted Hutu; it also refuses to acknowledge widespread criticism of *gacaca*, which largely failed to provide fair trials in accordance with international human rights norms.[117] Silence further surrounds the political and economic dominance of returned Tutsi exiles from Uganda, who have been particularly advantaged in the post-1994 era.[118]

The museum's silence regarding RPF war crimes in Zaire is especially deafening.[119] Within a week after the installation of the RPF regime in Kigali, over a million Rwandans fled across the border to North and South Kivu Provinces in Zaire because of fear of retribution.[120] The exodus to Zaire included several thousand former members of the Hutu militias, as well as former officers and soldiers of the Forces Armeés Rwandaises (FAR), who strategically located themselves in the hastily formed refugee camps. By October 1994, they began to launch attacks across the Rwandan border in a continuation of the war between the former Hutu-dominated regime and the newly established RPF government. Partly out of frustration with Mobutu's military support of the former FAR, the RPF helped engineer the creation of a new Congolese rebel force, the Alliance of Democratic Forces for the Liberation of the Congo-Zaire (AFDL), to be led by Laurent-Désiré Kabila, a longtime rebel soldier who had fought in various rebellions and mini-rebellions in the 1960s and 1970s. Kabila's march against the crumbling Mobutu regime is termed the

First Congo War (1996–1997). The Rwandans not only offered Kabila substantial logistical and military support but also took a leading role in military decisions; Jason Stearns describes the AFDL as a mere "fig leaf" for Rwandan involvement.[121] Uganda's role in the First Congo War was less overt than Rwanda's, but Museveni's government did provide troops and artillery.[122] Although Zairians widely perceived Kabila as a Rwandan puppet, the RPF regime successfully installed him as president in 1997. Kabila subsequently renamed the country the Democratic Republic of the Congo and promised a "rebirth" at his inauguration. Numerous spectators openly jeered.[123]

The carnage of the First Congo War was staggering. The death toll included the estimated 300,000 deaths of Rwandan Hutu refugees in the former Zaire, whose desperate flight through the equatorial Zairian rain forest is eloquently narrated by Marie Béatrice Umutesi in her memoir *Surviving the Slaughter: The Ordeal of a Rwandan Refugee in Zaire*.[124] In addition to being relentlessly targeted by Mobutu's forces and the RPF/AFDL, the refugees were dismissed by the international community as genocidaires despite the vast numbers of innocent civilians trapped in horrific conditions. The Congolese Hutu—many of whom had migrated to North Kivu during the colonial era as part of the Belgian resettlement scheme previously discussed—were the victims of what might be considered genocide. Evidence provided by the UN 2010 "mapping report" strongly indicates that the RPF and the AFDL killed Hutu civilians (both Zairian and Rwandan) indiscriminately as part of their official mission to wipe out the former FAR and members of the Interahamwe militia groups who had fled to Zaire, in what Lemarchand calls "a genocide of attrition."[125]

An even larger conflict was on the immediate horizon. A year later, Africa's "world war" (also called the Second Congo War, 1998–2003) broke out when Kabila expelled the Rwandan and Ugandan forces that had brought him to power. Rwanda and Uganda promptly engineered another rebellion through the newly formed Rally for Congolese Democracy (RCD) in another bid for control of the Congolese state.[126] Several African countries, with Uganda and Rwanda at the helm, rushed into the fray to support either one of the rapidly multiplying rebel forces or the Congolese government, which by 2001 was headed by Kabila's son, Joseph Kabila, who had taken power upon the assassination of his father.[127] Whereas the first war had a modicum of sense behind it insofar as Mobutu's ostentatious and inept despotism was an embarrassment to the entire region, the Second Congo War took the appearance of a free-for-all to seize control of the Congo's mineral riches.[128] Even the staunch

Uganda/Rwanda alliance broke down over access to diamond deposits, leading to a weeklong battle in 2000 between the former allies in Kisangani; an estimated 760 Congolese civilians were caught in the crossfire and killed.[129] The Second Congo War is widely described as the deadliest conflict since World War II; Congolese deaths have been estimated at 5.4 million.[130]

North Kivu and South Kivu were a nexus of conflict in both wars.[131] The Banyamulenge in South Kivu and other Tutsi who had migrated to Rwanda after 1959, whose claims to Congolese citizenship had been increasingly challenged in a series of legislative acts during Mobutu's era, had generally supported the RPF in its 1990 invasion of Rwanda.[132] Indeed, many had joined the RPF in its fight against Habyarimana's government and later joined the Rwanda-backed AFDL in its march against Mobutu. Congolese Tutsi also served as a core constituency of the RCD (which, readers will recall, was also supported by Rwanda) when it launched its war against Kabila's newly installed government from Goma in North Kivu in 1998. These tensions have crystallized into widespread hatred of Congolese Tutsi, who are perceived as a kind of "Trojan horse" that would allow the Rwandan government to annex the eastern region in order to return to the precolonial glories of "greater Rwanda."[133] Congolese Tutsi have undoubtedly committed numerous atrocities against Congolese civilians through their participation in various armed militias.[134] Nevertheless, Lemarchand contends that "few people have been dealt a harsher blow by history" insofar as they have been used by the RPF as "cannon fodder," on the one hand, and targeted by the ethnic hatred of fellow Congolese, on the other.[135]

In 1996, David Newbury coined the phrase "convergent catastrophes" to describe the violence in the former Zaire after the events of 1994.[136] Despite recent tentative moves toward regional stability,[137] the salience of the phrase continues to resonate at the time of this writing, more than twenty years after the Rwandan genocide. The Hutu militias operating in the DRC, which came together as the Democratic Forces for the Liberation of Rwanda (FDLR) in 2000, have played a key role in the Congolese conflict through their mass killings of civilians in North and South Kivu Provinces.[138] Despite the much-hailed surrender of approximately two hundred FDLR rebels in 2014, it remains one of the largest insurgency groups operating in the eastern Congo.[139] Although peace agreements were signed in 2003 and 2009, the eastern Congo continued to serve as a nexus of conflict as a result of at least thirty rebel armies; the Congolese army (Armed Forces for the Democratic Republic of the Congo, FARDC) and, to a lesser extent, UN peacekeepers have also contributed to the unrest through human rights abuses.[140] Meanwhile, Rwanda and Uganda continued to meddle in the region; the most recent manifestation was allegedly the M23 rebellion, which emerged in 2012 and rapidly moved to the forefront as one of the most powerful of the armed insurgencies before surrendering in late 2013. M23's official aim was to protect the Banyamulenge; its "protection," however, involved the displacement of hundreds of thousands of people, as well as summary executions, rape, and forced recruitment of civilians.[141] In 2012, the UN Group of Experts released a controversial report on the M23 rebellion that specifically named the Rwandan and, to a lesser extent, the Ugandan governments as key backers of the rebellion.[142] As even this brief summary indicates, the political leadership and top brass of Kinshasa, Kigali, and Kampala have played a crucial role in the convergence of catastrophe, in no small part through their manipulation of history and politicization of ethnicity.

The LRA serves as an especially notorious manifestation of transnational catastrophe. After terrorizing local populations in northern Uganda and southern Sudan from its inception in the late 1980s, the LRA crossed into the DRC in 2005 and established a base in Garamba National Park; it has not conducted operations in Uganda since 2006. After failed peace talks held in Juba from 2006 to 2008 and a UPDF-led offensive meant to rout LRA forces in Garamba, the LRA dispersed across the northeastern DRC, the southeastern Central African Republic (CAR), and the Western Equatorial Province of present-day South Sudan. Since then, it has resumed its campaign of violence beyond Uganda's borders. In late December 2008, the LRA carried out the notorious "Christmas massacres" in the Haut-Uele Province in the northeastern Congo, which left hundreds of people in the villages of Doruma, Duru, and Faradje dead; a year later, it committed the "Makombo massacres" in the villages of Mabanga Ya Talo, Makombo, and Tapili.[143] The LRA has also created havoc in the southeastern CAR through killings and abductions, particularly in 2012.[144] At the time of this writing, the LRA, which is believed to consist of one hundred to two hundred combatants and their dependents, continues to be most active in the northeastern DRC and in the eastern region of the CAR.[145] Mass publicity campaigns run by organizations such as Enough! and Invisible Children have galvanized US military intervention against the LRA, which, as argued by Kristof Titeca, has only intensified the waves of violence against civilians.[146] Even though its actual threat on the ground might be relatively minimal, the LRA occupies a starring role on the stage of empire, provoking a massive influx of foreign resources that Museveni has strategically used to shore up his friendly relations with the US government.[147] As this brief historical overview has repeatedly demonstrated, the exacerbation of violence and the extension of state power work in tandem, and ordinary Ugandans, Rwandans, and Congolese are caught in the ever-expanding crossfire.

One area of the Kigali Memorial Centre is devoted to "Wasted Lives," a comparative perspective on genocides throughout human history. In light of the multiple massacres and genocides that have occurred throughout the region, this area has the potential to be crowded with local references. One might anticipate, for example, that the mass killing of Congolese in the Congo Free State would help strengthen the master narrative of the perniciousness of colonialism and underscore the role of the Belgians as the original perpetrators. Instead, the memorial maintains a stringent silence regarding its neighbors. Panels are devoted to the violence of the Pol Pot regime in Cambodia in the 1970s, the Armenian genocide of 1915, the Balkans of the early 1990s, and the Holocaust (which receives the most discussion and coverage in the exhibit). The closest the exhibit approaches "home" is the German genocide of the Herero people in present-day Namibia, roughly 1,600 miles away. Despite the numerous episodes of mass violence that occurred just across the Congolese, Ugandan, and Burundian borders, the Gisozi memorial rigorously excludes all of them except the totalizing event of 1994. The remainder of this chapter touches on the political parameters of this deafening silence.

The Poetics of Recognition

The scale of the carnage in Rwanda in 1994, captured in the phrase "a million dead in a hundred days," would seem to assure the status of the country as the ultimate victim. Competition for victimhood, though, is rife throughout the region. The DRC aims to top Rwanda's rhetoric of one million dead through its claim of five million dead in the course of the Congo Wars; moreover, Congolese human rights organizations and political leaders regularly depict Rwanda as the perpetrator par excellence in order to topple Rwanda from its victimhood perch. Congolese Tutsi, in turn, might invoke the 1994 genocide as justification for their continued fighting in the Kivus. In addition, Kagame and Museveni's alliance has facilitated widespread regional beliefs about Uganda and Rwanda's joint efforts to propagate a "Hima-Tutsi" empire. Although these fears often manifest as a kind of free-floating paranoia that political leaders are quick to manipulate in order to exacerbate anti-Tutsi prejudice, the impact of the Kagame-Museveni alliance on the events of post-1994 Rwanda and the DRC is undeniable. The notion of an emerging "Hima-Tutsi empire," which has expanded to include Joseph Kabila through rumors of a Rwandan Tutsi mother, shores up the concept of a collective Bantu victimhood firmly rooted in colonialist Hamitic mythology. Critical engagement with these beliefs can be a fraught enterprise.

The term "genocide" also serves as a rhetorical weapon of choice in northern Uganda. Olara Otunnu, the former UN under secretary general and opposition presidential candidate, who hails from northern Uganda, has regularly charged Museveni's government with carrying out a genocide of the Acholi people through the appalling conditions of the IDP camps where the population was forced to relocate.[148] Through various inflammatory media forums, Museveni has also been accused of committing genocide against the Baganda in the Luwero Triangle through the actions of the NRM during the Bush War of the 1980s, in addition to participating in the 1994 genocide in Rwanda and the violence in the eastern DRC through his alliance with Kagame and the RPF.[149] Within northern Uganda, Acholi, Langi, and West Nilers compete over claims to victimhood, invoking their treatment during the regimes of Amin (for Acholi and Langi) or Obote (for West Nilers). More recently, tensions between Acholi and Langi have been exacerbated by what Langi people perceive as a disproportionate dispensing of aid to the Acholi subregion. Because the LRA originally emerged as an Acholi conflict before moving to the Lira subregion around 2001, some Langi are keen to position the Acholi as the perpetrators. Memories of the violence carried out by Tito Okello's troops in Lira during the 1985 coup add emotional fuel to the fire of ethnicity.[150]

In sum, fierce competition over definitions of victimhood characterize the Central African political landscape. Although I am attracted to Michael Rothberg's notion of multidirectional memory, which suggests that cataclysmic events such as the Shoah can contribute to an intercultural, productive use of memory characterized by a dynamic process of borrowing and cross-referencing, the generosity and optimism on which this concept depends are sorely lacking in the context of Great Lakes politics. Instead, the concept of competitive memory—the perception that one mass trauma can crowd out another in the public imagination—is more salient. Rothberg describes this kind of memory war as a "zero-sum struggle over scarce resources,"[151] but I suggest that it is precisely because of the scarcity of these resources that the war is sustained. The generosity inherent in multidirectional memory is a luxury that Central Africa cannot afford. This jockeying for victimhood might be likened to similar struggles that are carried out in the United States, in which marginalized populations often try to outdo one another on a scale of oppression in order to articulate claims for justice and reparation.[152] Wendy Brown's concept of wounded attachments is often cited in these discussions to theorize the deep investment of excluded populations in their history of suffering; the political scene requires that they brandish the wounds inflicted on their bodies and psyches in a bid for recognition.[153] The question is, how might political rights be achieved when the "logics of pain" work to resubordinate the subject that is ostensibly fighting its historical subjugation?[154]

To pursue this question in the context of the Great Lakes is to confront Brown's logics of pain on a staggering scale. For Rwandan Tutsi, for example, the "wound" in question is not just systematic disenfranchisement in political and economic life; it consists of the deaths of hundreds of thousands of people. Even though the application of Brown's exploration of contemporary US identity politics in late modern secular society to Uganda, Rwanda, and the DRC has clear limits, her linkage of wounded attachment to Nietzsche's concept of ressentiment, or moralizing revenge of the powerless, is still pertinent. Brown generally conceptualizes ressentiment in terms of the production of guilt; however, she also acknowledges "not only a psychological but a political practice of revenge, a practice that reiterates the existence of an identity whose present past is one of insistently unredeemable injury."[155] She continues, "The past cannot be redeemed *unless* the identity ceases to be invested in it and it cannot cease to be invested in it without giving up its identity as such, thus giving up its economy of avenging and at the same time perpetuating its hurt."[156] She calls attention to the sufferer's determination to locate an agent for her or his suffering, which, according to Nietzsche, helps to "deaden, by means of a more violent emotion of any kind, a tormenting, secret pain that is becoming unendurable, and to drive it out of consciousness at least for the moment."[157] Revenge does not simply satisfy a drive for retribution—it relieves pain. Brown's glossing of ressentiment helps clarify how victimhood is inextricably folded into a cycle of unending violence—or, as Mamdani famously put it, how victims become killers.[158] Nietzsche understood that the unendurable pain could be relieved only "for the moment," meaning that ressentiment calls for a perpetual cycle of accusations and blame.

Again, though, Brown's theoretical model falls short in the Great Lakes context, where the cause of moralizing revenge is not necessarily carried out by the powerless. Rather than seeking protection, as in the case of the US-based marginalized communities described in Brown's analysis, the RPF has assumed the reins of power. The state has accordingly moved swiftly to enact tight control over the narrative of exceptionalism; to question this narrative could lead to criminal charges of negationism—that is, of diminishing the horrors of those three months in 1994.[159] A particularly well known example occurred at the Kigali Memorial Centre when opposition figure Victoire Ingabire visited it in 2010. After placing flowers on the mass grave, she delivered a speech that included these damning remarks: "If we look at this memorial, it only stops at people who died during the Tutsi genocide. The Hutus who lost their loved ones are also suffering; they think about the loved ones who perished and are wondering, 'When will our dead ones also be remembered?' For us to reach reconciliation, we need to empathize with everyone's suffering."[160] The government responded by prosecuting her for genocide ideology and divisionism, and she was formally arrested later that year; she is currently serving a fifteen-year sentence. International organizations, such as Human Rights Watch (HRW) and the United Nations, are also not immune to government censure and are regularly accused of revisionism.[161] When the United Nations released its mapping report in 2010, which alluded to the possibility that the Rwandan government participated in acts of genocide against Hutu civilians during the First Congo War, as described earlier, the report predictably outraged the Rwandan government, which responded that such claims were tantamount to genocide denial. Certainly, denial of the Rwandan genocide does exist—revisionists claim, for example, that the Rwandan Tutsi victims of 1994 should be classified as casualties of the civil war between the Rwandan government and the RPF rather than as victims of a determined effort of systematic extermination. Furthermore, the throwing of grenades at the Gisozi memorial in 2008 and 2009 during the week of commemorating the genocide that occurs each April serves as a harsh reminder that anti-Tutsi ideology in Rwanda continues to simmer.[162] But because of the state's instrumentalization of the threat of denial to stifle opposition and dissent, attempts to situate the events of 1994 in a larger, transnational context that includes Burundi and the DRC run the risk of being criminalized.

But does the discourse of negationism explain the silence of international theatre artists? In light of the regularity with which categories of victims and perpetrators are blurred, why do western playwrights insist on clearly demarcated boundaries? Lynn Nottage's 2009 play *Ruined*, a daring exploration of sexual violence in the eastern DRC, drew on considerable research in Uganda, Rwanda, and Kenya, during which she interviewed a wide range of players in the theatre of war, from former LRA combatants to Congolese female refugees. What is striking, though, in the context of this chapter is the play's refusal to invoke Rwanda despite the country's looming presence in the conflict in the eastern DRC. In contrast, Uganda is mentioned several times in the play: the characters smoke Ugandan cigarettes, the characters speak of Kampala as an oasis of peace, and a rebel soldier scoffs at how the government troops "bring soldiers from Uganda, drive us from our land and make us refugees."[163] As explained previously, the Ugandan government was indeed a contributing factor in the two Congo wars; its role, though, was moderate in comparison with that of Rwanda.[164] I discuss Nottage's fascinating play in much more detail in chapter 4; here, my point is that the "routes" of violence are carefully ignored in favor of a more nation-centric and ultimately more contained concept of "roots." This hesitance is perhaps understandable given that any challenge to Rwanda's narrative of victimhood leaves a playwright vulnerable to charges of genocide denial, but these representations deny Rwanda's role as a regional heavyweight and the actions of Rwandan troops on Congolese soil. These silences run the risk of exacerbating regional resentment and competitive memory.

This artistic reluctance to address regional and transnational flows of violence resonates with the praxis of human rights, which is plagued by its own evasions and ironies. Chandra Lekha Sriram and Amy Ross identify nation-statism as the "central irony and challenge" of human rights discourse, noting that "crimes are on the one hand recognized as of international concern but, due to the state-centric nature of international legal mechanisms and responses, are often tailored in such a way as to exclude crimes committed outside a state territory or inside another."[165] In their analysis of northern Uganda and the DRC, they point out that although Kony is under investigation by the International Criminal Court (ICC) in The Hague, the ICC is limiting its investigations only to the crimes that Kony has committed in northern Uganda and not in southern Sudan, the DRC, and the Central African Republic. The "bizarre boundaries" created by the vagaries of international justice result in "zones of impunity" for certain individuals or crimes committed in certain countries.[166] Sriram and

Ross ask pointedly, "Once the zones of impunity have been recognized, what next?"[167]

What next, indeed? In closing, I consider the potential of anagnorisis, the Aristotelian term that Harrow invokes when he describes the Rwandan genocide as an anagnorisis in the narrative of exceptionalism. In *The Poetics*, Aristotle defines anagnorisis as "a change from ignorance to knowledge, leading either to friendship or to hostility on the part of those persons who are marked for good fortune or bad."[168] Harrow's use of the term invokes the negative outcome insofar as knowledge of the genocide generates hostility and territoriality. In contrast, how might playwrights and cultural workers adopt a more radical version of anagnorisis that harnesses the potential of recognition? In her memoir, Umutesi experiences such a moment when she gazes on a young female refugee dying during the flight across Zaire, whose body was being devoured by ants even before she had taken her last breath.

> I stood in a daze in front of this sixteen-year-old girl, lying in agony by the side of the road in the middle of the equatorial forest more than five hundred kilometers from home. As in 1993, when I heard about the extermination of my mother's family, as in 1994, when I saw the burned houses, the fear in the eyes of the fleeing Tutsi, and the arrogance and the hate in the faces of their executioners, as in 1995 when I saw pictures of women and children assassinated by the RPF in the camps at Birava, I was overcome by revulsion. What crime had all of these victims committed to deserve such a death? Where was the international community that talked about human rights but withdrew when they should have prevented the genocide of the Tutsi by the Hutu militias and when they should have condemned the massacres of the Hutu by the RPF?[169]

Umutesi does not just *see* the woman; she *recognizes* her as caught in a vast, interlocking web stained with the blood of Hutu and Tutsi victims, all of whom were shunned by the international community as unworthy of intervention. She also recognizes her powerlessness against "the death that lurked all around me." In this passage, she lingers on her feeling of revulsion; later, though, she acknowledges that "the only chance that we had of defeating [death], at least temporarily, was solidarity."[170] In an eloquent rumination on classical notions of anagnorisis, Piero Boitani writes, "Good recognition scenes are never cheap plot devices. They concern human beings and knowledge, not of abstractions or theoretical truths, but either of oneself or of another human being. They are charged with all the emotion and the ethical tensions this implies.... The processes of sense perception, memory, and reasoning become dramatic, anguishing scenes."[171] Similarly, Umutesi's experience is not a facile moment of identification but a deep and sustained engagement with another's sufferings that leads to the radicality of recognition. Boitani also points out that the Greek term literally means the "rising of knowledge." Here, as she does repeatedly throughout the book, Umutesi rises above the rhetoric of ethnicity.

Umutesi lives in exile in Belgium—she cannot speak of her recognition in Rwanda itself. It is easy to call for an end to competitive memory and to imagine a day when, for example, the 1972 genocide in Burundi will receive a panel on the top floor of the Kigali Memorial Museum and Umutesi's memoirs will be sold in its gift shop. Given the sustained intransigence of the government, I doubt that alternative narratives will be seen in official Rwandan space during my lifetime. Until then, though, anagnorisis is quietly occurring across Central Africa through the efforts of cultural workers, artists, and audiences. I am thinking here of my students at Makerere who interpreted *Ruined* in light of their experiences, memories, and postmemories of the LRA conflict or the Bush War of the 1980s.[172] I am thinking of the work of Victor Ocen and his Lira-based organization the African Youth Initiative Network, which organized a 2015 memorial ceremony of an LRA massacre that brought together war-affected people from across Uganda to facilitate a recognition of the mutuality of suffering from the Luwero Triangle to West Nile.[173] I am thinking of the Congolese choreographer Faustin Linyekula's renderings of economic crisis in the DRC as a means of calling attention to common roots of suffering that transcend colonialist notions of ethnicity.[174] The labor of transnational and regional history would help embrace the potential of anagnorisis, a form of engagement that leads to victim solidarity rather than competition. Tissues might still be useful, but so will the density of history.

Notes

1. The statistic of $2.5 million is provided in a Reuters news story, "Rwanda Rushes to Open Genocide Museum for Memorial," March 29, 2004. The budget has expanded greatly since the museum opened; in 2012, *Rwanda Focus* reported that Aegis Trust was raising $30 million for a peace-building education center and additional expansion plans (Jean-Christophe Nsanzimana, "Kigali Genocide Memorial to Be Expanded," *Rwanda Focus*, August 2, 2012). Aegis Trust lists several bullet points related to its overall mission of stopping genocide, such as "honour[ing] the memory for the victims of genocide," "help[ing] survivors

to rebuild their lives," and "bring[ing] the voices of those at risk to politicians, the media, and the public." The Kigali Genocide Memorial is a hallmark of the organization and features prominently in its website (www.aegistrust.org).

2. See Smith 2009 for a discussion of the series of events that led up to the establishment of the memorial center; a shortened version of this history is provided in the audio tour, which I listened to during my visit on August 18, 2015. See also Sodaro 2011, 78–79.

3. Rory Carroll, "In Memory of Murder," *Guardian*, March 24, 2004.

4. Her visit occurred on October 7, 2013. Aegis Trust posted a video of Power's remarks on YouTube, available at youtube.com/watch?v=GVekjP8ME6o, accessed July 13, 2015.

5. This comment was posted on April 29, 2015, available at www.tripadvisor.com, accessed July 13, 2015.

6. This paragraph is based on my notes and recollection of the center during my visits in July 2007, July 2011, and August 2015.

7. Sodaro 2011, 85.

8. See also J. Thompson 2009, 97–101, for a critique of the Kigali Memorial Centre and its manipulation of memory.

9. Harrow 2005, 224; see also Agamben 2005.

10. Aristotle uses the term catharsis only once in his treatise on tragedy, *The Poetics* (1449b21–28). Definitions of the term are widely debated; my notion of purgation is borrowed primarily from Ingram Bywater's interpretation and translation of catharsis as arising through "incidents arousing pity and fear, wherewith to accomplish its catharsis of such emotions," that is, the purification of negative emotions in general (Aristotle 1931). Bywater's translation is available online at http://www.gutenberg.org/files/6763/6763-h/6763-h.htm, accessed August 18, 2017.

11. See Verpoorten 2005 for a nuanced discussion of the death toll of the Rwandan genocide. She concludes that the number of Tutsi killed was between 600,000 and 800,000 but also notes the added difficulty in determining the number of Hutu deaths. She acknowledges Reyntjens's finding (1997) that the total number of Rwandans who "disappeared" from the population in 1994, whether Hutu, Tutsi or Twa, was between 1,050,000 and 1,150,000, but she goes on to explain that simple subtraction will not yield an estimate of Hutu casualties: "The disappearance of Hutu stems from several causes that cannot be disentangled: (1) killed by the perpetrators of the genocide, (2) killed by the RPF, (3) died from disease in refugee camps or, (4) fled to neighbouring countries (to escape prosecution)" (333n4). Note that this figure also includes the deaths of about 10,000 ethnic Twa, or about 30 percent of the Twa population in Rwanda (Beswick 2011, 495).

12. Lemarchand 1998. In the essay, Lemarchand identifies three separate genocides: of Hutu by Tutsi in Burundi (1972), of Tutsi and Hutu by Hutu in Rwanda (1994), and of Hutu by Tutsi in the DRC (1996–1997).

13. Anderson and Menon 2009, 13.

14. Rodríguez 2015, 24.

15. Ibid., 25.

16. Ibid., 19.

17. Gallie 1955–1956. My use of Gallie has been influenced by John Fletcher (2013, 51–52).

18. Gallie 1955–1956, 172.

19. The historiographical pitfalls of this approach should be acknowledged. Overstating the role of colonialism positions European conquest as a defining moment rather than contextualizing these fifty-odd years in the *longue durée* of African history, in which colonialism

"was but another incident in an ongoing drama that had begun decades before" (Glassman 1995, 270). In a sense, this overview caters to what David Newbury calls "the myth of colonial omnipotence" (2012, 48). He observes, for example, that "to say that the history of Rwanda in the first sixty years of the twentieth century consists only of the history of colonial administrators and colonial policy ignores African voices, denies African agency, and removes African participation from any of the transformations in Rwandan society over three generations of experience" (2012, 48). On a related note, this overview can be criticized as adhering to an elitist narrative of history given that the educated elites often seized on the political salience of colonial ethnic categories. My hope, though, is that this overview will help set the stage for the politics of competitive memory addressed in the final section, which draw on a colonial mentality of "divide and conquer" rather than seeking to build alliances of cosuffering. A more specific caveat in regard to this brief historical account is that I do not address the impact of the slave and ivory trade on the region. The slave trade was especially pervasive in the areas west of Lake Kivu; indeed, in the late nineteenth century, Leopold used the prevalence of slavery in the Congo as justification for his control of the region. See Médard and Doyle 2007 and Vansina 2010 for more information on the development, practices, and decline of slavery in the Great Lakes.

20. Chrétien 2003, 22.

21. See Hanson 2009, for example, for a discussion of how the broad label of dynastic kingship tends to obscure subtle articulations of heterarchy, such as the power of royal women, which previously ensured accountable governance in the Ganda kingdom.

22. See D. Newbury 1991 for a detailed case study of how kingship and clanship developed in a dynamic and complementary fashion on Ijiwi Island in Lake Kivu. This work challenges the prevalent historical narrative that primordial units of clan formation "evolved" into kingship in a linear fashion; instead, Newbury argues that they developed in tandem: "Clan differentiation . . . accompanied and facilitated the process of increased political centralization. . . . On Ijiwi, at least, these two forms of hegemony reinforced each other" (15).

23. The Nyiginya and Ganda kingdoms serve as especially prominent examples of active collusion between the local power structures and colonial administration. See Des Forges 2011 (especially chapter 5) for several fascinating examples of the careful dance of alliance that the Roman Catholic missionaries, the colonial administration, and the Nyiginya court executed in their combined attempts to strengthen control over peripheral areas. Similarly, the Baganda took advantage of their alliance with the British colonial administration to facilitate their expansion of power in the Ugandan Protectorate. Low 1971 and 2009 are especially useful sources on the collusion of the Ganda kingdom with the British administration. Baganda refers to the Ganda people, and Buganda refers to the Ganda kingdom; this chapter follows scholarly convention and uses Ganda as an adjective even though this term is rarely heard in Uganda itself.

24. Chrétien 2003, 42.

25. See Des Forges 2011; D. Newbury 2009, chaps. 8–11; C. Newbury 1988; and Vansina 2004.

26. See D. Newbury 2005 for a delineation of the reasons behind these multiple flows of refugees and migrants from Rwanda over the past few centuries, which included "to avoid famine, to seek more productive lands, to engage in commercial openings, to flee the process of precolonial dynastic centralization, to escape colonial impositions (including forced labor as well as taxation), [and] to establish or maintain ties among people arbitrarily defined as 'foreigners' by imposed colonial boundaries," among others (254–255). The Banyamulenge

serve as an especially prominent example of one wave of migration. D. Newbury traces their origins to the mid-eighteenth century, when they fled the expansion of the Nyiginya state; they ultimately settled on the Itombwe plateau west of Lake Tanganyika (1997, 216). For additional information on migrant movements within and from Rwanda, see Vansina 2004, especially chaps. 6 and 7; C. Newbury 1988; and D. Newbury 1991, 87–93.

27. The text of the speech, which was delivered on April 7, 2014, can be found at http://www.kwibuka.rw/speech, accessed July 13, 2015.

28. Cited in Chrétien 2003, 72; ibid., 283.

29. C. Newbury 1998, 11. Mamdani also argues that only in Rwanda and Burundi would the so-called Hamites, the Tutsi, be considered a separate race, even though the Hima and Ganda people in southern Uganda were also classified as Hamitic (2001, 35).

30. On a similar note, Chrétien emphasizes the more open environment inculcated by British indirect rule in Uganda, noting that numerous Hutu fled to Uganda in the 1930s to avoid the harshness of Belgian rule, in which forced labor and the whip were widely employed (2003, 280).

31. Vansina 2004, 164.

32. Ibid., 192. C. Newbury 1988, 111, notes that in Kinyaga, *ubureetwa* (also *uburetwa*) was imposed only on selected lineage groups; she credits colonial policy for formalizing the forced labor system on all adult male Hutu. See also pp. 140–144 for her discussion of *ubureetwa* during the colonial period, in which she notes that "it is difficult to exaggerate [its] exploitative character" (1988, 141). This emphasis on *ubureetwa* as a tool of ethnic stratification serves as a corrective to the work of Jacques-Jean Maquet, whose highly influential 1954 study *Le système des relations sociales dans le Ruanda ancien* foregrounds the significance of *ubuhake*, or cattle clientship, as a bedrock of precolonial Rwandan society. Maquet argues that *ubuhake* permeated all levels of Rwandan society and ensured social cohesion through a network of reciprocity between patrons and clients. Although C. Newbury 1988, among others, has thoroughly debunked the notion of *ubuhake* as widespread and universal—indeed, it "never affected more than a small percentage of Rwanda's population" (134)—Maquet's ideas, which bolster the concept of a cohesive, integrative precolonial Rwanda under Tutsi rule, continue to circulate in pro-RPF historiography. See D. Newbury 2009, 328–330, for a helpful summary and critique of Maquet's ideas, as well as Pottier 2002, 110–115.

33. C. Newbury 1988, 51. See also Vansina 2004, 23–43, for a discussion of how the terms Hutu and Tutsi might have emerged as a distinction between farmers and herders.

34. As Vansina has explained, "It is as though you would now write about the Holocaust and say that the cause is to be found in 1934, without looking a few centuries back" (Karel Arnaut and Hein Vangee, "History Facing the Present: An Interview with Jan Vansina," *H-Africa*, November 1, 2001, http://www.hnet.org/~africa/africaforum/VansinaInterview.htm, accessed December 15, 2015).

35. The diverse forms of political organization in the northern region, which ranged from military leadership of the Acholi to the relatively acephalous communities of the Teso in eastern Uganda, were generally homogenized in colonial discourse as uncivilized and barbaric. See Lamphear 1976, Tosh 1978, and Vincent 1982 as representative examples of in-depth analyses of how "stateless" societies organize themselves and how their complex systems of organization have changed over the past two centuries.

36. Atkinson 1994, 5. Note that the final sentence in this passage speaks to how the Ganda elite influenced British stereotypes of the north, or what Beverly Gartrell called the "Ganda-centric view of the north" (1983, 2).

37. Demonstrations of Acholi resistance to British rule include the Lamogi Rebellion in 1911, when Acholi rose up against the colonial administration to protest restrictions on the possession of firearms, as well as more general expressions of discontent against taxes, forced labor, and the appropriation of land. This event, in addition to the imprisonment of the Acholi leader Rwot Awich in 1912 in Kampala, continue to circulate in Acholiland as symbols of resistance.

38. See Roberts 1962 for further discussion of Ganda subimperialism and how British rule and Ganda expansion worked in tandem. I emphasize the Langi and the Acholi in this historical narrative because the politics of these two ethnic groups play a prominent role in postcolonial Uganda; I also frequently refer to them in my discussion of the LRA in chapters 2 and 5. The Teso, the Madi, and the Kakwa are just a few of the groups in northern Uganda that have been affected by the LRA conflict; these groups have also cultivated rich histories of resistance to colonial and postcolonial states (see, for example, Vincent 1982).

39. Mutibwa 1992, 4.

40. Vansina 2010, 8.

41. Ibid., 18.

42. Hochschild 1999, 4.

43. Vansina 2010. Similarly, Chrétien emphasizes the deadly impact of contagious disease that contributed to a demographic decimation of the entire region from 1890 to the 1930s (2003, 220–223).

44. Prunier 2009, 76.

45. Vlassenroot 2013, 17.

46. Kivu, the area west of Lake Kivu, alternated between district status and province status under the colonial administration (Lemarchand 1964, 62–65); after independence, Kivu was eventually divided into North Kivu, South Kivu, and Maniema. The resettlement policy that began in the 1930s, called Mission Immigration Banyarwanda (MIB), triggered considerable tension between the migrants and the local population because of the colonial administration's policies of favoritism toward the migrant Rwandans. The administration "appointed more people with Rwandan ancestry to the local administration, providing the whole group with better access to political and economic power than the indigenous Congolese received" (Autesserre 2010, 134). According to Stearns, "No historical event shook North Kivu as much, or reverberates as fiercely into the present," as the MIB project (2012b, 15); he adds that estimates of Rwandan migrants to the Kivus during the colonial period range from 150,000 to 300,000 (19). See also S. Jackson 2006 for a useful summary of the historical underpinnings of the ethnic politics of the eastern DRC.

47. D. Newbury 2012, 50.

48. Ibid., 50–51.

49. Ibid., 51.

50. For example, in the early 1950s, political opposition in Kinyaga (located in extreme southwestern Rwanda, an area that came under centralized Tutsi rule only during Rwabugiri's reign) was based on class rather than ethnic criteria (de Lame 2005, 49).

51. The two main parties at the time of the 1959 uprising were the monarchist Rwandan National Union (UNAR, founded in 1957) and the Party of the Movement for Hutu Emancipation (PARMEHUTU, also founded in 1957). Two additional parties that formed after the initial uprising were the Rwandan Democratic Assembly (RADER, founded in 1959) and the Association for the Social Promotion of the Masses (APROSOMA, founded in 1960). PARMEHUTU was to win elections in 1961 and 1962. By 1965, it was the only legal political party until Kay-

ibanda was overthrown by Habyarimana in 1973; it was replaced with the National Revolutionary Movement for Development (MRND). See Straus 2006.

52. Ibid., 179. Pages 177–183 provide a helpful summary of the events of 1959–1961.

53. Chrétien 2003, 305.

54. Cited ibid., 306. The original quote appeared in *Le Monde*, February 6, 1964.

55. D. Newbury emphasizes the differences between the events of 1959 and those of 1963: "Though often ignored by outsiders, the contextual distinctions between the events of 1959 and 1963 are important to historical understanding, for they represent both different scales of violence and different causes: 1959 saw few outright killings as part of a political conflict; 1963 saw killings on a massive scale in response to military intervention" (2012, 51).

56. Uvin 1998, 34.

57. Prunier 1995, 198. See also Lemarchand 2009 for a discussion of what he calls "the genocidal twins" of Burundi and Rwanda.

58. In "Precolonial Burundi and Rwanda," D. Newbury directly warns that these two states "were not simply reflections of each other, but different in organization and rationale." As representative examples of these differences between the two kingdoms, he invokes the "more numerous and more diverse" roles of ritualists in Burundi, as well as the more prominent role of Burundian elders, or *abashingantahe*, as intermediaries with the central power; both these examples suggest a less centralized power structure in precolonial Burundi than in Rwanda (2009, 301). In a direct rebuke to the present-day tendency to group the two countries together, he insists that "these were not 'twin states,' as outsiders often label them. . . . They did not have identical histories any more than they shared common cultural constructs or similar social processes" (315–316). He also acknowledges, though, that "that in postcolonial times, the recent political histories of Burundi and Rwanda have affected each other in what might be referred to as a 'mirror' effect" (408n67).

59. This quote by Stephen Weissman is cited in Lemarchand 2009, 71.

60. See Howard W. French, "Kagame's Hidden War in the Congo," *New York Review of Books*, September 24, 2009. Hundreds of thousands more fled to refugee camps in Tanzania, where Hutu extremism also took firm root (Malkki 1995).

61. Lemarchand 2009, 71.

62. Prunier 1995, 60–61; Lemarchand 2009, 115.

63. Chrétien 2003, 308.

64. See Desrosiers 2014 for a useful discussion of Kayibanda's and Habyarimana's regimes (called the First and the Second Republic, respectively).

65. Prunier provides a detailed discussion of the politically motivated agendas behind the statistics regarding the number of Tutsi refugees and argues for the number of 600,000 to 700,000 (1995, 63).

66. Autesserre 2010, 134. My presentation of the deepening divide between "indigenous" Congolese and the Banyarwanda relies primarily on this source.

67. Lemarchand 2013, 425. By 1971, Rwema held the title of chief of staff in the presidential office.

68. Lemarchand 2009, 12.

69. Mobutu seized power after a turbulent five-year period of independence, during which Prime Minister Patrice Lumumba was assassinated and Katanga seceded—events that prompted UN intervention from 1960 to 1964. Mobutu's regime lasted for thirty-two years. It should be noted that the Banyamulenge in South Kivu (the Banyarwanda whose claim to Congolese identity predates the colonial era) also found themselves favored when they turned

against the 1964–1965 Simba rebellion, a Maoist-inspired uprising against the government in which the Soviet Union and Cuba intervened on the side of the rebels, and Belgium and the United States intervened on the side of the government. Although the Banyamulenge initially supported the Simbas, they ultimately turned against them when their cattle were slaughtered to feed the troops; their loyalty was then rewarded by the Kinshasa government.

70. Autesserre 2010, 135.

71. Autesserre 2010. On a similar note, Lemarchand writes, "Only by taking into account the longue durée dimension of the crisis can one gain a proper handle on the dynamics of the violence in eastern Congo" (2013, 418).

72. Branch 2011, 155. For sources that complicate this emphasis on the northern/southern divide through an analysis of the politics of the western kingdoms of Ankole, Toro, and Bunyoro, see, for example, Low 2009, especially chaps. 6 and 7; and Steinhart 1978.

73. See Watson 1991, 6, for contextualization of this statistic. The Hima are a subgroup of the Ankole people, often perceived as an elite pastoralist group within the larger Ankole kingdom, and thus are linked with the "Hamitic" ideology propagated by the colonialists. See Otunnu 1999b for a discussion of the historical relationship between the Rwandan Tutsi and Ankole (3–5), as well as a fuller exploration of the role of Rwandan refugees and immigrants in Uganda.

74. Mamdani 2001, 167–170; Prunier 1995, 68–70. See D. Newbury 2005 for a useful summary of the various political climates that the Rwandan refugees in Uganda had to negotiate. For example, because the Rwandans were generally drawn to the opposition Democratic Party during Obote's regime, Amin saw them as an ally. But then, "as southwestern Uganda became a battlefield in the war to overthrow Amin during the late 1970s, the pendulum swung, and on Obote's eventual return to power in 1980, Rwandans tended to become targets of the new regime" (273). The literature suggests that Uganda was perhaps the most inhospitable country toward Rwandans in comparison with Tanzania, Burundi, and Zaire.

75. See Kasozi 1994, 111, for a list of various purges of Acholi and Langi. Of course, Amin did not confine state violence to Langi and Acholi troops. It is estimated that 100,000–500,000 Ugandans died as a result of his regime; 300,000 is the statistic most commonly cited. Readers might find it odd that I am passing so quickly over the specifics of Amin's rule in light of his reputation as one of the most brutal dictators on the continent. The mass expulsion of Asians that he ordered in 1972 serves as an especially vivid demonstration of the territorialization of identity; black Ugandans were categorized as "true" citizens in opposition to an Asian minority. However, I emphasize Obote in this narrative because Amin's notoriety has generally obscured Obote's version of state violence. Amin's expulsion of the Asian population, for example, was not necessarily a rupture in Uganda's postcolonial history but instead could be understood as an expansion of discriminatory policies established during Obote's first regime (E. C. Taylor 2013). For an excellent analysis of Amin's regime and tactics, see Decker 2014.

76. Essays by Low, Southall, and Kanyeihamba in the 1988 *Uganda Now* anthology delve into this complex period of Uganda's history in considerably more detail.

77. Simmering tensions between Acholi and Langi soldiers exploded in the aftermath of the coup, as discussed in briefly in chapter 5. See Lindemann 2011, 18–22, for an overview of how ethnic politics in Amin's and Obote's armies culminated in the 1985 coup.

78. See, for example, Refugee Law Project 2004, 11, for additional discussion of tensions between Langi and Acholi.

79. The armed wing of the NRM was called the National Resistance Army (NRA); for the sake of simplicity, I use the term NRM in this chapter. Several memorials to commemorate the dead were constructed in the Luwero Triangle, most of which are now in a state of shocking disrepair, as touched on in chapter 5.

80. Kasozi 1994, 6.

81. See, for example, Mutibwa 1992, 157. In 2004, Museveni alluded to this history at a memorial ceremony in Barlonyo (Lira) to commemorate the LRA's massacre of over three hundred Ugandans when he repeated a Ugandan proverb that effectively translates as "What goes around comes around." His statement, which provoked outrage among the mostly Langi mourners and survivors in attendance, was interpreted as a veiled message that the LRA massacre was a kind of cosmic payback for the killing of civilians in the Luwero Triangle carried out primarily by Langi and Acholi solders in Obote's army (Justice and Reconciliation Project 2009, 14). The actual proverb was "Lut ma opwodo kede neki ka pe ibolo i lum opwodi kwede," which the organization JRP translates as "If you do not throw away the stick that was used to beat your co-wife, it will also be used to beat you."

82. Mamdani 2001, 170.

83. Branch 2011, 58; see also Haggai Matsiko, "The Forgotten Original NRA 27," *Independent*, January 31, 2013.

84. Not all Rwandans in Uganda were refugees from the postcolonial waves of violence in Rwanda; some had lived in Uganda since the time of colonial partition or had moved there during the 1920s to the 1950s (Chrétien 2003, 279). Generally speaking, all Banyarwanda in Uganda were vulnerable to discriminatory practices and prejudice, although, of course, individual experiences varied greatly. I met Ugandan Tutsi returnees in Rwanda who spoke with fondness of growing up in Uganda and continued to follow Ugandan politics with avid interest.

85. Branch 2011, 63.

86. Ibid., 65.

87. Behrend 1999 is invaluable for its detailed examination of the conditions of Alice Lakwena's Holy Spirit Movement.

88. C. Dolan 2009, 45. Playwright Judith Adong boldly confronts this episode of Uganda's history in *Silent Voices*, as will be discussed briefly in the afterword.

89. Prunier 2009, 13.

90. Branch 2011, 61; see also Finnström 2008, 75; P. B. Jackson 2009, 324; and Otunnu 1999a, 32–33.

91. Museveni officially acknowledged some of these atrocities in a speech during NRM anniversary celebrations in January 2014; however, as Lino Owor Ogora points out in a detailed and thoughtful editorial in the *Monitor*, the acknowledgment stopped far short of a detailed investigation into multiple crimes in the area, as well as a full-scale apology (see "There's Need for an Official Apology for NRA Atrocities," *Monitor*, February 1, 2014).

92. Kony soon renamed his insurgency the United Democratic Christian Army (UDCA); it is unclear when he settled on the name Lord's Resistance Army. He was still calling his group the UDCA at the time of one of the earliest mass abductions in 1991, when over forty girls were kidnapped from the Sacred Hearts school in Gulu (Mutibwa 1992, 165n10). In general, the origins of the LRA are murky; the first major attack by Kony's forces occurred at Koch Goma in 1988, although the group may have formed as early as 1987. Useful chronologies of the LRA conflict are found in C. Dolan 2009, 43–57, and Branch 2011, 62–80; see also Refugee Law Project 2004 for a useful contextualization of the LRA conflict.

93. The LRA originally crossed into Sudan seeking respite from attacks by the Ugandan military. From about 1994 to 2002, the Sudanese government provided massive support to the LRA in exchange for its assistance in fighting the Sudanese People's Liberation Army/Movement. Although the LRA initially had cordial relations with the locals in southern Sudan, this relationship changed markedly after it received support from Omar al-Bashir's government. See Schomerus 2012 for more information regarding the impact of the LRA conflict in the former southern Sudan.

94. Prunier 2009, 82. The year 1994 often appears as a turning point in various chronologies of the LRA war; see, for example, C. Dolan 2009, 46, and Doom and Vlassenroot 1999, 24–25.

95. I have included rape on this list in light of the LRA's widespread practice of forced marriage; it should be noted, though, that the LRA banned civilian rape (see Annan et al. 2011).

96. Branch 2011 is arguably the most authoritative source on the IDP camps. Additional references to the camps are found in chapters 2 and 5.

97. D. Newbury 2005, 275–276.

98. Reed 1996, 486. See Reed 1996 for a discussion of how the RPF emerged out of the more radical Rwandan Alliance for National Unity, which called for the establishment of a socialist state in Rwanda. Reed also clarifies how the RPA emerged as a parallel structure to the RPF. Other useful sources include Otunnu 1999a.

99. Mamdani 2001, 175. The emergence of a more militant bent is ambiguous; see, for example, Prunier 1995, 70–71. Although Prunier implies that the RPF had settled on the need for return at the time of its founding, he also alludes to a sense of ambivalence among refugees in Rwanda in the early 1980s: "Many of the young men, like Fred Rwigyema and Paul Kagame, had felt that Rwanda was an old story, their parents' story, and that they were now Ugandans. And then they suddenly discovered that people among whom they had lived for thirty years were treating them as hated and despised foreigners" (70). See also Prunier 1998 for a discussion of how the reneging of the Ugandan government crystallized the RPF's desire to return to Rwanda, which was originally seen by many Ugandan exiles as "too dangerous and difficult" (127).

100. As is the case with just about any statistic associated with the RPF and the Rwandan refugees, even this number is contested, apparently because an unknown number of Rwandan noncombatants accompanied the RPF troops to the border to celebrate the possibility of a return to their homeland (Prunier 1998, 130; Reed 1996, 487–488). Since an armed return would have been to Museveni's advantage because it would have solved his "Rwandan problem," as well as ensuring a strong ally to the south, it is widely believed that Museveni knew about and even encouraged an RPF invasion of Rwanda. See Prunier 2009, 13–14, for a discussion of this invasion; for a Ugandan perspective, see Ssemujju Ibrahim Nganda, "Open Secrets: Museveni's Untold Role in RPF War," *Observer*, July 8, 2009.

101. Lemarchand 2002, 309; see also Straus 2006, 46–49.

102. As Jennie Burnet points out on the basis of a Human Rights Watch report, many of these claims were greatly exaggerated (2012, 58, citing Human Rights Watch, *Beyond the Rhetoric: Continuing Human Rights Abuses in Rwanda* [New York: Human Rights Watch, 1993]; see pp. 22–23 in the HRW report for a discussion of RPF killings and executions in northern Rwanda).

103. Mamdani 2001, 203; Des Forges 1999, 48, 168.

104. Stearns 2011, 18.

105. Des Forges 1999, 182. The devastation wrought in Burundi deserves far more attention than I give it here. Perhaps because the killing in Burundi does not correlate well with Shoah-centric ideas of genocide, it has been largely ignored by an empire of trauma. In addition, the Burundian state has generally avoided the Rwandan emphasis on official memorialization, which causes the country to recede even further from the international gaze. An exception is the widespread attention in the United States paid to the best-selling nonfiction book by Tracy Kidder, *Strength in What Remains* (New York: Random House, 2009), which tells the story of Deogratias Niyizonkiza, a survivor of the Burundian violence. Kidder's narrative, as well as the marketing of the book, relied heavily on its overlap with the more famous Rwandan example in order to edge its way into the trauma limelight.

106. Des Forges 1999, 186-243. This account also includes a discussion of the famous "Dallaire fax" of January 1994, in which Dallaire cited verified information by an informant in Habyarimana's regime about what appeared to be plans for Tutsi extermination (203-204).

107. In 2012, the Trévidic report, which was released by two French judges, concluded that the plane must have been shot down by Hutu forces since the missile was launched from Hutu-held Kanombe camp. The 2012 report, "Rapport D'expertise: Destruction En Vol Du Falcon 50 Kigali (Rwanda)" is available at http://ddata.over-blog.com/xxxyyy/2/93/44/38/rapport-ballist-attentat-contre-habyarimana-6-4-19-copie-1.pdf, accessed August 18, 2017.

108. Burnet 2012, 60. Des Forges 1999, 298, provided further details about how the genocide spread outside Kigali as early as April 7. Estimated numbers of Rwandans who participated in the killing range up to the state's claim of four to five million (Mamdani 2001, 266). Straus provides the most persuasive statistic of 175,000-210,000 perpetrators (2006, 117).

109. Des Forges 1999, 420-421.

110. RTLM stands for Radio Télévision Libre des Mille Collines. See Eltringham 2004, 19-25, for several quotations of racist propaganda and rhetoric from 1963 to 1994; the "pretty little nose" reference is cited on page 25. The quote about the Nyabarongo River, cited on page 93, is from a notorious 1992 speech by Léon Mugesera. In 2016, Mugesera was sentenced to life imprisonment by a Kigali court.

111. Des Forges 1999, 383-384; see also 483 and 770.

112. The Belgian peacekeepers had been assigned to protect Prime Minister Agathe Uwilingiyimana, who was assassinated by government troops on April 7.

113. Des Forges 1999, 962-963. See also chapter 8 in Prunier 1995.

114. See, for example, Stearns's interview with former FAR official Paul Rwarakabije, who disdained the genocide, seeing it as a distraction of resources from the "real" war against the RPF (2011, 16).

115. Des Forges 1999 provides an especially useful discussion of this complex issue. She explains how the RPF first attempted to thwart the genocide and offered a proposal to create a coalition with UNAMIR; however, when this proposal was rejected, the RPF understandably "undertook on its own to halt the genocide" (1060). What is more controversial, though, is that even when the UN proposed to send a much more substantial force to stop the killing, called UNAMIR II, at the end of April, the RPF categorically rejected these plans, which would have saved tens of thousands of lives. Des Forges questions the RPF's official explanation that "all the Tutsi were already dead," noting that "the tragic reality that hundreds of thousands had already been slain in no way negated the need to rescue tens of thousands of others who were still alive" (1063). See Prunier 2009, 19, and Reed 1996 for a harsher assessment of the RPF's reluctance.

116. D. Newbury 2005, 277.

117. See Ingelaere 2016 for more information on *gacaca*.

118. Hintjens 2008, 13. This chapter just scratches the surface regarding the "silences" of the Kigali memorial; for example, see Beswick 2011 for a discussion of the continued discrimination against the Twa and the refusal of the postgenocide state to recognize their rights as an ethnic minority. Another silence looms regarding the 1995 massacre in Kibeho, in which RPF troops opened fire on an IDP camp in southern Rwanda and killed thousands of civilians. The Kibeho massacre of 1995 is discussed in more detail in chapter 3.

119. Although this section emphasizes the impact of the genocide's immediate aftermath on eastern Zaire, it should be stressed that the region had already experienced multiple repercussions of the Rwandan civil war before the outbreak of genocide. As Autesserre summarizes, the war "fueled local antagonisms and widened the split within the Banyarwanda community" (2010, 140); for example, massacres that broke out in March 1993 in North Kivu, which resulted in the deaths of approximately fourteen thousand people, were connected to these heightened tensions. The Hutu Banyarwanda sought to cast themselves as "indigenous" since most of them had arrived during the colonial period, as opposed to the Tutsi, who had arrived after 1959; indigenous Congolese, though, "increasingly radicalize[d] against all 'Rwandans,' Tutsis as well as Hutus, refugees or not" (ibid., 141). Not surprisingly, Congolese Tutsi generally supported the RPF, and Congolese Hutu often sided with the Habyarimana government. These tensions added to Mobutu's well-established track record of exploiting and exacerbating ethnic divisions.

120. Again, the statistics are vexed. Stearns provides the number of a million refugees, although he notes the lack of a census in the camps (2011, 349n11). Mamdani writes that it was a "million plus" (2001, 234); Reyntjens states that it was one and a half million (2009, 43). Another estimated million refugees fled to Tanzania; about 250,000 of them crossed the Rusomo bridge in twenty-four hours.

121. Stearns 2011, 42, 53.

122. Although its role was less overt than that of Rwanda in the First Congo War, Uganda was instrumental in some key battles; Reyntjens credits UPDF troops with taking Kasindi and helping take some key cities, such as Bunia (2009, 55, 59). Museveni also reportedly offered some crucial advice to Kagame and introduced him to Kabila. See Reyntjens 2009, 58–60, for a more extensive discussion of Uganda's role in the first war. During the Second Congo War, the role of the UPDF became even more pronounced because its troops controlled much of the northern region.

123. James C. McKinley Jr., "Taking Office, Congo's Ruler Promises Vote," *New York Times*, May 30, 1997. McKinley observes that much of the heckling came from about a thousand supporters of the opposition leader Étienne Tshishekedi, who had opposed Mobutu's regime since 1980 and enjoyed a wide following in the country.

124. Umutesi 2004.

125. The UN mapping report stopped just short of accusing the RPF of genocide, noting that "the apparent systematic and widespread attacks described in this report reveal a number of inculpatory elements that, if proven before a competent court, could be characterized as crimes of genocide" (14). The English translation of the report can be found at http://www.ohchr.org/Documents/Countries/CD/DRC_MAPPING_REPORT_FINAL_EN.pdf. See also Emizet 2000. The "genocide of attrition" reference can be found in Lemarchand 2009, 105.

126. The French name on which the initialism is based is Rassemblement Congolais pour la Démocratie. Susan Rice coined the phrase "Africa's World War" (quoted in Lynne Duke, "Congo Allies Beef Up Anti-guerilla Forces," *Washington Post*, October 24, 1998).

127. See Prunier 2009 for a useful delineation of these various countries as "Kinshasa's friends" (Angola, Zimbabwe, Sudan, Chad, and Libya), "Kinshasa's foes" (Rwanda, Uganda, and Burundi), "fence sitters and well wishers" (Zambia, Tanzania, Kenya, and Congo-Brazzaville), and, finally, "the major outside presence" of South Africa (187–202).

128. Rwanda and Uganda reaped considerable profits through their illicit trafficking in Congolese diamonds, gold, and coltan. See Prunier 2009, 197–198, for an explanation of Uganda's fluctuating gold exports during and between the two Congo wars. See also a damning 2002 UN report on how the Ugandan, Rwandan, and Burundian governments benefited from the mineral wealth of the DRC ("Report of the Panel of Experts on the Illegal Exploitation of Natural Resources and Other Forms of Wealth of the Democratic Republic of the Congo," available at http://www.pcr.uu.se/digitalAssets/96/96819_congo_2002 1031.pdf).

129. Prunier 2009, 242; Stearns 2011, 247. The number of casualties is reported in the UN Security Council's "Report of the Inter-agency Assessment Mission to Kisangani" (December 5, 2000), available at http://reliefweb.int/report/democratic-republic-congo/report-inter-agency-assessment-mission-kisangani. Stearns devotes a chapter to the breakdown of the Uganda/Rwanda alliance, which exploded in Kisangani (2011, 235–248); see also Prunier 2009, 241–242. The Kisangani conflict was preceded by the breakup of the RCD into RCD-Goma (backed by Rwanda) and RCD-Kisangani (backed by Uganda) in 1999.

130. This statistic will be discussed further in chapter 4.

131. Readers should note that this brief historical overview bypasses the many differences (and tensions) between North Kivu, whose Banyarwanda population is primarily Hutu, and South Kivu, whose Banyarwanda population is primarily Tutsi. See Mamdani 2001, 235–236, for a helpful overview; see also S. Jackson 2006.

132. The 1964 constitution granted citizenship only to those who could prove ancestry before 1908; in 1972, the tide shifted in favor of selected groups of migrating Rwandans when a law was passed that granted citizenship to those who had arrived before 1950, which, of course, excluded the fifty-niners. In 1981, a law was passed (but not implemented) that revoked citizenship for all Congolese who could not prove that they had been present in Congolese territory at the time of partition in 1885; this law was upheld in 1991 and generated considerable insecurity among the Banyarwanda. The timing coincided with the outbreak of civil war in Rwanda. Even though the Banyamulenge should have been excluded from this law, their pre-colonial origins were often contested.

133. See D. Newbury 1997 for a critique of Rwanda's claim on the eastern region.

134. Congolese Tutsi have been implicated in, for example, the AFDL and M23, as well as M23's forerunner, the CNDP, the French initialism for the National Congress for the Defence of the People.

135. Lemarchand 2009, 11.

136. D. Newbury 1996; he further expands on his concept of convergent catastrophes in D. Newbury 1997.

137. Developments such as the establishment of a more robust African peacekeeping force and the signing of the Peace, Security, and Cooperation Framework Agreement by thirteen countries have helped facilitate a modicum of stability in the eastern DRC, prompting Stearns to write, "For the first time in seven years, there are signs of a serious peace process, with strong international involvement, aimed at addressing the real causes of conflict in Congo" (2013, 107). Stearns and Cristoph Vogel also note that Rwanda now lacks a serious ally in the region due to the demise of M23: "Even if Rwanda wanted to mobilize again, it would not be easy: Congolese Tutsi and Hutu occupy prominent positions in [the Congolese army] but

many of them harbor deep resentment against their erstwhile allies in Kigali" (2015, 5). Despite such promising developments, the Allied Democratic Forces, a group that emerged in Uganda in the late 1990s, has become increasingly implicated in a series of attacks in Beni in North Kivu. At the same time, though, researchers have cautioned that the identity of the perpetrators of these attacks is unclear; see, for example, Human Rights Watch, "DR Congo: Protect Civilians in Beni from Attack," October 7, 2016, available at https://www.hrw.org/news/2016/10/07/dr-congo-protect-civilians-beni-attack, accessed August 18, 2017.

138. The FDLR was, however, only temporarily unified; it eventually split into four factions—FLDR/FOCA, FLDR/Mandevu, FLDR/RUD, and FDLR/SOKI.

139. It should be noted that the remaining members of the FDLR, estimated between 1,000 and 2,500 troops, might no longer pose a serious threat (Stearns and Vogel 2015, 5). See Jean-Baptiste Baderha, "Is FDLR Surrender Serious?," *Independent*, June 8, 2014. Stearns, in his post "How Not to Write about the Congo," cautions against the tendency to homogenize the FDLR as genocidaires. "Yes, anti-Tutsi diatribe is still prevalent among the FDLR, but the group has also included a few Tutsi officers in the past, and has collaborated with Tutsi groups such as the Banyamulenge in South Kivu and RPR in North Kivu. So be careful not to conflate them with *genocidaires*" (congosiasa.blogspot.com, February 19, 2011).

140. FARDC is the French initialism for the Armed Forces of the Democratic Republic of the Congo. Stearns 2013 describes several of these armed groups as "ragtag bands of a few dozen men" (106) and noted that these groups work in tandem with the state rather than in opposition to it because of complex patronage networks among insurgents, the national army, and politicians. On the role of the FARDC and the UN peacekeeping mission, called MONUC and later MONUSCO, see Amnesty International's 2013 annual report on the DRC, available at http://www.amnesty.org/en/region/democratic-republic-congo/report-2013.

141. See Human Rights Watch, "DR Congo: M23 Rebels Kill, Rape Civilians," July 22, 2013, available at http://www.hrw.org/news/2013/07/22/dr-congo-m23-rebels-kill-rape-civilians. M23's original leader, Bosco Ntaganda, is currently being tried by the International Criminal Court (ICC) for his role as a perpetrator of human rights abuses, including rape, pillage, murder, and abduction, that occurred when he was the leader of another rebel group, the Forces Patriotiques pour la Libération du Congo, in North Kivu in 2002 and 2003. Other key leaders of Congolese rebellions that had previously received Rwandan backing include Laurent Nkunda and Thomas Lubanga. Lubanga was convicted by the ICC of war crimes in 2012; Nkunda has been held under house arrest in Rwanda since his arrest by Rwandan troops in 2009.

142. See Stearns 2012a for a thorough discussion of the M23 rebellion. As was the case in the First Congo War, Ugandan involvement was more nebulous, whereas Rwanda's role was "decisive" (52); see pp. 47–48 for more information regarding the ambiguities of Ugandan involvement in M23.

143. The Christmas massacres took place from December 24 to December 27, 2008; the Makombo massacres occurred from December 14 to December 17, 2009. This list of villages attacked by the LRA is not exhaustive; see Human Rights Watch, "Trail of Death: LRA Atrocities in Northeastern Congo," March 28, 2010, available at https://www.hrw.org/report/2010/03/28/trail-death/lra-atrocities-northeastern-congo, for more information. Bas-Uele Province has also been hard hit by the LRA; see Ledio Cakaj, "This Is Our Land Now: Lord's Resistance Army Attacks in Bas Uele, Northeastern Congo," Enough Project, August 10, 2010, available at http://www.enoughproject.org/files/thisisourlandnow.pdf, accessed October 31, 2017.

144. See Human Rights Watch, "Central African Republic: LRA Attacks Escalate," April 20, 2012, available at https://www.hrw.org/news/2012/04/20/central-african-republic-lra-attacks-escalate, accessed October 31, 2017.

145. In 2014, estimates of the size of the LRA ranged from 100 to 220 combatants (see Edward Ssekika, "LRA Resorts to Farming," *Observer*, February 13, 2014). In 2015, this number might have been reduced to around 120. A spate of abductions that occurred in 2016 in the CAR have been interpreted as the LRA's attempt to replenish its ranks.

146. See Kristof Titeca, "The (LRA) Conflict: Beyond the LRA Lobby and the Hunt for Kony . . . and towards Civilian Protection," *African Arguments*, May 17, 2013. Titeca explains that the United States' overwhelming focus on rooting out the LRA in the DRC has allowed numerous players in the eastern region, most notably the Congolese army, to profit from the situation "by copying LRA attacks, in order to put the blame on the LRA." Titeca provided statistics indicating that in 2011, 48 percent of all incidents against civilians were committed by individual Congolese soldiers, while 17 percent were caused by the LRA. See also Titeca and Costeur 2015. In March 2017, the US withdrew its troops with the argument that the LRA was no longer a threat; the UPDF called off the search for Kony the following month.

147. See Titeca and Costeur 2015 for a helpful contextualization of regional violence that sifts through the often feverish rhetoric around the LRA.

148. Otunnu 2006; see also Alfred Nyongesa Wandera, "Otunnu Unleashes Dossier on Alleged Acholi Genocide," *Monitor*, January 5, 2011.

149. As an example of this kind of inflammatory media chatter, see "Bantu People Should Vigorously Respond to Museveni for His Insults," *Rising Continent*, April 8, 2014, available at therisingcontinent.wordpress.com, accessed July 15, 2015.

150. Acholi/Langi tensions came to the fore in a riot that broke out in the town of Lira after the Barlonyo massacre in 2004; see Michael Dynes, "Peaceful Protest in Uganda Descends into Bloody Riot," *Times*, February 26, 2004. See also Refugee Law Project 2004, 38–40, for a discussion of anti-Acholi sentiment among the Teso and Langi.

151. Rothberg 2009, 3.

152. See, for example, Moses 2012 and Hankivsky and Dhamoon 2013.

153. Brown 1995.

154. Ibid., 55.

155. Ibid., 73.

156. Ibid. Emphasis in the original.

157. Nietzsche 1969, 127, cited in Brown 1995, 68.

158. Mamdani 2001.

159. See Waldorf 2009, 105–107, for a useful discussion of how negationism is used by the Rwandan government to silence critics.

160. The English translation of her Gisozi speech is available on Ingabire's website, http://www.victoire-ingabire.com/Eng/victoires-quotes/, accessed July 15, 2015.

161. In 2008, the late Alison Des Forges, HRW's senior adviser on the Great Lakes and a leading authority on Rwanda, was twice blocked from entering the country; in 2010, HRW's senior researcher on Rwanda, Carina Tertsakian, was denied the renewal of her work visa. See "Rwanda: Allow Human Rights Watch to Work," posted on hrw.org on April 23, 2010. See also Thomson 2011 for a gripping account of the Rwandan government's intervention in her research.

162. James Munyaneza, "Grenade Attack at Genocide Memorial Kills Policeman," *New Times*, April 12, 2008; James Karuhanga, "One Injured in Grenade Attack on Gisozi Genocide Memorial," *New Times*, April 16, 2009; Irene V. Nambi, "Another Attack on Gisozi Memorial," *New Times*, July 22, 2009.

163. Nottage 2009, 78.

164. The Ugandan references could be explained by the play's setting in Ituri Province in the northwestern DRC because Uganda is just across the border; however, Rwandan troops were also deeply implicated in the conflict in Ituri. The Human Rights Watch report "Ituri: Covered in Blood," released in July 2003 and available at https://www.hrw.org/reports/2003/ituri0703/DRC0703full.pdf, accessed August 15, 2017, is helpful in delineating the extent of Rwandan and Ugandan involvement in Ituri. It may also be significant that Nottage chose to set the action of the play in Ituri rather than in North or South Kivu, which tend to dominate analyses and media representations of the conflict. The Ituri Province is known for its conflict between the pastoralist Hema and the agriculturalist Lendu rather than warring factions of Congolese Tutsi and Hutu; by focusing on the Ituri conflict, Nottage was able to sidestep any complications of Tutsi victimhood. See Pottier 2010a for background on the conflict (1999–2007), which can be roughly traced to the colonialist rhetoric that perceived the pastoralist Hema as "Hamitic" and thus superior to the Lendu. Interestingly, the character Salima, who is discussed in more detail in chapter 4, is a Hema, and the Lendu soldier who appears in the play boasts to her about his massacre of Hema miners; in other words, the Hema are much more sympathetically portrayed than the Lendu, and thus the play "sides" with the (pastoralist) Hema.

165. Sriram and Ross 2007, 55.

166. Ibid., 46, 65.

167. Ibid., 65.

168. Aristotle, *Poetics* 1452a, cited in Le Huenen 2013, ix.

169. Umutesi 2004, 166.

170. Ibid., 171.

171. Boitani 2013, 5.

172. See Hirsch 2008 for a discussion of postmemory.

173. See africanyouthinitiative.org to learn more about Ochen's work; my comments here are also based on conversations with Ochen in Kampala in February 2013 and in Lira in April 2013. The 2015 memorial ceremony, which was held at Barlonyo in Lira, will be discussed in more detail in chapter 5.

174. Linyekula's work will be discussed in more detail in the afterword. I am thinking of other works here as well, but I do not wish to name them because of their political sensitivity. The politics of anagnorisis often operates as subtext.

2

MARKETING TRAUMA AND THE THEATRE OF WAR IN NORTHERN UGANDA

In late 2003, the UN under secretary general of humanitarian affairs, Jan Egeland, famously called the war in northern Uganda "the worst humanitarian crisis in the world today."[1] In the coming year, he employed a range of rhetorical devices in his efforts to propel the region more firmly into the trauma limelight, calling it "the worst forgotten crisis on Earth," "the biggest neglected emergency and humanitarian crisis in the world," "a moral outrage," and "worse than Darfur."[2] Of course, the fact that Egeland was speaking of the so-called invisible war with so much urgency indicated that it was beginning to shed that status.[3] This chapter focuses on my encounter with the empire of trauma in the critical moment of 2004, just before widespread international publicity generated by the Gulu Walk and the screenings of *Invisible Children: Rough Cut*.[4] As northern Uganda hovered on the brink of international consciousness, visibility was paramount even at the cost of catering to empire's whims.

The World Vision Children of War Rehabilitation Centre, located in the town of Gulu, offered a vivid glimpse of these dynamics.[5] The center, arguably the most prominent of eight such centers established across war-affected districts in northern Uganda, was meant to help children and youth transition from serving in the LRA to family life through a variety of mental health and resettlement services.[6] A focal point of the center was the counseling room, which was decorated with a series of paintings that condensed the children's pasts into a single tale of terror, hardship, and restoration.[7] The story began with an image titled "A Peaceful Acholi Home," which depicted children playing outside the kind of circular, thatched-roof hut that is ubiquitous in the region. After an attack by the LRA rebels, signified as such by their trademark dreadlocks, the abducted children were marched to a rebel camp and trained to fight the Ugandan military (Uganda People's Defence Force, or UPDF). These same UPDF soldiers were transformed into liberators when they rescued the children and transported them to the World Vision center, where they received medical treatment, counseling, and job training. After this humanitarian intervention, they were reunited with their families, and the archetypal Acholi home was restored.

Variations of this linear narrative repeatedly materialized in Ugandan representations of the LRA war. Its dominance excluded bewildering complexities, such as the UPDF's pattern of killing abducted children as well as rescuing them, the substitution of IDP camps for the "peaceful Acholi home," and the intensity of faith among some captives, who came to believe in the LRA movement and the spiritual powers of its leader, Joseph Kony.[8] In place of the "epistemic murk" of terror-warfare, the linear sequence of serenity, suffering and terror, intervention, and restoration was laboriously sustained despite the chaos and confusion that surrounded its production.[9]

I might dismiss this tale as an inevitable effect of narrative's capacity to domesticate lived experience into a simplistic story of good versus evil.[10] To do so, though, would overlook the intersection of this narrative with the politics of empire. I suggest that its dominance resonated with local understandings of the global market—a market in which LRA rebels, international humanitarian organizations such as World Vision, and Acholi civilians all competed for recognition and resources. As Clifford Bob points out in *The Marketing of Rebellion*, the marketing economy ensures that "worst-off groups" do not necessarily gain the most assistance; instead, groups and individuals must "scramble for scarce resources in a setting thick with similar aspirants."[11] This framework clarifies how northern Ugandans sought a foothold in an economic wasteland relatively isolated from the flows of transnational capital. Given that they were often limited to the rhetoric of humanitarianism as a means of entering the global market, narrative served as a crucial resource.

Narration caters to empire, but it also serves local needs for coherence, viewability, and order. In the first section of this chapter, I focus on the appropriation of arts therapy, specifically drama, in the World Vision rehabilitation center as a method of self-promotion on the global stage. In the second section, I discuss how the forces of empire fail to explain fierce local investment in linear narratives and the trappings of realism. Lastly, I contend that former LRA captives used Acholi dance to carve out a space in which alternative narratives of humanitarianism and terror-warfare unfolded. But even as these alternative narratives were embodied and performed, they were insistently appropriated as manifestations of humanitarian intervention. Creativity and resilience were omnipresent, but so was empire's shadow.[12]

In unpacking the contours of narrative, this chapter also attends to the complexities of spectatorship in theatres of war. Spectators in northern Uganda included the former captives at World Vision, fellow Acholi, southern Ugandans, NGO representatives, and foreigners such as myself who came to Gulu as one of the few places where one could "experience" the war in relative safety; a shadow audience consisted of imagined and idealized western spectators keen to offer financial support or at least a modicum of humanitarian pity. These layers of spectatorship speak to the adroitness with which a theatre of war caters to empire, on the one hand, but also responds to local needs and agendas, on the other. The expansiveness of terror-warfare, which systematically dismantles the boundaries of private/public and local/global in its destructive wake, ultimately generates a capacious audience to which the multifaceted form of performance might be uniquely equipped to respond.

An Acholi legend about the origins of Gulu illuminates the double nature of performance in the context of war. According to this legend, as explained to me by Okello Kelo Sam, who hails from Pader District, a hidden city exists beneath the town of Gulu. This city was created many centuries ago when a snake came out of the ground, leaving a hole that was filled with a rainbow. From the rainbow, a magical city came into being. Inhabitants of this underground city periodically rise to the surface and are glimpsed on the streets of Gulu as specters of another world.[13] In a sense, one might consider these otherworldly inhabitants as Michel de Certeau's walkers, the "ordinary practitioners of the city [who] live 'down below,' below the thresholds at which visibility begins."[14] I am often reminded of the Gulu legend in my attempts to come to terms with the dynamics of performance in contexts of sustained violence. Although performance is vulnerable to the harshness of co-option, it also contains a hidden realm in which holes speak not of emptiness but of possibility.[15] In contrast to frameworks of hybridity, which emphasize the potentiality of intermingling and mutual transformation, I suggest that these two realms remain relatively impermeable, save for occasional sightings of ghosts on the surface level. The legacy of these ghosts—that is, their lingering effects—remains an open question. De Certeau suggests that the walkers of the city ultimately participate in "a manifold story that has neither author nor spectator, shaped out of fragments of trajectories and alterations of spaces: in relation to representations, it remains daily and indefinitely other."[16] Like de Certeau's city, the protean space of performance takes on a life of its own that simultaneously insinuates and secretes.

Humanitarian Heroes and the Global Gaze

The LRA's ruthlessness serves as its trademark. As described in the previous chapter, the LRA emerged from the specific circumstances of Uganda's colonial and postcolonial history, channeling reserves of resentment cultivated through decades of marginalization and tension between northern and southern Uganda. The emphasis in this chapter, though, is on how the LRA's tactics of mutilation, mass murder, and abduction borrow from and participate in transnational codes of what Mary Kaldor has called the "new wars" of the late twentieth and early twenty-first centuries.[17] Under the terms of these wars, which increasingly target civilians instead of combatants, insurgency and counterinsurgency forces seemingly compete to outdo one another in the production of atrocity. In her landmark study of the Mozambican civil war, for example, anthropologist Carolyn Nordstrom has analyzed the public displays of atrocity practiced by the Renamo insurgency forces as a strategy meant to diminish local capacity for resistance.[18] Through forcing others to witness the atrocities inflicted on neighbors and loved ones, Renamo sought to "unmake the world" for victims and spectators alike, clearing the way for eventual surrender and defeat.[19] In a similar vein, Anthony Vinci points out that the extreme unpredictability of the LRA, which some observers have associated with Kony's seeming irrationality and even madness, facilitated the creation of a "pervasive climate of anxiety throughout the civilian and military population."[20] In other words, the seeming madness had considerable method in it.

The unmaking of the world plays out before the world. Witnesses and victims provide testimony to the international observers dotting the modern African warscape, who repackage this testimony for the global stage in the format of human rights reports, world news, and international aid policy. This expanded audience provides crucial context for the scripting and performing of terror-warfare. The terrorizing of civilians on a massive scale elicits attention from the worldwide press, which inadvertently encourages even more graphic acts of violence in a cyclical media machine. Several LRA tactics during the conflict suggested careful study of the international scripts of terror-warfare; for example, its practice of cutting off the lips, ears, or noses of civilians may have been borrowed from the example of the Renamo forces in the 1980s.[21] In 2004, the LRA still had not achieved as much notoriety as insurgencies in Sudan, Angola, and Somalia. The pressure to attract international attention might explain some of the LRA's improvisational tactics, such as padlocking the lips of civilians, which seemed to be a phenomenon unique to northern Uganda. My point is not to erase the historical and cultural specificity of these acts of violence but to emphasize the global stage on which they play out.[22]

In a study of the civil wars in Sierra Leone and Liberia, Danny Hoffman identifies a particularly insidious intent behind these spectacles of violence, arguing that combatants purposefully target civilians in order to gain access to international aid.[23] He found that the rebel soldiers of these West African countries were keenly interested in comparing their atrocious acts with those of their predecessors in Mozambique, Angola, Sudan, the DRC, and Somalia. He writes that "one tenet of this travelling knowledge of other African movements was that, when the international community responds to African crises, the more atrocious the conflict, the greater the level of aid."[24] Although the complexity of the LRA's motives should not be reduced to a desire for material gain, Hoffman's work helps explain how the politics of civil war and international aid intersect in African contexts.[25] In the streets of Gulu, the allure of aid money was repeatedly displayed as Land Cruisers and Pajeros belonging to the World Food Programme, the World Health Organization, Médecins Sans Frontières, various branches of the United Nations, CARE International, and World Vision drove past the locals on foot or, at best, on bicycles. These signifiers of wealth provide an impoverished population with tantalizing glimpses into the seemingly limitless flow of Eurocash, as if to affirm Michael Hardt and Antonio Negri's categorization of international humanitarian organizations as "among the most powerful and prominent in the contemporary global order."[26]

For World Vision's rehabilitation center, however, the Land Cruiser provided only a veneer of prosperity. Although the worldwide organization attracted massive funds, some of which were directed to its stately office in the capital city of Kampala in southern Uganda, the center occupied a marginal status.[27] Its facilities were run down, the children were crammed into battered

UNICEF tents, the latrines overflowed, and the counselors' wages, though undoubtedly superior to those of many northern Ugandans, were still insubstantial. The center's marginalized status in the humanitarian hierarchy meant that it, like the LRA, had to cater to multiple audiences, albeit through the medium of humanitarianism instead of terror-warfare. Nordstrom, who writes passionately and persuasively about how ordinary Mozambicans created "codes of creative worldbuilding" as a response to the decimation and terror of war, coins the following stirring phrase: "It is in creativity, in the fashioning of self and world, that people find their most potent weapon against war."[28] But in the LRA war zone, the codes of empire ensured that this creativity was carefully circumscribed. The staff of World Vision seemed intent on playing to the world in addition to rebuilding it.

Conveniently, the world often showed up on its doorstep. As one of the largest and best-known rehabilitation and reception centers for former child combatants in Uganda, the World Vision center received considerable attention.[29] Every two to three days during my stay in Gulu, visitors ranging from US military officers and foreign ambassadors to church groups appeared at the center, usually with little advance warning. When they arrived, scheduled activities invariably stopped, and the staff rushed to provide the visitors with a tour, an assembly of the children in the common hall, and a dance performance. These visitors took immediate precedence as the staff sought to shore up the center's image as a worthy recipient of international funds.

Arts therapy played a critical role in the center's production of humanitarian narratives. Although westerners champion this methodology as an alternative to "talk therapy," in which children are supposed to come to terms with their traumatic pasts through talking about their experiences with a counselor, my research indicated that arts therapy in northern Uganda was valued primarily as a means to market trauma.[30] The mostly Acholi staff members at World Vision invariably began the tours in the counseling room decorated with the series of paintings mentioned at the outset of this chapter.[31] After explaining that a former captive had produced the paintings—a piece of information that endowed them with a sense of authenticity—the counselor serving as the guide used the series as a template for describing the children's collective experience of trauma followed by rehabilitation. The guide then invited the visitors to peruse the stacks of drawings scattered around the room, allowing the visitors to become voyeurs of the children's experiences of LRA brutality that many of the drawings depicted. These works did not function as

Fig. 2. Poster created by children at the Gulu Save the Children Organisation (GUSCO), July 2004.

personal expressions of trauma and healing; instead, they were assimilated into the master narrative of war.[32] The counselors used representations of life in captivity as evidence of past suffering, whereas lighthearted drawings of trees, sunshine, and smiling people served as affirmations of World Vision's success at rehabilitation. As a mark of their value as a marketing tool, World Vision reproduced these drawings in the organization's brochures and on its website in the pages devoted to northern Uganda.[33] The weight that these drawings carry helps contextualize the ways in which the children's artistic expression was circumscribed. As the visitors examined the paintings and drawings, the counselors did not mention their tendency to grade the children's work—a practice that seems antithetical to therapeutic discourse, which calls for traumatized victims to purge their painful memories in a space that is ostensibly free of evaluation and judgment. In the midst of personal and cultural destruction, private expressions of pain are luxuries that northern Uganda could not afford.

Drama was acutely vulnerable to co-option by the machinery of empire and war. As part of the children's rehabilitation at the World Vision center, music, dance, and drama (MDD) were supposed to be included on a regular basis. Thursday afternoons and Saturday mornings were set aside for MDD. Despite the inclusiveness of this phrase, I found that drama was consistently omitted from the equation, passed over and even resisted in favor of Acholi dance. Although Liesbeth Speelman, a Dutch expatriate working for World Vision, had invited Robert Ajwang, a Tanzanian musician and dancer, and me to the center to organize drama workshops for the children, our attempts to organize these workshops were repeatedly turned aside. Granted, the center was subjected to constant disruption by the many national and international visitors. The center's activities typically ground to a halt during these visits, and the children would gather in the open-air common hall to listen to the visitors' expressions of sympathy and prayer. Even if these frequent displays of charity and compassion are taken into consideration, however, it became increasingly clear that our work was being pushed aside. We would be told that the children were "too tired" for dramatic activities, only to find those same children spontaneously performing a vigorous Acholi dance a few minutes later. Although multiple interpretations of this reluctance, indifference, and resistance are possible, this response suggests that drama was considered an insignificant activity in the context of daily life at the center. Drama was deemed useful only if the outside world was watching—a powerful outside world, which I believe that Ajwang and I did not signify since we lacked links to international donor agencies and other development organizations that the official visitors, for whom all other activities stopped, possessed.[34]

When the outside world did summon drama for its consumption, the staff was quick to respond. The center received two invitations during my stay to perform for official events attended by government officials, representatives of NGOs, local schoolchildren and their teachers, and European and US expatriates. In response to these prime opportunities for marketing and promotion, drama was abruptly rehabilitated as several members of the staff discarded their usual routines and devoted their time and energy to the creation of plays. Both the plays and the rehearsal process demonstrated the constraints on the children's creativity in a culture of war and the transformation of representation into what Michael Taussig calls a "high-powered medium of domination."[35]

Ironically, both occasions were meant as celebrations of children's empowerment. For the first event, a group of about twelve children from World Vision joined a few hundred schoolchildren at Karo Abili Primary School to commemorate children's rights.[36] After a grand procession, government officials, schoolmasters, staff from local NGOs, and a few foreigners watched as groups of children who represented primary schools throughout the district performed songs, plays, and dances related to the theme "The African Child, Family, and HIV/AIDS." As will be addressed in more detail, speakers and performers alike used the Acholi language.

The second event took place at the prestigious Acholi Inn, an elite hotel where foreigners and national figures regularly stayed. The focal point of the occasion was a photography exhibition titled *Armed with Resilience*, a remarkable collection of photographs by war-affected girls of northern Uganda. In keeping with the theme of the exhibit, the invitation requested that former female captives staying at World Vision perform dance and drama related to the theme of female roles in peace building.[37] In addition to two other groups from local secondary schools, the World Vision girls performed for a select audience of approximately fifty spectators that included government officials, NGO representatives, and several western foreigners. In reflection of the international tone of the event—the organizer of the exhibit, Jessica Lenz, was from the United States—a translator helped ensure that all members of the audience understood the speeches, though not the plays.

Despite the variations in context, the two plays that World Vision created were strikingly similar. For the children's rights festival, the play focused on a family living in an IDP camp. To the family's dismay, the older son spends his days drinking and carousing with girls. Amid this confusion, a World Vision counselor escorts a former female captive home. After a joyful reconciliation scene, the girl lectures her brother about the dangers of AIDS and explains that she learned about such matters during her stay at the World Vision center. The boy ignores her advice, only to meet dire consequences, since he dies in the final scene. Perhaps in keeping with the theme of building peace, the play performed at the Acholi Inn assumed a more optimistic tone. Although it also depicted a confident former female captive returning from World Vision to a troubled family at the IDP camp, the problem consisted of excessive drinking by the girl's father and brothers rather than sexual promiscuity. Like her counterpart in the AIDS play, she delivers a lecture about the folly of drinking; this time, the lecture produces the desired effect as her father and brothers decide to give up drinking. The play ends on a note of harmony as the family gathers together for a celebratory meal.

Both plays resonate with Anne Orford's analysis of humanitarian narrative. She identifies a consistent story line that recurs in stories of foreign intervention, in which a disruption of (Third World) order calls on (First World) "knights in white armour" to rescue the victims, who are uniformly cast as symbols of helplessness.[38] On the surface, the World Vision plays complicate this standard humanitarian narrative since the former female captives deliver their homilies about the dangers of AIDS and drinking from a position of authority and confidence rather than helplessness and passivity. But this strength does not stem from their experiences of war, their kin networks, or their cultural identity; instead, it is credited to World Vision, and the girls serve as emissaries of humanitarian enlightenment. Although these characters expand the convention of white humanitarian heroes swooping down to save troubled Third World nations, they dovetail with Orford's description of "active, humane savior[s] intervening to help people in trouble spots, obscuring other sets of relations between those who identify with the international community and those targeted for intervention."[39] The quarrelsome families that serve as the recipients of World Vision's wisdom are isolated, and sociopolitical context concerning the cramped, often shocking conditions of IDP camps and the utter failure of the state to protect its citizens is erased. The families, lacking agency and cultural resources, simply wait for World Vision's guiding hand, which they ignore at their peril, as the first play made abundantly clear through the brother's death.

The singularity of the humanitarian narrative was the outcome of a stringent rehearsal process. Although the children were the actors, the rehearsal process took place in an environment in which the counselors determined all aspects of the text and staging. The counselors conferred only with one another on the choice of topics, the casting, and the dialogue. Once the rehearsals began, the counselors exerted careful control over the words and delivery of the performers, emphatically telling them what to say and how to say it.[40] In a western context, this approach would be relatively unremarkable; in the context of Central and East African theatre, in which an atmosphere of collaboration and improvisation prevails, I found it startling. In her analysis of the Mozambican war, Nordstrom theorizes the prevalence of silence in cultures of terror as a means of guarding critical information; in other words, silence serves as a mode of survival in dangerous times.[41] In the creation of the World Vision plays, the staging methods served to silence the children's voices as their ideas about children's rights or peacemaking were never solicited. Instead of speaking as commentators on war, they served as the mouthpiece of preordained messages. Although I found the rehearsals difficult to watch, the situation in which the silencing occurred demands that I recognize the authoritarian approach to staging as indeed a mode of survival in dangerous times. Information was not so much guarded as it was painstakingly edited and shaped. In the charged atmosphere of Gulu, drama could not assume the connotations of children's play but was caught in the politics of war.

The hegemonic apparatus was not by any means absolute. For the first event, the reliance on the Acholi language (and the lack of translation for foreigners in the audience) might seem counterproductive. Why not ensure that the foreigners in the audience understand their message? Their reliance on Acholi prioritized the many locals in the audience, which included representatives of government, the UPDF, and NGO staff.[42] The center not only was dependent on international charity but also cooperated with district authorities and the military on the children's transfer to the center and their return to their families. The sympathies of high-ranking government officials from the region—who served as guests of honor at both events—were vital to the center's operations. Given the center's dependence on the generosity of other NGOs—for example, donations of mattresses and food from UNICEF and the World Food Programme—the NGO representatives in the audience also served as potential targets.[43] World Vision prides itself on its close ties to local communities; for example, the center trained a few hundred volunteers in Gulu District to help keep track of the children's progress once they were reunited with their families. A reputation for excellence among all the constituencies concerned was a key component of World Vision's success in negotiating these networks of interdependency.

But to be Acholi in 2004 was to be war affected. The organizers' reliance on the Acholi language suggests a degree of seclusion and privacy in the events despite their grandness, and thus I must acknowledge and account for an investment in linearity that demands a more nuanced explanation than the usual suspects of empire, globalism, and hegemony. Thus far, I have emphasized repression and domination at the risk of upholding master narratives of empire as a homogenizing force. But in teasing out how narratives of war overlap with the genre of realism, the next section touches on the potential of cultural memory.

Circulations of Realism in Theatres of War

Anthropologists and theatre scholars alike typically disparage realism as a medium for the representation of violence because it normalizes and perpetuates a seamless social order that disallows intervention and resistance.[44] Michael Taussig singles out realism for a harsh critique in the context of cultures of terror, calling it a kind of "hermeneutic violence" that "flatten[s] contradiction and systemitiz[es] chaos."[45] Although scholars such as Vivian M. Patraka, who cautiously suggests that "there are conditions [in the representation of violence] under which the traditional techniques of realistic identification may be useful," complicate this line of argument, realism is generally understood as a conservative ideological weapon that domesticates and contains the destruction left in violence's wake.[46] Since each of the dramatic and cinematic representations of the LRA war discussed in this chapter use conventions associated with realism, the overlap between war narrative and this distrusted genre calls for closer examination.

Ugandan theatre history helps contextualize the significance of the relatively stringent genre of realism on which representations of the LRA war depended.[47] As in the case of other East African countries, spoken drama in the realistic vein was strongly encouraged, if not enforced, in the Ugandan colonial school system in the late nineteenth century and the first half of the twentieth century.[48] In the postindependence era, Ugandan playwrights such as Robert Serumaga, Rose Mbowa, and Byron Kawadwa sought to transform this colonialist style of theatre by drawing upon Uganda's complex traditions of indigenous music, dance, and folklore. Even in contemporary works that might be loosely categorized as realistic, meaning that they construct a dramatic narrative that adheres to a rational, causal sequence of events, performers regularly break into song or speak directly to the audience. Such conventions both disrupt the veneer of illusionism and demonstrate the well-theorized capacity of sub-Saharan Africa to transform western ideas and conventions to suit local tastes and desires.[49]

In dramatizations of the LRA war, however, this expansive interpretation of realism yielded to an orthodox version that resists ruptures of the linear narrative.[50] This shift in the politics of representation raises a crucial question, given the limitations of the form and its dependence on a rational cause-to-effect progression of events. Why this preference for a form that belies, if not suppresses, the murk and mayhem of this war? At first glance, the indomitable force of empire presents itself as a logical explanation for this pattern. In other words, the use of realism might be theorized as a capitulation to a global marketplace that uses the mirage of objectivity to convey the horror of the LRA war to southern Uganda and beyond.

A 2004 film titled *War Child: Abducted*, directed and produced by Robert E. Altman, serves as a classic example of how realism works to confine and domesticate atrocity.[51] *War Child* relies on a visceral level of realism to tell the story of the LRA's abduction and military training of an eight-year-old boy named Okello. After a lengthy introductory sequence that emphasizes the serenity of Okello's village in rural Gulu, LRA rebels kidnap him and his older brother from the local schoolhouse. Both boys, as well as their classmates, are marched to a rebel base in southern Sudan and provided with military training.[52] After being subjected to sustained trauma at the hands of a brutal rebel commander, who forces him to kill his best friend, Okello manages to escape along with one of his schoolmates. They make their way to Gulu, where a UN worker brings them to a rehabilitation center that strongly resembles the one run by World Vision. In the final scene, his mother tracks him down at the center, and the two are reunited in a joyful embrace. Although the murders of Okello's father and brother in the course of the film preclude a seamless restoration of the social order, the film still upholds a sense of reaffirmation since Okello's prewar quality of innocence remains intact. The film, funded by Hallmark Entertainment, was clearly aimed at a western audience and therefore constructed a classic example of "an essentialized portrait of the universal sufferer, an image that can be commodified, sold, and (re)broadcast to global audiences who see their own potential trauma reflected in this simulation of the modern subject."[53] The mechanics of realism, which positioned Okello as the sympathetic protagonist in contrast to the otherness of the malevolent rebels, provided smooth terrain for this process of commodification and identification to occur.

Although the film was originally intended for US audiences, local investment in the trappings of realism played a key role in the film's conventions. On May 21, 2004, the film received its Uganda premiere at an international film festival in Kampala, a thriving metropolitan center where locals pride themselves on their cosmopolitan attitudes and practices.[54] Kampala residents, who are predominantly from southern Uganda, were relatively indifferent to the war; a visitor to the city at that time could easily remain unaware of the war decimating the northern part of the country.[55] Given this context of apathy, the film's Kampala premiere marked a key opportunity to raise awareness and perhaps cultivate empathy. Okello Kelo Sam (who was mentioned in this chapter's introduction) and Milton Obote, both of whom participated in the filmmaking and actively contributed to the writing of the script, responded to questions from the audience after the showing of the film.[56] One of the earliest questions, asked by an audience member whose accent and appearance conveyed a southern Ugandan identity, questioned the "truth" of the film in a skeptical tone of voice. Sam responded immediately and firmly, "This is not fiction. This is fact." Sam, who is intimately acquainted with the paradoxes and ambiguities of this war,[57] elided its complexity in a straightforward declaration that conflated realism with reality, or perhaps the reality that he wanted the spectator to believe, one that boiled down the murk of war to the issue of an innocent child trying to survive. Both Sam and Obote then invoked their experiences of having immediate family relatives abducted as a means of shoring up their authority to pronounce on the veracity of the film. The medium of realism was conflated with reality in a collaborative effort to overcome the disbelief and indifference of southern Uganda.[58]

This investment in realism might be linked to the genealogy of a global trend that encompasses imperial, colonial, and postcolonial cultures and states.[59] In his analysis of the pervasiveness of realism in representations of violence in Northern Ireland, Allen Feldman calls attention to the impossibility of determining a single origin for such a complex phenomenon: "The molding of realistic modes of depiction into a hierarchy of credibility and fact-setting and as a public form of truth-claiming and depictive legitimation was a long and fragmented historical labor that emerged in a variety of discontinuous but overlapping social sites—and not all at one time if we consider the respective development of state archiving, juridical rules of evidence, popular media, optical experimentation, art movements, and the commodification of visual experience."[60] I would add humanitarianism as another factor in the privileging of realism to Feldman's list of cultural, legal, and artistic discourses, all of which coalesce to ensure its global dominance. Although humanitarianism is more readily linked to the visual practice of photorealism, in which images of suffering are meant to trigger a sense of moral outrage, its master narratives also resonate with the politics of identification that underpin realistic drama insofar as the spectator is invited to imagine herself in the role of the hero who ultimately restores the social order.[61] Trauma and realism are fused in the circulation of visual and performative cultures.

Although the globalization of realism partly explains its pervasiveness in northern Uganda, my experiences at the World Vision center suggested that cultural issues were also at stake. I contend that the rationality of linear narrative becomes entangled in cultural memory as a mode to make things thinkable, to render the senselessness of the war intelligible and remake the world, however provisional the result.[62] The role of western arts activism helps clarify the intensity of this local investment. Children as Peacebuilders (CAP), a children's theatre group based in Gulu that included several former LRA captives, aimed to raise awareness in the IDP camps about the harsh conditions that child combatants endure.[63] For its first major production, which was created and performed in 2002, the group adhered to the conventional war narrative of home life, abduction, escape, and reintegration into home communities. In an interview conducted with a Canadian journalist, members of the group pointed to their ability to make the audiences cry as a sign of their success.[64] Instead of packaging this story for the international community or southern Uganda, the children used the techniques of realistic drama to provoke sympathy and identification with the plight of these children among fellow Acholi.

In 2003, foreigners deliberately intervened in the children's reliance on realism. Speelman, previously mentioned as a Dutch expatriate at World Vision in Kampala, contracted two Dutch acrobats to teach CAP members circus techniques such as acrobatics and juggling in order to expand their repertory of performance skills. The children strongly resisted the idea of incorporating circus techniques since they believed that this would diminish the seriousness of the story they were telling. Speelman admitted that the children were more or less "forced" to learn the techniques, and at the end of the monthlong workshop, they produced a play in which juggling, pyramid building, and plate spinning were integrated into the usual tale of abduction.[65] For example, in a scene in which a female abductee frantically attempts to start a fire under the orders of an increasingly impatient rebel soldier, the performer used the technique of plate spinning to help convey her sense of tension.[66] Although the resulting production provides a rare example of an experimental approach to the grim subject matter, it occurred only under western duress.[67]

The forces of imperialism and memoralization coalesce in a tale of culture clash, in which nonlinear techniques of representation confronted the monolith of realism. This particular tale, however, complicates the usual connotations of culture clash as the west versus Africa. On the one hand, the reaction of the children refutes popular and academic discourses of globalization as an indefatigable external force, given their collective unwillingness to capitulate to the imported European experts and their trendy performance techniques.[68] On the other hand, grassroots globalization and hybridity also falter as theoretical frameworks since these bottom-up models depend on the adaptation and transformation of dominant (western) cultural forms. In this instance, the requisite transformation did not occur. Unlike the indigenized versions of realism that postindependence Ugandan playwrights developed, the children's reliance on realism might be more easily categorized as a throwback to the colonial era than as a manifestation of local creativity.

My attempts to work with war-affected children clarified the limitations of these theoretical models. The reluctance that Ajwang and I had previously encountered turned into active resistance once we finally managed to work with the children. As a theatre scholar and practitioner well schooled in a distrust of realism, I confess that I was also keen to introduce experimental theatrical techniques. Not surprisingly, once we finally managed to organize a workshop, the counselor assigned to work with us responded with considerable resistance to our ideas.[69] Although her reaction invites a variety of interpretations, it was commensurate with widespread preferences for linear narrative and realistic representation characteristic of dramatizations of the LRA conflict.[70] The insistence on this pattern leads me to speculate on the possibility of a deep-seated cultural investment and to theorize this moment as an example of how genre plays out in the construction of cultural memory.

In consultation with the staff, we proposed working with a preexisting script that a counselor had composed based on the biblical story of the Prodigal Son. This parable is rich in significance for northern Ugandans because of its narrative emphasis on forgiveness and reintegration. It not only speaks to former captives, who might confront complicated homecomings when they are reunited with their families, but also resonates on a larger scale with the granting of amnesty to LRA combatants.[71] We suggested that we expand the parable using techniques that East African cultural nationalists have established as the hallmarks of an indigenous African theatre—storytelling and integration of music, dance, and drama.[72] The counselor immediately expressed strong resistance. She insisted that we would not be following the story if we used these techniques. She was particularly perturbed by my suggestion to introduce a flashback approach in which the story unfolded through the remembrances of the Son. While the children watched and waited, much of our workshop consisted of our joint efforts to persuade her to let us try this approach. Although we finally convinced her, or so we thought, the Prodigal Son never made it home since we succeeded only in workshopping the first two scenes.[73]

This encounter cannot be explained as another manifestation of the marketing of trauma. No NGO representatives or other VIPs were watching—just the children themselves. Still, Ajwang and I could not be left to our own experimental devices; instead, we were confronted with the absolutism of linearity in which the son is restored to the father's embrace through a series of causally related actions. It is significant that this story manipulates the classic humanitarian tale of suffering followed by external intervention to emphasize the internal role of forgiveness. The closing scene of restoration in the parable, faithfully reproduced in the counselor's script, allows the social order to be reasserted through the internal decision of the father. This narrative twist marginalizes and perhaps even excludes the role of humanitarianism, which depends on the act of external intervention, and instead underscores indigenous strength and resolve. The counselor's insistence on this story line suggests that she was invested in the terms of representation not only as an employee of World Vision but also as a war-affected Acholi woman whose Christian faith served as a source of strength.[74]

The formation of a narrative to make sense of traumatic events is not, in itself, surprising. Shoshana Felman and Dori Laub argues that in order to come to terms with trauma and transform it into a relatively contained memory of the past, "a therapeutic process—a process of constructing a narrative, of reconstructing a history and essentially, of *re-externalizing an event* has to be set in motion."[75] In her study of postwar reconstruction in Peru, Francine A'ness thoughtfully elaborates on Felman and Laub's work, noting that the production of testimony requires an atmosphere of stability: "In order to speak about the traumatic event a victim needs to feel safe. She needs to know that what happened in the past has come to an end and, moreover, that the listener before whom she testifies is someone who will listen and in whom she can trust."[76] As children continued to be kidnapped and people massacred—indeed, the famous Barlonyo massacre had occurred the previous February—these narratives played out where the population was most assuredly *not* safe.[77] The narrative, though, with its promise of restoration, held out a cultural lifeline that placed survival in local hands as opposed to those of the capricious and indifferent state, the United Nations, and international charities.

Emphasizing local agency runs the risk of overlooking the hierarchies that pervade its articulations. As the three of us attempted unsuccessfully to come to an agreement about the dramatic interpretation of the Prodigal Son, the children simply watched our negotiations. They willingly, even enthusiastically, participated as requested, but their interpretation of the biblical story is not known. Although I have called attention to instances of indigenous strength in the LRA theatre of war, the former captives have remained largely silent throughout this chapter. In the final section, I discuss how these children, particularly the girls and young women, overcame these various modalities of oppression through the forum of Acholi dance. Their reclamation of complexity and rescripting of humanitarian narrative clarified the creative and community resources at their disposal.

Restoring the Past

One of the demands of humanitarian discourse is to represent the traumatic past as a time of unrelenting terror and suffering. To complicate that image is to run the risk of diminishing the emotional responses that might generate charitable contributions. But as children's rights activist (and organizer of the photography exhibit previously described) Jessica Lenz argues, these discursive moves negate the skills that child soldiers and other abductees cultivate during captivity. Speaking specifically of the experience of female abductees in northern Uganda, Lenz explains, "During the process of reintegration and rehabilitation, far too often, we suppress and undermine skills and strengths that have enabled these girls to survive in the first place."[78] Lenz found, for example, that abductees developed a range of skills during LRA captivity, such as cartography, soldiering, spying, teaching, accounting, nursing, and public speaking; many also took on leadership roles in the military or in camp life in Sudan.[79] To emphasize these strengths is to intervene in the seamless representation of victimhood and begin to script an alternative narrative of war.

Lenz facilitated the creation of these narratives in her organization of the photography exhibit that showcased the work of twenty-six girls, who included former female captives of the LRA and other war-affected teenagers.[80] The exhibit, which I previously mentioned in the context of the two World Vision plays, marked the culmination of a six-month project in which they were trained in photography and encouraged to take photos that conveyed images of female strength. In addition to capturing a variety of powerful images, the photographers wrote brief commentaries about their role in peace building that vividly illustrated their capacity for sociopolitical commentary, as well as their desire to reclaim the complexity of their pasts. One former captive who participated in the project wrote, "Sometimes they say 'forget your past' to those who are formerly abducted. . . . It is important to remember [these] times, the times that made you strong. Like me, I remember what is most important, my strength that kept me alive."[81] This refusal to categorize herself as a helpless victim of LRA violence might not market well on the global stage, but it carves out a space in which the epistemic murk of war and abduction might be acknowledged rather than suppressed.

Lenz's ideas provide fresh theoretical space for understanding how the former female captives undermined the dominant narrative of war. Although the girls of World Vision did not participate in the photography project, they found other ways to reclaim the complexities of their pasts. In the play that they performed at the exhibition, the girl who played the alcoholic father wore a black rubber anklet. These anklets, which were endowed with Kony's spiritual power, were given to the girls as part of their indoctrination into the LRA. Several of the children at World Vision, particularly the child mothers, continued to wear them despite the staff's efforts to persuade them otherwise. This subtle visual cue in the performance conveyed a sustained belief in Kony's powers, a sign that World Vision's attempts at rehabilitation and intervention could not extinguish. Clearly, the anklets confound attempts to classify them simply as markers of resistance since they also served as reminders of LRA brutality; indeed, the girls' attachment was linked to fear of harmful spiritual repercussions if they were removed. But in light of the obvious confidence and sense of agency that these girls regularly demonstrated at the center, I contend that these anklets hinted at a counterculture amid humanitarian intervention.

Acholi dance allowed the counterculture to burst forth. In contrast to the careful restraints in which drama and arts therapy operated, enthusiastic and impromptu performance of these dances flourished at the World Vision center. Artistic skill and Acholi identity coalesced in these spontaneous performances to produce a creative commentary on war. Although the official timetable scheduled MDD only two times weekly, the children daily practiced dance steps and taught one another drumming rhythms. Boys participated as musicians for official events or during the scheduled MDD activities, but the older girls consistently initiated and led the informal performances; they also served as drummers. This distinction became especially prominent during one of the regular Monday-afternoon debate activities. For this debate, which addressed the value of formal schooling, the common hall that served as the nexus of the center contained only boys. The debate provided a picture-perfect moment for the global gaze as a well-run rehabilitation activity in which the counselors led the terms of the debate and guided their charges on the path to recivilization. Meanwhile, a group of about fifteen girls disregarded the formal schedule and performed a playful rendition of the *apiri* dance in front of the dormitories.[82] These parallel activities illustrate a classic dichotomy of official versus unofficial cultures, in which male-dominated official culture was juxtaposed to a female counterculture that played out on the margins.

But the enthusiastic participation of the World Vision female counselors in the dancing complicates this straightforward interpretation. The blurring of boundaries between staff and clients forged a democratic space that overturned the center's conventional hierarchies. Instead of maintaining a sense of professional detachment, the three counselors danced with energy and passion alongside the girls, who clearly were in command. As was customary in these performances, one of the girls served as the dance captain, using her whistle to determine transitions in the rhythms and movements. Although a participatory, democratic atmosphere is hardly unique in the context of African performance, it stood out in the context of World Vision, where anxiety over the terms of representation dominated artistic expression. This celebration of shared Acholi identity temporarily displaced the center's hierarchical structures and challenged the classic narrative of war that situates not only the former captives but also the Acholi people as victims of terror and oppression. In a moment of solidarity, female staff and former captives collectively displayed their cultural resilience and, at least temporarily, rebuilt their world.

This blurring of hierarchies and boundaries was not confined to the center itself. During a scheduled MDD afternoon, female dancers and musicians performed at the adult rehabilitation center, which housed adult male LRA combatants who had surrendered to or had been captured by the UPDF.[83] Master narratives about the LRA war might characterize these men as the cruel oppressors who abducted the girls and forced them into sexual slavery. As the testimony of hundreds of former female captives indicates, these narratives often reflected reality insofar as female abductees regularly experienced beatings, deprivation, and forced marriages as part of their indoctrination.[84] Given that an unspecified majority of LRA soldiers had once been abducted children themselves, however, the distinction between captive and rebel cannot be easily made. This zone of ambiguity provides critical context for the performance at the adult center, which hinted at the nuances and complexities of the relationships between "rebels" and "captives."

A particularly charged moment of the performance occurred during the *larakaraka*, a popular courting dance. As several Acholi enthusiastically explained to me, in the prewar era, villages organized major performances of *larakaraka*, which allowed visitors from other villages to investigate potential marriage partners. Typically, male musicians and female dancers use the medium of dance as an opportunity to flirt and convey their interest.[85] But during this particular performance at the adult center, the young boys who served as musicians were not the objects of the girls' affection; instead, sexual tension played out between the adult male spectators and the dancers. In a classic example of how the LRA war confounds simplistic oppositions between oppressor and victim, mutual relationships between rebels and captives occasionally developed.[86] New relationships also emerged during the rehabilitation phase; in order to sustain these ties, some girls were known to slip away to the adult center to visit their boyfriends. The *larakaraka* produced a unique moment in which a sanctioned, formal activity provided a veil for this undercurrent of attraction. Far from serving as a reification of tradition, these dances were adapted to serve a culture of crisis in which conventions of courtship occurred in war rehabilitation centers instead of rural villages.[87]

In addition to negotiating the demands of the present, these dances bore witness to the complex range of the girls' experiences in captivity. Their assured confidence in executing the steps was a legacy not so much of their preabduction upbringing as of the LRA camps in the former Sudan, where captives and combatants taught each other Acholi dances.[88] These dances not only allowed Acholi identity to exceed the parameters of war but also reinscribed a past of resourcefulness. Humanitarian discourse dictated that the life of LRA captivity must be represented as one of seamless oppression in which the innocent victims were subjected to relentless oppression and terror. These tropes were perhaps necessary in order to raise international awareness, but they also undermined the girls' memories of the times that made them strong, to rephrase the photographer quoted earlier, and the skills that they cultivated during their experiences. These dances expanded the single tale of hardship and humanitarian restoration into a discursive realm that encompassed complex pasts and complicated futures.

Even amid these celebrations of resilience, however, the forces of empire intruded. The march of humanitarianism ensured that the dances became entangled in its narratives through the force of appropriation. With their usual savvy comprehension of international aid politics, the staff members skillfully incorporated these moments of counterintervention into the narrative of rehabilitation. The dancers and musicians were regularly trotted out for the entertainment of official visitors, and their enthusiastic renditions of *larakaraka* and *bwola* were appropriated as spectacles for the global stage. Although the energy of the performances might have posed a challenge to the visitors' preconceptions of oppressed and downtrodden LRA victims, the staff readily invoked the children's high spirits as evidence of the success of rehabilitation. A Ugandan journalist who expressed amazement at the happiness of the World Vision dancers was informed that "the joy we could see was after days and weeks of counseling by World Vision staff."[89] Resilience was repackaged as a picture-perfect "after" moment in the makeover narrative of World Vision.

But stopping the analysis here would utterly deny the active engagement and intensity that generally characterize Acholi attitudes toward their indigenous dances. In a workshop that Ajwang and I arranged at GUSCO, the other major rehabilitation center in Gulu, we anticipated that our attempts at arts intervention might be more productive if we focused on dance choreography instead of drama.[90] In the renditions of *larakaraka* that we observed at both rehabilitation centers, the children employed a circular formation in which the male musicians surrounded the female dancers and effectively obstructed the spectators' view. Ajwang, who was trained in Tanzanian dance and choreography, proposed that he and the GUSCO staff and children collaborate on an alternative version of *larakaraka* for official performances that would open up the choreography to the spectators' gaze. Both the GUSCO counselor and the children responded to his suggestion with a distinct lack of enthusiasm. Given the cultural ability to adapt and reinvent their dances to suit the demands of the moment, this resistance cannot be chalked up to a reified notion of tradition as a museum piece to be protected from change. Instead, it suggests that even in the economy of spectacularization, limits were placed on the extent of commodification. Cultural definitions of what it meant to be Acholi were clarified among staff and children alike in response to external intervention.

It is a truism that global and local cannot be placed in opposition because of the intensity of mutual infiltration. In his study of the Kabre people of northern Togo, a world "in which sacrifice and MTV, rainmakers and civil servants, fetishists and catechists exist side by side and coauthor an uncontainably hybrid cultural landscape," Charles Piot emphasizes the theoretical impossibility of separating tradition from modernity: "Where does the 'traditional' end and the 'modern' begin? Where is there an 'outside' to modernity's 'inside'? Where is there a 'local' that is not also 'global'?"[91] These compelling questions drive countless in-depth studies of postcolonial and neoliberal cultural formations throughout the continent. But I continue to be drawn to Sam's image of Gulu's hidden city as a model that more thoroughly captures these dynamics of empire and performance. The dances served as fodder for an empire of trauma in addition to nourishing a vibrant subculture in which the children commemorated and celebrated their strength. The forces of empire and cultural memory might have coexisted, but they did not intertwine and intersect in a union of hybridity—they remained stubbornly, even protectively, sealed off and contained. Once the official visitors to the World Vision center had departed, the dances simply continued. In these moments, not only was the representational frame of trauma exceeded, but also the hidden city itself burst forth.

One day when I was in the World Vision counseling room, I saw two girls, newly arrived at the center, pointing at the paintings that circled the room and whispering.[92] Were they using the paintings to make sense out of their recent experiences? To flatten and homogenize them, perhaps, but also to make them bearable? Were they comparing the series of linear, causally related images to a disjointed reality? The girls were animated but hushed; even if I had known Acholi, I would not have understood their words. Their analysis of this particular representation of war was muted as if in awareness of the loaded context in which they spoke, in which a white foreigner was observing even a private conversation. It is tempting to position these girls as caught between western and Acholi anxieties, each side intent on using artistic expression to realize its own particular agendas. This reductive opposition, of course, does not do justice to their capacities to reclaim cultural and individual pasts and contextualize them in the epistemic murk of war. To return to Nordstrom, creativity not only served as "their most potent weapon against war" but was also a weapon coveted by a variety of players on the global stage of northern Uganda.

Notes

1. His statement, which he made after his visit to Kitgum in November 2003, was widely reported in the international press. See, for example, "Ugandan Paper Urges Government to Accept Foreign Assistance in Ending War," *BBC Monitoring Africa*, November 11, 2003.

2. See, for example, "Uganda: Dozens Slaughtered in 'Worst Forgotten Crisis on Earth,'" *National Post*, November 19, 2003; "Uganda Dismisses UN on LRA," *Monitor*, October 25, 2004; "'Outrage' over Uganda Crisis," *Western Mail*, October 25, 2004; and "Rebellion in Uganda 'Worse than Darfur War,'" *Daily Telegraph*, October 23, 2004.

3. Although Egeland did not call the conflict an "invisible war," this term was picked up by the media; see, for example, "The Invisible War," *BBC News*, October 22, 2004. Note that the DRC was in competition with northern Uganda for this label; see, for example, "The Invisible War," *Globe and Mail*, April 4, 2003.

4. The first Gulu Walk, which was organized by University of Toronto students Adrian Bradbury and Kieran Hayward to raise awareness about the night commuters, occurred in July 2005; a Global Gulu Walk was organized for the following October. *Invisible Children: Rough Cut* was first screened in 2004, but widespead screenings in the United States did not occur until 2005.

5. The town of Gulu is located in Gulu District in the north central part of the country; unless otherwise specified, Gulu refers to the town only. The Children of War Rehabilitation Centre, originally called the Gulu Traumatised Child Project, opened in 1995 at a time when the number of abductions dramatically increased. At the time of my visit in 2004, it provided shelter, medical treatment, and counseling to approximately four hundred former captives of the LRA, a number that constantly shifted because of the steady stream of arrivals and departures. Stays at the center varied from a few weeks to a few months, depending on the length of captivity and the level of difficulty in tracing the child's relatives. It should also be noted that the term "children of war" encompasses infants and toddlers born in captivity to older teenagers on the brink of adulthood. Some of the "child mothers," the term used to describe abducted girls who were forced into marriage and made to bear children, had been in captivity for so many years that they were more accurately classified as young women at the time of their escape or surrender. Although the center continued to call itself the Children of War Rehabilitation Centre, it began to shift toward serving young men around 2011, whereas women and children were sent to the Gulu Save the Children Organisation (GUSCO). When I returned to Gulu in January 2013, the bustling center had become a veritable ghost town because the number of returnees had plummeted to twelve adult male LRA fighters who had returned from the DRC. In the same month as my visit, World Vision announced plans to close the shelter because of the low numbers of returnees ("Rehabilitation Centre for Uganda's LRA Returnees to Close," *IRIN*, January 18, 2013). By June 2013, though, Invisible Children had reopened the center through a partnership with World Vision (see "Coming Home: Life after the LRA," June 20, 2013, on the Invisible Children blog at https://invisiblechildren.com/blog

/2013/06/20/coming-home-life-after-the-lra/). The center was redesigned as a forum for community support, offering classes, counseling, and medical care for returnees (see "Reintegration: Supporting Youth Recovery," November 5, 2013, at http://invisiblechildren.com/blog/2013/11/05/reintegration-supporting-youth-recovery/). It also stepped in when Ugandan LRA members surrender in the DRC or the CAR and are transported home (see Julius Ocungi, "11 Years Later, LRA Captives Return Home," *Monitor*, January 5, 2014). Although the center is still listed as a rehabilitation program on Invisible Children's website (see "Rehabilitation Projects," https://invisiblechildren.com/program/rehabilitation-project/, accessed August 9, 2017), its status at the time that this book is going to press is unclear.

6. As Chris Blattman and Jeannie Annan caution, "The total number of abductees is difficult to ascertain, and any figure is at best an educated guess" (2010b, 135). They provide an estimated number of 66,000 Ugandan abductees; this number is now widely cited by organizations such as Invisible Children. In a 2007 study, Phuong Pham, Patrick Vinck, and Eric Stover raised the estimate to 24,000–38,000 children and 28,000–37,000 adults, or up to 75,000 people by 2006 (3). See also C. Dolan 2009, 74–75, which draws attention to the large numbers of adults who have been abducted and thus complicates the commonly held image of the LRA as focusing primarily on abducting children.

7. The paintings were intact during my visit in 2013; director Susan Alal confirmed that no one had yet identified the original artist.

8. These statements are a compilation of various observations I gathered during two months of research conducted in Uganda from mid-May through mid-July 2004, particularly the three weeks I spent in Gulu from June 23 to July 14. Because of the sensitivity of these topics, much of this information was gathered through informal conversations with the staff and the children at the Children of War Centre. Instead of recording interviews, I kept detailed field notes throughout my stay. Although I did not engage an official translator, the staff and some of the children spoke English, and I was often able to communicate through my associate, Robert Ajwang, a native speaker of Luo, which bears close linguistic similarities to Acholi. I have omitted the names of World Vision staff in Gulu and of the children.

9. See Taussig 1986, 121.

10. I am borrowing here from Nordstrom's statement "Narrative domesticates experience" (1997, 22).

11. Bob 2005, 6, 7–8.

12. My narrow focus on the World Vision rehabilitation center means that I am addressing only a microlevel of the layers of domination that the LRA conflict contained. By focusing on the counselors, who, like most Acholi, were also victims of the LRA war, I risk negating their dedication and labor. An overtly anticolonial perspective might instead emphasize the larger forces that sustained the conflict, such as the US "war on terror," which allowed Museveni to shore up friendly relations with the Bush and Obama administrations through labeling the LRA a terrorist organization. Even researchers such as myself who are allowed free access to the children with minimal supervision should be implicated in the forces of domination in which these children are caught. But in a kind of homage to Taussig's concept of epistemic murk, my work bears witness to the extraordinary complexities of terror-warfare by attending to the formations of hierarchies among its victims.

13. Sam shared this legend in Tallahassee, Florida, in October 2004, when we were developing the script of *Forged in Fire*, a play about the LRA conflict that is discussed in more detail in chapter 5. The story of the hidden city is mentioned briefly in the play when the Tour Guide

makes a comparison between the ghosts from the hidden city and the night commuters in Gulu.

14. de Certeau 1984, 93.

15. The metaphor of Gulu's "hidden city" resonates with James Scott's concept of "hidden transcripts" (1990), that is, "discourse that takes place 'offstage,' beyond direct observation by powerholders" (4) and articulates "a sharply dissonant political culture" (18). I prefer the spatial parameters of Sam's metaphor, though, because it offers the possibility of exit from empire rather than resistance to it. A hole in the ground serves as a potential gateway to another realm.

16. de Certeau 1984, 93.

17. See Kaldor 1999 and 2013 for further information on the concept of "new war," which emphasizes the role of globalization in so-called local wars, as well as the blurring of lines between protracted violence and formally declared war.

18. Nordstrom 1997.

19. Nordstrom borrows the phrase, "unmaking the world," from Scarry 1985. Whereas Scarry conceptualizes the "unmaking" as playing out within the immediate social world of the torture victim, Nordstrom expands the notion to include the witnesses as well: "In Mozambique, it is not the victim that is hauled off to an isolated room, but the torture that is hauled into the center of home and community" (1997, 169).

20. Vinci 2005, 372–373. Although the LRA was ostensibly fighting to overthrow Museveni's government, the UPDF was seldom directly attacked during the LRA's prolonged operations in Uganda. Instead, the LRA preferred to attack Acholi homesteads and, once most of the homesteads were deserted, the IDP camps. The testimonies of former captives and commanders indicate that Kony, who comes from Odek in Gulu District, justified these attacks on his own people as a method to purge them of wrongdoers and thus pave the way for the creation of a new Acholi people who would rule Uganda. See Human Rights Watch 1997.

21. Nordstrom 1997, 165.

22. See Doom and Vlassenroot 1999, 27, for a discussion of cultural meanings behind the LRA's mutilations of civilians.

23. Hoffman 2004. For similar studies of how international aid politics helps facilitate atrocity, see Uvin 1998 and Gundel 2003.

24. Hoffman 2004, 216. Interestingly, the LRA did not even register on the West African soldiers' scale of violence, despite the length of the war and the extremities of their tactics, an omission perhaps explained by the fact that Hoffman conducted most of his research before the films and media stunts of Invisible Children.

25. Material goods served as a prime target of the rebels, who regularly conducted raids on IDP camps. Writing in the late 1990s, Doom and Vlassenroot imply that impoverishment was a primary motivation of the rebels: "For the majority of the rank and file, [rebellion] is a survival strategy, a way to obtain things which are out of reach by all normal means: consummatory rewards as ideological drive" (1999, 36). See Finnström 2010 for a more substantive discussion of the LRA's aims based on a study of a series of manifestos released since the late 1990s.

26. Hardt and Negri 2000, 313.

27. World Vision's "2004 Annual Review" listed its annual income as $1.5 billion. Available at http://www.wvi.org/publication/2004-annual-review, accessed July 31, 2016. I was not able to find out how much World Vision allocated to northern Uganda in 2004; however, it

seemed clear that the center was operating on a shoestring. Humanitarian aid was running short in the region; in 2004, UN agencies issued a collective appeal for $112.4 million to meet basic needs of people in the IDP camps.

28. Nordstrom 1997, 12, 4.

29. See Pham, Vinck, and Stover 2007 for an overview of several reception centers in the region. It should also be noted that the majority of returnees did not pass through these centers (Annan et al. 2011, 885).

30. Opiyo and Hepner (2013) comment on "the plethora of cultural and arts-based NGO interventions in northern Uganda today," which "suggests a shift in the last two decades, in which aid programming increasingly values creative and cultural expression" (180).

31. The only non-Acholi I encountered among the counselors and other staff members, such as the cooks and medical personnel, was a Lango counselor. See chapter 5 for a discussion of how the Langi people were also affected by the LRA conflict. At the time of my research, Langi abductees were mostly served by the Rachele Rehabilitation Centre in Lira, which opened in 2003.

32. See Opiyo and Hepner 2013 for a sensitive discussion of the ethics of visual art as a means of therapy; they note that "transplanted visual art initiatives are most likely to breach Acholi norms pertaining to expression, especially of traumatic events, and prematurely request and expect visual depictions of such events" (188).

33. See, for example, the 2004 World Vision report "Pawns of Politics: Children, Conflict and Peace in Northern Uganda," available at http://resourcecentre.savethechildren.se/library/pawns-politics-children-conflict-and-peace-northern-uganda, accessed July 31, 2016.

34. Although my racial phenotype alone would have signified wealth to individual Acholi, my lack of organizational trappings of wealth, such as a Pajero bearing the name of an international NGO, meant that I did not represent the kind of international power with which World Vision is accustomed to dealing.

35. Taussig 1986, 121.

36. This festival occurred on July 9, 2004.

37. The exhibit took place on July 11, 2004. Its complete title was *Armed with Resilience: A Photographic Dialogue with Girls Affected by the Conflict in Northern Uganda*, and it was funded in part by Save the Children in Uganda, Quakers Peace, and Social Witness. Children's rights activist Jessica Lenz was the project leader who raised the funding and organized the training of the photographers. This fascinating exhibit is discussed in more detail in the final section of this chapter.

38. Orford 2003, 158–185. As mentioned in the introduction, Teju Cole would famously term this trope the "white savior industrial complex" (Teju Cole, "The White-Savior Industrial Complex," *Atlantic*, March 21, 2012).

39. Orford 2003, 165.

40. This statement is based on my observations of the rehearsals of the two plays, which took place on July 8 and 10, respectively.

41. Nordstrom 1997, 81–83.

42. The use of Acholi was, of course, a practical issue as well, since most of the actors spoke little English. That said, I found it significant that the counselors seemed unconcerned with making sure that the foreigners in the audience understood the plays.

43. The sponsor of the children's rights festival was GUSCO, which operated the other major children's rehabilitation center in Gulu.

44. Anthropologists such as Taussig, Nordstrom, and Allen Feldman, all of whom are united in their distaste for realism as a method for representing violence, have engaged in insightful theoretical discussions of antirealisms as useful alternatives. Taussig, for example, invokes Brecht's *Verfremdungseffekt* as a method for "transmitting and transforming the hallucinatory reality of Putumayo terror" (1986, 133). Nordstrom was intrigued by the possibilities of Bakhtin's theory of the grotesque as a means of resisting terror-warfare (1997, 171–172), and Allen Feldman discusses Dada and surrealism as means of critiquing "the festishized integration of realist aesthetics into warfare and the structure of everyday life" (2000, 71).

45. Taussig 1986, 132.

46. Patraka 1999, 45. See also Diamond 1997, 38, and Carlson 2003. Carlson complicates the "pornographic" connotations of theatrical representations of torture and violence, suggesting that "even with psychological realism, the actor is perceived alongside the character" and therefore creates the potential for "self-aware complicity for the spectator" (392).

47. For a basic summary of developments and trends in Ugandan theatre, see Banham, Hill, and Woodyard 1994, 121–126; see also Kasule 2013 for a more comprehensive discussion of postcolonial Ugandan theatre. Much of the scholarship on Ugandan theatre focuses on theatre for development; see, for example, Breitinger 1994 and Frank 1995. See also the following PhD dissertations: Kaahwa 2001, Mulekwa 2012, Seremba 2008, and von Fremd 1995. For additional discussions of Ugandan dramatic literature, see Ntangaare and Breitinger 1999 and Mbowa 1998.

48. Here I depart slightly from Karin Barber's historical account of African realism. She interprets the development of Nigerian realism in the colonial era as part of a "general representational shift which took place across Africa" (2000, 352), implying that the shift was more an organic response than an imposed style. Although I agree with her point that scholars cannot assume that European modes of representation were simply "transferred wholesale to the rest of the world" (358), the anxiety of postindependence playwrights to counteract this style indicates that the violence of the colonial encounter played a key role in the East African context.

49. See Barber 1997 for a useful summary of the various theoretical trends in theorizing African popular culture and its transformational capacity. See also Barber 2000, 352–361, for a thoughtful analysis of the incarnation of realism in Nigerian popular theatre, which manipulates European versions of realism in order to emphasize reflections of moral agency. As a representative example of the expansive conception of realism in Ugandan theatre, on June 13, 2004, I attended a Luganda play by the group Afri-Talent at Bat Valley Theatre in Kampala titled *Gogolimbo* (The intrigue). At first, the play, which depicted the various shenanigans that played out among staff and guests in a hotel lobby, progressed in what my western perspective characterized as a classic fourth-wall realistic style, both in production style and in script. As the play continued, however, the fourth wall was often punctured when the actors began to lip-sync popular songs that were played over the sound system, as well as slipping in an occasional aside to the audience.

50. In addition to the examples that I discuss in this chapter, I have also researched *The Aboke Girls*, a play developed by a Dutch children's theatre company called Het Waterhuis about the famous abduction of 139 girls from one of the most elite secondary schools in northern Uganda (see also chapter 5 for a discussion of the Aboke girls). This play is decidedly nonrealistic, consisting of a series of monologues written in lyric poetry. After performing it in the Netherlands in 2001, the company toured it in Uganda in 2002. According to Dragan

Klaic, "After holding workshops for professional and semi professional actors, Het Waterhuis has handed over the production to a Ugandan cast who will perform the play in a local language" (2003, 33). My research, however, indicated that the play was not performed again once the Dutch performers returned to Europe. See Klaic 2003 for a discussion of this play.

51. The film is available at https://vimeopro.com/handmadetv/war-child, accessed July 30, 2016.

52. As mentioned in chapter 1, from the mid-1990s until around 2002, the Sudanese government provided massive support to the LRA in exchange for its assistance in fighting the Sudanese People's Liberation Army/Movement (SPLA/M); in fact, some of the returning child soldiers reported spending more time fighting the SPLA/M than the UPDF.

53. Hinton 2002, 26. Although Hinton specifically refers to the representation of refugees in mass media, this passage can be easily applied to the univeralism of Okello's character. It should also be noted that although Hallmark sponsored the film, the network chose not to air it because of the violence of the subject matter (e-mail communication with Robert Altman, December 15, 2004).

54. The Amakula film festival took place primarily in the National Theatre from May 21 through May 30, 2004. I attended this premiere.

55. To describe Kampala's population as predominantly southern is not, of course, to ignore the fact that many northern Ugandans of various ethnicities lived in Kampala. But northern perspectives on the LRA conflict were frequently lost in the overall atmosphere of indifference. As late as 2012, this apathy apparently manifested itself during the premiere of Judith Adong's *Silent Voices* at the National Theatre in Kampala, which addresses the human rights violations committed by Museveni's military in Acholiland. As described on the *Silent Voices* Facebook page, the audience often laughed in response to the serious subject matter. Although I hesitate to categorize the reasons for this laughter, it is telling that Adong perceived it as a manifestation of southern indifference.

56. Their names would clearly mark Sam as an Acholi and Obote as a Lango to a Kampala audience.

57. Several informal conversations and formal interviews with Sam in Tallahassee in October 2004 revealed that his experiences of war speaks powerfully of Taussig's epistemic murk, which the film, in which Sam played the role of the rebel commander, belied.

58. Although the presence of Altman, a New York City–based director, might indicate that this realistic style was more his choice than that of the Ugandan actors, Sam informed me that Altman relied heavily on the actors' participation in the shaping of the script. The few nonrealistic elements in the film, such as the incorporation of a soundtrack that juxtaposed scenes of horror to compelling, haunting Ugandan music, were clearly added after the filming and could be more safely classified as a western choice.

59. See Rothberg 2000 for a pertinent discussion of "traumatic realism," in which he explains that realism in relation to the Holocaust entails "an epistemological claim that the Holocaust is knowable and a representational claim that this knowledge can be translated into a familiar mimetic universe" (3). Similarly, my usage of the term "realism" in this chapter is predicated on the idea of knowability, familiarity, and linearity. Linearity here might seem to promise an end to the violence.

60. Feldman 2000, 60. To help illustrate the multiple manifestations of realism in colonial and postcolonial eras, Feldman also provides a useful summary of scholarship in this area (59–60).

61. See Malkki 1995, 11, for a discussion of dominant images used in humanitarian refugee discourse.

62. The idea of thinkability is borrowed from de Certeau. The original quote is describing historical work, which is "organized . . . by the will to make all things thinkable" (de Certeau 1988, 44).

63. Children as Peacebuilders, "Reconciliation," n.d., http://www.childrenaspeacebuilders.ca/resources/pdf/youth/26.pdf, 128–131, accessed December 9, 2004. The description of the 2002 project is based on this report. As of 2017, this link was no longer working, but a 2005 World Vision report in which CAP is discussed is still accessible; see Valarie Vat Kamatsiko, "Small Feet, Deep Prints: Young People Building Peace with World Vision East Africa," World Vision, 2005, 61–71, available at at http://www.wvi.org/africa/publication/small-feet-deep-prints, accessed August 10, 2017. The group, which was founded in 2000, was still active as late as 2013, when the members started a blog (http://capuganda.blogspot.com/).

64. Children as Peacebuilders, "Reconciliation," 131.

65. Personal conversation in Kampala, July 7, 2004.

66. I viewed a videotape of the performance that was filmed during its premiere on May 29, 2003, in Gulu.

67. Interestingly, the children kept the play in their repertory and continued to perform it for at least a year after the workshop, which suggests that they shed at least some of their anxiety over this method of staging. The videotape of the premiere performance depicted a highly enthusiastic crowd, which might have lessened the children's concerns over diminishing the seriousness of the subject matter.

68. Although they yielded in the end, this compliance should be viewed in the context of their low-ranking position within a hierarchy of national and international organizations. Children as Peacebuilders is linked to a Canadian-based NGO that is sponsored by Defense of Children International and funded by the Canadian International Development Agency (http://www.childrenaspeacebuilders.ca/home.htm, accessed December 9, 2004).

69. This "workshop" took place on July 1 and 2, 2004. See chapter 6 for a critical look at the kind of theatre activism that Ajwang and I were practicing; that chapter also includes a critique of the workshop mentality.

70. An example of alternative interpretations includes that of authorial integrity; that is, the counselor might have been reacting as a playwright to my rearrangement of her script. Although this explanation is certainly feasible, a strict adherence to notions of authorial integrity would be at odds with the majority of my experiences in East and Central Africa, where playscripts tend to be treated as expressions of a collective voice. Another interpretation is that, as a devout Christian, the counselor was uneasy with the rearrangement of the biblical version. She herself, however, had freely updated the parable by setting it in northern Uganda, which suggests that she was not bound to strict, literal translations.

71. In contradiction of widespread perceptions that former LRA captives were ostracized when they returned to their families, Blattman and Annan find that "community acceptance of former abductees is high, and they report similar levels of social support as do nonabductees" (2010a, 883). The child mothers at World Vision, though, conveyed considerable anxiety about returning home, suggesting that the Prodigal Son story still held particular significance. Lenz 2004 also indicates that the return home could be a mixed experience.

72. Tanzania and Uganda both serve as representative examples of former British colonies that sought to transform the colonialist style of theatre into one that reflected indigenous

modes of performance. In addition to the Ugandan sources listed in note 47, see Mlama 1991 for a discussion of these issues in a Tanzanian context.

73. They also ensured that Ajwang and I remained in the role of observers for the two plays created for the two events previously described, which perhaps indicated that we were not to be trusted in this sensitive task.

74. The religious and cultural significance of the Prodigal Son parable was clarified in 1999 when the archbishop of Northern Uganda, John Baptist Odama, used the Prodigal Son as a metaphor to suggest that the LRA combatants should be "forgiven and welcomed back into the fold." See "New Archbishop Seeks to End Conflict in Northern Uganda," All Africa News Agency, April 5, 1999.

75. Felman and Laub 1992, 69. Emphasis in the original.

76. A'ness 2004, 398.

77. The Barlonyo massacre, which occurred on February 21, 2004, is discussed in more detail in chapter 5.

78. Jessica Lenz, "Resiliency," *AUP Magazine*, Fall 2003, 6.

79. Lenz 2004, 150–155. As Lenz explains, the leadership roles that many of these girls fulfilled during captivity can make returning to socially ordained gender roles at home a fraught experience: "Females who decide to speak out against the abuses they receive from the community may be labeled unfit for society, where in actuality they may have gained more assertiveness, confidence, and a feeling that they have the right to express their opinions" (2004, 22). See also Lenz 2017.

80. Fourteen girls were former captives who participated in Lenz's in-depth research and interviews; four were coresearchers; and eight were recruited from six different peace clubs within Gulu District who had not necessarily been formerly abducted (Lenz 2004, 112).

81. Caption on untitled photograph, *Armed with Resilience*.

82. This combination of debate and dancing occurred on July 5, 2004.

83. This visit occurred on June 24, 2004.

84. Human Rights Watch 1997; see Blattman and Annan 2010a, 2010b; Annan et al. 2011; and Lenz 2004 for more judicious discussions of abductees' experiences. For example, their findings suggest that the rate of atrocities committed by the abductees has been overstated (Blattman and Annan 2010b, 136). Lenz 2004 sheds considerable light on the range of experiences of abducted girls; those who were kept on the move in Uganda experienced greater hardship than those who lived more settled lives in the camps in Sudan. See also note 88.

85. See Girling 1960, 68–69, for a description of *larakaraka* in the late colonial era.

86. After capture or surrender, former captives and their abductors occasionally formalized their relationship through legal marriage. One could argue that the former female captives had limited choice given the social disapprobation regarding their pasts; however, to insist on this perspective negates both the ambiguities of the situation and the agency of the former captives. See also Annan et al. 2011, 884, in which a former female captive comments on the possibility of mutual affection between herself and her "bush husband": "We got along well. You know, he was abducted like me." The authors also observe, though, that only 5 percent of LRA forced wives remained with their bush husbands after their return to civilian life.

87. One might argue that the girls served as a spectacle for the men; to do so, though, negates the participatory atmosphere that is typical in East African performance. In this performance, two of the men joined the drumming and displayed their skill in what might be seen as a courting move of their own.

88. The LRA generally kept their "wives" and children at villages and encampments in the former southern Sudan. From 1994 to 1997, about three thousand to four thousand fighters were established at Aru-Kubi, nicknamed "New Gulu" or "Kony Village." Later, after this camp was overrun by the SPLA, semipermanent bases were established around Jebel Lin, Pager, Rubangateka, Magwi, Gambera, Illyria, and the Imatong Mountains (Schomerus 2012, 126). Festivals and celebrations were often organized at the camps to mark military victories or holidays. These events often included both modern and traditional dancing. Lenz reports that in her study, 21 percent of her interviewees mentioned singing and dancing both modern dances and traditional dances (2004, 171).

89. Julius Mucunguzi, "A Visit to Uganda's War Children Is Humbling," *Monitor*, October 28, 2004.

90. This event occurred on July 7, 2004.

91. Piot 1999, 173.

92. This incident occurred on June 25, 2004.

3

TRAUMA, INC. IN POSTGENOCIDE RWANDA

Guilt and Rwanda are joined at the hip. The UN decision to sharply reduce troops at the onset of the 1994 genocide has triggered countless excoriations over the past twenty years. "There is no country today ... which can wash its hands of Rwandan blood just by saying sorry," Roméo Dallaire, the commander of the UN peacekeeping contingent during the genocide, proclaimed on the occasion of the tenth commemoration.[1] Ten years later, UN secretary general Ban Ki-Moon also acknowledged the international legacy of the genocide, albeit in more judicious tones: "The shame still clings, a generation after the events."[2] The battle cry of "a million dead in a hundred days" is cited not only to remember and honor the victims but also to elicit guilt in the international community, which might have rewritten this equation of brutality had it only intervened.

The Rwandan government is adept at using the proliferation of guilt to render the world submissive to its whims in a dynamic commonly called the genocide credit. Filip Reyntjens coined the phrase within two years after the genocide to describe the government's uncanny ability to escape international censure despite its violations of human rights both within Rwanda and across the border in the DRC.[3] In 2004, Reyntjens more fully defined the genocide credit as "a source of legitimacy astutely exploited to escape condemnation," explaining that "the 1994 genocide has become an ideological weapon allowing the RPF to acquire and maintain victim status and, as a perceived form of compensation, to enjoy complete immunity."[4] The idea of the genocide credit has gained considerable traction among scholars and journalists to reference Rwanda's curious impunity on the international stage.[5]

But, with apologies to Emily Dickinson, Rwanda is also the thing with feathers. The Rwandan state not only circulates narratives of guilt but also presents itself as a beacon of hope. The Rwandan PR machine serves up a range of statistics as evidence for the country's seemingly miraculous rise from the ashes of the genocide: Rwanda has more women in parliament than any other country in the world; nearly 98 percent of Rwandans have health insurance; the gross domestic product has more than tripled.[6] In a 2012 *Foreign Policy* op-ed, former British prime minister Tony Blair and philanthropist Howard Buffet touch on several high points of the Rwandan success story, such as new infrastructure, a functioning internet, and improved state transparency. They proclaim that "in the last five years, Rwanda has lifted 1 million people out of poverty, created 1 million new jobs, and is poised to meet most of the U.N. Millennium Development Goals."[7] Blair and Buffet smoothly transition from one million killed to one million lifted out of poverty in a masterful spin that could be termed Rwanda's hope credit.

But how useful is the notion of credit in light of Rwanda's complex and shifting international relations? In 2008, President Paul Kagame felt compelled to respond to those who "claim that we are trading in the genocide for political gain" in his annual genocide commemoration speech, caustically noting that "those who say so probably need to have genocide in their own countries so that they too can enjoy those profits."[8] "Credit" is a multifaceted word that refers to the trustworthiness of one's reputation and thus resonates with the moral authority of the RPF, which has been hailed as a collective hero for ending the genocide in July 1994 upon its capture of Kigali and the subsequent declaration of a cease-fire. But Reyntjens tends to prioritize the economic connotations of credit; for example, he regularly describes the RPF as "exploiting" the credit—a term that the *OED* defines as "to make capital out of."[9] In her analysis of how the Rwandan government continues to receive aid despite mounting international criticism, Eugenia Zorbas glosses genocide credit as "large aid flows," which suggests a straightforward equation: guilt=credit=aid.[10] Similarly, Jason Stearns comments on the economic advantages of Rwanda's trafficking in hope: "If the Rwandan government today attracts Starbucks and Rick Warren and Tony Blair, it's not because it's such a great economic opportunity, it's because people see it as a symbolic beacon of hope in Central Africa."[11] The hope credit helps generate an alternative revenue stream from western countries seduced by the narrative of an African success story.

But use of the term credit indicates a finite amount that at some point will expire. When Reyntjens introduced the phrase, he indicated that it was "rapidly eroding"; in 2000, he described the credit as "diminishing."[12] Similar claims were periodically made in the years that followed.[13] These predictions stemmed from occasional suspensions of aid and expressions of criticism in response to Rwandan military intervention in the DRC and the repression of democratic freedoms in presidential and parliamentary elections.[14] Each time, however, the suspension of aid was more symbolic than material, and Rwanda deflected criticism like water off the proverbial duck's back. After the release of a UN report in 2012 that condemned Rwandan support of the M23 rebellion in the DRC in particularly harsh terms, several donors suspended funding, an action that led to predictions that the genocide credit was "running on fumes."[15] Again, though, these censuring moves were tentative and were often reversed; by February 2013, aid had resumed despite the lack of evidence that Rwanda had withdrawn support from M23.[16] The genocide credit continues to survive the crossfire of aid cuts and recriminations, somewhat battered but still intact.

Two decades after the genocide, the concept of the genocide credit cannot fully capture the curious foothold that Rwanda has cultivated and maintained in an empire of trauma. The RPF might be masterful at pulling the west's emotional strings, but the west seems unduly eager for its strings to be pulled. I suggest that the west is attached to genocide in ways that exceed rational explanations and sociopolitical contexts. My use of attachment, a term that emerges from psychological studies of mother/child relationships, builds on the theoretical work of Wendy Brown, Sally R. Munt, and Lauren Berlant.[17] They consider cultural and political attachments that are built into "the very structure of *desire*," that is, as a fundamental process of identity formation.[18] Attachments are inextricably bound up "within a circulation of emotion that we barely perceive" and thus are pervaded with ambivalence and contradiction insofar as the emotions generated by attachment operate "ideologically, somatically, and unconsciously."[19] Analyzing Rwanda's grip on the international imagination through the lens of attachment clears theoretical space for the economy of emotion in international relations with Rwanda. Unlike credit, an attachment is not a finite amount that will at some point run out—it can only find new objects for its affections.

So what is empire attaching to, twenty years after the genocide? Cultural theorists of attachment can be roughly divided into two camps: the first draws on the work of Foucault and Judith Butler to emphasize the idea of subjugation to the attachment object; the second, characterized primarily by the work of Berlant, theorizes attachment as generating a sense of fantasy and optimism.[20] In tracking the contours of genocide attachment, I find both dynamics at work. I repeatedly came across a Janus-faced attachment in which empire indulges in a masochistic wallowing in guilt and shame, on the one hand, and basks in the light of optimism and hope, on the other. Empire consumes Rwanda's genocidal past as a source of guilt but depends on its seemingly bright future as a wellspring of hope—a double-edged narrative that satisfies the curious western penchant for pleasure and pain.[21]

This chapter explores the cultivation and manipulation of genocide attachment. Two Rwandan celebrities serve as focal points in an expansive analysis that draws on political speeches, genocide memoirs, a Catholic retreat, an off-Broadway play, and a BBC documentary. The first section discusses Kagame—a head of state but also a world celebrity—whose theme song is less the manipulation of guilt than a nuanced understanding of the politics of shame. Kagame skillfully invokes the moral authority of Tutsi collective victimhood to cast empire in a surprisingly submissive role. I then turn to Immaculée Ilibagiza, arguably the best-known Rwandan genocide survivor in the world because of her best-selling 2006 memoir *Left to Tell: How I Found God amidst the Rwandan Holocaust*. Since the publication of her book, she has gained fame as a self-help guru who proclaims the gospel of love and forgiveness as the key to self-realization and success. In contrast to the shame-wielding Kagame, Ilibagiza offers love as a balm of redemption to her western followers. The dynamics of shame and forgiveness work together to satisfy empire's contradictory appetites.

But Ilibagiza's story does not stop there. She quietly uses the genocide attachment to redefine national identity and religious subjectivity in the context of an authoritarian state.[22] On the one hand, Ilibagiza demonstrates clear and unquestionable loyalty to the RPF; for example, she praises Kagame as a "miracle" who helped unite all Rwandans, and First Lady Jeannette Kagame's ringing endorsement, which appears on the back cover of *Left to Tell*, folds the book into a master narrative of reconciliation and patriotism: "I hope that all can experience Immaculée's profound spiritual transformation and be inspired to work for a united and lasting nation."[23] On the other hand, Ilibagiza's self-performance intervenes in the production of "Rwandanicity," a term that Ananda Breed uses to theorize the performativity of a post-1994 Rwandan identity.[24] The intensity of Ilibagiza's Catholic faith exceeds the reach of state and empire and recasts the genocide attachment as an attachment to the nation itself.

More recently, Ilibagiza's writing and public appearances have increasingly focused on the southern town of Kibeho, which became famous in the early 1980s as a site of apparitions of the Virgin Mary. Kibeho's dense history, in which religious miracles and mass killings intersect, provides rich terrain for her reinventions of Rwandan identity. The final section of this chapter delves further into the politics of Kibeho, focusing on its appearances in the controversial documentary *Rwanda's Untold Story* and Katori Hall's play, *Our Lady of Kibeho*, both of which premiered in late 2014. From the BBC to off-Broadway, the genocide attachment reinvents itself with dogged determination. Its fierceness will not be denied.

Kagame and the Politics of Shame

When it comes to Rwanda, guilt is in the air. Why doesn't the west condemn Kagame for his invasions of the DRC and support for rebel militias? Why weren't any members of the RPF indicted for war crimes in the Arusha trials? Why isn't the government censured for its repression of opposition political parties? Why did the UN give Rwanda a seat on the Security Council? Across the board, scholars and journalists consistently point to the overriding factor of guilt.[25] Zorbas comments that references to the 1994 genocide "elicit strong feelings of guilt among major western donors—even many years afterwards."[26] The repercussions of international guilt, which has allowed Rwanda free rein despite its repressive tendencies at home and its destructive campaign in the DRC, are potentially massive. When a 2012 US intelligence report suggested that Rwanda would be a failed state in 2030, Chris McGreal of the *Guardian* suggested that "the bloody legacy of Anglo-American guilt" might be to blame.[27] In other words, if the Rwandan state does fail, the west will be guilty of its guilt.

But in regard to Rwanda, guilt is, strangely, nowhere. The evidence for the actual existence of guilt is relatively scant. Zorbas, for example, quotes two diplomats who used the words "discomfort" and "some responsibility" in relation to the genocide, which hardly add up to "strong feelings of guilt."[28] More striking is Pottier's adamant assertion that Boutros Boutros-Ghali, who was the UN secretary general during the genocide, was caught "red-handed" with his admission of guilt in May 1994.[29] Boutrous-Ghali's statement, though, is more easily interpreted as rhetorical spin: "We are all responsible for this failure, not only the world powers but also the African countries, the NGOs, the entire international community."³⁰ Although Boutros-Ghali did acknowledge responsibility in this remark, that responsibility was immediately diffused as broadly as possible across the globe; it is unclear how this statement translates to being caught red-handed.³¹ To insist on the prevalence of guilt glosses over the refusal of the international community to admit to its existence. As legal scholar Nesam McMillan points out, "Despite ... widespread criticisms of the international response [to the Rwandan genocide], there have been no legal consequences flowing from this event—no countries have been prosecuted or punished for their failure to fulfill their legal obligation to prevent the crime of genocide."³² To acknowledge guilt is tantamount to admitting accountability.

Scholars find themselves on firmer empirical terrain when the issue of the government's manipulation of guilt is raised. Reyntjens, for example, points to the regime's response to a 2001 Amnesty International report that underscored the "devastating human toll" of Rwanda's occupation of the eastern DRC; the report was called "an insupportable insult to the memory of the more than a million victims of the 1994 genocide."³³ In 2008, when the United Nations released a report that accused Rwanda of funding and arming the CNDP, a rebellion in the eastern DRC led by Laurent Nkunda, the state immediately lashed out.³⁴ Minister of Information Louise Mushikiwabo called the report a "continuous ploy by powerful countries," which "have decided to undermine any truth as regards to Rwanda to hide their guilt after they abandoned Rwandans during the Genocide."³⁵ In 2010, the regime again invoked the UN failure to intervene during the genocide in order to discredit an even harsher UN report that accused the Rwandan military forces of systematic massacres of Congolese civilians.³⁶ Given the consistency with which the RPF invokes guilt, state officials clearly see it as a salient strategy in international relations. In his 2009 commemoration speech, Kagame proclaimed that "there is a lot of guilt. Guilt is written all over, the world is guilty no doubt."³⁷ His insistent and repetitive naming of guilt summons it into existence.

But the emphasis on guilt conceals a more complex dynamic at work. I suggest that rather than guilt, shame is a more salient framework for understanding the international community's submissive posture in relation to Rwanda. In making this assertion, I am participating in a "broad shift ... away from the 'moral' concept of guilt in favor of the ethically different or 'freer' concept of shame," as Ruth Leys put it in her aptly titled book *From Guilt to*

Shame.³⁸ The transition from the rhetoric of guilt to the discourse of shame entails a "shift of focus from actions to the self that makes the question of personal identity of paramount importance."³⁹ In contrast to guilt, shame is an amorphous, navel-gazing creature that neatly evades issues of legal accountability and responsibility in exchange for sentiment and hand-wringing. In the Rwandan context, the framework of shame helps explain the difficulty in finding clear-cut evidence of the seemingly all-pervasive guilt. To admit guilt is to open the door to legal accountability, whereas expressions of shame might leave the western self feeling appropriately cleansed and ready to continue on a hegemonic, globalizing path. An analysis of Kagame's strategic manipulation of the rhetoric of shame provides new insights into his famous PR machine but also underscores the west's investment in this rhetoric. The empire weeps for shame in order to be reassured by its goodness; meanwhile, the Rwandan state proceeds on its merry authoritative way. The shift from guilt to shame also resonates with the dynamics of attachment. The material benefits of a genocide credit are finite and tangible; likewise, guilt is more easily located in a specific action and thus can be purged through an act of atonement. Shame and attachment work in tandem because both operate at the mercurial level of irrationality and sentiment and thus are more fluid and elusive.

To rephrase: when it comes to Rwanda, shame is in the air. In her analysis of the international response to the Rwandan genocide, McMillan draws on theories of shame to explain how these "questions of legal accountability ... have been sidelined, in favour of an emphasis on the social and moral implications of this event."⁴⁰ For example, she argues that international apologies, which stop short of acknowledging responsibility for the Rwandan deaths, should instead be understood as confessions.⁴¹ Her analysis of speeches by former UN secretary general Kofi Annan, former US president Bill Clinton, and former Belgian prime minister Guy Verhofstadt reveals a "confessional logic" in which they "seek to acknowledge their personal failures regarding the Rwandan genocide in order to be freed of such past sins."⁴² Perhaps the most famous confession is that of US president Bill Clinton in a speech that he delivered at the Kigali airport in 1998, in which he did not apologize for his failure to intervene but instead diffused the responsibility, as Boutros-Ghali did in 1994, across "the international community, together with nations in Africa."⁴³ The text of the speech lists three general actions that this expansive "we" did not do: "We did not act quickly enough after the killing began. We should not have allowed the refugee camps to become safe havens for the killers. We did not immediately call these crimes by their rightful name: genocide." In archival footage of this speech, he delivers these dry statements in a monotone.[44] Once he turns to a confessional mode in which he frames his inaction as a personal failure, the language becomes more poetic, and his vocal quality attains emotional depth and passion: "It may seem strange to you here, especially the many of you who lost members of your family, but all over the world there were people like me sitting in offices, day after day after day, who did not fully appreciate the depth and the speed with which you were being engulfed by this unimaginable terror."[45] Whereas he appears emotionally detached during his brief acknowledgment of guilt, he seems to relish the performance of shame. Unlike the legal implications of guilt, shame serves as a pathway to personal redemption, signified as such by Clinton's broad smile when he concludes his speech.[46]

The narrative of shame helps ensure the centrality of empire.[47] Phil Clark points out in a review of the 2004 film *Hotel Rwanda*, "The problem here is that the narrative of non-intervention is all about the west, in the same way that the cowardly motivations behind non-intervention were all about the west."[48] Excessive hand-wringing distracts attention from the estimated 800,000 victims, and the west's domination of the global limelight is assured once again. This navel-gazing narrative helps explain how Dallaire, who is often lionized as a hero of the Rwandan genocide despite his refusal of that label, has been positioned as "the human symbol, the embodiment, the very face of the Rwandan genocide."[49] White shame prevails at the expense of black suffering.

The Rwandan PR machine obligingly responds. As previously mentioned, the postgenocide state does not hesitate to invoke western inaction during the genocide as a means of gaining political capital. What is striking, though, is that the machine has shifted to charges of racism and imperialism. These latter charges are shame friendly, so to speak, in that they invoke pervasive structural exploitation rather than specific actions, or the lack thereof, in 1994. Why did French judge Jean-Louis Bruguière accuse Kagame of the missile attack on Habyarimana's plane? Racism.[50] Why is the west criticizing the lack of freedom of speech in Rwanda? Imperialism.[51] Why did the Swedish government expel Rwandan diplomat Evode Mudaheranwa? More racism.[52] I have personally experienced how accusations of racism are used to shut down critical dialogue regarding Kagame's emphasis on economic security over political freedom; the surprisingly effective argument is that to criticize Kagame is to succumb to racist notions that Africans cannot effectively serve as heads of state. This strategy can help silence those citizens of empire who might not feel directly implicated in the events of 1994 but who are vulnerable to anxiety over being called racist.

Focusing on Kagame clarifies how the tactics of shame and guilt intersect and overlap. His commemoration speeches leave no emotional stone unturned: the Xinhua News Agency reported his 2004 speech for the tenth commemoration as blaming the entire international community, the *Boston Globe* and the BBC singled out his accusation of the French government, and the *Daily Telegraph* and Reuters emphasized his charge of racism.[53] Although these speeches are often quixotic and mercurial—much like Kagame himself—a shift in tone has occurred over the past several years.[54] After his long-winded invocation of guilt in 2009 previously cited—"The world is guilty no doubt"—he began to favor more subtle barbs about the patronizing attitude of the west in relation to human rights. "What freedoms are you teaching me?" he demanded in 2010. "If you can't take full responsibility for what you did, for the politics that killed one million people of Rwanda, why do you teach me freedom yet in that freedom you don't want me to put the blame on you, and rightly so?"[55] In 2011, he sardonically referred to genocidaires roaming in "the same capitals of the world that try to give us lessons about human rights, rule of law and justice" and called for Rwandans to "go about our business—the business of giving our dignity back to ourselves."[56] In embracing the rhetoric of anticolonialism and anti-imperialism, he has assumed the role of a martyr standing up to the bullying west, adding new layers of authenticity to his former standing as "the only man alive who can claim to have stopped a genocide."[57] Now he is also a victim of the racist, colonialist, imperialist west, which, as he pointed out in 2012, values Rwandan lives less "than the lives of their citizens."[58] Faced with this newly authenticated Kagame, the west would, one imagines, bow its collective head in shame, implicated as beneficiaries of historical domination. Kagame subtly reminds it of what Timothy Bewes calls, in an expansion on Jean-Paul Sartre's concept of shame, a "primary or fundamental shame, rooted in our definition as embodied, inter-subjective beings, [that] is at the origin of the history of colonial domination."[59] In Kagame's strategic hands, shame is harder to deflect because of its insinuating nature as opposed to a frontal, adamant accusation of guilt.[60]

Like any good entrepreneur, Kagame knows his consumer base. Rwanda is widely celebrated for its pro-business attitude; Kagame, who calls entrepreneurship the "backbone of a new Rwanda," has taken unprecedented steps to ease the financial and bureaucratic burdens to facilitate start-ups in hopes that supporting these initiatives will help "to unlock people's minds, to allow innovation to take place, and to enable people to exercise their talents."[61] Kagame's performance on the global stage demonstrates his innovative and strategic thinking. Instead of adhering to clichéd human rights categories of heroes, victims, and perpetrators, he straddles multiple and overlapping roles.[62] As an entrepreneur of Trauma, Inc., he teases out empire's short attention span through the development of new and innovative scripts.

He generates one such script through his carefully cultivated relationship with the famous US evangelist Rick Warren. Through their interactions, Kagame provides a warm and fuzzy alternative to his usual tongue-lashing approach. The combination of guilt and shame is a homogeneous repast that will not satisfy the capacious demands of the west's genocide attachment. A surfeit of discomfort calls for a therapeutic dose of sentiment and hope, which Kagame has proved to be surprisingly adept at providing.

It might seem at first that Warren is the dominant player. As Warren tells it, he received a letter from Kagame in 2004 that invited him to "come help rebuild our country. . . . We'd like to build a nation of purpose."[63] A "nation of purpose" refers to Warren's international best-seller, *The Purpose-Driven Life* (2002), which outlines a forty-day plan for learning and realizing what Warren has identified as God's five purposes: worship, fellowship, discipleship, ministry, and mission.[64] In 2008, Kagame and Warren together launched the "40 Days of Purpose" campaign in Rwanda, in which "the entire nation is encouraged to study [Warren's] book as if it is a national manifesto."[65] Warren crafted new language for the campaign: in addition to his five purposes and forty-day plan, he compiled a list of the "five global giants"—spiritual emptiness, selfish leadership, hunger, sickness, and illiteracy—to be overcome through the PEACE plan: Plant churches, Equip servant leaders, Assist the poor, Care for the sick, and Educate the next generation.[66] By 2013, approximately 1,300 volunteers from Warren's Saddleback Church had traveled to Rwanda to join the campaign, scattering across villages to install water-purification systems, develop livestock-distribution programs, legalize marriages, and baptize converts.[67] Several journalists have commented on Warren's expansion of a US evangelical Christian empire through the PEACE plan; James Cowan of the *National Post*, for example, notes that "his ministry has extended itself into almost all aspects of Rwandan civil society."[68] Warren's PEACE plan intends "to turn every single Christian church on earth into a provider of local health

Fig. 3. Paul Kagame and Rick Warren at Amahoro Stadium in Kigali, July 2005, during Warren's visit to launch his PEACE plan. Courtesy of Getty.

care, literacy and economic development, leadership training and spiritual growth."[69] Rwanda serves as ground zero in Warren's campaign.

What interests me here, though, is not Warren's appropriation of Rwanda but Kagame's appropriation of Warren.[70] Warren might "dream of a global expansion of God's kingdom," but Kagame has a more practical aim in mind.[71] Although he is frank about his lack of religious convictions, he has expressed strong appreciation for "high-powered" PEACE volunteers, who "use their contacts to draw on resources and attract investment. I can't have anything better than this."[72] He has also commented on Saddleback's ability to connect Rwanda's tourism and investment sectors to powerful business leaders in the United States.[73] In contrast to western governments, these high-powered and influential Saddleback members are far less likely to read the growing pile of UN Group of Experts critical reports, especially when their beloved pastor insists that Kagame "is going to be more important to Africa than [Nelson] Mandela" and that "he's the George Washington of Africa."[74] Indeed, Warren's endorsement helped Kagame gain a coveted spot in *Time*'s list of the one hundred most influential people in 2009.[75] In 2008, Saddleback allocated $13 million to Rwanda as part of the PEACE plan; that same year, Sweden and the Netherlands announced that they were withholding a total of about $15 million in aid to Rwanda in response to a UN report about Rwanda's meddling in the DRC.[76] Kagame's capitulation to the white savior industrial complex has been amply rewarded insofar as Saddleback provides a relatively steady stream of revenue that helps compensate for the vagaries of international aid.[77]

To reward the Saddleback community for its contributions, the famously stiff Kagame unbends and offers up sentiment and gratitude. Less than three weeks after he gave the speech for the twentieth commemoration of the genocide in Kigali, he visited Warren's Saddleback Church in the United States. In contrast to his speech in Rwanda at the commemoration event, in which he expounded at length on Rwanda's colonial history, he referred only briefly to the genocide in order to focus on the promise of Rwanda's future. This in itself was not unusual since Kagame regularly emphasizes Rwanda's achievements; what stood out is that Saddleback Church received star billing as a reason for Rwanda's success:

> Today, things are different and again thank you Saddleback members for providing this meaningful new partnership. Today, faith in God is again a source of comfort for millions of Rwandans. Saddleback's decision to accompany Rwandans on their journey has played an important role. More than 2000 members of this church as already mentioned have served in Rwanda as part of the PEACE plan. We thank you. You served in every part of the country; you lived and worship with Rwandans from all walks of life. You have seen the new Rwanda both our achievements and our struggles. You know what we have gone through and you are still with us.[78]

Although Kagame could hardly be described as effusive, he went on to repeat "thank you" three more times in the remaining minute of his speech. His brief acknowledgment of Saddleback's role in Rwanda's success was amply repaid; once he finished the speech, Warren proclaimed Rwanda's leadership as the main reason for the country's rapid success. He repeated it once more as the crowd cheered: "I know the first reason and it's leadership!"[79] Warren scoffed at Rwanda's critics with the repeated statement that "they are not God." He went on to offer a public prayer that Kagame, along with the rest of his administration, would not be swayed by critics.[80] In a particularly inspired burst of PR, Warren proclaimed that "God chose a nation the world turned its back on during its darkest hour to give the world a new model."[81] Kagame received generous compensation in exchange for toning down his anticolonial rhetoric. If Rwanda was chosen by God, then Kagame is his angel.

Immaculée Ilibagiza and the Politics of Love

When it comes to Rwanda, love is in the air. Such was the case at the UN launch of Kwibuka20, an umbrella term for events around the world to commemorate the twentieth anniversary of the Rwandan genocide, at its headquarters in New York City.[82] UN-sponsored events to commemorate the Rwandan genocide often include a survivor as a panelist, whose testimony adds moral weight and authenticity to the menu of official speeches.[83] Ilibagiza, who had assumed this role for the 2014 launch, spoke briefly about how she survived the genocide by hiding in a Hutu pastor's bathroom with six other women and a young girl. For most of her speech, though, she elaborated on her call for unity and love. "The world is divided into two parts," she told the audience, "those who take the side of love and those of hate." She explained that once she took the side of love, along with Nelson Mandela and Mother Teresa, she found "great peace." She reminded everyone in the audience that they would die one day, but that "what lives forever is the love in our hearts, the loving actions we do." She briefly acknowledged her gratitude to the current government for its strides in bringing progress to Rwanda, specifically improved educational opportunities at the secondary and tertiary levels, but soon returned to the theme of love: "We are capable to do good, we are capable of love, we are capable to forgive one another, we are capable [of] peace." When she finished, she received a standing ovation. In the words of self-help guru and author Wayne Dyer, one of her strongest supporters, "Immaculée not only writes and speaks about unconditional love and forgiveness, but she radiates it wherever she goes."[84] The radiance of this love outshone the specific details of her experiences.

In contrast, an excruciating level of detail can be found in Ilibagiza's memoirs.[85] *Left to Tell: Discovering God amidst the Rwandan Holocaust* includes graphic descriptions of the deaths of her immediate family members, as well as the horrors that she witnessed through the window of the bathroom where she was hiding. When the genocide broke out on April 6, 1994, she was on holiday from her studies at the national university in Butare in southern Rwanda and was visiting her family in her hometown of Mataba, located in western Rwanda in the former Kibuye Province, where the genocide was carried out with particular speed and efficiency.[86] Kibuye was also included in the so-called humanitarian zone known as Operation Turquoise established in southwestern Rwanda by French troops. These troops provided Ilibagiza and her fellow survivors with temporary refuge when they left the pastor's bathroom, only to desert them in front of a Hutu militia.[87] In her second memoir, *Led by Faith: Rising from the Ashes of the Rwandan Genocide*, she writes eloquently of despair in the years after the genocide—both her own and that of her fellow Rwandans—as she sought to create a new life in Kigali. Although her memoirs contain shades of what Julie Salverson might call an "erotics of injury," which caters to "a preoccupation with the experience of loss and a privileging of trauma," they are also fascinatingly complex and often unflinching.[88] Ilibagiza forcefully and consistently articulates agency in the face of overwhelming circumstances, in which the genocide was only the beginning of a series of challenges as she sought to build a new life without the protection of family members in postgenocide Rwanda.

Led by Faith deviates from the standard genocide narrative through its nuanced portrayal of relationships between Hutu and Tutsi, as well as its depiction of tensions among and between Tutsi returnees and survivors like herself. For example, in her discussion of Burundian Tutsi returnees such as her friend Anne, who articulates a strong thirst for revenge against Hutu, she expresses anxiety that Burundian Tutsi might bring "new hatred and violence" to Rwanda.[89] She also depicts her former boyfriend, a Hutu, in a complex light; his bystander status during the genocide, in which he observed the killing but did not intervene or participate, carves out a complex middle ground between notions of Hutu "moderates" and perpetrators. She also writes with sensitivity and compassion regarding the suffering of Rwandan Hutu who returned from the refugee camps in Zaire.[90] Although she stops well short of implicating the RPF, she repeatedly expands the framework of victimhood to include all Rwandans and thus broadens mainstream narratives of the genocide. In her recollections, despair crosses ethnic boundaries with ease.

This interpretation is, however, checked by the realities of the US consumption machine. In 2006, when I accessed the listing for Ilibagiza's book on Amazon.com, I clicked on the link for "similar books" out of curiosity. I expected to find trade publications about the genocide, such as Philip Gourevitch's *We Wish to Inform You That Tomorrow We Will Be Killed with Our Families: Stories from Rwanda* or Samantha Power's *"A Problem from Hell": America and the Age of Genocide*; instead, I was invited to peruse a range of self-help books such as Dyer's book for children, *Incredible You! 10 Ways to Be Happy Inside and Out*. That a book that includes graphic descriptions of horrific deaths, torture, and suffering would be equated with helping US children attain a state of happiness speaks of the voracious appetites of the self-help industry and its capacity to appropriate others' pain. Trauma memoirs have long relied on descriptions of excessive pain as a means to gain a foothold in the public consciousness and make a profit; context is blithely and enthusiastically evacuated in the quest for new narratives of personal redemption in which even genocide cannot keep a good change agent down.[91] Perhaps it is a sign of desperation in these increasingly uncertain times that the genocide serves as reassurance that the privileged life is indeed worth living.

Excavating agency in the context of the US consumption of trauma can be an exercise in theoretical quicksand. An analysis of Ilibagiza's self-performance, in which she shuns the politics of guilt and shame in favor of the pleasurable affect of love, forgiveness, and prayer, deepens an understanding of the genocide attachment and how it exceeds the scope of international politics to operate in the populist sphere of US self-help. Ilibagiza works within this highly scripted discourse to articulate a specifically Catholic worldview as a means of countering the growing dominance of Pentecostal Christianity both in the United States and in Rwanda. In other words, she explains how to be an incredible *Catholic* you, and thus her cultural production helps delineate the complexities of a neoliberal era in which various Christian denominations battle for Rwandan hearts and minds.

In *Left to Tell*, Ilibagiza resolutely credits her strength in the face of adversity to divine intervention and the power of prayer. When she is struck with flashes of insight—for example, she urges Pastor Murinzi to conceal the door to the bathroom where the women were hiding with a tall wardrobe—she credits God for giving her the idea.[92] When she manages to land a coveted job at the UN in Kigali thanks to the intervention of Pierre Mehu, a UN spokesman for the UN mission in Rwanda, she positions this moment as an apex in a long line of divine interventions: "God had brought me a long way from the bathroom, and He'd walked with me every step of the way: saving me from the killers; filling my heart with forgiveness; helping me learn English; delivering me to safety; providing me with friendship, shelter, and food; and finally, introducing me to Mr. Mehu and my dream job."[93] When this "dream job" makes her vulnerable to rape by a high-ranking UN official in a locked hotel room, she calls out to God for the strength to stand up to her attacker, and she successfully deters his plans.[94] My point is not whether this framework of divine submission negates her personal agency but that it makes her extraordinary capacities accessible to anyone who is willing to open herself to the power of a Christian faith.[95] As she assures her readers, "Faith has transformed my life, and it can transform yours."[96] Ilibagiza casts herself as a messenger of divine love instead of a global heroine.

As if to ensure the purity of this message, she carefully avoids the politics of guilt and shame. In *Left to Tell*, for example, she devotes one scant paragraph to the refusal of the international community to get involved.[97] This brief acknowledgment, however, is embedded in her expressions of gratitude to the UN for providing her with employment. When demonstrators in Kigali throw rocks at the UN van taking her home from work, she acknowledges the reasons for the seething anger against the UN but insists, albeit rather feebly, "I thought that the demonstrations overlooked the good work the UN was doing in our country."[98] The attempted rape by a UN official, instead of being viewed as a sign of institutional corruption, serves as another opportunity to explain how God provided her with the strength to resist. Her frequent references to the transformative practice of forgiveness occur only in the context of forgiving the genocidaires who killed her family and friends. Even the Operation Turquoise troops who protected her for weeks, only to abandon her at a crucial moment in front of a Hutu militia, did not need to be forgiven. The westerners who appear in her narrative are collectively exempt from guilt; so too are her western readers.[99]

Instead, she invites these readers to join her in victimhood. In her emphasis on forgiveness, she offers a capacious definition of victimhood to which anyone can belong. She urges her readers and interlocutors to forgive just as she had forgiven those who murdered her family. She explains: "The story of Rwanda is one that belongs to us all. We don't have to experience genocide to know the darkness in which murder is born. Hatred, anger, mistrust, and fear enter our lives every day in a thousand different ways. We're all wounded by these evils, but we can all be healed through the power of love and forgiveness—a power readily available to all of us when we have faith."[100] Her message of forgiveness becomes especially potent through casting her western readers and spectators in the role of victims like herself; the rhetoric of forgiveness ameliorates shame and guilt. Her moral authority as a genocide survivor allows her followers to detach from the shame of geopolitical privilege and join a community of victims with the charismatic Ilibagiza at the helm. At her speech at the Kwibuka20 launch, the United Nations was invited to join this community as she pleaded with everyone to join on the side of love and learn the lesson of forgiveness. Whom did Ban Ki-Moon sitting at her side have to forgive?

The fulfillment of dreams is the icing on the Immaculée cake. Prayer not only provided her with the ability to survive the genocide but also brought her a husband, a dream job, and a best-selling book. Particularly in *Left to Tell*, she adds a rhetorical spin of positive thinking to the rhetoric of prayer, asserting that positive thinking and prayer "really are almost the same thing."[101] When she receives the coveted job at the United Nations, she credits both forces for her success: "I envisioned it, I dreamed it, I prayed for it, and now I had it!"[102] A similar dynamic occurs when she explains how she met her future husband: "Once I was clear on what I wanted, I began to visualize it, believing in my heart that it had already come to pass.... Three months later, he [appeared]: Mr. Bryan Black, who was sent by God, courtesy of the UN, all the way from America!"[103] These messages resonate with the notion of self-help as a neoliberal technology in which an individual's ability to think positively (rather than agitate for public health care and social services) serves as the cure for all social and economic ills.[104] If the techniques of prayer and positive thinking helped Ilibagiza overcome the trauma of genocide to attain a green card, a beautiful family, and financial security, then what could it help her US-based readers achieve in a post-Fordist era of temporary contract labor and shrinking welfare?

The innocuousness of her message helps ensure a wide audience that includes a range of Christian, "spiritual," and secular readers alike, from Rick Warren, whose endorsement is splashed across the front cover of *Led by Faith*, to self-help guru Martha Beck, who describes Ilibagiza as "a master of oneness."[105] Playwright and actress Leslie Lewis Sword, who has shaped *Left to Tell* into a one-woman show called *Miracle in Rwanda*, explains Ilibagiza's tale of survival in terms of psychological control: "She realized that her mind would kill her before the killers ever did.... She told herself that she had to control her mind."[106] An occasional note of resistance to Ilibagiza's message can be found in reviews of Sword's play—the *Village Voice*, for example, comments that "if, as [Ilibagiza] presents it, God protected the room in which she and her companions were huddled, one might wish he'd done something similar for the 400,000 Tutsi outside."[107] These exceptions aside, the play's emphasis on the revolutionary power of forgiveness has been mostly embraced, particularly in a revival at the 2015 Grahamstown National Arts Festival in South Africa.[108]

With increasing persistence, though, Ilibagiza redefines her celebrity in terms of her Catholic faith. Her more recent writing has rejected the generic rhetoric of positive thinking in favor of the specificities of Catholic worship. In *Our Lady of Kibeho: Mary Speaks to the World from the Heart of Africa* (2008) and *The Rosary: The Prayer That Saved My Life* (2013), she emphasizes Mary's love and the power of the rosary. At the end of *The Rosary*, she compiles a list of miracles that have resulted from praying to the rosary among her followers; she assures her readers than even her Protestant fans have experienced miraculous transformations through this method.[109] These miracles are made accessible on her website, which sells a multitude of rosaries at prices ranging from $15 to $160; both *Our Lady of Kibeho* and *The Rosary* include detailed instructions on how to pray the rosary, complete with illustrations.[110] Her website also lists her many speaking engagements, in which appearances at self-help conferences organized by Hay House alternate with explicitly Catholic settings, such as Catholic high schools and Catholic antiabortion rights and anti-LGBTI conferences.[111] The specificity with which she increasingly articulates a conservative Catholic identity makes her story less easily appropriated and perhaps less marketable. Instead of Rick Warren's genial, benevolent God "who wants to be your best friend,"[112] she summons forth a God who will punish with genocide if his will is not obeyed.

Ilibagiza leads Catholic retreats across the United States in which participants gather for two days to hear her usual message of love and forgiveness, with a special emphasis on the power of Mary. In March 2015, I attended one of her retreats at Cranberry Park, Pennsylvania, and watched the audience of a few hundred people (mostly white women) fall under Ilibagiza's charismatic spell.[113] Despite the obvious eagerness of the participants to learn more about her specific experiences during the genocide, Ilibagiza said relatively little about her Rwandan past and instead deflected questions to refocus on the miracle of Mary and the significance of the rosary. When she was asked about reconciliation in Rwanda after the genocide, for example, she simply noted that "Hutu and Tutsi all suffered," but that they have learned to "answer Mary's call" and have brought Rwanda "back to life." The grand finale consisted of a ritual procession in which all the participants were invited to place flowers in vases at the foot of a statue of Mary, thus creating an improvised altar in her honor. Ilibagiza prayed aloud throughout the procession for everyone in the room who might be suffering from emotional or physical pain. These retreats can be interpreted as Ilibagiza's attempt to inflect and particularize dominant

Fig. 4. Immaculée Ilibagiza praying at a Catholic retreat in Cranberry Park, Pennsylvania, in March 2015.

Catholic discourses with a lay version of Marian devotion, in which she channels the moral authority of her traumatic past.[114]

But Ilibagiza adds another layer to her theology—that of Rwandan nationalism. When we arrived at the retreat, we were requested to wear blue rubber bracelets that bore the phrase "OLK Loves Me," followed by a website address: ourladyofkibeho.com. Our Lady of Kibeho refers to a series of Vatican-approved Marian apparitions in the southern town of Kibeho, currently located in Nyaruguru District in the Southern Province, in the 1980s. The bracelets not only indicated that we had paid the conference fee but also served as a strategic way of interpellating us as believers in this particular incarnation of the Holy Mother. As the next section seeks to explain, Our Lady of Kibeho serves as a keystone in Ilibagiza's project of Rwandanicity.

Staging Kibeho

Kibeho rose to international fame in the early 1980s. In late 1981 and early 1982, three girls studying at the College of Kibeho, a Catholic school that trained girls to be secretaries or primary-school teachers, began to have visions of Mary, who proclaimed herself as the Mother of the Word. These three girls, Alphonsine Mumureke, Anathalie Mukamazimpaka, and Marie-Claire Mukangango, were eventually joined by four girls from outside the college—Valentine Nyiramukiza, Stéphanie Mukamurenzi, Vestine Salima, and Agnes Kamagaju—as well as a teenaged boy named Segatashya who had visions of Jesus.[115] Thousands of pilgrims, including Ilibagiza and her family members, gathered at the college to hear the visionaries in their trance-like states. Seven years after the genocide, in 2001, Kibeho became the only Vatican-approved site of Marian apparitions on the African continent, on a par with Lourdes and Fatíma, both of which attract millions of tourists and pilgrims. Ilibagiza aims to make Kibeho as famous as these other shrines: "I wanted the whole world to know about the Kibeho visionaries. . . . I wanted the whole world to share my love of the Virgin Mary. And I wanted the whole world to travel to Rwanda and visit Our Lady's remarkable shrine . . . to feel the power and purity of her love in that holy place for themselves."[116] Kibeho serves as a focal point in which Ilibagiza's devotion to Mary and her homeland can intersect. Instead of hailing Rwanda's uniqueness in the African continent because of its economic progress and stability, Ilibagiza promotes Rwanda as a divine site chosen by Mary herself.[117]

To "know" Kibeho, though, is to encounter a vortex of narratives and counternarratives of genocidal and postgenocidal Rwanda. Kibeho has indeed gained a measure of international fame as the site of Mary's visitations, but it is also notorious as a killing field.[118] The town fairly bursts at the seams with dramatic moments and performative strategies as church, state, and citizen-subjects seek to claim and co-opt the meanings of its past and present. Ilibagiza's counterappropriation of Kibeho takes full advantage of the Holy Mother's megastar status to blot out the tensions of the town's history and recast the genocide attachment as Christian devotion.[119]

A brief summary of Kibeho's extraordinary history will help clarify the boldness and significance of Ilibagiza's counternarrative.[120] Within months of the first apparition, the visionaries became the focus of machinations and appropriations. In May 1982, the Rwandan Information Office provided the college's courtyard with a sound system so that the large crowds of gathering pilgrims could hear the visionaries' reports of their conversations with Mary; in July, the church built a platform on which the visionaries received their visions in full view of the crowds.[121] Meanwhile, government-run newspapers and radio stations publicized the apparitions throughout Rwanda. According to Ilibagiza, "By the late spring of 1982, Alphonsine, Anathalie, and Marie-Claire were household names and practically celebrities."[122] She listened avidly to these nightly broadcasts as a young girl. Gerrie ter Haar interprets these official interventions as attempts to domesticate and contain the radical religious ecstasy of these eight youths, who commanded a sense of power and agency in their direct interactions with the crowds: "The visionaries form the centre of a religious drama which takes place in the open air where they address the crowd as mediators between God and man, blessing them in the name of Christ, and . . . they lay on hands independently."[123] A more violent drama simultaneously played out as male investigators examined the girls in full view of the crowd. In order to ascertain the authenticity of the visions, they poked twigs in the girls' eyes, held open flames to their arms, and jumped on their chests. The visionaries, deep in their trances, did not react.

A turning point occurred on Assumption Day, August 15, 1982, when an estimated twenty thousand pilgrims witnessed five of the visionaries relating apocalyptic visions: "The children saw terrifying images, a river of blood, people who killed one another, cadavers abandoned without anyone to bury them, a tree all on fire, a wide open chasm, a monster, decapitated heads."[124] As Timothy Longman explains, "The fact that the role of prophet was taken up by poor children in an obscure corner of the country," half of whom he describes as Tutsi, "seemed a threat to the Catholic hierarchy."[125] Seven schoolgirls and an illiterate boy who herded sheep were mounting a subtle challenge to the Catholic Church's authority in a context where "struggles for increased power within the religion realm were . . . intimately connected to the struggles for state reform."[126] In light of these tensions, it was undoubtedly best for the girls' safety that most of the apparitions ceased in 1983.[127] Eight years later, in 1991, Augustin Misago, a priest who had participated in one of the Church's investigations of the Kibeho apparitions, published a lengthy book on the apparitions that was guardedly sympathetic toward the visionaries; a year later, he was appointed as the bishop of the Gikongoro diocese.[128] Longman suggests that Misago's appointment "may have been a means of bringing the Marian devotions under control, since his pronounced sympathies for the movement would give him the legitimacy to restrict its independence and impose orthodoxy on it."[129] The oscillating forces of local fervor and official control repeatedly surface in retellings of the apparitions.

According to Ilibagiza, one of the final visions of Mary was broadcast live on the radio during the genocidal months of 1994. In *Our Lady of Kibeho*, she quotes Nyiramukiza's message from Mary, which she heard on the radio while she was hiding in the pastor's bathroom: "The gates of heaven are open, and your brothers and sisters are with me tonight. Do not cry for the ones you have lost; cry for those who are left behind."[130] Ilibagiza interpreted this statement as a divine message that her family was "in the arms of the Blessed Mother, who was still reaching out from Kibeho to tell me that I was loved," reaffirming and strengthening her faith in a moment of extreme crisis.[131] This apparition, which occurred in May 1994, was reportedly the last of the public Marian visions in Rwanda; Nyiramukiza soon left the country and eventually settled in Belgium, where she continues to receive visions.

Meanwhile, Kibeho went up in flames. According to African Rights, "The massacre in this préfecture [Gikongoro] was carried out systematically and speedily, to an extent unmatched elsewhere except for Kibuye and Cyangugu."[132] During the genocide, approximately ten thousand to twenty thousand Rwandans perished in the church, the college, the hospital, and additional school buildings.[133] On April 15, the church was turned into a "crematorium" when the genocidaires set it ablaze to kill the remaining people trapped inside.[134] Alison Des Forges ranks the killing at the Kibeho church as among the "most devastating" massacres that occurred during the genocide.[135] Like churches and schools throughout Rwanda, the church had served as a place of refuge for Rwandan Tutsi during previous outbursts of ethnic violence; in 1994, though, these former havens were transformed into stages for some of the most graphic acts of genocidal slaughter, often with the tacit or even active support of the local clergy.[136] Protestant ministers and Anglican clergy also participated in the slaughter; however, given that Rwanda's population was approximately 80 percent Catholic at the time of the genocide, the Catholic Church looms especially large in narratives of the Rwandan genocide because of the scale of its ethical and moral failure.[137]

Just over a year later, the RPF committed its own moral and ethical failure in Kibeho. In response to a tense climate of fear and distrust, about eighty thousand to one hundred thousand Rwandans, mostly Hutu, had gathered in an IDP camp in Kibeho, refusing the RPF's orders to return home.[138] In order to close the camp, the RPF adopted increasingly coercive means, such as herding the refugees close to the center of the camp and cutting off food and water supplies; RPF troops also occasionally fired into the air. Tensions exploded on the morning of April 22, 1995, when RPF soldiers opened fire on the crowds of IDPs and killed an estimated five thousand men, women, and children. The

RPF used what Pottier described as "surreal diplomacy" to shrug off the incident, claiming that only 338 were killed, and that they all deserved their fate as genocidaires.[139] Although the 1994 massacre at Kibeho is openly discussed and commemorated, the events of April 1995 cannot be broached in public.[140] The impact of these tumultuous years left most of the visionaries either killed or scattered; only Mukamazimpaka, one of the original three visionaries, remains in Kibeho at the time of this writing.

The RPF picked up the task of Kibeho's domestication. In September 1994, just three months after the RPF had declared victory over the genocidal regime, Radio Rwanda journalist Dominique Makeli was arrested on charges of inciting genocide. Makeli was well known in Rwanda for his extensive coverage of the Kibeho apparitions; significantly, the prosecution cited his coverage of the Marian apparition that had occurred during the previous May as the reason for his arrest.[141] In contrast to the message that Ilibagiza recalled overhearing while hiding in the bathroom, Makeli reportedly claimed that Mary offered the more ambiguous statement "The parent is in heaven."[142] As explained by Reporters Without Borders, which sharply criticized Makeli's arrest, "The prosecutor insisted that, in the context of that moment, this was taken to mean, 'President Habyarimana is in heaven' and was interpreted as a message of support for Habyarimana and, by extension, the policy of exterminating Tutsis."[143] Although the vagueness of the evidence against Makeli was not unusual in light of the thousands of arrests made in the months after the RPF came to power, his case clarifies how Kibeho was a lightning rod for controversy in the post-1994 era.

An even more controversial arrest related to Kibeho occurred in 1999. That year, the government selected Kibeho as the site of the five-year commemoration of the genocide—a charged move that decisively claimed the town as a site of Tutsi victimhood. In his speech, President Pasteur Bizimungu dismissed the 1995 massacre victims as members of the Interahamwe, which, as Jennie Burnet points out, "contributed to the erosion of distinctions between Hutu civilians who did not support or participate in the genocide and those who did and played into the globalization of blame to all Hutu."[144] Bizimungu singled out one particular Hutu for censure: Bishop Misago, who had been accused as early as 1996 of involvement in the 1994 genocidal killings in Kibeho. Bizimungu "shocked the gathering" when he pointed out Misago, who was seated near him among other honored guests, as a genocidaire.[145] "Will the Catholic Church continue to ignore accusations by Christians of the church against Bishop Misago, accusations which have continued to grow in number? . . . The Rwandan state did not place Bishop Misago above the law and is not afraid of him."[146] Within a week, Misago was arrested, receiving the dubious distinction of being the only Roman Catholic bishop to be charged with genocide. As *Newsweek* noted drily in reference to the tense relations between Rwanda's post-1994 government and the Catholic Church, "It wasn't clear whether [Misago] or the Roman Catholic Church as a whole was in the dock."[147] Although Misago was eventually acquitted, competing narratives of his involvement in the 1994 genocide continued to proliferate.[148]

Upon his release from prison in 2000, Misago moved swiftly to reclaim his authority. In 2001, he claimed a new measure of fame as the author of the published Vatican statement "The Declaration of Definitive Judgment on the Apparitions of Kibeho." The timing of this report, a year after his release, was charged with Church politics. Not only was Misago rehabilitated, but also Kibeho was brought firmly and emphatically into the Catholic fold as the only Vatican-approved site of Marian apparitions in Africa. The relative speed with which the site was authenticated—only twenty years after the apparitions originally appeared—marks yet another claim on the meaning of Kibeho.[149] In addition to citing reasons such as the "tangible character of the ecstasies" and the eloquence and consistency of the messages, the Vatican statement also refers to the apocalyptic visions that the women experienced in 1982 as evidence, noting that they "proved to be prophetic due to the human dramas in Rwanda and throughout the countr[ies] of the Great Lake[s] region in recent years."[150] Given that Marian apparitions across the globe have included apocalyptic predictions, particularly in contexts of cultural stress, it seems possible that Misago borrowed from the genocide credit in order to hasten the authentication process.[151] How could the Vatican refuse his findings in light of its burden of guilt?

This multilayered history can be discerned in the town of Kibeho itself, which reads like a jigsaw puzzle in that the pieces of its past are compartmentalized but also juxtaposed. Its fame as the site of the apparitions is showcased in a stunning plateau marked with sacred sites for prayer and reflection.[152] The girls' dormitory where the visions first appeared has been memorialized as the Chapel of the Apparitions, an intimate space where people come to pray in private. A much grander place of worship can be found in next door at the Church of Our Lady of Sorrows, which seats up to a thousand people; finally, an outdoor

Fig. 5. Our Lady of Sorrows church in Kibeho and plateau.

amphitheatre, just across from the entrance to the cathedral, helps accommodate the tens of thousands of worshippers who gather at Kibeho to celebrate major Catholic holidays and other events specific to Kibeho. Just the day before my arrival, an estimated thirty thousand visitors, many of whom had come from Uganda, Burundi, the DRC, and Tanzania, had gathered in Kibeho to celebrate Assumption Day.[153] Despite the massive crowds that had gathered in that spot just the day before, the plateau gleamed with cleanliness and order.

Another clearing, located less than a five-minute walk away from the sanctuary, marks one of Kibeho's killing fields. I refer here to the site of the parish church where thousands of Tutsi died in 1994; today the church is used for both worship and memorialization. During the restoration of the building after 1994, sections of the brick walls were painted purple to mark where the genocidaires had hacked their way into the building.[154] At the far end of the church, a room, sealed off from the main hall of worship, contains a mass grave and a glass case with twelve skulls; a banner reads, "Turasaba ko abicanyi bahanwa bakanabuzwa

Fig. 6. The Catholic parish church in Kibeho, originally built in 1943, which serves as both a place of worship and as a memorial for the genocide. The newer building to the left houses victims' remains.

gusibanganya ibimenyetso," which Burnet translates as "We ask for the murderers to be punished and prevented from erasing the signs."[155] In a pristine white building adjacent to the church, visitors descend a flight of stairs to a kind of crypt, where skeletal remains are displayed on a series of shelves. Their appearance and the smell of preservative recall the more famous site of Murambi, but the smaller setting and the dark, cellar-like room convey a greater sense of intimacy.[156] White lace curtains hang on each shelf, offering a modicum of privacy and dignity not afforded to the Murambi victims. The day before my visit, the memorial had received numerous visitors from surrounding East and Central African countries who had come to celebrate Assumption Day, many of whom, according to the caretaker, had experienced intensely emotional reactions on hearing the narrative of the Kibeho massacre and witnessing the victims' remains.

The Kibeho massacre of 1995, of course, is not memorialized, and I did not ask about it—my visit was too brief and the subject matter much too sensitive. Although the location of the 1995 killing field is unclear, it seems likely that the apparition grounds were central to the unfolding of the tragic events.[157] What is especially striking, though, is that relatively accessible internet sources such as Wikipedia claim that Marie-Claire Mukangango, the third visionary, was killed by the RPF during the 1995 massacre.[158] Perhaps I should not have been surprised to hear this explanation of Mukangango's fate repeated during my Kibeho visit in response to my purposefully vague questions about the visionaries and their current whereabouts. The ambiguity of the visionaries' ethnicities strengthens their potential as a tool of unification, at least among Catholics and perhaps among other followers of the Christian faith. This narrative of Mukangano's death also allows a reminder of the 1995 massacre to coexist, albeit quietly, with the genocide in 1994.

In her celebration of Kibeho, Ilibagiza takes on a multiheaded narrative beast. She briefly acknowledges the complexities of Kibeho's history; for example, she mentions the genocidal state's appropriation of Nyiramukiza's final vision and fleetingly refers to the 1995 massacre as another example of bloodshed in Kibeho.[159] Although these horrific events would seem to work against her ultimate vision of miraculous love—in other words, Mary failed to protect her devoted followers—she adroitly turns them into stepping-stones on the pathway of conversion thanks to the apocalyptic prophecy that occurred in 1982. In Ilibagiza's interpretation, the Holy Mother foresaw what was going to happen and tried to warn her followers; she did not desert them in their time of need but instead did her best to save them. In a documentary about Kibeho that Ilibagiza coproduced, Ilibagiza visits the memorial at Nyamata church; the camera pans the benches lined with piles of clothes, the bullet holes in the ceiling, the bloodstains on the walls, and the shelves containing rows of skulls. In a voiceover, Ilibagiza asks, "You may ask, where was God? How could He let this happen? The truth is, He tried to stop it. He sent his mother to Kibeho with a clear message about what was coming, and how to avoid it."[160] As ter Haar observes, "Miracles in Africa, as elsewhere, are performed not for their own sake, but with the purpose of building faith."[161] In postgenocide Rwanda, where the former Catholic stronghold is giving way to a more multifaceted landscape that includes Pentecostals, Seventh-Day Adventists, Muslims, and atheists, the miracle of the Kibeho prophecy could help renew and reenergize Catholic Rwanda.[162]

Ilibagiza positions the genocide as the climactic moment of the Kibeho story, but she does so in a way that includes Hutu victimhood. Although she does not hesitate to identify the ethnicity of the various Rwandans who appear in her memoirs, she does not make a single reference to the ethnicity of the visionaries. Mukamurenzi "disappeared during the holocaust and has never been heard from again," whereas Mukangango is described as having been slain when she attempted to save her husband when he was targeted by gunmen.[163] More vaguely, she notes that Salima "survived the genocide but became ill soon afterward and passed away."[164] This ambiguity allows the power of the visionaries to be accessible to all Rwandans regardless of ethnicity and thus facilitates her project of alternative Rwandanicity.

The purity of Mary's message is meant to blot out the machinations of the genocidal and postgenocide state. Ilibagiza does not explicitly refer to either Makeli's or Misago's arrests; instead, she simply puts forward her interpretation of these events. Her lengthy quotation of what she remembers Mary saying through the radio broadcast of Nyiramukiza's vision serves as her quiet corrective to the genocidal state's appropriation of the apparitions. Similarly, she subtly dismisses the controversy that has swirled around Bishop Misago when she warmly thanks him in *Our Lady of Kibeho* for his dedication to the Kibeho site: "No doubt God has wisely chosen you to be the shepherd of His flock in this special place."[165] As a genocide survivor, her expression of gratitude is tantamount to an absolution of whatever failings or misdeeds he committed in 1994. In her coproduced documentary film about Kibeho, *If Only We Had Listened*, even the state begins to recede in response to the intensity of Marian love. Whereas she had previously lionized Kagame in *Led by Faith* as a miracle of Rwanda,[166] she now gives the Virgin Mary full credit. "Without Kibeho," she states confidently, "forgiveness would not be as prevalent in Rwanda as it is today. Peace would be impossible."[167] The miracle of Kibeho flattens the multiplicity of experiences in Kibeho and tames the multiheaded beast. The village of Kibeho, rather than the government in Kigali, can lead the world.

In the intensity of her devotion, her earlier rhetoric of forgiveness yields to the discourse of guilt. As marketed by Hay House, she might be the paragon of love and forgiveness; however, in her 2009 book, also titled *If Only We Had Listened*, the sweetness of her message takes on a decidedly harsher tone. "If we had listened to [Mary] in Rwanda, the million people who died during the genocide would be alive today."[168] The "we" is implied to be the Rwandans who listened to the Marian apparitions, both in person and throughout the country via state-run radio. Ilibagiza is nothing if not inclusive—instead of collective victimhood, she now casts herself and her fellow Rwandans as perpetrators. In the documentary *If Only We Had Listened*, her voiceover broadens the "we" to a global audience: "What happened here could happen anywhere, if people do not come back to God and put him first in our lives."¹⁶⁹ She expertly turns the dryness of a "genocide credit" into a religious theology in which all of us will suffer unimaginable loss if we do not atone for our sins: "The time to repent is now!"¹⁷⁰

Her counternarrative is audacious. In the Kibeho documentary, she muses on the "million and more" of the victims and then suggests that "maybe the blood of the innocent people [was] shed for the salvation of Rwanda." Such interpretations of catastrophic events are commonplace in a Christian framework in which the suffering of Christ paved the way for redemption. Even secular commentators borrow from this logic, as seen in Philip Gourevitch's discussion of the 1995 Kibeho massacre, in which he implies that the killing of thousands of Hutu served as a moment of purification that allowed the wisdom of Kagame's governance to triumph.¹⁷¹ Unlike Gourevitch, though, Ilibagiza speaks with the moral authority of a survivor and a borderline saint. Her beloved parents and brothers, among countless other relatives, friends, and neighbors, died for no less than the glory of God's kingdom, conveniently located in Rwanda. The fierceness of her attachment rewrites the vocabulary of trauma.

Kibeho, 2014

As 2014 drew to a close, Kibeho made two more dramatic appearances that clarify the persistence of the genocide attachment. On October 1, the BBC broadcast the controversial documentary *Rwanda's Untold Story*, which sought to challenge the "accepted story" of the 1994 genocide.¹⁷² In the film, journalist Jane Corbin interviews several opposition figures and other critics of Kagame's regime; the result claims to expose the "untold story" of both Kagame and the RPF and attempts to topple them from their heroic pedestals. The documentary puts forth several accusations, which range from the relatively well-accepted points about the government's role in exacerbating the violence in the DRC to the highly contested theory that the RPF shot down Habyarimana's plane. As described in the *Telegraph*'s review, "The allegations kept coming: of rigged elections and political oppression, of pressure put on official investigations into the genocide, assassination attempts on Kagame's exiled ex-colleagues, and Rwanda's role in the deaths of five million people in the wider conflict in the Congo region."¹⁷³ Aside from brief acknowledgments of Rwanda's achievements in economic development and health care, this particular story emphatically portrays Kagame as a dictator and a war criminal.

The intensity of the documentary's critique indicates a crack in the west's genocide attachment. No longer were counternarratives about Kagame and the RPF circulating primarily in academic scholarship; they were broadcast on a relatively mainstream television channel. The documentary's BBC affiliation is especially significant in light of the United Kingdom's sympathetic stance toward Kagame over the past twenty years. The outcry was immediate: protesters against the BBC filled the streets of Kigali, the government banned the Kinyarwanda broadcasting of the BBC and launched a commission of inquiry, and an international petition demanding that the BBC apologize to the Rwandan people began circulating on change.org.[174] But the furor over the documentary has only called more attention to its critique. The *Telegraph*'s positive review of the documentary concludes, "The numbers were mind boggling, the answers few, the claim that the UK is the largest contributor to the near £500 million annual foreign aid that helps keep Kagame in power, deeply concerning."[175] In his speech at the 2015 genocide commemoration, Kagame seemed pushed into an unusually defensive position, speaking at length against accusations of Rwanda's alleged support of M23; he also discarded his usual veiled references to his critics and specifically invoked *Rwanda's Untold Story* as a film that "depicted the victims, those who were being hunted, as having caused the genocide."[176] The documentary's existence, in addition to the tumult it unleashed, invites the obvious question, has the fabled genocide credit truly begun to expire?

I find a partial answer in the film's depiction of Kibeho. The multiple narratives of Kibeho are cherry-picked to serve the producers' intent to expose the postgenocide state. Predictably, the tale of the Marian apparitions is ignored in favor of the 1995 massacre in which an estimated five thousand Hutu refugees at the Kibeho IDP camp were killed.[177] Corbin describes a few seconds of blurred footage as showing the actual massacre; although I found this segment impossible to decipher, what *is* clear is the footage that depicts corpses and wounded children who were victims of the attack. An unidentified British UN peacekeeper then explains in excruciating detail how a woman who was surrendering to the RPF was brutally shot down. In this part of the film, the producers invoke Kibeho as a corrective to the RPF's preferred tale of heroism and celebration.

But the arc of the film undermines this potential. The Kibeho footage occurs immediately after what is arguably the most controversial moment of the film, when political scientist Allan Stam confidently puts forward his highly contested theory that only 200,000 Tutsi and 800,000 Hutu died during those months of the genocide, based on research conducted by Christian Davenport and himself.[178] Although a majority of the points raised in the film are grounded in at least a modicum of peer-reviewed scholarship, Stam and Davenport's assertions mark an example of genocide denial despite Stam's insistence to the contrary.[179] To position the 1995 Kibeho massacre—the evidence of which is so persuasive that even supporters of the postgenocide state have acknowledged its occurrence—immediately after Stam's "evidence" serves to undercut and question the event as portrayed in the film.[180] High-profile attacks on the film have invoked its representation of the Kibeho massacre, claiming, for example, that the film does not mention that the camp "was heavily militarised and continued to pose a grave national security threat."[181] The blurriness of the Kibeho footage is emblematic of how the film destabilizes the actual event.

Reyntjens appears in the documentary immediately after the discussion of the Kibeho massacre. After being described as a leading expert on Rwanda who can no longer travel to the country because of accusations of genocide denial, Reyntjens explains his concept of the genocide credit: "Someone criticizing the RPF for its human rights record is immediately accused of being a genocide denier. Rwanda has been benefitting from what I call genocide credit. The RPF has such moral high ground, it's unchallengeable."[182] It is curious that his explanation of the genocide credit is put forward in the middle of a relatively mainstream film that consists of a sustained critique of the RPF, which undermines the very idea of the genocide credit and discredits his theory. Further, the film draws problematic narrative and visual connections between Stam and Reyntjens—for example, both of them are described as researchers who can no longer travel to Rwanda because of their research, and both are filmed as gazing at colorful, digitized maps of Rwanda—and thus their research can be cast in the same questionable light. Even though Reyntjens, who is indeed a leading scholar of the Great Lakes region, has dismissed Stam's work as "flirt[ing] with genocide minimization or denial," the documentary positions their work as linked.[183] The film tars academic critics of Kagame with the same narrative brush. The crack that appears in Rwanda's master narrative seems to be of hairline width.

The same month in which *Rwanda's Untold Story* was broadcast, *Our Lady of Kibeho* premiered in the off-Broadway Signature Theatre. While the BBC aimed for an edgy and overtly political tone, playwright Katori Hall took a gentler, more mainstream approach to Kibeho, the genocide, and

Kagame's regime. Hall chose to write about the three original visionaries of Mary as "a back door [or] a side door" to the genocide; the apocalyptic visions that the girls experienced in 1982 serve as the climax of the play.[184] *Our Lady of Kibeho* is unique among western representations of Central African trauma in its direct exploration of the power of religious belief and the presence of the divine. The play uses elaborate special effects that seek to erase any doubt about the authenticity of the Marian apparitions; the girls speak in tongues, fall into deep trances, and even levitate in the spectacular end of the first act. Although I appreciate Hall's exploration of postsecular territory and her determination to bring an extraordinary moment of Rwanda's history to a wider audience, the play ultimately clarifies that even a side door ultimately leads to a well-worn path. In the end, *Our Lady of Kibeho* leaves the master narrative of the Rwandan genocide intact.

The play focuses on the three original visionaries—Alphonsine, Anathalie, and Marie-Claire—in order to tell what one critic called "a holy prelude to a tragedy."[185] It depicts the turmoil and controversy that the visions generated among the staff and students, the violent attempts of the Vatican to authenticate the visions through graphic scenes of torture, and the media circus that sprang up in Kibeho as news of the apparitions traveled. Hall skillfully uses the framework of a linear, realistic play to foreground the looming presence of the genocide, which becomes especially explicit in the climactic scene when the girls experience apocalyptic visions. Instead of the relatively ambiguous descriptions of skulls and blood that are described in the historical record, Hall's visionaries proclaim, "The hills of Rwanda will be littered with graves. . . . Sons will slaughter their fathers, husbands will rape their wives, babies will have their brains dashed out by mothers."[186] As Father Flavia, the investigating priest from the Vatican, warns, "There is something dangerously specific about this vision."[187] Indeed, at the end of the play, Father Tuyishime, the Tutsi priest, leaves for Uganda in order to avoid the bloodshed described in the girls' final vision. Charles Isherwood of the *New York Times* observes in his glowing review, "The play has the gripping intensity of a thriller, in part because pricking at the edge of our consciousness throughout is the knowledge of the horror that engulfed the country a little more than a decade after the events in the play take place."[188] The script's foreshadowing of genocide was often singled out by critics as a narrative thread that they clearly grasped and understood.

Ethnic tension is a constant refrain. In contrast to the ambiguity that marks Ilibagiza's retelling of the apparitions, the three visionaries are clearly

Fig. 7. Production of *Our Lady of Kibeho* by Katori Hall at the Signature Theatre, 2014. The (Hutu) head nun glares suspiciously at the three (Tutsi) visionaries. Photo by Joan Marcus.

identified as Tutsi. Alphonsine is mocked as "Tutsi Lying-Through-Her-Teeth Alphonsine" by a classmate, and another student refers to Anathalie's "ugly Tutsi teeth."[189] Even the bullying Marie-Claire, who passes as Hutu and relentlessly ridicules Anathalie and Alphonsine, reveals herself to be Tutsi once she falls prey to the apparitions herself. Head nun Sister Evangelique, who favored Marie-Clare as a fellow Hutu, confides, "At least I can rejoice that the Virgin Mary does not only favor the Tutsi. She has chosen another Hutu to spread Her message. At least I can share in that victory." She is "stunned" by Marie-Claire's revelation that she is also Tutsi; Marie-Claire also murmurs that "truth and the morning become light with time."[190] The play delineates a clear boundary between the marginalized, truthful Tutsi who receive glimpses of the divine light and the resentful, mocking Hutu. Although the Hutu students come to believe in the visions, they are excluded from the transformative experience of seeing Mary for themselves.

The lobby display at the Signature Theatre bolstered mainstream narratives of the Rwandan genocide.[191] The display provided two timelines, one that outlined events of the genocide and the other the story of the Kibeho visionaries;

neither offered a hint of the 1995 Kibeho massacre or any other information that might complicate the standard understandings of the genocide. The postgenocide state was, predictably enough, described in a positive light. Hall offered her own ringing endorsement in a quote that was emblazoned in large lettering along the top of the display: "In my opinion, there has been a huge act of performing forgiveness (in Rwanda). . . . I think that can be applied to a lot of moments in history when it comes to atrocities—from Bosnia to the Holocaust." The complexities of Kibeho are flattened into a simplistic narrative of which the RPF would heartily approve as its policies of reconciliation are held up as a beacon to other war-torn parts of the world. Audience members crowded around the display after the show, consuming the classic tale of how morally upright Tutsi triumphed over Hutu murderers in the end.

To be clear, I am not taking Hall to task for shaping the raw material of the Kibeho story into a gripping and highly successful drama. My point is that these artistic choices sharpen the contrast between her play and Ilibagiza's project. Hall's play hardens ethnic distinctions and notions of Tutsi superiority, whereas Ilibagiza advances a relatively expansive notion of Rwandanicity that allows for coexisting narratives. Ilibagiza's reluctance to identify the visionaries' ethnic identities, coupled with her emphasis on the shared need for forgiveness, facilitates nuance rather than certainty. In the politics of post-1994 Rwanda, ambiguity and love can be startlingly bold.

Certainty, though, is what sells. Hall's play clarifies the stubborn endurance of genocide narratives, attachments, and credits. In the Signature Theatre production, the pilgrims who had traveled to Kibeho were positioned along the aisles that ran between and alongside the audience; the spectators were thus surrounded by their excitement and sense of wonder generated by the visions. At the performance that I attended, a majority of the audience members raised their arms to the ceiling in mimicry of the pilgrims who raised their arms in a gesture of awe at Mary's appearance. In light of the deep western attachment to the 1994 genocide, I am tempted to interpret their upraised arms as an eagerness to seek absolution in Rwanda's moral purity.[192] This collective gesture paid homage not only to the power of the Virgin Mary but also to the genocide attachment.[193] Twenty years after the genocide, the narrative of Rwanda continues to seduce its audience and generate awe. Its shelf life remains to be seen.

Notes

1. "Rwanda Marks Genocide Anniversary," *BBC News*, April 6, 2004.
2. "Rwanda: Genocide Anniversary," 2014.
3. Reyntjens 1996, 249.
4. Reyntjens 2004, 199.
5. Some of the more recent examples of how Reyntjens's concept of genocide credit circulates in scholarship on Rwanda include Beswick 2010; Goodfellow and Smith 2013; Stys 2012; and Wilén 2012. Even if the phrase "genocide credit" is not explicitly mentioned, similar understandings of international guilt as a source of state exploitation can be found in, for example, Prunier's reference to the RPF's careful design of a "propaganda line to exploit the outside world's guilt" (2009, 20). Similarly, Peter Uvin has noted that "within the international human rights community, it is now common to state that Rwanda, like Israel, is skillfully using the genocide, and the general imagery of victimhood, to justify brutal politics and deflect international scrutiny" (2001, 179).
6. By Rwanda's PR machine, I am referring only in part to the efforts of the UK-based firm Racepoint, which includes the Rwandan government among its many prominent clients (Robert Booth, "PR Firms Make London World Capital of Reputation Laundering," *Guardian*, August 3, 2010). I think of Rwanda's PR machine in broader terms, similar to what Susan Thomson calls "the RPF's longstanding disinformation campaign that has relied on exchange students, public relations firms, commemorative events, and a whole host of other techniques to craft an idealized and often invented version of what Rwanda was like before the onset of colonialism and what it has become since the 1994 genocide" (Susan Thomson, "Rwanda's Twitter-Gate—The Disinformation Campaign of Africa's Digital President," *African Arguments*, March 17, 2014). Tony Blair and Howard G. Buffet, "Stand with Rwanda," *Foreign Policy*, February 21, 2013, available at foreignpolicy.com, and Crisafulli and Redmond 2012 can be interpreted as just two representative products of this surprisingly far-reaching machine; see also Farmer et al. (2013), which provides several of this chapter's cited "hopeful" statistics in an upbeat article about Rwanda's health-care system. Donald G. McNeil Jr., "Rwanda's Health Care Success Story," *New York Times*, February 4, 2013, subsequently reported on this article and provided further spin.
7. Blair and Buffet, "Stand with Rwanda."
8. Edwin Musoni, "Fight for Your Dignity," *New Times*, April 8, 2008. The following year, Kagame again referred to the genocide credit: "Deniers of genocide, cynics and others—some of them are so-called scholars, or experts of some kind, who are given a lot of airtime to express their views; I don't mind that—have accused us of exploiting the guilt of those who could have done something about what happened here in Rwanda—the genocide." See http://www.presidency.gov.rw/speeches/201-nyanza-memorial-site-kicukiro-kigali-7-april-2009xx.
9. Definitions of "credit" and "exploit" are taken from the *Oxford English Dictionary* at www.oed.com, accessed July 7, 2014. Examples of his use of the term "exploit" can be found, for example, in Reyntjens 2009, 184n47, and 2013, 128.
10. Zorbas 2011, 115n5. In particular, Zorbas references the high amounts that the United Kingdom's Department for International Development has pledged to Rwanda in the form of direct aid (2011, 106–107); the department has admitted that its amount of assistance to Rwanda is "higher than Rwanda's population and level of poverty might suggest" (quoted in Zorbas 2011, 107; DfID 2004, 17).

11. Robert Daguillard, "Activists Urge US to Push Rwanda to Help Bring Peace to DRC," *Voice of America*, September 19, 2012.

12. Reyntjens 1996, 249, quoted in Muniini K. Mulera, "Uganda: Bizimungu Quits, Truth Takes Over," *Monitor*, March 30, 2000.

13. In 2004, Heidy Rombouts (148) observed that the genocide credit was being "devalued"; a year later, Alison Des Forges described it as "running out" (quoted in Stephanie Nolen, "Is the 'Genocide Credit' Used Up?," *Globe and Mail*, January 22, 2005). In 2009, Mark A. Drumbl suggested that it was "expiring" (499). See also Danielle Beswick, "20 Years On, Rwanda Exhausts Its 'Genocide Credit' with Donors," *Conversation*, April 4, 2014.

14. For example, Des Forges was referring in part to the United Kingdom's announcement in late 2004 that it would cut one-quarter of its general budget support to Rwanda in response to Rwanda's open declaration that it was considering another invasion of the DRC. See Zorbas 2011, 111–112, for more information on this cut.

15. The UN report (S/2012/348, "Letter Dated 21 June 2012,") can be found at http://www.securitycouncilreport.org/atf/cf/%7B65BFCF9B-6D27-4E9C-8CD3-CF6E4FF96FF9%7D/DRC%20S%202012%20348.pdf, accessed August 12, 2017. This observation was made by the editors of *Rwanda Fast Forward* in a 2012 blog entry ("The Changing Veneer of Rwanda," *Long Term Thought*, July 31, 2012, http://longtermthoughts.wordpress.com/category/rwanda/). It should be noted that in August 2012, the government launched the Agaciro Development Fund, a campaign to collect donations from Rwandan citizens that was meant to lessen Rwanda's dependence on foreign aid. The timing of Agaciro's launch indicates that the government was reacting to the pressure of the cuts that were instituted after the June 2012 report.

16. The United Kingdom in particular waffled to an extreme as it suspended, released, and then resuspended $16 million in direct budget support (David Smith, "UK Blocks £16m Aid to Rwanda," *Guardian*, July 27, 2012; "UK Unfreezes Aid to Rwanda," *BBC Monitoring Africa*, September 5, 2012; Mark Tran, "Andrew Mitchell: 'Restoring Rwanda Aid Not the Act of a Rogue Minister,'" *Guardian*, November 8, 2012). Meanwhile, the United States weighed in with only paltry amounts as it cut $200,000 in military support in 2012 (Katrina Manson, "US Warns Rwanda over Alleged War Crimes," *Financial Times*, July 25, 2012). In August, according to Jason Stearns in a post on his *Congo Siasa* blog (October 30, 2013, http://congosiasa.blogspot.com/), active military support was continuing to bolster M23's ranks. Stearns goes on to suggest that Rwanda did eventually withdraw support, which helped bring about M23's surrender in November 2013, but the connection of this withdrawal to international pressure is not conclusive.

17. Brown 1995; Munt 2008; Berlant 2011.

18. Brown 1995, 62; emphasis in the original.

19. Munt 2008, 12; here she also draws on the work of Ahmed 2004.

20. See Butler 1997, 2004b; Berlant 2011; and Berlant and Edelman 2013. I am playing a bit fast and loose with complex and nuanced arguments; Butler and Berlant do not fall into polarized camps. Berlant, for example, is more interested in opening up concepts of attachment rather than rejecting the idea of subjection and subjugation wholesale. See Duschinsky, Greco, and Solomon 2015 for a useful overview of Butler and Berlant's approaches to attachment.

21. Zorbas's explanation of "Rwanda's paradox," a phrase she uses to theorize Rwanda's ability to draw aid despite widespread criticism, touches on Rwanda's multifaceted emotional appeal (2011). She acknowledges Reyntjens's genocide credit but also invokes the western de-

sire for African success stories, admiration for the RPF, and the government's strategic use of donor-friendly language. In other words, her explanation goes beyond the "feeling bad" principle of guilt to consider how Rwanda also makes the west, in effect, "feel good." But even in the midst of careful, nuanced explanations, her use of the term "paradox" suggests that a fundamental irrationality is still in play.

22. Her quiet politics is only slightly louder than the "amplified silence" described in Burnet 2012. Burnet observes that "rather than actively resist [the state-ordained] monolithic history, many women choose to remain silent, preserving the singularity of their experiences in private" (12). See also Thomson 2013 for a discussion of how Rwandan peasants "whisper their truth to the power of the postgenocide regime" through everyday acts of resistance (9).

23. Ilibagiza 2008a, 71.

24. Breed uses the term "Rwandanicity," which appeared in a 2005 article in the *New Times*, to consider how Rwandan identity is created and performed in a variety of cultural contexts (2014, 7).

25. Representative examples of these arguments can be found in "Q & A on the United Nations Human Rights Mapping Report," *Human Rights Watch*, October 1, 2010; Peskin 2011, 173; "Rwanda: Where Opposition Means Guilty of 'Divisionism and Genocide'?," *Africa Faith and Justice Network*, April 9, 2010; Jennifer Fierberg, "Rwanda, M23 and the UNSC," *African Arguments*, August 30, 2013; and "Support Free and Fair Presidential Elections in Rwanda to Prevent Another Genocide," *Targeted News Service*, March 10, 2010. The Arusha trials refers to the International Criminal Tribunal for Rwanda, which was established in November 1994 and closed in December 2015; see Cruvellier 2010 for more information on the UN's "court of remorse." Also, it should be noted that international guilt is not just linked to the lack of intervention during the genocide but is also traced to the outpouring of international aid devoted to the Zairian refugee camps in the genocide's aftermath. As Tom Goodfellow and Alyson Smith point out, "As it became evident that the donor community was indirectly funding elements associated with the genocidal former regime via the camps, the RPF-led government began gaining the moral imperative, which laid the foundations for Rwanda's subsequent strategy in its engagement with donors over the longer term" (2013, 3190). Kagame invoked this particular incarnation of guilt in a 1997 interview with Gourevitch: "I think we should start accusing those people who actually supported those camps—spent one million dollars per day in those camps, gave support to these groups to rebuild themselves into a force, militarized refugees. . . . Why shouldn't we accuse them? And this is the guilt they are trying to fight off" ("Letter from the Congo: Continental Shift," *New Yorker*, August 4, 1997, 55, cited in Prunier 2009, 156).

26. Zorbas 2011, 106.

27. Chris McGreal, "Rwanda's Genocide and the Bloody Legacy of Anglo-American Guilt," *Guardian*, December 12, 2012.

28. Zorbas 2011, 106.

29. Pottier 2002, 156.

30. Ibid. Pottier is citing an article on Boutros-Ghali's press conference of May 25, 1994, that appeared in the May 27, 1994, issue of *Libération*. In a video of the press conference that is available on C-SPAN, Boutros-Ghali describes the failure of the international community in even grander terms: "It is a failure not only for the United Nations but it is a failure for the international community. And all of us are responsible [for] this failure, not only the great powers but the African powers, the NGOs, all the international community" (available at http://

www.c-span.org/video/?57228-1/secretary-general-news-conference, accessed August 1, 2016). Interestingly, he went on to describe the genocide as a personal failure because of his inability to persuade the UN Security Council to commit troops and thus adhered to the confessional logic described in McMillan 2008. It should also be noted that Boutros-Ghali was harsher in a report submitted to the Security Council on 30 May 1994: "We all must recognize that ... we have failed in our response to the agony of Rwanda, and thus have acquiesced in the continued loss of human lives" ("Report of the Secretary-General on the Situation in Rwanda," S/1994/640, May 31, 1994, 12, available at http://www.un.org/Docs/secu94.htm, accessed August 12, 2017).

31. Pottier 2002, 147, 160. As further evidence of guilt, Pottier cited a 1995 *De Standaard* article in which Faustin Twagiramungu, the Hutu prime minister of the new postgenocide government, who was forced out of office after just over a year, explained, "That the international community did not prevent the genocide has hit her deep in the stomach.... She feels guilt and in debt to the RPF—which did end the genocide—and eases her conscience with a variety of aid programmes" (147). Certainly, Twagiramungu possessed intimate knowledge of the workings of the Rwandan government; however, Pottier's reliance on this quote as evidence of international guilt suggests that concrete manifestations of guilt are hard to find.

32. McMillan 2008, 4.

33. Amnesty International, "Democratic Republic of Congo: Rwandese-Controlled East; Devastating Human Toll," 2001, available at http://www.amnesty.org/en/library/info/AFR62/011/2001/en, accessed October 31, 2017; both this report and the government's response, "Response to the Amnesty International Report," are cited in Reyntjens 2013, 129.

34. CNDP is the French initialism for the National Congress for the Defense of the People.

35. "UN Report 'Part of West Conspiracy against Rwanda,'" *Rwanda News Agency*, December 15, 2008.

36. The mapping report, "Democratic Republic of the Congo, 1993-2003," which is dated August 2010, can be accessed at http://www.ohchr.org/Documents/Countries/CD/DRC_MAPPING_REPORT_FINAL_EN.pdf, accessed August 12, 2017. See Howard French, "U.N. Congo Report Offers New View on Genocide," *New York Times*, August 27, 2010, for a useful summary of the report.

37. Paul Kagame, "Speech at the 15th Commemoration of the Genocide against the Tutsi at the Nyanza Memorial Site in Kicukiro, Kigali," speech at Kicukiro, Kigali, April 7, 2009, available at http://www.presidency.gov.rw/speeches/201-nyanza-memorial-site-kicukiro-kigali-7-april-2009, accessed July 11, 2014.

38. Leys 2007, 7.

39. Ibid., 11; Bewes 2011, 28.

40. McMillan 2008, 4.

41. McMillan 2010, 86, 91.

42. Ibid., 91. Verhofstadt's speech, as McMillan notes, was the most "frank" in its admission of international guilt (ibid., 90). See Hayman 2010 for a discussion of Belgium's unique "soul searching" over its role in the 1994 genocide; this process culminated in Verhofstadt's speech in 2000.

43. For text and video of Clinton's speech, see William J. Clinton, "Remarks to the People of Rwanda," speech in Kigali, Rwanda, March 25, 1998, available at https://millercenter.org/the-presidency/presidential-speeches/march-25-1998-remarks-people-rwanda, accessed October 20, 2017.

44. This moment occurs at approximately the 6:00 mark in the video of the speech.

45. This moment occurs at approximately the 8:20 mark in his speech.

46. His moment of "feeling bad" efficiently clears the way for "feeling good" as he begins to speak hopefully about how the US government can work together with Rwanda toward a peaceful future: "And if we set about the business of doing them together, you can overcome the awful burden that you have endured. You can put a smile on the face of every child in this country, and you can make people once again believe that they should live as people were living who were singing to us and dancing for us today." Clinton is smiling broadly at this point. He has passed through the gateway of shame and now basks in the balm of redemption.

47. Elizabeth Povinelli has persuasively used a postcolonial lens to explore theories of shame in her analysis of two high-profile Australian land disputes in which indigenous Australians laid claim to state land. She argues that state rhetoric of shame over the appropriation of indigenous land operates as a demarcation point between the imperial brutality of the past and the newly enlightened nation that will not repeat past mistakes (1998, 586). In this context, the collective expression and purging of shame over the colonial past pave the way for a "new abstracted national membership" that putatively includes the former colonial subject (580). The expansive presence of Rwanda in what Olesen (2012) has called a "global memory" indicates that the role of shame in identity formation exceeds the level of the nation-state; Rwanda serves as a point of cohesion in the formation of empire's unwieldy global self.

48. Clark 2005, 121.

49. Gerry Caplan, "The Hero and the Horror," review of *Shake Hands with the Devil: The Failure of Humanity in Rwanda*, by Roméo Dallaire, *Globe and Mail*, November 1, 2003, D14.

50. David Kabuye, "Judge Bruguiere; Fighting for Mother France," *New Times*, November 27, 2006.

51. Stephen Kinzer, "End Human Rights Imperialism Now," *Guardian*, December 31, 2010. The rhetoric of imperialism is not, of course, limited to Rwanda; the Ugandan state-sponsored newspaper *New Vision*, for example, routinely portrays human rights activists and donors who criticize Uganda's harsh antihomosexuality legislation as imperialists.

52. Andrew M. Mwenda, "Inside the West's Double Standards," *Independent*, March 17, 2012. Mwenda refers to this particular incident in vague terms; more information can be found in United States Department of State, *Human Rights Reports—Rwanda*, http://allafrica.com/stories/201304231135.html.

53. "West Is to Blame for Rwandan Genocide in 1994—Rwandan President," *Xinhua News Agency*, April 7, 2004; Carter Dougherty, "Rwanda Marks Genocide Anniversary; Victims, Heroes Honored; Criticism Directed at France," *Boston Globe*, April 8, 2004; Anton La Guardia, "Was World's Failure to Act Racism? Asks Kagame," *Daily Telegraph*, April 6, 2004; Matthew Green, "Rwanda's Kagame Scolds Outside World over Genocide," *Reuters News*, April 4, 2004.

54. Ibreck 2012, 101–107, provides a useful and nuanced summary of Kagame's speeches that speaks to their mercurial nature and the difficulty in ascertaining clear patterns or narratives over the years.

55. Paul Kagame, "Speech at the 16th Commemoration of the Genocide of the Tutsi," Kigali, April 7, 2010, available at http://www.presidency.gov.rw/speeches/332-speech-by-president-paul-kagame-at-16th-commemoration-of-the-genocide-of-the-tutsi-kigali-7-april-2010, accessed July 10, 2014.

56. Paul Kagame, "Speech by President Kagame at the 17th Genocide Commemoration Ceremony," Kigali, April 7, 2011, available at http://www.presidency.gov.rw/speeches/434

-speech-by-president-kagame-at-the-17th-genocide-commemoration-ceremony-kigali-7-april-2011, accessed July 10, 2014.

57. Rabbi Shmuley Boteach, "Elie Wiesel and Kagame of Rwanda Discuss Genocide & Syria," *Jewish Press*, September 30, 2013.

58. Paul Kagame, "Speech by H.E. Paul Kagame, President of the Republic of Rwanda, at the 18th Commemoration of the Genocide against the Tutsi," Kigali, April 7, 2012, available at http://www.paulkagame.com/index.php/speeches/630-speech-by-he-paul-kagame-president-of-the-republic-of-rwanda-at-the-18th-commemoration-of-the-genocide-against-the-tutsi-amahoro-stadium-7-april-2012, accessed July 12, 2014.

59. Sartre 2003, 245–246; Bewes 2011, 165.

60. Kagame makes frequent references to racism and imperialism in speaking to international audiences. See, for example, his speech at Oxford University, in which he discussed the "context of imperialism" behind charges about the Congo ("Standing Ovation for Kagame at Oxford University," *News of Rwanda*, May 18, 2013). See also his interview with the *Guardian* in which he called the attacks racist: Chris McGreal, "Is Kagame Africa's Lincoln or a Tyrant Exploiting Rwanda's Tragic History?," *Guardian*, May 18, 2013. Of course, anticolonial discourse is commonly used by African heads of state as a means of appealing to popular sentiment; my focus here is on how Kagame uses it to manipulate global sentiments of shame. Rwanda's "Twittergate" scandal in 2014 is a particularly timely and relevant example. This scandal, in which internet troll @RichardGoldston, who had regularly attacked critics of Kagame, was traced to the president's office itself, has been discussed in a variety of sources; see, for example, Susan Thomson, "Rwanda's Twitter-Gate: The Disinformation Campaign of Africa's Digital President," *African Arguments*, March 17, 2014. Goldston's profile seemed uniquely designed to reach out to citizens of donor countries such as the United Kingdom that are not directly implicated in Rwanda's colonial past. In a bio on the now-deleted Twitter account, Goldston described himself as "a descendant of an English imperialist," explaining that "i [sic] regret every deed that imperialistic policies did to Africa. I am on a mission to clear my conscience." (A screenshot of his bio can be found at https://medium.com/@steveinafrica/richardgoldston-backstory-part-1-f25542c88786, accessed November 16, 2016.) That this background would be perceived as a means of legitimizing Goldston's attacks on Kagame's critics indicates that at least someone in the president's office viewed imperialist shame as a potent strategy.

61. Kagame 2009, 14, 12. In 2013, the World Bank and the International Finance Corporation rated Rwanda among the top ten countries in the world in which to start a business. Their report, "Doing Business 2013: Smarter Regulations for Small and Medium-Size Enterprises," can be accessed at http://www.doingbusiness.org/reports/global-reports/doing-business-2013, accessed August 12, 2017.

62. Mutua 2001, 201, 230. The RPF is generally described as embracing the role of victim; for example, Reyntjens emphasizes how the post-1994 regime "acquire[s] and maintain[s] victim status" (2004, 199) through its exploitation of the genocide credit. An oft-cited example of the government's exploitation of victimhood is its official change of the name of the Rwandan genocide to the Tutsi genocide in 2008, meaning that "Tutsi victimhood is now firmly established in the public discourse" (Ibreck 2012, 104). But the RPF also readily invokes the categories of "hero" and "savior" when it suits its collective purpose.

63. James Cowan, "A Purpose Driven Country," *National Post*, April 28, 2008.

64. See Rick Warren, *The Purpose Driven Life: What on Earth Am I Here For?* (Grand Rapids: Zondervan, 2002), 3.

65. Cowan, "Purpose Driven Country." See also Eugene Mutara, "'40 Days' Crusade to Promote Pastor Warren's Teachings," *New Times*, March 31, 2008.

66. Ann Pepper, "Pastor Lays Out a Global Vision," *Orange County Register*, April 17, 2005. The developmental rhetoric of the PEACE plan was strengthened when Warren changed "Plant churches" to "Promote reconciliation" in the fall of 2007, when he launched a revised version of the PEACE plan through "PEACE 2.0" (Timothy Morgan, "Rebooting PEACE," *Christianity Today*, May 28, 2008). Currently, on the website http://saddleback.com/connect/ministry/the-peace-plan, the "P" is described as "Planting churches that promote reconciliation," accessed August 12, 2017.

67. Descriptions of these programs can be found in "Church, Community, Country: 2013 Rwanda PEACE Plan Report," available at http://rwandaupdate.wordpress.com/, accessed July 10, 2014. An internet search in August 2017, as this book was going to press, revealed that Saddleback's PEACE activities in Rwanda had sharply diminished; however, the organization had scheduled an "HIV/AIDS and Orphan combo trip" for singles, to take place in October and November 2017 at an unspecified location in Rwanda; see http://saddleback.com/connect/ministry/the-peace-plan/trip/36372164122/36372164122, accessed August 12, 2017.

68. Cowan, "Purpose Driven Country." A particularly revealing statement of the PEACE plan's imperial bent can be found in *Time* magazine: "[Warren] convened 1,700 pastors from the purpose-driven network to Saddleback and urged them to send out teams as part of the 'PEACE Coalition.' 'There was a lot of energy afterward,' he says. 'Guys with tears in their eyes. A guy was going, 'I'll take Mozambique,' and one was going, 'I'll take Nigeria.' They were dividing up the world" (David Van Bierna, "The Global Ambition of Rick Warren," *Time*, August 7, 2008). See also Gilbert Ndikubwayezu, "Rwanda: RNP Officers Train on Criminal Investigation," *New Times*, March 11, 2009; and Florence Mutesi, "Police Benefit from Pr Warren's Peace Project," *New Times*, March 12, 2008.

69. Van Bierna, "Global Ambition of Rick Warren."

70. Kagame's embrace of Warren's Pentecostal faith should also be understood in relation to the state's hostility toward Catholicism. Ostensibly this hostility stems from the reprehensible behavior of numerous priests and nuns during the genocide, as well as the cozy relations between Habyarimana's regime and Catholic authorities. A more controversial interpretation, though, is that Catholicism continues to be associated with the majority Hutu population, as well as opposition politics (see, for example, Zorbas 2011, 111). In a thoughtful article about Saddleback's interventions in Rwanda, Gwendolyn Driscoll quotes an anonymous human rights expert living in Rwanda as stating, "The Catholic Church still represents an alternative power base.... So by welcoming in the evangelical churches (Kagame is) simultaneously showing the West (his) openness to ideas and (he's) weakening (his) opposition" (Gwendolyn Driscoll, "The Pastor and the President," *Orange County Register*, December 24, 2006). The article situates Warren as a pawn in a high-stakes Rwandan political game.

71. This quote of Warren's is in Gwendolyn Driscoll, "Saddleback Church: 25th Anniversary Celebration," *Orange County Register*, April 18, 2005.

72. Van Bierna, "Global Ambition of Rick Warren."

73. Ibid.

74. Rick Hampson, "Americans Finding Purpose in Hopes for Africa's Future; Rwanda Sees Revival of Dreams for Prosperity," *USA Today*, July 22, 2008, A1.

75. Rick Warren, "Leaders and Revolutionaries: Paul Kagame," *Time*, April 30, 2009.

76. Van Bierna, "Global Ambition of Rick Warren"; "Rwanda to Set Up Development Fund Following Aid Withdrawal," *BBC Monitoring Africa*, December 19, 2008.

77. The reference to the white-savior industrial complex, as noted in previous chapters, is drawn from Teju Cole, "The White-Savior Industrial Complex," *Atlantic*, March 21, 2012. The 2013 report on Rwanda's PEACE plan is vague about dollar amounts but is filled with statistics relating to renovations, construction of buildings, and education and health programs, all of which add up to a substantial financial investment. I accessed this report from peaceplan.org in 2014; by August 2016, the website had been moved to http://saddleback.com/connect/ministry/the-peace-plan, and the report was no longer accessible.

78. The text of his speech can be found at http://en.igihe.com/news/president-kagame-s-speech-during-kwibuka20-held.html, accessed July 10, 2014.

79. A video of the speech and the exchange between Warren and Kagame is available at https://www.youtube.com/watch?v=VLsUNBmsbGg, accessed August 12, 2017. This video also includes Warren's prayer described in the next sentence.

80. Warren's comments before Kagame's speech, in which he keeps insisting that Kagame's critics are not God, can be found at https://www.youtube.com/watch?v=deNHZQRm9Ws&index=29&list=UUFyumXCzCahOP-UznvpByuA, accessed August 12, 2017.

81. "Resilience of Rwandans Kept Nation Alive—Kagame," *New Times*, April 27, 2014. This comment does not appear on the YouTube videos of the event, but it was widely circulated in the *New Times*; Kagame's website, Pantheos.com; and the *Christian Post*.

82. The archived webcast of the UN event is available at http://webtv.un.org/watch/launch-of-kwibuka20/3267564158001/, accessed July 7, 2014.

83. The roster of Rwandan genocide survivors who have spoken at the UN commemorative events at the New York City headquarters makes up a distinguished group. They include Kizito Kalima, Eugenie Mukeshimana, Virginie Ingabire, Jacqueline Murekatete, and Marie Claudine Mukamabano (who did not speak but instead sang in Kinyarwanda at the opening and closing of the 2009 event). Several of these speakers have made more than one appearance; Ilibagiza, for example, also spoke in 2011 at the April commemoration event. Rarely do these panelists provide a detailed recounting of the horrors they experienced; instead, they use this moment on the global stage to denounce negationism (Mukeshimana in 2008), recount the names of their many family members who died (Ingabire in 2009), or urge greater social services and protection for genocide survivors (Murekatete in 2010). Webcasts of several of these events can be accessed at http://www.un.org/en/preventgenocide/rwanda/commemoration/pastcommemorations.shtml.

84. Ilibagiza 2006, xii.

85. All the books discussed in this chapter except her 2009 book *If Only We Had Listened* are credited by Ilibagiza with Steve Erwin, a Canadian journalist based in New York City who previously served as the New York correspondent for the Canadian Broadcasting Corporation.

86. African Rights 1995, 394. According to 1991 census data, Kibuye had the highest population of Tutsi in the country at the time of the genocide, with a population of 252,000. According to African Rights, "By the end of June 1994 there were only between seven and eight thousand Tutsis left alive" (394). In this chapter, I occasionally cite African Rights, a UK-based organization that authored several reports on the events in 1994; however, it should be noted that the organization has been exposed as actively complicit with the RPF (Reydams 2016). Butare was officially renamed Huye in 2006; however, I follow popular usage and continue to refer to it as Butare.

87. Kibuye also included the famous resistance site of Bisesero, where several thousand Tutsi fought off Hutu militias during April and May 1994 from their vantage point on Muyira Hill; Operation Turquoise troops are strongly implicated in the story of their ultimate defeat in June.

88. Salverson 2001, 121.

89. Ilibagiza 2008a, 64–65.

90. Ibid., 66–71.

91. Gilmore 2010, 659.

92. Ilibagiza 2006, 82.

93. Ibid., 190.

94. Ilibagiza 2008a, 118–119.

95. Ilibagiza's deferral to divine will would generally discredit a notion of agency as such since it is couched in the framework of submission to religion rather than the empowerment of herself as an individual. But, as Sarah Bracke points out, an understanding of feminist agency in a postsecular age must draw forcefully on Foucault's theory of subjectivity, which allows scholars to "trace how the very conditions that bring about subordination are themselves a source of subjectivity and hence agency." She adds, "This point of departure allows for different (non-liberal, non-secular) understandings of the capacity to act and shape the world" (2008, 63–64). To contextualize Ilibagiza's agency in "an economy of profound love and yearning for God" (Bracke 2008, 63) does not negate the extraordinary risks that she took both during the genocide and in the following years, as well as her boldness in cultivating a life and livelihood for herself as a survivor of genocide.

96. Ilibagiza 2008a, 192.

97. Ilibagiza 2006, 104. Also, in *Led by Faith*, she mentions western inaction briefly in the context of the Hutu refugees fleeing to Zaire: "The great irony was that the west had sat by and done nothing during the Tutsi slaughter yet came to the rescue of the refugees in Zaire" (2008a, 61). I should acknowledge, though, that Ilibagiza was surprisingly forceful in her criticism of the United Nations during the retreat that I attended, described later in this chapter. In response to a participant's question about the role of the United Nations, she stated with uncharacteristic forcefulness, "The UN failed us big time." This statement stood in marked contrast to her praise of the UN in her published work.

98. Ilibagiza 2006, 112–113.

99. If her western readers do feel a touch of guilt, it could be resolved through consumer activism given that the proceeds from her book go to provide scholarships to Rwandan orphans through her Left to Tell Foundation. Originally, the foundation was intended to help children who were orphaned by the genocide; however, the language has become more inclusive given that many of those children are now over twenty years of age. For more information about the foundation, see http://www.immaculee.com/charity/, accessed July 16, 2014.

100. Ilibagiza 2008a, 192.

101. Ilibagiza 2006, 190.

102. Ibid.

103. Ibid., 207.

104. See Ehrenreich 2009 for a lively critique of the ideology of positive thinking.

105. See Martha Beck, *Finding Your Way in a Wild New World* (New York: Free Press, 2011), 116.

106. Sam L. Marcelo, "God in the Midst of Genocide," *Business World*, July 16, 2010.

107. John Beer, "Survive, She Said," *Village Voice*, April 25–May 1, 2007, 46.

108. For a highly positive review of the Grahamstown performance that touches on the play's resonance for South Africa, see "Immaculate Performance," *Cue*, July 5, 2015, available at http://cue.ru.ac.za/2015/07/immaculate-performance/. I regret that I have been unable to obtain a copy of the script. In March 2017, Sword (who now goes by the name Leslie Lewis) performed the play for a two-week run at Passage Theatre in Trenton NJ.

109. Ilibagiza 2013, 238.

110. Ilibagiza 2008b, 186–198; 2013, 19–36; see also Ilibagiza 2009, 99–113.

111. Examples of her varied appearances can be found at www.immaculee.com/events/appearances.php. When the site was accessed on July 21, 2014, events included speaking at the Cornerstone Catholic Conference: Building a Culture of Life (October 2014), speaking at the Christ Our Life Catholic Regional Conference (September 2014), and several weekend retreats. In July 2014, she spoke at a Catholic "healing" conference that urged the path of chastity to men and women who experience same-sex desire; see Lou Baldwin's "People with Same Sex Attraction Find Courage at Conference, *Catholic Philly*, June 22, 2014, available at http://catholicphilly.com/2014/07/news/local-news/people-with-same-sex-attraction-take-courage-at-conference/, accessed August 11, 2017.

112. Warren 2002, 85.

113. The retreat took place on March 20–21, 2015.

114. As explained by Manuel A. Vásquez and Marie F. Marquardt, Marian devotional practices are linked to the Catholic Church's New Evangelization project launched in 1983, which sought not only to gain new converts and renew the faith of nominal Catholics but also to reaffirm the Church's "unity, universality, and hierarchical authority" (2000, 131–132). They ask, "How can the Church reconcile the need to proselytize with renewed fervor, which requires active work from the laity, with the Vatican restoration and its call for unity and universality in the face of the fragmentation produced by globalization?" (132). The widely adored figure of Mary provides a means to negotiate tensions between what they call the "global scripts" of religious theology and lived religious practices.

115. After Segatashya began experiencing visions, he added the name Emmanuel.

116. Ilibagiza 2011, 6.

117. See Skrbiš 2005 for a discussion of how Marian apparitions are folded into nationalist discourse; both the apparitions and nationalist imagining presuppose "the idea of election/chosenness and an associated perception of divinely ordained specialness" (445).

118. Recent academic publications on Marian worship indicate that Kibeho continues to be marginalized as an apparition site. Rarely was Kibeho mentioned in the Marian scholarship I consulted, even in those publications dated well after 2001, the year in which the apparitions were authenticated. For example, Kibeho does not appear in the publications *Moved by Mary: The Power of Pilgrimage in the Modern World* (Hermkens, Jansen, and Notermans 2009) and *The Mystery of the Rosary: Marian Devotion and the Reinvention of Catholicism* (Mitchell 2009).

119. Hermkens, Jansen, and Notermans 2009, 1.

120. For additional information about the apparitions at Kibeho, see Longman 2010; ter Haar 2003; Saur 2004; and Burnet 2005. French sources include Maindron 1984 and Misago 1991.

121. Saur 2004, 213. Sources do not agree on this point. Burnet states that ORINFOR provided both the sound system and the platform (2005, 198), whereas Ilibagiza states that the Church authorized both when Kibeho was pronounced a site of public devotion (2008b, 101).

I am emphasizing Saur's interpretation because he provides more detail than either of these sources; for example, he mentions that Chrisophe Mfizi, the director of ORINFOR, wired the platform for sound, and that the bishop (presumably Bishop Gahamanyi) had the platform built (2004, 213). This uncertainty is perhaps emblematic of the close connections between the Catholic Church and the state at this time, as Burnet indicates (2005, 198n153).

122. Ilibagiza 2008a, 100. Given the intended US readership, I assume that by "late spring," she means April or May.

123. ter Haar 2003, 431, 422. Saur interprets these actions to promote the visionaries as manifestations of the close ties between the Catholic Church and Habyarimana's regime (2004, 213); indeed, Habyarimana's family members were frequent pilgrims to Kibeho. Saur also links the intensity associated with the apparitions to the Catholic Charismatic Renewal movement that began in 1967, in which Catholic worship borrowed from Pentecostal fervor as a means of reinvention and rejuvenation.

124. Maindron 1984, quoted in Longman 2010, 31.

125. Longman 2010, 146. It is unclear why he identifies half of them as Tutsi.

126. Ibid.

127. In 1989, Ilibagiza made her first visit to Kibeho; in *Our Lady of Kibeho*, she vividly describes her sense of ecstasy when Nyiramukiza, under divine instruction, singled her out from the crowd to bless her with a drink of holy water (Ilibagiza 2008b, 170). By that time, Nyiramukiza was the only visionary of the original eight who had continued to receive public visitations. In the documentary *If Only We Had Listened*, Ilibagiza interviews visionary Agnes Kamagaju, who indicates that she continues to receive private visitations from Mary and Jesus; it should be noted that Nyiramukiza also continues to receive visitations in Belgium on May 15 each year.

128. See Misago 1991. The Gikongoro diocese was established in 1992; previously, Kibeho had belonged to the Butare diocese.

129. Longman 2010, 157.

130. Ilibagiza 2008b, 174.

131. Ibid.

132. African Rights 1995, 290.

133. Burnet provides the statistic of 10,000 (2005, 175); a sign that used to be displayed pointing visitors to the memorial (which had been removed by the time of my visit in 2015) stated that 25,000 victims died. None of the visionaries perished at Kibeho—indeed, Kamagaju tells Ilibagiza in the documentary *If Only We Had Listened* that she took shelter at the parish church but managed to escape. Segatashya, however, was shot during the genocide, and Mukamurenzi "disappeared during the holocaust and has never been heard from again," according to Ilibagiza (2008b, 175). Mukangango also died in Kigali during this time, apparently in defense of her husband (ibid.); however, as will be discussed in more detail, rumors that Mukangango died in the 1995 Kibeho massacre circulate to this day.

134. Gourevitch uses the term "crematorium" to describe the Kibeho church (1998, 198).

135. Des Forges 1999, 301.

136. Jean-François Kayiranga, Eduoard Nkurikiye, Consolata Mukangango (Sister Gertrude), Julienne Mukabutera (Sister Maria Kizito), and Wenceslas Munyeshyaka are just a few of the better-known names of these abettors.

137. See Longman 2010 and Rittner, Roth, and Whitworth 2004 for a much more thorough discussion of Church complicity and participation in the genocide; see also Carney

2014 for the historical context of Catholic politics in Rwanda during the colonial period up to 1962.

138. The camp originated as a "safe zone" during Operation Turquoise. According to one newspaper source, the IDPs gathered in Kibeho because it was perceived as a place of protection due to its association with the apparitions. See Karen Middleton, "Calm after the Storm—Strife Brewing Again for Rwanda," *Age*, February 4, 1995.

139. Estimates of Kibeho's 1995 death toll vary widely, from the official statistic of 338 up to 8,000 (Pottier 2010b, 189); the statistic of 5,000 comes from Prunier 2009, 41. The reference to "surreal diplomacy" is found in Pottier 2002, 160; for further information on the 1995 massacre, see Adelman and Suhrke 1996, 61–64; Burnet 2005, 175–204; O'Halloran 2010; and Pickard 2008.

140. Burnet explains, "The vast majority of survivors of this second massacre refused to speak with me about the genocide, the second Kibeho massacre, or their experiences since the genocide and war. The few who did mention what happened at Kibeho in 1995 or who talked about acts of vengeance they had suffered at the hands of certain genocide survivors did so in hushed tones and cryptic metaphors or euphemisms, and with a look of terror on their faces lest someone else hear them" (2005, 178).

141. Reporters Sans Frontières, 2002.

142. According to Alison Des Forges, RTLM announcer Valerie Bemeriki, one of the most prominent voices of "hate radio" during the genocide, also invoked the apparitions in her reporting; she "maintained that the Virgin Mary, said to appear from time to time at Kibeho church, had declared that 'we will have the victory'" (1999, 357). Bemeriki was sentenced to life imprisonment in 2009.

143. Although Reporters Without Borders repeatedly criticized Makeli's arrest, the Rwandan state resolutely ignored international appeals on his behalf for fourteen years. Even when Makeli was acquitted by a *gacaca* court and released in 2008, the court subsequently retried his case in 2009 and sentenced him to life imprisonment. The charges had far exceeded the reporting of the Marian apparitions at this point. According to the organization, "The former journalist was convicted of inciting genocide on the national radio station and holding meetings to plan genocide and attacks on Tutsi in the central city of Kabgayi. The court also found him guilty of criminal association, attempted murder and being a member of the highest level of genocide planners" ("Government to Demand Exorbitant Sums to Launch New News Media," *Reporters Sans Frontières*, September 24, 2009). Makeli then fled to Kampala, where, according to the *Observer*, he was the target of a failed abduction in 2010 by Kinyarwanda-speakers (Peter Beaumont, "Paul Kagame: A Tarnished African Hero," *Observer*, July 17, 2010).

144. Burnet 2005, 193.

145. Misago had long been a figure of suspicion. The African Rights report singles out Misago for his apparent complicity in the genocide and provides a list of seven accusations against him (African Rights 1995, 899–900); however, the objectivity of this report has been thoroughly called into question (see n86).

146. "Content of President's Speech to Mark 1994 Genocide Broadcast," *BBC Monitoring Africa*, April 7, 1999.

147. Tom Masland, "The Bishop in the Dock," *Newsweek*, September 27, 1999.

148. Longman acknowledges that he "found clear evidence of his cowardice in the face of the genocide but no evidence of his direct involvement.... The Misago case seems... to have served as a symbolic trial of the Catholic Church for its complicity" (2010, 158). In reference to Misago's trial, Burnet comments, "The trial divided Rwandans as many people believed that

Misago was guilty while others believed that not only was he innocent but that he had saved thousands of lives" (2005, 180n141). Misago died of natural causes, still in office, in 2012.

149. At the time of this writing, the Catholic Church has continued to reserve judgment on the apparitions at Medjugorje in Bosnia, which also began in 1981.

150. The report does not quite toe the line of state narratives of the genocide. Misago's reference to "other countries" that were affected by the genocide is undoubtedly a veiled reference to the DRC; even more daring is his explicit reference to the 1995 massacre when he calls Kibeho "a scene of a double racist massacre in April 1994 and April 1995." The report can be found at http://kibeho-sanctuary.com/index.php/en/introduction/archives.

151. The Kibeho apparitions share several commonalities with broad patterns of other Marian apparitions. For example, as Nicholas Perry and Loreto Echeverría describe in *Under the Heel of Mary* (1988), the visionaries are usually poor, marginalized young women or girls, the messages often include apocalyptic warnings, Mary is often described as a beautiful, glowing woman, and miracles are often reported by the visionaries and their followers. See also Matter 2001; Matter notes that the surge of apparitions of the Virgin "has become a cultural phenomenon of its own, with certain increasingly expected motifs and characteristics" (128).

152. In addition to the facilities described here, a well-marked path called the Way of the Rosary leads visitors to a small pool, the "Source of Mary," in which a well gushes water that is considered holy; visitors gather the water in jerricans to use for healing and personal blessings.

153. I visited Kibeho on August 16–17, 2015. Despite much discussion in the Rwandan press about the need to "develop" Kibeho as a tourist site and provide appropriate accommodation, many pilgrims simply sleep on the ground or stay awake to pray. The *New Times* published an unusually lengthy feature about the 2015 Assumption Day celebration in Kibeho; see Solomon Asaba, "The Long Journey to Kibeho to Celebrate Assumption Day," *New Times*, August 23, 2015.

154. At Kibeho, according to testimony gathered by African Rights, genocidaires included militia members, police, soldiers, and local residents (African Rights 1995, 291–315). Haunting photographs of the Kibeho memorial can be found at "Through a Glass Darkly Project," http://genocidememorials.cga.harvard.edu/kibeho.html. These photographs date from the time at which the crypt was a shed instead of a permanent memorial.

155. Burnet 2005, 176. This room marks a compromise between the Catholic authorities, who wanted the building to be restored solely as a place of worship, and survivors of the genocide, who pushed for the entire building to serve as a memorial, similar to the Nyamata or Ntarama churches outside Kigali. Burnet notes that the banner serves, in part, as a "reproach" to the Church for wanting to remove the memorial outside the church (ibid.)

156. The memorial of the Murambi Technical School, in which dozens of corpses are laid out in a series of classrooms, is discussed in chapter 6.

157. The website for the Kibeho sanctuary states categorically that the 1995 massacre occurred "on the esplanade, where the apparitions had taken place, when people [robbed] of their homes took refuge in Kibeho." See http://kibeho-sanctuary.com/index.php/en/apparitions/overview, accessed January 14, 2015; its open claim on this controversial event raises multiple questions. See O'Halloran 2010 for photographs of the Kibeho IDP camp that show a small church—apparently an earlier version of the Church of Our Lady of Sorrows—positioned as a central landmark in the IDP camp (131); the parish church is also seen in the background (136, 138). A map situates an unnamed church as adjacent to the actual massacre site in the camp (151).

158. See, for example, Wikipedia, "Our Lady of Kibeho," available at https://en.wikipedia.org/wiki/Our_Lady_of_Kibeho, accessed September 14, 2015. The source for this piece of information is a relatively obscure article about the making of the documentary about Kibeho that Ilibagiza coproduced, which states only that "[Mukangango] would later be killed in the massacre at Kibeho in 1995" (Lois Rogers, "Our Lady of Kibeho," *Monitor* [Trenton, NJ], January 20, 2012). I suspect that the writer is simply confusing the two massacres; this piece of information is not based on an original investigation. The Kibeho website is more thorough but also contains shades of ambiguity. After explaining that Mukangango lived in Kigali with her husband, it goes on, "They were caught off guard by the genocide of 1994. Together with many other war displaced, they were taken towards Byumba, which was supposed to be a secure zone. There, a great number of unarmed civilians was slaughtered. The exact date and circumstances of their death are not (yet) elicited. Witnesses say that Marie Claire was killed in an attempt [to] defend or to find her husband kidnapped and lead [sic] together with other victims to an unknown destination" (http://kibeho-sanctuary.com/index.php/en/apparitions/visionaries, accessed September 14, 2015). This particular explanation is echoed in Ilibagiza's version described below, albeit in truncated form.

159. Ilibagiza 2008b, 176.

160. Ilibagiza and Bloomfield 2011. The documentary, *If Only We Had Listened*, was broadcast on EWTN on November 28, 2012, and on the Catholic TV Network on February 9 and February 12, 2014.

161. ter Haar 2003, 419.

162. See Gwendolyn Driscoll, "An Evangelical Explosion," *Orange County Register*, December 17, 2006; Stephanie Agletti, "Evangelism Booms, Catholicism Suffers in Post-genocide Rwanda," *Independent*, April 19, 2014; and Craig Nelson, "Washed in Blood," *Atlanta Journal-Constitution*, April 24, 1994.

163. Segatashya is perhaps the most readily interpreted as Tutsi because he was shot by a death squad during the genocide; even in Ilibagiza's book dedicated to Segatashya, though, she does not identify his ethnic background (Ilibagiza 2011). This evasiveness follows a certain precedent; Gabriel Maindron (1984) and Augustin Misago (1991) similarly avoid references to the ethnicity of the visionaries in their accounts of the apparitions.

164. Ilibagiza 2008b, 177.

165. Ibid., 204. A cheerful photo of Ilibagiza and Misago also appears in Ilibagiza 2008b (photo insert) as another mark of her endorsement of Misago.

166. Ibid., 71.

167. Ilibagiza and Bloomfield 2011. In *Our Lady of Kibeho*, she quotes Misago as telling a crowd of approximately fifty thousand worshippers who were celebrating the twenty-fifth anniversary of Mary's first appearance at Kibeho, "Our Lady of Kibeho is a beacon of hope, a light for all of Africa and the world!" (2008b, 182). In light of the regularity with which Rwanda has been called a "beacon of hope," the wording is especially evocative.

168. Ilibagiza 2009, 117. Unlike her previous books, this book was not published by Hay House; instead, it was published by a Catholic publishing house, Ignatius Press.

169. Ilibagiza and Bloomfield 2011.

170. Ilibagiza 2009, xix.

171. Gourevitch 1998, 187–188.

172. *Rwanda's Untold Story*, BBC Two, 2014. The opposition party RDI-Rwanda, founded by former prime minister Faustin Twagiramungu, posted the documentary to Vimeo in 2014 (http://vimeo.com/107867605, accessed August 3, 2016).

173. Gerard O'Donovan, "This World: Rwanda's Untold Story, BBC Two, Review—'Intense,'" *Telegraph*, October 1, 2014.

174. "'Angry' Rwanda Protest against BBC Documentary on 1994 Genocide," *BBC Monitoring Newsfile*, October 22, 2014; Stephen Rwembeho, "Anti-BBC Demos Spread to Countryside," *New Times*, November 10, 2014; Dugald Baird, "Rwanda Bans BBC Broadcasts over Genocide Documentary," *Guardian*, October 24, 2014. The petition is available at https://www.change.org/p/bbc-trust-bbc-trust-should-apologise-to-the-rwandan-people-over-rwanda-the-untold-story-documentary, accessed January 5, 2014, at which time it had gathered a relatively paltry 826 supporters. (The petition closed with 829 in total.) See also "BBC Genocide Film—Protest Letter by 38 International Researchers and Historians," *New Times*, October 15, 2014; and "Genocide Survivor Organisations in Rwanda Outraged by BBC This World Genocide Denial Film," October 3, 2014, http://www.kwibuka.rw/bbc-genocide-denial-film, accessed January 5, 2015. See Reyntjens 2015 for a thorough discussion of the aftermath of the airing of the documentary.

175. O'Donovan, "This World: Rwanda's Untold Story."

176. Paul Kagame, "President Kagame's speech at the 21st Commemoration of the Genocide against the Tutsi," Kigali, April 7, 2015, http://www.paulkagame.com/index.php/speeches/national-events/1513-president-kagame-s-speech-at-the-21st-commemoration-of-the-genocide-against-the-tutsi, accessed August 3, 2016.

177. On the Vimeo version, the documentary's discussion of Kibeho begins at the 32:42 mark.

178. Ibid. This statement is made at the 30:32 mark.

179. Stam and Davenport have made their findings available on their website, http://genodynamics.weebly.com/, accessed January 5, 2015. For criticisms of their work, see Marijke Verpoorten, "Rwanda: Why Claim That 200,000 Tutsi Died in the Genocide Is Wrong," *African Arguments*, October 27, 2014, africanarguments.org, accessed January 5, 2015.

180. Gourevitch 1998, 188–194. It is noteworthy that the Kibeho massacre is not mentioned in "BBC Genocide Film—Protest Letter by 38 International Researchers and Historians."

181. David Mwaniki, "A Tale of Two Genocides—and the Poor Attempt at Revisionism," *New Times*, October 14, 2014. See also Edwin Musoni, "BBC Documentary Targeted Person of President Kagame, Says Expert," *New Times*, November 22, 2014; this story was picked up by the BBC: "Ex-Journalist Says Archive Footage in BBC Film Was Doctored," *BBC Monitoring Newsfile*, November 22, 2014.

182. This statement occurs at the 34:30 mark.

183. Filip Reyntjens, "Rwanda's Untold Story: A Reply to '38 Scholars, Scientists, Researchers, Journalists and Historians,'" *African Arguments*, October 21, 2014, africanarguments.org, accessed January 4, 2015. See also Reyntjens, "'Rwanda: The Untold Story': Facts and Fabrication," *Open Democracy*, October 26, 2014, for a more sustained critique of Stam and Davenport's research. The three scholars are linked in Musoni, "BBC Documentary"; see also Andrew Wallis, "Rwanda's Untold Story: Questions for the BBC," *Open Democracy*, October 6, 2014, which dismisses Reyntjens as "a long-term advisor to Habyarimana . . . [who] has not been in Rwanda for twenty years."

184. Hall made these remarks in a promotional video about the play released by Signature Theatre, available at https://www.youtube.com/watch?v=_JVLzh4_NHk, accessed January 5, 2015. The production was directed by Michael Greif and ran from October 28 to December 14, 2014.

185. Michael Dale, "Our Lady of Kibeho Tells of a Holy Prelude to Tragedy," *Broadway World*, December 2, 2014. The quote appears only in the headline, not in the review itself.

186. Hall 2015, 90.

187. Ibid.

188. Charles Isherwood, "'Our Lady of Kibeho,' a Katori Hall Drama Set in the 1980s," *New York Times*, November 16, 2014.

189. Hall 2015, 76.

190. Ibid., 88.

191. My observations about the lobby display and the production are based on my attendance on December 6, 2014.

192. Although some of these audience members might have been expressing devotion to the Holy Mother through this moment of public display, I think that it is safe to categorize a typical off-Broadway audience as a relatively secular group. The Signature Theatre is dedicated to supporting the work of US playwrights of a wide range of aesthetic styles; it often devotes an entire season to a single playwright's work.

193. I should acknowledge that this story of Kibeho has an open-ended closure because the actors in *Our Lady of Kibeho* proceeded to undercut this moment of seduction in the curtain call. In response to widespread evidence of police brutality in the United States, the actors raised their arms in a gesture of solidarity with the late Michael Brown of Ferguson, Missouri. This gesture caused momentary confusion both for me and my companions since it mimicked the raised-arms gesture that occurred during the play as an expression of awe. The actors abruptly reminded the audience of the context of police brutality and racial oppression in a jarring, even Brechtian moment that counteracted the atmosphere of prayerful contemplation. Given that part of the US attachment to Rwanda stems from the need/desire to contain trauma in distant, "tiny" Rwanda, it seems painfully fitting that the cast undercut this attachment by reminding the audience of the precarity of safety and security for black and brown bodies "at home." My thanks to Jean and Brian Graham-Jones for their thoughtful remarks on the production.

4

REPETITION, RUPTURE, AND *RUINED*

Narratives from the Congo

In 2008, US playwright and feminist activist Eve Ensler, founder of the organization V-Day, penned a series of poems in reaction to the rape epidemic of the DRC. In her poem "Baptized," she commands her (western) readers to "think of your luxuries as corpses" and continues:

> Count the bodies
> 30 hacked children for Jed's new play station
> 20 tortured women so you can text photos from the party
> 50 amputated men, waving their missing limbs as sweet Andrew bounces his rubber ball.[1]

After linking electronic devices of the early twenty-first century to the suffering of Congolese women and children, Ensler abruptly takes a historical detour. The fifty amputees serve as a pointed reference to the Congo Free State, in which King Leopold II of Belgium ruled over the vast territory of the Congo River basin as his personal kingdom from 1885 to 1908. In the early twentieth century, the Congo Free State became notorious for the widespread brutality inflicted on the Congolese people to force them to gather wild rubber. The amputation of hands and feet was an especially notorious tactic; the "sentries" hired by the rubber companies, as well as members of the state army, cut off the hands and feet of living Congolese, supposedly to account for the use of bullets. The poem emphatically sutures the violence against Congolese civilians to the insatiable western hunger for material goods. Ensler's poem exemplifies her earnest determination to prod westerners into awareness of their complicity in Congolese violence—or, as she put it, "It isn't over there / The Congo / It's inside everything you touch or do / Or do not do."[2] Here, Ensler disdains subtlety and nuance. Readers of the poem are expected to plunge into the depths of consumer guilt and imperial shame as a prelude to their support for V-Day's advocacy for Congolese victims of sexual violence.

Ensler's sudden swerve from the contemporary moment to the historical is what catches my attention. The poem erases differences between western habits of consumption of the early twentieth centuries and those of the present; Congolese bodies and limbs simply continue to accumulate. This rhetorical gesture positions Congolese victimhood on a timeless continuum of "one hundred years of darkness," to borrow the title of Marcus Bleasdale's book, which uses quotations from Joseph Conrad's Heart of Darkness as captions for his photographs of the eastern DRC.[3] This historical move might seem justified in light of obvious parallels between the forced extraction of rubber in the Congo Free State and the exploitation of "conflict minerals" (primarily tin, tantalum, tungsten, and gold) from the eastern region of the DRC. In both cases, the so-called resource curse has exacerbated violence and mass death. John Prendergast of the Enough Project, a US-based organization that has spearheaded a conflict-minerals campaign, makes a similar move when he draws a connection between Enough and the Congo Reform Association (CRA), which famously sought to raise awareness about the horrific conditions of Leopold's Congo through an outpouring of lectures, books, and pamphlets. Prendergast boldly proclaims, "A century ago, thousands of people across the globe joined together in what became one of the 20th century's first great international human rights movements in protesting the bloody reign of Belgium's King Leopold II over the Congo.... A century later, the people of the Congo need a new popular movement to end the atrocities once and for all."[4] The implication, of course, is that the Enough Project will step in as the new CRA. Again, the move from the past to the present is seamless and abrupt in its erasure of the intervening years from 1908, when Leopold relinquished control of the Congo Free State to the Belgian parliament, to 1996, when Laurent Kabila led a rebellion against Mobutu's regime. The erasure of this multifaceted history, which includes the violence of Belgian colonialism, the struggle for independence, the tumultuous events that followed the achievement of independence in 1960, Patrice Lumumba's assassination, and the rise of Mobutu's regime, is, of course, blatantly colonialist.

One might argue, though, that this move is justified in light of scholarship that identifies strong continuities between the past and present of humanitarianism. In *Humanitarianism and Suffering*, Thomas Laqueur writes that "like violins in the age of Stradivarius, sad and sentimental tales as a form reached perfection very early in their history."[5] In the same volume, editors Richard Ashby Wilson and Richard D. Brown suggest that humanitarian campaigns have relied on a "proven method" of "arousing sympathy and awakening moral qualms, and connecting them to real and imagined self-interest," which has inspired "legions" of followers to answer the humanitarian call to ease distant suffering.[6] On a similar note, Peter Stamatov comments on "the remarkable persisting patterns that still continue to inform action on behalf of distant strangers," suggesting that these continuities help clarify "deeper causal processes and structures that cumulatively have shaped our current interest in distant people and our efforts to support and advocate their rights."[7] These threads of continuity in humanitarian discourse might justify a century-long leap from the CRA campaign against Leopold's "red rubber" to Enough's campaign against "blood minerals." Certainly, both have been startlingly effective at gaining international attention and advocacy; sensationalist imagery and narratives of Congolese victimhood dominate both campaigns in an attempt to shock outsiders into action. Perhaps the empire of trauma could be figured as an ahistorical force blundering its way from the early twentieth century to the present, with only slight changes in appetite as it moves from the consumption of male amputees to female rape victims.

But given the radically changed nature of empire in the twenty-first century, how could it *not* be different? Recall that Hardt and Negri insist on a rupture between the "old" empire, which relied on territorial expansion, clear hierarchies, and formal declarations of sovereignty, and the newer, slicker version that spreads its tentacles in postmodern, rhizomatic fashion. In a neoliberal age characterized by flexibility, mobility, and nimbleness, how has empire accordingly adapted? To follow Hardt and Negri's lead would perhaps emphasize the straightforward clarity of the CRA campaign, which sought to wrest territorial control of the vast Congo Free State from Leopold and hand it over to the Belgium government as a legitimate colony. In contrast, the conflict-minerals campaign takes a subtler approach in which it seeks to instill a collective sense of shame. The catchphrases that have sprung up around the movement—"blood in the mobile," "blood on your laptop," "your cell phone, Congo's misery"—serve as graphic reminders that to go about one's daily electronic and social media activities is to be complicit in horrific violence.[8] These media catchphrases reassure ordinary westerners of their soft power and ethical selfhood through the inculcation of shame.

This chapter explores repetitions as well as ruptures. In an oft-cited essay, "An Acoustic Register, Tenacious Images, and Congolese Scenes of Rape and Repetition," Nancy Rose Hunt juxtaposes images and narratives of suffering of the Belgian Free State to those of the current violence in the eastern DRC. She aims at a nuanced "tethering" of the past to the present in order to "interrogate the nature and modalities of spectacular violence among Congolese people," not in order to make historical connections but to help "sort the debris."[9] In order to pursue repetitions and discontinuities across these two humanitarian movements, I consider how the demands of capital shape the images that are available for empire's consumption. In particular, I find that the campaigns against red rubber and blood minerals operate in tandem with the gendered politics of labor. Changing preferences for Congolese "poster children" are linked to shifting concepts of productivity.

This chapter lingers on the present moment. The discussion of the Congo Free State is meant primarily to set the stage for an analysis of the Enough Project and V-Day campaigns to end sexual violence and the trade in conflict minerals. My emphasis on the present-day conflict is extended in the final section, in which I address Lynn Nottage's 2009 play *Ruined*, a critically acclaimed and commercial success. After its off-Broadway run, the play went on to become one of the most produced plays in US regional theatre in the 2010–2011 season; at the time of this writing, it continues to appear regularly on professional and university stages.[10] Although *Ruined* perpetuates certain narratives of what Jason Stearns, borrowing from Binyavanga Wainaina, calls "How Not to Write about the Congo," the play takes a cue from neoliberalism and is not nearly as predictable as one might assume.[11] Ultimately, it untethers the colonial past and exposes the workings of the trauma market. To return to Ensler's poem, the Congolese characters count their own bodies and rewrite the equations of pain.

Red Rubber and the Aesthetics of Victimhood

The figure of King Leopold dominates historical narratives of the Congo Free State.[12] Certainly, a Leopold-centric narrative has the advantage of establishing a clear villain in a sordid tale. As was addressed briefly in chapter 1, the Congo Free State was conceived through King Leopold II's behind-the-scenes machinations to gain control of ten million acres of land, which he ruled as

IN THE RUBBER COILS.

Scene—*The Congo "Free" State.*

Fig. 8. *Punch* cartoon by Linley Sambourne, November 28, 1906. Courtesy of *Punch*.

his personal domain. The Congo Free State became synonymous with brutality in light of the harshness of the quota system and the forced labor imposed on the local population in the gathering of wild rubber; it is believed that millions of deaths resulted from a combination of direct and indirect repercussions of Leopold's rule. In a 1906 *Punch* cartoon, "In the Rubber Coils: Scene—The Congo 'Free' State," Leopold is portrayed as a hybrid of a rubber vine and a python that has entrapped an adult African male in his lengthy coil. Although his muscular victim strains mightily against his bonds, the malevolent Leopold beast, looming over the victim's exposed throat, is overpowering and heartless. In the background, a woman clutching an infant has attempted to flee the scene; however, she has turned back to look, and she seems frozen with fear in midstride. This prescient detail indicates the waves of violence that encompassed Congolese women, men, and children in the wake of Leopold's greed.

The actual violence was carried out by microvillains. Gathering rubber, a labor-intensive process that required the tapping of rubber vines that reached upward at least a hundred feet, was perceived as men's work, and local Congolese males were widely conscripted as sources of labor. In order to "encourage" the gathering of rubber, Leopold's Force Publique soldiers and local sentries hired by the rubber concessions attacked villages and held relatives hostage until quotas had been satisfied. Whipping, hanging, shooting, and the severing of hands also served as notorious tactics of control.[13] Although European officers regularly participated in the atrocities, the sentries were often depicted in the humanitarian literature as the sine qua non of savagery.[14] Testimonial evidence of their actions evokes a macabre déjà vu when it is read alongside much more recent accounts of sexual violence in the eastern Congo; cannibalism, torture, and sadism were endemic regardless of the gender or age of the victim. Joseph Conrad, who first visited the Congo Free State in 1894 as the commander of a steamboat, published *The Heart of Darkness* in 1903 as an anguished response to the atrocities he witnessed. In a fascinating portrayal of the complexities of empire, the character Marlow describes European imperialism as a kind of "flabby, pretending, weak-eyed devil of a rapacious and pitiless folly."[15] Like the *Punch* cartoonist, Conrad summons the image of a monstrous creature in an effort to capture the horror of the Congo Free State. In Conrad's rendering, though, the beast is "flabby" and "weak-eyed" rather than invincible. Its rapaciousness is perhaps its undoing.

Enter an army of British heroes to fight the Leopold beast. Historical narratives have long emphasized the starring role of two British men, Edmund Dean Morel and Roger Casement, in the struggle against Leopold's rule.[16] As early as 1890, Morel, who was a shipping clerk for the Liverpool company Elder Dempster, began publishing anonymous attacks on the Congo Free State.[17] A growing chorus of concern, in which Morel was an especially insistent and passionate voice, achieved concrete action in 1903 when the United Kingdom sent British consul Roger Casement to investigate. Casement submitted his detailed report, which included lengthy passages from Congolese testimonies, in February 1904; the very next month, as a result of prior conversations between Morel and Casement, the UK-based Congo Reform Association was established with Morel as its secretary. In late 1905, another report, reluctantly commissioned by Leopold in the face of mounting pressure, confirmed much of Casement's report. By December of the following year, Leopold agreed to Belgian annexation of the Congo Free State, although the actual transfer of power did not take place until mid-1908. By 1913, after a series of reports on the apparently improved conditions in the renamed Belgian Congo, the CRA declared victory and dismantled itself. Scholars have lauded Casement and Morel's work as an example of nascent human rights advocacy; for example, Sharon Sliwinski proclaims that both Casement's report and Morel's writings "offer a complex indictment that can be regarded as a forerunner to the work of present-day humanitarian groups such as Human Rights Watch and Amnesty International."[18] An obvious caveat about this celebratory narrative is that Casement and Morel were hardly advocates of Congolese self-governance. They perceived Leopold's rule as an aberration that would be set to rights by Belgian trusteeship and thus were fully invested in the trappings of European colonialism.

More recently, the cast of heroes has broadened to include Protestant missionaries.[19] Although individual missionaries, particularly Baptists from the United States, spoke out against the abuses of Leopold's regime as early as 1890, protests grew in strength as Leopold's regime sought to "stifl[e] their work of proselytization" through intimidation and exclusion.[20] The CRA included Grattan Guinness, a leader of the Congo Balolo Mission (CBM), at the helm; he had reluctantly joined forces with Morel in light of Leopold's continued resistance to the expansion of the Protestant missions.[21] The uneasy alliance between Morel and Guinness was formed because although Morel distrusted the missionaries' religious agenda, he was eager to take advantage of their wide audience appeal. In 1904, two CBM missionaries, John and Alice Harris, who were based at a station in Baringa in present-day Équateur Province, began to send accounts and photographs of Anglo-Belgian India Rubber Company (ABIR) atrocities to Morel, who published them in the *West African Mail*.[22] After they returned to England in 1905, the Harrises delivered "Congo Atrocity Lectures," in which they presented "magic-lantern" slides of their photographs, displayed whips made of hippopotamus hide commonly used by the Force Publique, and sang hymns. Their role in the London auxiliary of the CRA was formalized in 1906 when they became the joint organizing secretaries. Indeed, the Harrises became the public face of the campaign; from October to December 1907, they gave over fifty public appearances, in contrast to Morel's fewer than fifteen.[23] Tensions between John Harris and Morel eventually came to a head, and the Harrises departed from the CRA in 1910.[24]

Among these missionaries, Alice Harris has increasingly moved into the limelight.[25] Although she rarely received credit during her lifetime, many of the best-known atrocity photographs are generally believed to be hers.[26] These photographs appeared in pamphlets, books, and newspaper articles and most famously in the magic-lantern lectures, in which slides of atrocities were projected. The Harrises became especially well known for their lectures on the Congo atrocities, of which they presented over three hundred in 1906 alone.[27] To help keep up with the demand, sixty slides and the text of their lecture were marketed as a package, "Lantern Lecture on the Congo Atrocity," to encourage other activists to speak in support of the movement.[28] Scholars frequently comment on the revitalizing role that the images and the atrocity lectures played in the faltering Congo reform campaign; for example, Hunt notes that "Harris' photographs and the magic lantern shows ... enabled Morel's relentless humanitarian propaganda machine to gather force and move an ever-larger British and North American public."[29] In order to demonstrate the impact of the photographs, scholars of the campaign consistently invoke Mark Twain's harangue against the Congo Free State, *King Leopold's Soliloquy*, which he published in 1905 in order to express his support for Morel's cause. Writing in the first-person voice of a petulant King Leopold, Twain rails against the "incorruptible kodak," which he calls "the only witness ... that I couldn't bribe."[30] This quotation is ubiquitous in the scholarly literature as evidence that the photographs facilitated or even caused Leopold's loss of the Congo.[31]

A sizable category of these photographs depicts mutilations or amputations of limbs, which serve as iconic representations of Leopold's cruelty.[32] The victim is commonly wrapped in a white cloth against which his (or, much less often, her) mutilated arm can be clearly displayed, a trope that "reif[ies] a notion of a maimed, disfigured, individualized body" because the photos are cropped to foreground the victim's isolation.[33] Occasionally the hand is maimed from gunshot wounds; these photos, however, are not reprinted nearly as often as the more graphic documentations of amputation. Hunt dismissively summarizes these images as "a mute row of male atrocity victims with mere stumps for arms."[34] The photographs are indeed almost all of male victims, a pattern that could be chalked up to the relative lack of worth of female victims on the early twentieth-century humanitarian scale. That is, only males were deemed valuable enough to photograph, and the mutilated (or otherwise violated) women were relegated to the margins of media invisibility. To subscribe to this reasoning, though, would position the shift in focus to Congolese female victims that occurred a century later as a sign of teleological progress that equates visibility with worth rather than recognizing how visibility works in tandem with commodification, surveillance, and confinement. A more interesting question, to borrow from Rey Chow's reading of Deleuze, is, how might these photographs, and the CRA campaign more generally, speak to the complexity of the relations between the sayable and the visible?[35] What are the conditions of victimhood as perceived in the media glare of the early twentieth century?

Although other atrocities are also documented in the photographs, the photographs of amputees are ubiquitous in the CRA books, pamphlets, newspapers, and lecture slides.[36] The majority are drawn from a collection of about eight identified males, whose faces and names become familiar to those perusing the CRA reform literature. Four members of this group are young boys—Impongi, Epondo, Lokota, and Yoka—who look out at the viewer with expressions ranging from stalwart to forlorn and, in Epondo's case, even a bit mischievous.[37] Another subset of photos depicts two males, Mola and Ikabo, who appear to be older, perhaps in their late teens.[38] Finally, Lomboto and Isekausu (also called Isekansu) round out the cast of characters as two adult men who make regular (if less frequent) appearances in the CRA publicity materials.[39] Among all the named male victims, Impongi, who appears exceptionally young and vulnerable, is most frequently trotted out; he is unusual among the cast of victims in that he suffered the loss of both a hand and a foot.

The combination of his extreme youth and the double amputation undoubtedly contributed to his ability to serve as a "poster child" of the movement; the term, as explained by Robert Bogdan, was originally coined to refer to an ill or disabled child with a disease or disability whose picture was used by particular charities to encourage donations.[40] Unlike his fellow sheet-wrapped victims of amputation, Impongi wears a tailored white shirt and cutoff pants, which speak of his assimilation into European ways and thus might have increased his worth on the early twentieth-century trauma market.

Amid these boys and young men, Boali stands out as the only female victim in the entire corpus of atrocity photographs who bears the dignity of a name.[41] As a known female victim of sexual violence as well as mutilation, she has attracted considerable critical attention.[42] According to her testimony to the 1905 Commission of Inquiry, she lost her foot when she refused to submit to a sentry's demand for sex; he then shot her in the stomach and cut off her foot to steal her anklet.[43] Her haunting image, in which she looks out calmly at the viewer, holding a staff to keep her balance and clothed at the waist, appears with surprising frequency in the literature, such as the "Congo Atrocities" lecture, a 1906 issue of the *Graphic*, various CRA pamphlets, and Twain's 1907 edition of *King Leopold's Soliloquy*.[44] Her image is frequently paired with Impongi's, and I suspect that she achieved a level of fame equal to his. Whereas Impongi's mute innocence and properly clothed figure slide easily into humanitarian narratives, Boali's photograph "was an ambiguous, perhaps even troubling image" because her near nakedness and obvious strength serve as a rebuke to colonialist ideas of womanhood.[45] Impongi's overt innocence might have lessened any discomfort associated with her frank gaze. At the very least, Boali's quietly insistent presence in the publicity materials makes it difficult to dismiss the atrocity photographs as a homogenized portrayal of victimhood.

Perhaps, though, this seeming diversity of victimhood is meaningless because the colonial gaze infantilized all Africans as "childlike." Bogdan explains that "poster children" dominated charity fund-raising campaigns because images of children were deemed the most effective strategy, even when the condition or illness was primarily associated with adults, as in blindness or arthritis campaigns.[46] One might argue that all victimized Congolese, regardless of age, served as potential poster children. This perspective would also explain a famous montage of nine atrocity photographs that was reprinted in publications ranging from the 1905 edition of Twain's *Soliloquy* to Arthur Conan Doyle's 1909 diatribe *The Crime of the Congo*. Although this montage gestures to a curious egalitarianism of victimhood insofar as it contains photographs of four boys, two youths, two adult men, and one adult woman—almost as if the unknown creator of the montage deliberately sought broad representation—it is noteworthy that the victims are never identified in the montage. Individual names and stories are erased; they are significant only through their shared experience of acquired disability. They can be read simply as "children whose limbs have been cut off," according to a caption at Anti-Slavery International, even though the central photograph is clearly that of an older woman—the only other representative of female victims of mutilation in the entire CRA literature in addition to Boali.[47] Unlike the nearly naked, full-length shot of Boali, she is more demurely clothed in the usual white cloth wrapped around her torso. She looks at the photographer with weariness, as if she is tired of the entire atrocity business that effaces individual stories and complexity.

The "tenacity of the visual" tends to blot out the prodigious number of books and pamphlets that the CRA produced.[48] The plethora of texts helps clarify the significance of the sayable in tandem with the visible and suggests that adult Congolese men did indeed have a specific purchasing power in the Congo reform campaign. Although Morel himself became keenly aware of the value of the photographs—indeed, the publication and crediting of the photographs became a point of contention between Morel and Guinness, indicating that both men perceived their value—the collection of photographs was but one of many weapons in the CRA's arsenal.[49] Twain's fictional king does indeed complain about the "incorruptible kodak," but he also objects to the CRA pamphlets and Morel's *West African Mail*: "They write tons of these things! They seem to be always around, always spying, always eye-witnessing the happenings; and everything they see they commit to paper."[50] Leopold expresses annoyance about the pamphlets throughout the book, whereas his irritation at the photographs is confined to a single paragraph toward the end. It should be noted that many, if not most, of the CRA publications did not include photographs at all or included photographs that were not immediately identifiable as documentations of atrocity.[51] What is to be revealed if we avert our gaze from the visual archive of mutilation? What if I follow Hunt's lead and "push beyond the shock of the photographic that tends to blot out all else"?[52]

Many of these texts extol the morality of free labor. Just scratching the surface of Morel's writing reveals an intensity of rhetoric devoted to this topic as he relentlessly attacks the Congo Free State's reliance on forced labor. The

Belgian regime justified the use of forced labor as a disciplinary tool that would compel the "essentially lazy and indifferent" Congolese subjects to work; in response, Morel insisted that the native's ability to hire out labor for appropriate wages was a fundamental right and indeed a pillar of civilization.[53] On this front, Morel and the missionaries were in clear agreement because "no issue was of greater importance than labor."[54] To free the Congolese from forced labor would introduce Adam Smith's invisible hand of the market and allow the so-called savage to be "disciplined as both a producer and a consumer."[55] In order to refute the notion of the "idle native" on which the Belgian system of forced labor depended, Morel sought tirelessly to provide evidence of the Congolese subject's aptitude for work. He rhetorically asks in *The Tragedy of the Congo*, "Is the Congo native deprived of the commercial instinct commonly known to man?"[56] He proceeds to respond indignantly, "Certainly not," citing explorers and missionaries who testify to the natives' industriousness. He quotes, for example, the explorer Henry Morton Stanley's description of the Congolese as "keen, enterprising, high-spirited peoples" in 1884 arguing that the Belgian authorities abruptly changed their tune after 1903 in order to justify "a policy of wholesale robbery and enslavement."[57] Elsewhere, he resorts to ancient history to make his case, invoking accounts about the eagerness of West Africans to trade with the ancient Carthaginians as evidence of African commercial instincts that predated the Christian era.[58] He also draws on the British and French experiences in West Africa as evidence of the productivity of the "natives" in these contexts; the implication, of course, was that Leopold's mismanagement and brutality were to blame for failing to generate similar results in the Congo.[59] For Morel, the inherently productive Congo subject served as a linchpin in his thinking in order to justify the establishment of the free-trade and labor system, overseen, of course, by a benevolent colonial power.

Specifically, the productive Congolese was gendered as male. In the opening pages of *King Leopold's Rule*, Morel imagines an idyllic Congolese scene before European contact. As "the men-folk hunt or fish, weave mats, make knives, [and] work brass wire" and the children play, the women "attend to household matters" and "spend many an hour over the intricacies of their *coiffure*."[60] Again, he seeks to persuade the reader that Congolese men are intrinsically hard-working, whereas women and children fall neatly into seemingly preordained (western) roles. Although women receive an occasional acknowledgment of their protective role as mothers and their embodiment of the "noblest virtues of womanhood," women and children were usually linked as evidence of the state's depravity since neither group was spared from either forced labor or extreme physical violence.[61] The text of "The Congo Atrocities: A Lecture," which contained slides of both the child Impongi and the adult Isekansu, carefully differentiates between the two victims. When the lecturer projects the slide of Isekansu, the text of the lecture reads, "You will naturally be surprised to see men mutilated in this way, and of course it is not common. Men are too valuable to be damaged. You would never injure a workable machine!"[62] A few slides later, though, when the painfully young Impongi is shown with his missing foot and hand, the text is much briefer, noting only that the "poor lad" Impongi was only six or seven years old when he was "shamefully mutilated."[63] In Impongi's case, the crime is obvious, whereas Isekansu's atrocity needs to be explained. Each experienced a specific form of violence through the violent act of mutilation: Impongi lost innocence, and Isekansu lost the potential of productivity.

The rhetoric of labor informs my reading of the photographs, revealing motifs beyond that of mutilation and other overt manifestations of physical violence. CRA pamphlets or books regularly include images of a small group of Congolese simply looking at the viewer without any obvious signs of injury. Although these photos bear the markings of the quasi-ethnographic approach that was typical of colonial photography, the framework of atrocity adds a new slant.[64] The atrocity lay in their seeming paralysis and inability to serve as productive subjects. The women in Morel's "Wretched Mongo Women," a photograph of two women with quizzical expressions and elaborate scarification marks, are less wretched when they are perceived as examples of colonial anthropology. But once they are situated in *King Leopold's Rule in Africa*, they are cast in the role of victims, prevented from carrying out appropriate forms of female forms of labor, such as pottery and weaving.[65] In other words, these photographs mark a subtler form of "atrocity"—that of unproductivity, or what one might call laborlessness. Even those photographs that presumably capture them in the moment of forced labor are strangely marked by the absence of labor. A frequently printed photograph, for example, shows men holding empty baskets, ostensibly ready to collect rubber.[66] Again, this photograph is marked with motionlessness, a negation of potential.

Only the imposition of a kinder, gentler colonialism would restore these men to the status of "workable machines." In *Affairs of West Africa*, Morel serves up several photographs of well-run (that is to say, British) colonies in

Africa in which men are presented as hard at work, making palm oil, fishing, and washing rubber; these photographs capture the men in the moment of physical exertion rather than stillness.[67] Not to be outdone, supporters of Leopold's regime were also at pains to show photographs of men gathering and drying rubber.[68] One such photograph shows two men gathering rubber with relatively cheerful expressions. Clearly, they are thriving rather than suffering under King Leopold's hand, which is leading them to new heights of sustainable production.[69]

The attitude toward female labor was more ambivalent. In 1886, Francis de Winton delivered a paper at the National Geographic Society titled "The Congo Free State," in which he acknowledged a curious reversal of the labor of the sexes. The women "do all the hard work and the agricultural labour while the men look after the children and do what sewing is required."[70] Apologists for the Congo Free State went a step further; in their view, the women simply did all the work while the men lazed about.[71] Morel acknowledged the prevalence of this belief, noting that defenders of the Congo Free State "allege that in his natural condition, the native of tropical Africa is content to smoke and drink all day, while his wife labours."[72] To the European frame of mind, this pattern was clearly understood as an aberration from the natural order of the sexes. A similar sentiment can be discerned in the horror of the reformers toward the conscription of women as porters by the Congo Free State, which Alice Harris described as "the most revolting form of 'corvée' ever witnessed" in her pamphlet *An Appeal to British Women*; this particular outrage was ranked just after a lengthy description of how the women were raped and sold into sexual slavery.[73] Images of "appropriately" colonized Congolese women showcased them as practicing the domestic arts of sewing, weaving, and making pots, thus channeling their potential into Eurocentric categories of feminized labor.[74]

The final slides of the atrocity lecture present a textbook version of the gendered politics of productivity. In this section, titled "Philanthropy That May Be," the lecture narrative assures the spectators that happier conditions in the Congo would reveal the "keen, enterprising, high-spirited man Stanley described him to be" and goes on to project three slides of this enterprising Congolese male in action: "Natives Making Bricks," "Natives Making Palm Oil," and "Sawing Timber."[75] Then, the lecture provides a glimpse of the appropriately colonized Congolese female: "Schoolgirl's [sic] in Prize Dresses." The narrative explains that "the missionary offers clothes as prizes to the girls, and the girls eagerly compete for them."[76] It is noteworthy that the Congolese girls are not portrayed as sewing the clothes but simply as modeling them. These final images demonstrate a neat division of labor into the working male and displayed female as if to set right a world gone astray. This short series of slides provides a fitting prelude for the final image, "The Last Resort," in which a picture of a British warship suggests that military force might be necessary to allow these images of hard-working men and demurely clothed girls to prevail.[77]

In the end, the warship was not needed because Leopold finally capitulated to domestic and international pressure. The Belgian Congo was ushered into existence, and the CRA declared a successful close to its campaign in 1913. This celebratory account downplays the "enormous ideological and structural continuities" from Leopold's regime to the Belgian Congo.[78] The python might have been dispatched, but practices of forced labor continued, albeit in more subtle form. As the value of wild rubber plummeted after 1910, the Belgian colonial administration increasingly embraced the potential of copper, gold, and diamonds as a new means of turning a profit; plantations of coffee, tea, quinine, and cotton were also established as a source of income.[79] Its master plan was stymied, however, by the sustained refusal of its Congolese subjects to enter colonial wage systems of labor in the mines and the plantations. As Julia Siebert explains, Congolese had developed a profitable trade and agricultural economy of their own and disdained the poor wages, dangerous working conditions, and isolation from family that the colonial system provided as an alternative. In order to combat a severe labor shortage, subtle and not-so-subtle forms of forced labor developed in the 1920s, ranging from the use of the whip to tricking illiterate villagers into signing contracts.[80] The racist stereotype of African laziness was again invoked in order to justify the intensity of the violence.[81] The inclusiveness of the forced-labor policies erased distinctions of gender and age; men, women, and children were all forced to work the plantations, build infrastructure, and dig for minerals. Like the Belgian Free State, the Belgian form of colonialism practiced an all-inclusive form of colonial exploitation. Meanwhile, the colonial administration continued to churn out images of sewing women and men laboring in the mines in order to celebrate its progress in civilizing the recalcitrant natives.[82]

Before I consider repetitions and continuities of the "red rubber" campaign in today's conflict-minerals campaign, the most famous photograph in the entire campaign should be addressed. This photograph, taken by Alice

Fig. 9. Nsala of Wala. 1904 photograph by Alice Harris. Courtesy of Anti-Slavery International.

Harris, depicts a father named Nsala seated on her veranda, staring at a small hand and a foot, the only remains of his young daughter who had been killed and eaten by the ABIR sentries who attacked his village. Compared with the shock value of the mutilation photographs, the subject material of this photograph is subdued; it is not obvious that the two objects that captivate Nsala's, and thus the viewer's, attention are human remains. Like the image of Boali, this image has attracted considerable scholarly attention; its measured composition, for example, has raised speculation that Harris staged the photograph for maximum viewer effect.[83] What strikes me, though, is the portrayal of grief. Judith Butler's famous question "What makes for a grievable life?" is pertinent here in light of the sustained dehumanization of the Congolese that the CRA was attempting to refute. As Butler explains, "If a life is not grievable, it is not quite a life; it does not qualify as a life. . . . It is already the unburied, if not the unburiable."[84] The onslaught of publications and photographs could be understood as a sustained effort to convince readers and auditors that Congolese lives were, if not grievable, perhaps pitiable; at the very least, they were worth a modicum of emotional and financial investment. But the photograph of Nsala raises a different question: what makes for a grieving life? Again, the photograph is one of stillness; in this context, though, stillness conveys dignity. Grief, Butler reminds us, is fundamentally nonproductive; one cannot apply oneself to the task "and endeavor to achieve the resolution of grief."[85] Instead, "one finds oneself fallen."[86] The photograph adds nuances of victimhood beyond that of helplessness or laborlessness insofar as it reminds the viewers of the intricate networks of community and family to whom Nsala is attached and in which he is undone. Nsala dwells in grief. The photograph serves as a powerful testament that his daughter possessed an inestimable worth that exceeds and predates the crudeness of imperialism and colonialism. His grief makes the narrative falter.[87]

This discussion sets the stage for an exploration of the circulation of victimhood in the late twentieth and early twenty-first centuries. Although the campaigns of "red rubber" and "blood minerals" are easily fused in today's humanitarian discourse, the machinery of what Butler calls "derealization," the stripping away of the realities of other lives, is far more efficient today.[88] Congolese men exist not to be grieved or even pitied but only to be demonized as perpetrators, whereas the NGO gaze has settled its sights on Congolese women as the new "workable machines." In contrast to Conrad's day, empire is no longer flabby.

Neoliberal Poster Children of the DRC

A century later, the Leopold python has become a multiheaded hydra; the singular villain has spiraled into multiple insurgency and counterinsurgency groups. In 2003, the International Rescue Committee (IRC) published a report that calculated that 3.3 million "excess deaths" occurred as a result of the conflict from 1998 to 2002, most of which were due to preventable and treatable conditions, such as malnutrition and increased rates of disease, rather than direct violence; the death toll was raised to 5.4 million in 2007.[89] The report included the lengthy statement that "it is believed that the death toll from the war in the DRC has exceeded that of the Biafran conflict as the highest death toll ever attributed to a war in Africa, or indeed anywhere in the world since World War II."[90] This sentence was quickly condensed to the catchy soundbite "the deadliest war in the world since World War II."[91] From CNN to Slavoj Žižek, this statement has been repeated like a mantra.[92]

In the battle of catchphrases, "the rape capital of the world" has edged out "deadliest conflict."[93] Despite the IRC's insistence on the impact of structural violence on the escalating carnage, and its particular impact on children, the female victim of sexual violence has taken center stage. Maria Ericksson Baaz and Maria Stern theorize this singular obsession as a classic example of the "othering" of Africa; they draw on Trinh T. Minh-Ha's work to observe that Congolese women are appropriated as "'private zoos' . . . as objects whose sufferings are there to be consumed by a Western audience."[94] Séverine Autesserre goes a step further and suggests that the notion of rape as "the ultimate violation of self" generates considerable emotional impact among westerners.[95] She explains, "The narrative resonates with audiences from all nationalities, as sexual abuse takes place everywhere."[96] This dynamic of identification resonates, for example, in the acclaimed 2007 documentary *The Greatest Silence*, in which filmmaker Lisa Jackson, herself a survivor of gang rape, was moved to make a film about Congolese rape survivors as a gesture of solidarity. Similarly, Ensler, also a survivor of sexual violence, has vividly described her identification with Congolese women.[97] This singular focus could lead to coalition-building strategies that undo the tired binary of what Gayatri Spivak calls the "fitter Self" from the north and the "victim other" from the global south.[98] As persuasively articulated by Baaz and Stern, though, this singular focus on the damage of rape nullifies the complicating factors of insecurity, economic inequality, and structural violence in which sexual violence is inextricably caught. It also erases the shocking extent to which Congolese boys and men have been traumatized and killed: "The visitor/spectator is there to attend to stories about the woman's rape . . . not to the killing of her son or her husband."[99]

The international gaze registers the son or husband only if he committed rape or carries a gun. To return again to the *Punch* cartoon, the youthful, muscular man struggling against King Leopold has become pigeonholed as the perpetrator, and the young woman in the background has taken center stage as a victim awaiting humanitarian aid. In Ensler's poem quoted in the introduction to this chapter, it takes fifty men from the Congo Free State to equal the horror of twenty women in the present; the children fall somewhere in between. Even the children who blithely consume the products from the DRC and thus are complicit with the body count are gendered as male ("sweet Andrew" and Jed). Although Ensler's vivid imagery and lack of subtlety make her perhaps a too-obvious example of how Congolese men are derealized, she is only a single thread in a widespread pattern of media stereotypes.[100] The female rape victim has become the new poster child of Congolese victimhood.

To enhance her photogenic appeal, she also suffers from traumatic fistula. Although obstetric fistula, a hole in the birth canal caused by difficult labor that can lead to incontinence, occurs throughout the developing world, the term "traumatic fistula" refers to a hole between the vagina and bladder or rectum that is caused by especially violent forms of rape. The translation of sexual violence into a physical wound requiring medical intervention expands on Miriam Ticktin's useful argument about the medicalization of rape in discourses of war: "Medicalisation has allowed the victim of sexual violence to be cleaned up—to be rendered palatable, legitimate, even sympathetic. She becomes another suffering body, someone innocently infected with HIV/AIDS, the passive victim of war, of sexual harm. Sex here is a medical issue, about disease and survival. She is a patient, seen in isolation from other injustices or forms of exploitation, and she requires care, not justice."[101] Although Ticktin does not comment specifically on traumatic fistula, her ideas clarify the "need" for fistula in order to "clean up" the Congolese woman.

This curious need predominates in Ensler's video poem "Fistula," which provides a voyeuristic, arguably obscene, gaze for the western feminist viewer as the camera depicts an operation on a Congolese woman for fistula. Footage of the operation is intercut with the lines of Ensler's poem, which emphasize the dimensions and facticity of the wound: "During the operation I looked inside her / and saw the hole/in the lining / it was undeniable . . . it was almost a perfect circle / the size of a quarter maybe / too big / to prevent things from getting in / to keep things from falling out."[102] In this context, rape is directly translated into an "undeniable" physical wound requiring surgery, and thus the medicalization of rape par excellence has occurred. The implication, of course, is that rape alone is not enough to wrench Congolese woman out of the quagmire of invisibility; their vaginas must be mutilated in order to give these women sufficient gravitas.

Ensler works tirelessly on behalf of Congolese rape victims. Her work as a playwright on *The Vagina Monologues*, which premiered in 1996, inspired her to found the organization V-Day, a global activist movement to end violence against women, in 1998.[103] In 2007, the violence in the eastern DRC caught her attention, and she assumed a leadership role in the US-based movement to end what she called "femicide."[104] She championed the work of Panzi Hospital in Bukavu, where gynecologist Denis Mukwege operates on women suffering from fistula; in 2009, she traveled throughout the United States with Mukwege on a "Turning Pain to Power" tour to raise further awareness.[105] In 2011, she went a step further with the opening of the City of Joy, also in Bukavu, which serves as a safe space for sixty to ninety survivors of sexual violence through a six-month program. A page on the City of Joy's website is devoted to explaining how the center stands apart from the usual patronizing approach of humanitarian aid: "It does not use a sponsorship model, and it does not view the women it serves as individuals that need to be saved; rather, the City of Joy aims to provide women with the opportunity to heal and redirect themselves *in a community, on their own terms*" (emphasis in the original).[106] Healing is achieved through a range of activities and programs, including self-defense, agriculture, computer literacy, and theatre arts. This training, explains the website, helps the participants be "vagina warriors," and these warriors will leave the City of Joy with the capacity to become leaders in their communities.[107] The *Guardian* enthused, "Their big idea is not aid, but empowerment. If we accept that rape is a violent expression of the power imbalance between men and women, then you prevent rape by helping women get more power."[108] Curiously, the article champions this approach as a version of "Congolese feminism" despite its origins as a US-led intervention and the clear western bias inherent in the programming.[109]

Although Ensler is arguably the most prominent US activist working to "save" the Congo, the dashing John Prendergast is a close second. His organization, the Enough Project, was founded in 2007 with the aim of working to end crimes against humanity in Somalia, Sudan, the Central African Republic, and the DRC through lobbying US politicians and publishing reports.[110] He also regularly makes high-profile trips to these countries with celebrities such as Angelina Jolie, Don Cheadle, and George Clooney. My focus here is on Enough's conflict-minerals campaign, which originated in 2009 with the release of Prendergast's report "Can You Hear Congo Now? Cell Phones, Conflict Minerals, and the Worst Sexual Violence in the World." The report directly links western consumption of electronics to sexual violence in the eastern region, as Prendergast straightforwardly explains:

> Armed groups from Congo, Rwanda, and Uganda finance themselves through the illicit conflict mineral trade and fight over control of mines and taxation points inside Congo. . . . But the story does not end there. Internal and international business interests move these conflict minerals from Central Africa around the world to countries in East Asia, where they are processed into valuable metals, and

then onward into a wide range of electronics products. Consumers in the United States, Europe, and Asia are the ultimate end-users of these conflict minerals, as we inadvertently fuel the war through our purchases of these electronics products.[111]

He identifies the key conflict minerals as the "three T's" (tin, tantalum, and tungsten) and gold and then reassuringly explains how to break this link: "It can be stopped by a combination of focused consumer pressure and enlightened government action. If women and girls are to be protected and empowered in Congo, one of the most important priorities is to end the deadly trade in conflict minerals. Take away the fuel and the violence will be much easier to end."[112] The campaign successfully advocated for a specific provision in the 2010 Dodd-Frank Wall Street Reform and Consumer Protection Act that required companies registered on the US stock exchange to certify to the Securities and Exchange Commission that their products did not contain conflict minerals from the DRC or neighboring countries.[113] Although this provision (section 1502) did not explicitly ban the use of conflict minerals, it sought to "name and shame" companies that were complicit in the conflict-minerals trade.

Ensler's and Prendergast's visibility and fame allow V-Day and the Enough Project to wield considerable influence in the shaping of US foreign policy.[114] In May 2009, Ensler and Prendergast served as panelists for a hearing of subcommittees of the US Senate Foreign Relations Committee on sexual violence in Sudan and the DRC.[115] Ensler opened the panel with a passionate appeal in which she included numerous graphic stories about Congolese victims of sexual violence and insisted that the DRC was the "worst" country in this regard. Her fervent emotion served as a foil for the calm and measured Prendergast, who concluded the panel with his customary equation of conflict minerals and sexual violence and urged support for the Congo Minerals Act (a forerunner to Dodd-Frank). Their ability to toe the line of gendered behavior (the emotional Ensler versus the rational Prendergast) undoubtedly enhanced their legibility in the legislative sphere. The Sudanese and Congolese female activists who appeared on the panel were sandwiched between Ensler and Prendergast, who acted as bookends for the panel in a mark of their authority.[116]

Whereas Ensler seeks to empower Congolese women, Prendergast aims to galvanize western consumers. Ensler recites litanies of horrors that the women endure; in contrast, Prendergast reassures his listeners of their collective ability to make a difference. At the Senate hearing, Ensler claimed that King Leopold's "terrible legacy of genocidal colonialism" was "now lodged in the DNA of the worst perpetrators" and thus seamlessly conflated historical context with a biological, inherent propensity to rape.[117] In contrast, Prendergast simply called attention to the advocacy movement that supposedly brought Leopold to his knees and thus appropriated the CRA movement as a symbol of hope.[118] This approach offers potential supporters a choice between the instant gratification of donating to the City of Joy and Panzi Hospital (in Ensler's case) and a relatively sustained approach that includes writing to conflict-mineral campaigns, researching the list of companies provided on Enough's website, and making careful consumer choices (Prendergast's). To build on the ideas of Lilie Chouliaraki, these options dovetail with what she terms "the marketization of humanitarian practice" in offering consumer choice on how to achieve ethical personhood.[119]

At the same time, though, the Enough Project and V-Day campaigns share the markings of neoliberalism through their emphasis on individual choice and empowerment. The political consumerism that underpins the conflict-minerals campaign has been thoroughly critiqued for its complicity in sustaining late capitalism. On the one hand, political consumerism can be linked to a version of civil society in which consumers are encouraged to intervene in the complexities of the global economy; on the other, it can "reduce local, national, and global processes to a simple producer-consumer dichotomy" in which "end-consumers appear as the only individuals with agency."[120] The agency of the western consumer can reach dizzying extremes, as articulated in Peter Eichstaedt's widely cited book *Consuming the Congo*: "Each time we use a mobile phone, use a video game console, or open a tin can, we hold the lives and deaths of the eastern Congolese in our hands."[121] One could become drunk on the implications of power that these mundane actions contain.

Ensler's rhetoric of empowerment also resonates with neoliberal ideology. In the City of Joy, rape survivors are separated from their home communities and subjected to a variety of intervention techniques in order to "turn pain to power." Thus the experience of rape becomes the trauma card that paves the way to economic development through the benevolence of foreign aid. Both NGOs and the women become complicit in what Baaz and Stern have called the "commercialization of rape," a system in which humanitarian organizations compete fiercely for funding for victims of sexual violence and in which the women "feel forced to present themselves as rape victims in order to gain access to basic services and assistance."[122] The plethora of humanitarian interventions offered to female rape survivors, such as medical care, school fees, microcredit, and housing, invites the question, "Are (raped) women rendered vehicles of *good* (Western?) governmentality?"[123] The "commercialization of rape" can also be understood as the "neoliberalization of rape" insofar as the sexually violated (and medicalized) Congolese woman is deemed suitable for a host of intervention strategies that will foster nimble, information-rich individuals who can move into the global economy, armed with their newfound vocational and literacy training provided courtesy of City of Joy.[124] It is also noteworthy how often Ensler assures her auditors of the resilience of Congolese women; speaking at the hearing of the 2009 US Senate Foreign Relations Committee, she passionately exclaimed that Congolese women "are simply the strongest, most gorgeous, resilient women in the world," as if to reassure the senators in the room that these women are indeed worth saving.[125]

This account of the blood-minerals campaign suggests a relatively cut-and-dried case of an empire of trauma. The ponderous beast's appetite might have altered slightly over the past century, moving from a taste for mutilated boys to one for sexually violated women, but in general, the narrative lends itself to a sense of continuity stretching over this period. In an article that compares the atrocity photographs of the Congo Free State with images of rape survivors in the eastern Congo, Aubrey Graham emphasizes this sense of continuity: "Where a white sheet was once used as a background in images portraying bodily mutilation, now the contrast is reversed—white medical gauze or bandages often signify the injury that lies beneath."[126] The woman with a traumatic fistula serves as the new poster child for humanitarian capital. Any sense of discontinuity between the two campaigns could be chalked up to neoliberalism and its discourse of individual empowerment. From a colonialist crusade against red rubber to a neoliberal campaign against blood minerals. From mutilated limbs to mutilated vaginas. Case closed.

But does neoliberalism fully explain dehumanization? The V-Day campaign is a blatant example of how Congolese men are homogenized as perpetrators through its rhetorical emphasis on "femicide," which forecloses the possibility of male victimhood and erases the thousands of boys and men who have been systematically tortured and/or killed by armed groups. Ensler also participates in this homogenizing move in her famous description of the eastern DRC as the "rape mines of the world."[127] This sensationalist phrase indicates that mining is inextricably sullied by rape; legitimate miners and mass rapists are tarred with the same brush. But the Enough Project also participates, more insidiously, in the derealization of Congolese men. The campaign's efforts to criminalize unregulated mining in the eastern DRC means that the miners (invariably perceived as male) are also criminalized.[128] Enough regularly emphasizes the role of forced labor of women and children in the mines; for example, its 2015 report "Grand Theft Global" explains, "It begins at mine sites, where armed groups and Congolese military officers control minerals through the use of terror and physical violence. Civilians, including women and children, are forced to mine for minerals, and those minerals are sold along trading routes that are controlled, taxed, and protected through the use of force and psychological coercion."[129] This seemingly logical argument excludes the crucial fact that small-scale mining is a primary form of income generation in the eastern DRC, where sustained conflict has made more traditional forms of livelihood, such as farming, untenable because of instability and displacement. In 2010, when the government of the DRC enacted a de facto embargo on mineral extraction from the eastern region in response to international pressure, as well as the Dodd-Frank legislation, the result was economic devastation and drastically decreased quality of life in many mining communities.[130] Such nuances are erased in Enough's depiction of these miners either as coerced women and children or as armed men seeking to exploit the mines.

The conflict-minerals campaign has generated an onslaught of criticism. Laura Seay, for example, points out that the notion that "cell phones=rape" is based on the assumption that sexual violence is most prevalent around unregulated mines, even though evidence strongly suggests that sexual violence is endemic in the DRC regardless of the proximity of mining, illegal or otherwise.[131] Autesserre, another outspoken critic of the conflict-minerals campaign, argues that its window-dressing approach not only ignores the root causes of the conflict (such as land disputes and structural violence) but also has "exacerbated the problems that they aimed to combat."[132] For example, she observes that attempts to regulate the exploitation of resources have enabled armed groups to strengthen their control over mines.[133] The intensity of the criticism of Dodd-Frank grew to the point that the Enough Project's campaign faltered slightly in 2014 as it sought to respond to critiques of the legislation.[134] In the

Repetition, Rupture, and *Ruined* | 185

end, though, its publication of "Grand Theft Global" in 2015 indicates that its customary narratives remained firmly intact.

Photographs generated and circulated by the Enough Project campaign reinforce these narratives. The work of photojournalist Marcus Bleasdale, a senior fellow of the Enough Project, is particularly pertinent to this discussion given that his photographs often appear in Enough's publications and websites, as well as in national and international publications. Many of his DRC photographs that are reprinted and circulated by the Enough Project fall into a categorical division between adult male perpetrators and female victims. In a 2014 TEDx talk about conflict minerals, he presented about a dozen photographs over the course of his lecture. Both the images and the text of the lecture reinforced the dominant narrative of the conflict-minerals campaign; images of child labor, soldiers, and female victims of sexual violence dominated.[135] In these iterations of humanitarianism, even the laborlessness that appeared in the photographs circulated in the CRA campaign has been disallowed. The stillness of the men in the atrocity photos from the Congo Free State gestures to a kind of potential that has yet to be realized; in the early twenty-first century, even the potential has been erased. Instead, the only labor that the adult Congolese male is allowed to perform is that of violence.

Certainly, a more diverse range of photographs exists. Bleasdale has published an extraordinary collection of photographs, *The Rape of a Nation*, which is dedicated to images of the eastern DRC. Aside from the problematic title, which invokes a metaphorical use of sexual violence that diminishes the specificity of the act of rape, the collection veers into surprising new territory with its depiction of Congolese people simply living their lives with all the dignity that they can muster. The book closes with a stunning series of six photographs that depict the death, burial preparations, and funeral of an eight-month-old girl named Sakura Lisi, who died of malaria.[136] Perhaps the most vivid photograph depicts Sakura's relatives washing her body for burial; the hands of Sakura's relatives and the streaming water surround her minute figure in a loving benediction and farewell. In addition to the sense of intimacy and nuance that pervade these six photographs, I am also struck by their captions, every one of which describes Sakura as the daughter of a miner.[137] For example, the photograph of the washing of her body is captioned as "The washing of the body at the burial of the eight-month-old Sakura Lisi, the daughter of a gold miner in Mongbwalu, northeastern Congo." Another photograph is

186 | Performing Trauma in Central Africa

Fig. 10. Burial of the daughter of a gold miner in Mongbwalu, northeastern Congo. Photo by Marcus Bleasdale.

described as "Parents say their final goodbyes at the burial of the eight-month-old Sakura Lisi, the daughter of a gold miner in Mongbwalu, northeastern Congo," which is followed by "Carrying the coffin to the grave at the burial of the eight-month-old Sakura Lisi, the daughter of a gold miner in Mongbwalu, northeastern Congo."[138] The repetition of "daughter of a gold miner" relentlessly inscribes her father into a landscape of loss. The final image of this series shows a grieving man standing in the deep grave looking down at the small wooden coffin; he is wiping his eyes. Although the caption does not identify his relationship to the infant, the man's profound grief is etched into the photograph and into the mind of the viewer. Here is the twenty-first-century parallel to Nsala; here stands a grieving life. The display of grief holds the viewer in thrall.[139] I only wish that he was named.

The usual culprit of good intentions, though, has curtailed the potential of Bleasdale's images. From 2009 to 2014, Enough partnered with a photography exhibit titled *Congo/Women*, which toured throughout the United States and Europe.[140] One of its earliest stops was the US Senate building, where it was displayed during the Foreign Relations Committee hearing on sexual violence previously described. This exhibit included thirty-seven photographs by Bleasdale, Lynsey Addario, Ron Haviv, and James Nachtwey to depict "the story of daily life in the Congo—political, economic, cultural, medical and personal."[141] In a sense, *Congo/Women* served as a modern version of the magic-lantern show. Instead of the spoken lecture that accompanied the lantern slides of the Congo Free State, the exhibit included a series of short essays that were displayed alongside the photographs, as well as captions for the images that sought to provide context for the grief and suffering. The exhibit also included eight color photographs of female suffering that had been enlarged to life size in an attempt to "increas[e] the visibility of conflicts—quite literally."[142] The haunting photographs are, as the website describes them, "gorgeously composed, highly aesthetic, and full of humanity."[143] The curators excluded some of the more sensationalistic photos from the photographers' archive, choosing those that endowed the women with a sense of dignity.[144] That said, the selected photographs betray a certain rigidity of categories because the Congolese subjects can be readily divided into (female) victims or (male) perpetrators. Only one photograph provides a glimpse of an adult male Congolese in the context of mining. This particular image (number 3), also by Bleasdale, depicts a gold miner in the northeastern region; the miner is looking off in the distance, seemingly dwarfed by the huge cliff that serves as a backdrop. Despite the apparent vulnerability of the miner in the photograph, the caption assures us that "most of these miners are combatants who exploit mineral rich areas through illegal exportation" and thus closes the door to further considerations of these men and their contribution to the Congolese economy.[145] Even more telling is how the curators framed the extraordinary image of the bathing of Sakura Lisi's body described in the previous paragraph. In the context of *Congo/Women*, the caption has been edited to read, "The body of eight month old Sakura Lisi is washed for burial. She died of anemia brought on by malaria, a preventable yet common affliction in a region with almost no healthcare."[146] The reference to Sakura as the daughter of a gold miner has been cut; a father's searing loss has been erased, and he is disallowed the humanity of grief. The sharply edited caption speaks of a refusal to acknowledge an expansive comprehension of the suffering and grieving that exceeds that of raped women and children. Although the dehumanization of African men is an old song, my point is to clarify its forcefulness. The complexity of Bleasdale's original photograph is chewed up and spit out, and its gorgeousness serves not to commemorate a father's child but rather to uphold narrative demands.

The exception helps prove the rule. In 2013, *National Geographic* devoted an extensive essay to the conflict-mineral campaign, "The Price of Precious," which included numerous photographs by Bleasdale along with an essay written by Jeffrey Gettleman of the *New York Times*.[147] In a seemingly surprising twist, the prose and several of the photographs depict Congolese men as workers rather than as perpetrators. The accompanying text describes this labor in colorful language: "The mountainside was crawling with young, hulking men wearing rags and headlamps, hammering, digging, shoveling, scooping, scraping, and hauling away every possible speck of yellowish cassiterite rock, or tin ore. Their cheeks bulged with chunks of sugarcane for energy."[148] These men, the article explains, worked at a mine at Nyabibwe, which is held up as an example of a properly regulated mine in which bags are labeled with plastic tags certifying that they are conflict free. I am reminded of the early twentieth-century photographs of laboring Congolese men who are allowed to exist only in the context of "legitimate" colonialism; here, though, they exist only when multinational mining companies properly regulate them.[149] In a context in which adult Congolese men are criminalized, only multinational corporations have the power to govern and humanize them.

One might argue that the forces of global capitalism are summoning women as a more easily exploitable labor force, newly groomed by the likes of humanitarian organizations such as the City of Joy. Images of productive eastern Congolese women thus serve as a nexus of humanitarianism and neoliberalism; they demonstrate the efficacy of NGO intervention and uphold the structures of late capitalism. This argument would dovetail with the much-heralded exploitation of female labor in the global economy, or what has been called the feminization of labor. As Pheng Cheah explains, "Female labor is preferred in export-oriented industries and newly established industrial zones because women workers are cheaper, and perceived as more flexible, that is, more subservient to managerial authority, less prone to unionization and easier to dismiss and replace, and because of their greater manual dexterity."[150] Men are thus excluded from the picture as a matter of economics. A reliance on female labor also sanitizes the practice of global capitalism because corporations can present their employment of women as a sign of their support for the worldwide advancement of gender equality.

Again, though, neoliberalism falters as an explanatory catchall. I find it curious that these images of productive Congolese women bear a striking resemblance to those of their early twentieth-century colonized counterparts.

In other words, they sew. Despite V-Day's emphasis on the computer classes and agricultural training that Congolese women receive at City of Joy, images of women with needle and thread dominate the website.[151] Similarly, the single photo in *Congo/Women* that exceeds the framework of female victimization depicts women who are busily sewing. This black-and-white photograph by Bleasdale, captioned as "Women in a church run a help center for victims of sexual violence," is cropped so that the central focus is on the women's busily sewing hands; the caption also firmly connects their labor to the humanitarian narrative of sexual violence.[152] I am aware that for women throughout Central Africa, vocational training in sewing is a greatly desired skill and can be seen as a potential livelihood. I am reminded, for example, of the female youth at A River Blue, an organization in northern Uganda described in the next chapter; these girls articulated a strong desire for their own sewing machines so they could help support their siblings. My point is that the prominence and repetition of the Sewing Woman as a complement to the Raped Woman in the midst of neoliberal rhetoric deserves further exploration.[153] The story of a downcast victim who has been rehabilitated into a smiling, active subject serves as a handy marketing strategy for all humanitarian organizations; what interests me is that the smiling, active subject is one who sews, knits, and weaves.

Hunt has commented on the implications of this image in a passage well worth quoting in full:

> But images of girls and women gathered in a Catholic, Caritas project are disconcerting. They are learning to sew. A few sewing machines suggest capital, a chance to learn an important money making skill alongside a technology that still costs dear. But these machines disappear quickly, and the dominant image becomes one of rows and rows of girls learning to embroider with needle, thread, and circular embroidery frame. This unsettling flashback to thousands of Belgian colonial domesticity training scenes, reinforces one more time an image of a Congolese woman as homemaker, helpmeet, dependent, and needy, obedient wife.[154]

Hunt interprets the Caritas project's reliance on this image as a manifestation of the colonial past, a remnant that explains limited roles for Congolese women beyond that of obedient, subservient wife and mother.[155] I would extend Hunt's observation and unpack further this stubborn colonialist throwback in the midst of lofty rhetoric regarding the empowerment of Congolese women. If men are deemed unproductive and women are allowed to be productive only in a domestic sphere, then all Congolese adults are excluded from participating in the global economy. Old-fashioned colonialism reigns in a pernicious example of the tenacity of the past.

So are we back to Laqueur's Stradivarius and the violins? Is this just a drawn-out iteration of the idea that *plus ça change, plus c'est la même chose*?[156] Am I suggesting that the easy conflation of the violence of today's DRC and yesterday's Congo Free State is justified? In a 2014 interview, James Ferguson expanded on how informal economies have displaced former ideas of wage labor in the developing world. After asking the rhetorical question "How do people make distributive demands if it is not in exchange for labor, that is, outside the traditional model of the labor market?" he suggests that one option is to make demands based on suffering or injury.[157] The sticking point is that in the DRC, this option is available only to women. Although Congolese men have also been raped, quite possibly in large numbers, their reluctance or refusal to come forward is invariably explained as the result of their sense of shame over their emasculation of manhood.[158] But in light of the increasing numbers of male rape victims who are coming forward in Kampala with the support of the Refugee Law Project, which has explicitly reached out to them through the provision of social services, perhaps Congolese men are not coming forward in the context of the DRC because they are savvy enough to know that their testimonies will not register.[159] Their testimonies are worthless as emotional currency because they cannot be exchanged for legal, reparative, or humanitarian aid.

At the Senate hearing in which Prendergast and Ensler testified, the *Congo/Women* exhibit was not the only artistic presentation of sexual violence in the DRC. Lynn Nottage's *Ruined*, which was then playing off-Broadway at the Manhattan Theatre Club, also made an appearance. At a reception that followed the panel, actress Quincy Tyler Bernstine, who played the character Salima, performed a monologue from the play.[160] This powerful monologue contains Salima's graphic description of how rebel soldiers murdered her infant girl and held her as a sexual hostage for five months; she returned home but was beaten and rejected by her husband. In addition to watching Bernstine's performance, audience members also heard remarks by photographers Bleasdale and Haviv and were invited to tour the exhibit afterward. Like the images in *Congo/Women*, Salima's monologue is horrifying but artistically wrought; for example, she describes one of the attacking soldiers as follows: "He was so heavy, thick like an ox and his boot was cracked and weathered like it had been left out in the rain for weeks. His boot was pressing my chest and the cracks in the leather had the look of drying sorghum."¹⁶¹ In the original script, the monologue is interspersed with supporting lines of dialogue from the character Sophie, who offers gentle reassurance and care as Salima works her way through her memories. At the reception, though, Sophie's character was excised from the script, and thus Salima was isolated and alone. This portrayal of her character resonated with the photographs of *Congo/Women*, in which the female victims of sexual violence are also depicted as isolated, with only dependent young children to keep them company. The seamlessness with which Salima's story of victimhood blended with the photographs reinforced the classic humanitarian narrative in which viewers are asked to step forward with assistance and, in this instance, legislation. The poetic imagery of the monologue and the powerful composition of the photographs added an aesthetic touch to the tales of horror that were shared in the actual hearing.

Nottage has often toed the line of the humanitarian narratives. *Ruined*'s emphasis on traumatic fistula dovetails with master narratives of Congolese violence. Indeed, Salima's final line, "You will not fight your battles on my body anymore," could have been borrowed from an oft-cited NGO report about sexual violence in the eastern DRC, "Women's Bodies as a Battleground," as if to strengthen the play's ties with dominant NGO rhetoric.¹⁶² When *Ruined* received the Pulitzer Prize for Drama, Nottage donated a portion of the prize money to Panzi Hospital,¹⁶³ and her suggested websites, included at the end of the published version of the play, include the Enough Project and V-Day. She also appears in Prendergast's *The Enough Moment* as one of "Congo's champions in the United States," and her statement follows the logic of the Enough Project's campaign: "Our silence on this issue means that every time we use our cell phones, we are inadvertently fueling a war that is being fought on the backs of women."¹⁶⁴ Furthermore, the play sidesteps controversial political territory. As discussed in chapter 1, it avoids naming Rwanda as one of the main instigators of the conflict in the eastern DRC, instead putting the blame primarily on Uganda.

Understood in its entirety, though, the play is a complex literary work that claims new ground for postcolonial identities. My analysis of the CRA, Enough, and V-Day campaigns helps clarify *Ruined*'s intervention in a colonial, humanitarian, and neoliberal imaginary. To return to Hunt's theories of historiography, the play does not simply sort through historical debris—it rejects it in a dramatic space-clearing move.

A Different Kind of Rape Story

Nottage has coined a strategic catchphrase to explain to the news media what she aimed to accomplish with her play *Ruined*. Whether speaking to Human Rights Watch, *The NewsHour with Jim Lehrer*, or Public Radio International, she explains that she wanted to "sustain the complexity of modern Africa."[165] With this phrase, she extricates herself from the legions of US writers and theatre makers who have diminished the continent's heterogeneity through stereotype, but she also reminds her auditors that the complexity is such that it cannot be captured but only "sustained."

Initially, Nottage planned to write an adaptation of Bertolt Brecht's classic antiwar play *Mother Courage* that would be set in the eastern DRC. Brecht's play, written in 1939, tells the story of the indomitable Mother Courage, who attempts to keep herself and her three adult children alive during the Thirty Years' War fought in seventeenth-century Europe. Although Mother Courage is indeed courageous in her quest for survival, the play also contains a harsh critique of her complicity in the economies of war. As a businesswoman who runs a canteen out of her wagon, she is determined not just to survive but also to earn a profit from the war. This determination leads to the deaths of all three of her children over the course of the play. Upon the death of her beloved daughter Kattrin, the third of her children to die, the play famously ends with Mother Courage taking up the wagon and resuming her quest for business: "I hope I can pull the wagon by myself. Yes, I'll manage, there's not much in it now. I must get back into business."[166] The play is also prescient in its implications of sexual violence; for example, Mother Courage explains Kattrin's muteness with the chilling statement that a "soldier stuck something in her mouth when she was little."[167] This statement appears in a scene in which Kattrin has just been assaulted and quite possibly raped: "There'll be a scar," Mother Courage laments, ostensibly referring to a wound on her head. "She needn't wait for peace now."[168]

Nottage has explained that she backed away from her original decision to write an adaptation of Brecht's play after listening to the testimonies of female refugees from the DRC, Sudan, and Somalia. In an interview with the *Guardian*, she states, "Almost all the women I interviewed had been sexually abused and assaulted in horrific ways. . . . [The women's] stories were so specific to Africa, and to that conflict, that the play had to be about them. I didn't need Mother Courage in the end. Theirs was the story that wasn't being told."[169] As the original source of inspiration, though, the legacy of *Mother Courage* lingers in fascinating ways. Mother Courage's dramatic parallel is Mama Nadi, who runs a bar and brothel in the Ituri rain forest that is patronized by rebel soldiers, government soldiers, and miners. Like Mother Courage, Mama Nadi serves all sides in the war in order to turn a profit and looks out for herself. As she explains to Sophie, "If things are good, everyone gets a little. If things are bad, Mama eats first."[170] Even Mother Courage's three children have Congolese counterparts: Salima, Sophie, and Josephine, the three women who work for Mama and depend on her for shelter, food, and clothing. (Although Mama Nadi makes several references to a total of ten girls who live at the brothel, only these three women appear in the action of the play.) Mother Courage's two male companions, Cook and Chaplain, have Congolese parallels in the characters of Mr. Harari, a Lebanese diamond merchant, and Christian, a local traveling salesman; both Harari and Christian seek to benefit from the war through their business dealings. In the opening scene of the play, Christian even sells Sophie and Salima to Mama Nadi as "two for the price of one."[171] Brecht's Marxist exposé of how war and capitalism intertwine resonates in Nottage's cynical portrayal of the human instinct to make a profit out of mass destruction.

Two primary shifts occur in Nottage's translation of Brecht to the eastern DRC. Brecht's subtle references to Kattrin's sexual trauma are put center stage; instead of muteness, Sophie suffers from traumatic fistula. In the opening scene, as Christian explains to Mama Nadi, Sophie has been "ruined" as a result of multiple rapes: "Militia did ungodly things to the child, took her with . . . a bayonet and then left her for dead."[172] Later in the scene, Mama Nadi underscores Sophie's physical condition: "It smells like the rot of meat."[173] The opening scene drives home the facticity of Sophie's disability, which promises to serve as a crucial narrative device in the unfolding of the plot. A second shift can be termed the sentimentalization of Mama Nadi. Unlike Mother Courage, who remains hard-bitten throughout the play, Mama Nadi becomes softer, more sentimental, to the extent of trying to pay for an operation for Sophie to repair her fistula. At the end of the play, she capitulates to Christian's gentle advances and allows him to kiss her. The two of them dance together in a moment of redemption that refutes the harsh cynicism of Brecht's *Mother Courage*, who pushes away her grief at the deaths of her three children and returns to pulling her wagon, still determined to capitalize on war.

It can be argued that the horror of the Congolese war has been sentimentalized and domesticated in order to "sell" the subject matter to western audiences. Indeed, despite its incessant references to maiming, murder, and rape, the play is surprisingly tasteful. As Ben Brantley of the *New York Times* puts it, *Ruined* is "a comfortable, old-fashioned drama about an uncomfortable of-the-moment subject."[174] Aside from Sophie's slight limp, for example, the medical symptoms of this condition—the leaking of urine and feces—are never shown on stage or even mentioned again after Mama Nadi's comment about the smell; even Sophie's limp became less pronounced over the course of the 2009 production that I saw at the Manhattan Theatre Club.[175] The play's portrayal of disability calls to mind David Mitchell and Sharon Snyder's concept of narrative prosthesis, in which disability "inaugurates the need for a story but is quickly forgotten once the difference is established."[176] Once Sophie's disability is well established, "difference is quickly nullified" in the narrative thrust.[177] In addition, the quasi-realistic format of the play domesticates and restrains the epistemic murk of the eastern DRC into a linear narrative, which, in the words of Michael Taussig, "flattens contradiction and systematizes chaos."[178] As pointed out by Jill Dolan on her *Feminist Spectator* blog, Mama Nadi's and Christian's romantic coupling at the end of the play "capitulat[es] to realism's mandate that narratives resolve with heterosexual marriage that solves everything." Mama Nadi and her girls "have been redeemed by a good man."[179] The ending also capitulates to a narrative of hope that Allen Feldman considers typical in stories of human rights violations, in which the "experiences of terror and abuse" are archived "as episodes scheduled for eventual overcoming through redemptive survival, recovery, and restorative justice."[180] A happy and tasteful ending prevails despite the extent of the hell that the characters endure. Indeed, one could arguably categorize the play as a sanitized representation of an intractable conflict that does little more than help your average privileged US spectator feel that she is assisting Congolese victims simply through her attendance. Heterosexist and ableist tropes serve as icing on the mainstream cake.

Ruined is a vexing play. In a thoughtful, persuasive analysis of the play's disability politics, Ann Fox writes of her initial negative response to the play: "Where friends who saw it were moved, I was angry: at the horrible violence against women, but also at the play's romanticized conclusion. Why would a work that had labored to expose the violence of a war fought for the economic gain of a mercenary few (and, thanks to the conflict minerals, our own ability to purchase cheap cell phones) become transformed in the end to an individuated, happily resolved love story?"[181] Here she refers to the denouement that marks Mama Nadi's capitulation to Christian's advances. Fox goes on to explain, though, that she "revisited the play over the coming months, not quite able to let it go," and concludes that the play's "representation of disability functions significantly as part of its political project, resisting the easy narrative closure of the ending."[182] She believes that Sophie, who watches as Mama Nadi and Christian dance, complicates the ending: "Sophie's body remains on stage in the play's final moment, still disabled. What has been done to her remains, and cannot be glossed over."[183] Like Fox, I believe that the ending exceeds a basic reiteration of heterosexual redemption. But in my interpretation, the ending contains a lesson in how to "work" an empire of trauma and use one's disability as a means of humanitarian currency. Ultimately, the play does indeed sustain complexity as it clears new ground in writing and performing the Congo.

Ruined articulates a rupture with the colonial past. The opening scene of the play evokes this past through Christian's presentation of Belgian chocolates to Mama Nadi; he hopes that they will soften Mama's resolve not to accept the "ruined" Sophie, who is revealed to be his niece.[184] He later explains how he became "stuck" with the chocolate: "Handmade. Imported. *Trés bon*. I hope you're impressed. A Belgian shopkeeper in Bunia ordered them. Real particular. I had a hell of a time trying to find these Goddamn chocolates. And then, poof, she's gone. And now I'm stuck with twenty boxes, I tried to pawn them off on Pastor Robbins, but apparently he's on a diet."[185] The Belgian shopkeeper has disappeared, leaving Christian to use the chocolates as a bargaining chip for his niece's safety. Later in the play, the dieting Pastor Robbins is dispatched even more brutally. His Protestant affiliation and Anglophone name call to mind the Protestant missionaries who attempted to reform Leopold's rule. Unlike the Protestant missionaries, who were lionized as heroes in the Free State campaign, Pastor Robbins is brutally executed and torn to pieces by government soldiers in retaliation for his providing medical care to rebels: "They cut him up beyond recognition. Cut out his eyes and tongue."[186] The news of his death, which occurs roughly in the middle of the play, generates the first real sense of fear in Mama Nadi, who "buries her face in her palms, overwhelmed."[187] The characters are pushed into new territory as the play jettisons the Congo's colonial past through the removal of these emblematic figures of commerce and Christianity.

Much of the plot revolves around a large diamond that has come into Mama Nadi's possession, which she keeps hidden away as her "insurance policy." As explained previously, diamonds served as a crucial export for the Belgian Congo and thus bear the legacy of "ordinary," legitimate colonialism, which, of course, depended on the violence of forced labor. By 1929, the Belgian Congo was the world's largest supplier of diamonds after South Africa; even today, the DRC serves as the third-largest exporter of industrial diamonds.[188] Like the Belgian shopkeeper and Pastor Robbins, Mama Nadi's diamond is abruptly removed from the world of the play when Harari steals it.[189] Again, Mama Nadi becomes temporarily unmoored as she must scramble for a new insurance policy in its absence.

Notably, she does not turn to NGOs for assistance. In the world of *Ruined*, humanitarian aid does not exist. In the third scene of the play, in an attempt to cheer up Salima, Sophie shows her a pile of cash that she has been stealing from Mama Nadi: "When there's enough we'll get a bus to Bunia."[190] Her reasons for wanting to go to Bunia are explained in a later scene, when Mama Nadi furiously confronts her about the stolen money. Sophie pleads in her defense, "A man that come in here said he can help me. He said there is an operation for girls. . . . He give [sic] me this paper."[191] This paper is hardly a ticket to an all-expenses-paid operation at Panzi Hospital; instead, it provides the name of a medical doctor who expects to be paid well for his services. In a turn of events that foreshadows Mama's growing sentimental streak, she conceives of the idea of using her precious diamond to pay for Sophie's operation. She urges Harari to take Sophie with him to Bunia and gives him Sophie's piece of paper: "It has the name of a man in Bunia, a doctor. . . . He won't trouble you with questions. . . . This [diamond] will raise enough money for an operation, and whatever she needs to get settled."[192] Even though the plan ultimately fails because Harari simply steals the diamond and leaves Sophie behind, it is noteworthy that hospitals such as Panzi that provide free operations for women suffering from fistula, championed by activists such as Ensler, are not even mentioned. Saviors such as Prendergast, Ensler, and Mukwege do not exist in *Ruined*. Even Mr. Harari's abrupt departure in an aid vehicle is symbolic of how humanitarian enterprises and theft can work in tandem.[193]

When aid organizations are mentioned, they are mocked as an option. When Mama Nadi learns of Sophie's medical condition, she scoffs, "I'm running a business not a mission. Take her to the sisters in Bunia, let her weave baskets for them."[194] As previously discussed, the ubiquity of sewing, knitting, and weaving Congolese women in the publicity materials of NGOs can be interpreted as the continuation of a Belgian colonial narrative in which sewing served as a hallmark of civilized (Christian) womanhood. Mama's statement evokes the Belgian colonial past, as well as the force of humanitarianism; she soundly rejects both. Similarly, Christian brushes aside Mama's suggestion that he take Sophie to the mission in Bunia, insisting that "here at least I know she'll be safe. Fed."[195] As described by Human Rights Watch, Bunia became notorious as "the bloodiest corner" of the DRC during the conflict; at least five thousand civilians died in a particularly fierce burst of fighting between Hema and Lendu militias from 2002 to 2003.[196] Meanwhile, the UN peacekeeping force, which was not authorized to intervene, "cowered under fire behind its razor-wire perimeter."[197] Christian's comment suggests that a brothel in the middle of the Ituri rain forest is a safer refuge for his niece than a major town. Like Christian, Sophie also expresses her faith in Mama Nadi's business as the best available option. When Salima states her desire to leave, Sophie cuts her off: "Look here, if you leave, where will you go? . . . Scrounge for food in a stinking refugee camp."[198] At Mama Nadi's, the necessities of food and water seem to be plentiful ("I bake bread and it goes stale," laments Mama), and each woman has her own bed.[199]

In the absence of colonialism and humanitarianism, the characters carve out a world in which entrepreneurship rules. Mama Nadi is the quintessential businesswoman, sweet-talking, flirting with, and scolding the soldiers and miners who come into the bar, as the situation demands. She proudly states, "I turned a basket of sweets and soggy biscuits into a business."[200] The characters are placed on a hierarchy based on their level of savvyness, ambition, and adaptability. Despite her "ruined" status, for example, Sophie is elevated above Salima and Josephine because she is a university student who can read and do accounting for Mama Nadi, who calls her "a *petit bureaucrat* in the making."[201] In contrast, Salima is treated with disdain as a "digger," an illiterate who "doesn't have much learning."[202] Whereas Sophie steals money, Salima sneaks food; in other words, Sophie thinks strategically, whereas Salima is governed by her physical appetites as well as her growing pregnancy. Sophie makes eager plans to move to Bunia, while Salima yearns for her village home and speaks nostalgically of her life as a farmer: "A peacock wandered into my garden, and the tomatoes were ripe beyond belief. Our fields of red sorghum were so perfect, it was going to be a fine season," she recalls as her last positive

Fig. 11. Sophie (Condola Rashad) and Salima (Quincy Tyler Bernstine) in the 2009 production of *Ruined* by Lynn Nottage at Manhattan Theatre Club. Photo by Joan Marcus.

memory of her former life as a wife and mother.[203] As a "digger," Salima is mired in the agrarian age.

Salima is also the only character who dies. Her husband, Fortune, who regrets his earlier treatment of his wife when she escaped from the rebels, arrives at the bar in search of her. Frustrated by Mama Nadi's refusal to allow him to see her, he eventually betrays Mama to Commander Osembenga of the government army by informing him that the rebel leader Jerome Kisembe had taken refuge at her business.[204] Osembenga and his soldiers promptly attack the brothel as revenge and prepare to rape Josephine, only to be stopped short by the sight of Salima entering, covered with blood. The pool of blood that has formed "in the middle of her dress" suggests that she has stabbed herself in the womb; she staggers onto the stage and dies after delivering her battlefield line quoted earlier.[205] The final scene of the play, set a few months later, shows the other three women moving on with their lives; Sophie and Josephine are busily cleaning the bar while Mama stands in the doorway, trying and failing to tempt the "blue helmets" (UN soldiers) marching down the road to patronize her business. When Christian expresses his sorrow about Salima, Mama is dismissive: "*C'est la vie*. Salima was a good girl."²⁰⁶

One could argue that Salima must die since she is not capable of shedding her agrarian, simple self and moving into the play's complicated interpretation of late capitalism. In this framework, Mama Nadi and Sophie are "good" neoliberals and thus are allowed to survive; even Christian passes muster as a salesman who manipulates the global commodities at his disposal, from Belgian chocolates to Ugandan cigarettes. The lack of support from the state, the United Nations, and the NGOs means that the characters must rely only on their wits. As Mathieu Hilgers put it, "Given a context of liberalisation with no or little help from the state, taking hold of one's own destiny—being an 'enterprising self' in the Foucauldian sense—can constitute a necessary condition for survival and success."²⁰⁷ Mama Nadi, Sophie, and Christian exemplify the neoliberal ideal of enterprising selves par excellence, and thus they are rewarded with their lives. By the final scene, Salima has been discarded with ease since she never belonged to this competitive world in the first place.

In my reading of the play, though, Salima dies because of another kind of ignorance. In her penultimate appearance in the play, Salima delivers her shattering testimony in the monologue that was presented at the US Senate hearing described earlier, a heartrending tale of how she was held by soldiers for five months, "chained like a goat," and repeatedly raped: "I lay there as they tore me to pieces, until I was raw."²⁰⁸ This monologue occurs in act 2, scene 2. Curiously, Salima then vanishes from the action of the play until she reappears, covered with blood, at the end of scene 6—her death scene and the climax of the play. In the world defined by an empire of trauma, one's tale of suffering is to be hoarded like Mama Nadi's diamond as an insurance policy. Salima's only asset is her story of pain; once the story has been shared, she is worthless and must be discarded. It is striking, for example, that Sophie never tells her story of how she came to be "ruined." When Christian starts to tell Mama Nadi what happened to Sophie, she cuts him off abruptly.²⁰⁹ Josephine, who bears a disfiguring scar on her stomach, gives only the briefest glimpse of what happened to her: "When the soldiers raided us, who was kind to me? . . . Did any of them bring a blanket to cover me, did anyone move to help me?"²¹⁰ She says nothing more about her past except for her incessant reminders that her father was the chief. Unlike Salima, the other women are savvy enough to keep their stories in reserve for those moments when their stories can be instrumentalized, commodified, and exchanged.

And thus Brecht's legacy is fully revealed. In the context of the DRC, to be "ruined" is less a disability than a condition to be appropriated as an asset. Sophie skillfully calls attention to her condition when it serves her advantage; in other words, the actual disability takes a backseat to how Sophie learns to use it as a bid for sympathy. When Sophie is caught stealing, Mama Nadi succumbs to complete rage: "I will put you out on your ass. I will let you walk naked down that road, is that what you want?" Sophie strategically defuses Mama Nadi's rage by explaining about the operation in Bunia: "Listen, listen, please listen, they can repair the damage."[211] Mama Nadi's rage accordingly dissipates; in a milder tone, she simply tells Sophie to bring her the books where she has hidden the rest of the money.[212] In these moments, Sophie uses her condition as a bargaining chip. Fistula becomes a commodity like Christian's chocolates.

Mama learns from Sophie's example. In the final scene, when Christian starts to leave out of frustration over Mama's lack of response to his courtship, Mama abruptly delivers an eleventh-hour revelation. "I'm ruined," Mama Nadi says, and then repeats the words: "I'm ruined." These two sentences directly quote Brecht's play when Mother Courage predicts imminent financial ruin. "I'm ruined," Mother Courage states dramatically when a truce is declared; she also claims that she will be "ruined" when the chaplain uses her supply of shirts as bandages for the wounded.[213] Even though Nottage is using "ruined" as a euphemism for fistula, Brecht's economic implications of the term still resonate. Christian comforts her, they dance, and the play's so-called happy ending is assured. Although her outburst could be interpreted as a manifestation of Mama's newly sentimentalized self, I suggest that her confession is a strategic move. Harari stole her diamond and left her in a state of economic vulnerability; furthermore, her business has not been going well. Christian, who has been absent for an unspecified length of time, enters the bar wearing a new suit for the first time in the play, and he implies that his wagon is well stocked.[214] Christian's relatively secure financial status makes him a viable business partner for Mama Nadi, and she uses the condition of being "ruined" accordingly as a bid for sympathy. "Go, Mama," are Josephine's last words as she and Sophie watch Mama and Christian dance.[215] Rather than celebrating this moment of love and redemption, they applaud her latest business move. As Mama and Christian dance, a silent parrot that has been onstage throughout the entire play suddenly cries out, "Mama! Primus! Mama! Primus!"[216] This final line can be understood as reminiscent of Mother Courage picking up her wagon and continuing her quest for a profit. Primus, the national beer of the DRC, is a key commodity that Mama sells to her customers; the parrot's outburst is a reminder of the business transaction that Mama has just skillfully negotiated with Christian.

One final intervention of the play concerns the miners. In this harsh, Brechtian-like world, Salima is not the only one to be punished; miners are also regularly exploited and marginalized. They are casually killed off, as seen when the soldier who traded coltan for Salima's sexual favors brags of his exploits: "Fifteen Hema men were shot dead and buried right in their own mining pit, in mud so thick it swallow them into the ground without mercy."[217] Whereas Mama behaves obsequiously to the soldiers, she bosses the miners around, chasing one out of the bar when he shows up with muddy clothes; similarly, a soldier drives a miner out of his seat, who accepts this insult with only the barest grumbling.[218] Mama Nadi's diamond was taken unapologetically from a miner in exchange for "one night of company and four beers not even cold enough to quench his thirst."[219] She mocks his foolishness: "It probably took him a half year of sifting through mud to dig it up."[220] In the first act, miners appear in half the scenes, drinking and playing pool in the shadows of the bar; it is striking, though, that the play does not allot them a single line of dialogue. To borrow (apologetically) from Spivak, the subaltern miner cannot speak. These miners cannot hold a candle to the enterprising, nimble selves of Mama, Sophie, Harari, and Christian; without access to the guns of the soldiers, they are powerless. Instead, like Salima, they serve as pawns. In the topsy-turvy world of Mama Nadi's bar, the miners are exploited rather than criminalized, and to be ruined is to come out on top.

Of course, to subscribe to this notion of ruined not only effaces the materialities of disability but also perpetuates an empire of trauma. Humanitarianism cannot be entirely rejected; like Brecht, its legacy lingers. In the off-Broadway production, this legacy became explicit through the guise of photography. When I was leaving the theatre at the end of the play, I noticed a series of six photographs of women hung in the lobby. Captions revealed that these photographs were portraits of the female refugees whom Nottage had interviewed in Uganda. Her husband, photographer and documentary filmmaker Tony Gerber, took these photographs "moments after the women shared their powerful stories."[221] The photographs depict six stalwart-looking women staring into the camera; the photos are cropped so that their faces fill the frame, conveying a sense of intimacy to the viewer. The photographs are clearly meant, like the play, to capture the power and resilience of the women. Indeed, two of the photographs bear a certain stylistic likeness to that of Boali, whose strength resonates across the century.

I can certainly sympathize with Nottage's desire for audience members and readers to be reminded of the actual women whose stories inspired the characters of *Ruined*. But in light of the historical trajectory of humanitarian photography and its demand for poster children, I contend that these photographs serve as a humanitarian stamp that diminishes the play's subtleties. The women are indeed gorgeous and powerful, but they are also isolated and detached from the complexities of their lifeworlds. The play's nuanced portrayal of gender politics, in which adult men are disenfranchised and female "ruination" becomes a strategy, is abruptly erased. For all of the play's attempts at rejection and space clearing, the tropes of victimhood that stretch over the past century remain firmly in place. Ruptures have a curious way of repeating themselves.

Notes

1. The text of this poem can be found at the V-Day 2009 Spotlight Video, available at https://www.youtube.com/watch?v=-JGL9ALaeKE, accessed July 17, 2015.
2. Ibid.
3. Bleasdale 2003.
4. John Prendergast, "Can You Hear Congo Now? Cell Phones, Conflict Minerals, and the Worst Sexual Violence in the World," Enough Project report, April 2009, 3–4, available at enoughproject.org, accessed August 14, 2017.
5. Laqueur 2009, 33.
6. Wilson and Brown 2009, 10.
7. Stamatov 2013, 10–11.
8. *Blood in the Mobile* is a 2010 documentary film produced by Koncern TV- og Filmproduktion, Denmark (see http://bloodinthemobile.org/). See "Conflict Minerals: Is There Blood on Your Laptop?," a video report of *Time* magazine, available at http://content.time.com/time/video/player/0,32068,594243401001_2013170,00.html. (The date of the video is unclear, but it seems to have been posted in August 2010.) See also Robin Wright, "Your Cell Phone, Congo's Misery," *CNN.com*, November 28, 2011.
9. Hunt 2008, 243. See Hunt 2016, especially 1–25, for an expanded discussion of her ideas of historiography.
10. See Theatre Communication Group, "Top 10 Most-Produced Plays," 2010–2011, available at https://www.tcg.org/publications/at/ATtopten.cfm, accessed July 17, 2015.

11. Jason Stearns, "How Not to Write about Congo," available at http://congosiasa.blogspot.com/2011/02/how-not-to-write-about-congo.html, accessed July 17, 2015; see also Wainaina 2005.

12. Hunt 2008, 224.

13. See Harms 1975, 79, for a detailed account of the harshness of the system and how the concession system was designed to maximize production.

14. Casement's report (2003) contains numerous references to these atrocities; see also Hochschild 1999, 166, for an account of the brutality of European colonial officers in the Congo Free State.

15. Conrad 1963 [1899], 17.

16. See Pavlakis 2010 for an overview of key historiographical narratives of the CRA. He also usefully delineated five phases of the reform movement: (1) from 1890 to 1900, when a humanitarian organization, the Aboriginal Protection Society, attempted to sway public opinion through relatively conservative means by lobbying King Leopold and the Foreign Office, under the leadership of Secretary H. R. Fox Bourne; (2) 1900–1903, when Morel and Bourne began publishing books and pamphlets; (3) 1904–1905, which included the founding of the Congo Reform Association and its US affiliate, as well as the publication of Leopold's commission report; (4) 1906–1908, when a popular movement spearheaded by missionaries took root; and (5) from 1908 until the dismantling of the CRA in 1913. See also Pavlakis 2016 for a detailed exploration of the origins, strategies, politics, and eventual folding of the CRA.

17. Morel based his determination of the conditions of the Congo Free State on his observations of the quantities of ivory and rubber shipped to Europe in exchange for shiploads of guns and ammunition shipped to the Congo. Much of the information in this paragraph is drawn from Síocháin and O'Sullivan 2003, particularly 28–32.

18. Sliwinski 2006, 334, see also Linfield 2010, 48–50, for an example of this argument.

19. My emphasis on the atrocity photographs precludes a discussion of several other missionaries who were instrumental in the reform campaign. Other noteworthy figures include E. V. Sjöblom of Sweden; William Morrison of the United States; William Sheppard of the United States, who was the first African American missionary in the Congo; and Daniel J. Danielsen of the Faeroe Islands.

20. Grant 2005, 41. T. Jack Thompson complicates Grant's argument that the missionaries were motivated to speak out as a result of Leopold's curtailment of their work, noting that "the opposite is at least partly true: that once they had begun to speak out, further land grants became very difficult to obtain" (2012, 174).

21. Grant 2005, 51. The CBM was founded by Guinness's father (also named Grattan Guinness); it later became part of the Regions Beyond Missionary Union, the name that was increasingly used from 1899 onward. It exists today as World Team.

22. Harms 1975, 83.

23. Louis 1968, 210.

24. See ibid., 204, for more discussion of the personal rift between Harris and Morel.

25. From January to June 2015, the International Slavery Museum in Liverpool held an exhibition, *Brutal Exposure: The Congo*, that praised Harris's photography as "a radical and significant shift in the representation and understanding of the impact of colonial violence in the Congo, and exposed the deep-rooted hypocrisy of so called 'colonial benevolence' which cost the lives of millions of Congolese" (http://www.liverpoolmuseums.org.uk/ism/exhibitions/brutal-exposure/index.aspx, accessed July 17, 2015).

26. The Reverend W. D. Armstrong has been credited with taking many of the earlier atrocity photographs while Casement was gathering testimony for his report; it is thought that he pioneered the convention of posing the victims of mutilation and amputation wrapped in a white sheet. (The photographs were not included in Casement's report but appeared later in pamphlets and books.) Óli Jacobsen (2014) argues that Daniel J. Danielsen, mentioned in note 19, should also receive credit for several of the more famous photographs. In addition to the substantial secondary literature on the atrocity photographs, this section draws on my analysis of the digitized collection of the atrocity photographs available at http://shop.anti-slavery.org/category/Images-Historical-Belgian-Congo/10, the Anti-Slavery Society slide collection at the Bodleian Library at Oxford University, a microfilmed version of the E. D. Morel Collection at the London School of Economics, and a review of numerous pamphlets published by the CRA. A special note of thanks is due to Hugh Cahill at Lambeth Palace Library for providing me with access to *The Camera and the Congo Crime* (Congo Reform Association 1906a).

27. Grant 2005, 71. Pavlakis observes that lantern lecturers seeking to educate or raise awareness for a cause usually kept up a similar brisk pace (2016, 188).

28. In 1906, Riley Brothers Ltd. assembled sixty slides under the title "Lantern Lecture on the Congo Atrocities." The text of the lecture survives in the E. D. Morel Collection; the microfilmed version is found on reel 2. As Grant cautions, the lecture "should not be treated as a universal script, but as one version among many produced by a group of reformers who struggled to appeal to the public without alienating or offending... in the face of atrocity" (2015, 81). Pavlakis (2016) also provides helpful clarification on the distribution and use of the Riley collection; he explains that the CRA had a set of the Harris slides to loan out for lantern lectures, in addition to the Riley slides (188–198). He also notes that the Riley collection emphasized a missionary perspective, whereas the Harris slides stressed a political solution.

29. Hunt 2008, 222. See also Hunt 2016, 27–60.

30. Twain 1905, 40.

31. References to this passage in *King Leopold's Soliloquy* appear in, for example, Geary 2003; Grant 2005; Sliwinski 2006; T. J. Thompson 2012; and Twomey 2014, 2015.

32. Mindful of Saidiya Hartman's warning against the "casualness" with which scenes of black suffering are circulated, which might "immure us to pain by virtue of their familiarity" (1997, 3), I decided against reprinting any of the famous mutilation photographs from the Congo Free State. With two exceptions (figures 9 and 10), I do not include any illustrations in this book that directly portray trauma. I realize, though, that the viewing of the photographs will clarify and deepen reactions to my analysis, so I encourage readers to visit the site of Anti-Slavery International: http://shop.antislavery.org/category/Images-Historical-Belgian-Congo/10. The website allows for more systematic viewing of the photographs than a general internet search, which will yield a flood of undifferentiated and uncontextualized images of suffering. I direct the reader to specific images in the Anti-Slavery International digitized collection in the following notes, referenced as ASI website. The site's framing of this collection as "shopping" serves as a reminder of the omnipresent commodification of these images.

33. Hunt 2008, 223. Photographs were altered so that they would conform to this aesthetic; for example, additional figures were removed, as in the case of the photograph of the unnamed young boy from Wambala (see note 40), or a white cloth was added, as in the case of Ikabo.

34. Ibid., 224.

35. Chow 2010.

36. A photograph of a man being whipped is particularly well known. See Peffer 2008 for a thorough discussion of this photograph; he persuasively argues that it was most likely staged. Another famous photograph, that of the grieving Nsala, will be discussed in more detail later in this chapter.

37. The ASI website includes Impongi ("Boy with Severed Hand and Foot"), Lokota ("Mutilated Child"), and Yoka ("Two Youths with Severed Hands"). Epondo can be seen in the montage photograph, "Children Whose Limbs Have Been Cut Off as Punishment," as the bottom-center image. The montage is discussed in more detail later in this chapter.

38. Mola is pictured in "Two Youths with Severed Hands," and Ikabo appears as the left-center victim in the montage (ASI website). The literature refers to them in diminutive terms as "lad" or "boy" even though Mola was old enough to have a wife (see Casement 2003, 159–164; Congo Reform Association 1905, 59; and Morel 1904, 376). One might believe that this pattern is simply reflective of the common racist tendency to demean black men; however, I think it more likely that this reflects a certain confusion among the writers about how to classify these youths, because adult men such as Isekansu were not referred to as "boy" or "lad" but always as a man.

39. Lomboto is pictured in "Man Shot in Wrist and Hand" and Isekansu in "Seated Man with Severed Hand" (ASI website). Lomboto and Isekansu (spelled Isekausu in the lecture) are featured in "The Congo Atrocities: A Lecture" (slides 26 and 36, respectively). Lomboto is unidentified in the lecture narrative; he is described only as "shot for climbing a tree," probably so that spectators will not confuse him with another "Lomboto" (slide 35), a "plucky native" who confronted the ABIR director at the Baringa hearing associated with the 1905 Commission of Inquiry (see also Twain 1905, image facing p. 50). (Incidentally, a third Lomboto is identified as Boali's husband; see Congo Reform Association 1905, 23 and 30, where he is also called Lonboto.) Other unidentified boys and men make occasional appearances in the literature; for example, a photograph of a young boy, presumably from Wambala in modern-day Équateur Province, is relatively common (see "Small Boy Mutilated," ASI website). An especially expansive collection of photographs can be found in the widely circulated pamphlet *The Camera and the Congo Crime* (Congo Reform Association 1906a, 18); Isekansu (as Isekausu), Nsala, Ikabo, Boali (as Boaji), Impongi (as Imponga), and Lokota all make identified appearances.

40. Bogdan, Elks, and Knoll 2012, 44.

41. "Mutilated Woman," ASI website.

42. See Hunt 2008 and Grant 2015 for insightful discussions that raise alternative perspectives about Boali's significance and visibility.

43. Cited in Hunt 2008, 225.

44. The *Graphic* was a British illustrated weekly magazine with wide distribution in the United Kingdom, North America, and the British Empire. Both Impongi and Boali lived at Baringa; the Harrises knew them both, although they apparently were not related. Their images appear in "The Congo Atrocities: A Lecture" as slides 34 and 40, respectively. Furthermore, Morel uses both photos as the two representative examples of amputations in his "Murderland: Startling Exposures of the Congo Atrocities" series that appeared in several August 1907 issues of *Penny Pictorial*. Impongi appears in the August 17 issue, 34 (429): 481; Boali is depicted in the August 31 issue, 34 (431): 51. Their images appear on successive pages in the 1907 edition of *King Leopold's Soliloquy* (opposite pp. 65 and 69) and in the pamphlets *Essential Facts on the Congo Question* (J. Harris 1908, 23–24) and *The Camera and the Congo Crime* (Congo Reform Association 1906a, 16–17). Impongi's image consistently precedes Boali's.

Finally, they both appear on the same page as the only two atrocity photographs at the end of *The Indictment against the Congo Government* (Congo Reform Association 1906b). Interestingly, the 1905 Commission of Inquiry's report also links Impongi and Boali in a grudging acknowledgment that Impongi's and Boali's mutilations did occur, but as a result of theft (because sentries cut off the limbs in order to gain Impongi's copper rings and Boali's anklet) rather than a state campaign of torture (*The Congo: A Report of the Commission of Enquiry* 1906, 102). The only instance I have found in which Boali appears without any reference to Impongi is in John Harris's "Dark Deeds in Darkest Africa: Scenes and Tales of Cruelty from the Congo Free State," published in a special supplement to the January 1906 issue of the *Graphic* (n.p.).

45. Hunt 2008, 242. The Harrises attempted to cloak Boali in a veneer of British-style morality in their descriptions of her. Grant 2015 is particularly helpful in tracing the various permutations of her original testimony to the Commission of Inquiry in 1905, the publication of her testimony in the CRA's *Evidence Laid before the Congo Commission of Inquiry* (1905, 23, 29–30), and the domestication and sanitization of her testimony for the lantern lecture (n.d., 19). As Grant explains, the sentry's demand for sex is replaced with a demand for food; Boali is "struck" with the gun rather than shot in the stomach; and a husband appears to protest her treatment and receives a whipping as a result. Grant comments that the lantern lecture attempts to "portray this Congolese woman as properly moral by British standards" and make Boali into a "woman worthy of compassionate empathy" (2015, 81).

46. Bogdan, Elks, and Knoll 2012, 44. An analysis of the CRA campaign's representation of disability has yet to be written. The disproportionate number of photographs of amputation that appear in the CRA literature calls out for such an analysis insofar that it speaks of an ableist fascination with acquired disability, which is generally perceived as more "tragic" than congenital forms. Such an analysis of the CRA campaign would help clarify the ways in which gender, productivity, and disability overlapped to help determine the victim's "worth" on the trauma market.

47. The caption can be found at http://shop.antislavery.org/product/Images-Historical-Belgian-Congo/Montage-children-whose-limbs-have-been-cut-off-as-punishment/122, accessed July 20, 2015. Jacobsen 2014, 99–101, provides a helpful analysis of this montage. He has tracked down the identity of four of the subjects (Epondo, Lokota, Mola, and Ikabo); the five unknown subjects include two male children, two unidentified men or youths, and one unidentified older woman. Jacobsen has helpfully located the woman as probably from Ikoko because of the background (2014, 101), but otherwise I have found no speculation about her in the scholarship.

48. Hunt 2008, 230.

49. Twomey 2014, 17. See also Pavlakis 2016, 184–185, for his clarification that Morel was initially reluctant to use photos, as demonstrated in *Affairs of West Africa*, which includes only one atrocity photo. When Morel delivered lectures on the Congo Free State, he did not use lantern slides, at least as of late 1906 (ibid., 188).

50. Twain 1905, 14.

51. Many of these pamphlets did not include either testimonies or photographs; see, for example, Morel 1907a and 1907b. Even Alice Harris's pamphlet, *Enslaved Womanhood of the Congo: An Appeal to British Women* (1908), includes no photos save for a cover image of three Congolese women adorned with jewelry and scarification marks gazing into the distance.

52. Hunt 2008, 230–231.

53. Morel 1908, 31; Morel is apparently citing a speech by King Leopold.
54. Grant 2005, 3.
55. Ibid., 19.
56. Morel 1907b, 13.
57. Ibid., 13, 14.
58. Morel 1903, 11.
59. Several pages in *King Leopold's Rule* are devoted to tables that show the regularity with which the value of imports exceeded those of exports in all the colonies in West Africa, with the Congo Free State as a glaring exception (Morel 1904, 49–58). Morel cheerfully extols the productivity of French and British colonies in West Africa (see, for example, 1904, 100). As Kevin C. Dunn observes, what was at stake was the entire colonial enterprise; he quotes Morel as describing Leopold's actions in the Congo as "befouling civilization, and jeopardizing the whole future of European effort in the Dark Continent" (*West African Mail*, February 24, 1905, 1103, quoted in Dunn 2003, 54).
60. Morel 1904, 33.
61. J. Harris 1908, 7.
62. "The Congo Atrocities: A Lecture," 20.
63. Ibid., 21.
64. See Geary 2003, 26–29, for a discussion of the exoticizing aesthetic of colonial photography. Geary also notes that even though the Kodak had been introduced in 1888, many photographers used the older style of cameras that required long exposure times, which might explain the quality of stillness that characterizes the atrocity photos. But this explanation falls short given that the photographs of "legitimate" colonialism fairly hum with activity and movement.
65. Morel 1904, "The Wretched Mongo Women from the Abir Concession," opposite p. 168.
66. For example, the *Essential Facts* pamphlet (J. Harris 1908) includes three photographs of rubber gathering in the Congo Free State, all of which are frequently reprinted in the literature: men holding empty baskets for gathering rubber (7), men holding full baskets (12), and an especially popular photograph of a listless young boy waiting for the rubber to be drained into the basket (8). In none of these instances do we see them gathering the rubber; these kinds of images are permitted only as examples of the legitimate colonialism described later in this chapter.
67. Morel's *Affairs of West Africa* (1902) includes, for example, photographs such as "On Fishing Bent—South Nigeria" (frontispiece), "Washing Rubber" (facing p. 122), and "Making Palm Oil" (facing p. 42), all of which depict busy, active British subjects in the "legitimate" colony of Nigeria.
68. Two of the better-known supporters of Leopold's regime were Frederick Starr, who wrote a series entitled *The Truth about the Congo* that was published in the *Chicago Tribune* and later published as a book in 1907, and Henry Wellington Wack, who published *The Story of the Congo Free State* in 1905. Both works depict Congolese in the act of gathering and processing rubber; see, for example, "Bachoko Bringing In Rubber, Djoko Punda" (Starr 1907, opposite p. 56), and "Melting Latex of Rubber in Forest of Lusambo (Lusambo-Kasai)" (Wack 1905, opposite p. 412).
69. Ironically, this photograph ended up in the Anti-Slavery International collection with the caption "Two men forced to collect rubber by ABIR in Belgian Congo." This photograph

appears in Wack 1905, opposite p. 280, as an endorsement of Leopold's rule, and it was also disseminated by the Congo Free State as propaganda (Geary 2003, 33–34).

70. de Winton 1886, 619.

71. See for example, Wack 1905, 154.

72. Morel 1904, 244.

73. A. Harris 1908, 5.

74. See, for example, the anonymous pamphlet *An Answer to Mark Twain*, which responded to *King Leopold's Soliloquy* through the publication of over sixty photographs that presented the Congo Free State as a model colony, as well as Wack's *Story of the Congo Free State*. Both texts include the same photograph of Congolese girls working at sewing machines (*Answer* 1907, 16; Wack 1905, opposite 242).

75. "The Congo Atrocities: A Lecture," 29. The slides are 54, 55, and 57.

76. Ibid., 30. The slide is 58. The slide images of laboring Congolese men are relatively easy to identify—a photograph of the men sawing timber, for example, is found at the ASI website as "Cutting Timber"; see also CRA 1906a, 22. Curiously, though, it is difficult to identify the slide of the girls in their prize dresses. The only candidate I have come across is located at the Bodleian Library at Oxford, titled "Coloured lady with native girls in training at Luebo, Kasai," which depicts Congolese girls standing in front of a school dressed in western-style dresses. However, the box in which this slide was stored was labeled 1911–1912, which considerably postdates the heyday of the CRA campaign (MSS. Brit. Emp. s. 17 / B7 1911–1912).

77. "The Congo Atrocities: A Lecture," 31–32, slide 60.

78. Siebert 2010, 375.

79. Harms 1975, 73–74. New and cheaper forms of rubber from plantations in South Asia became readily available, thus lessening the demand for Congolese and Angolan wild rubber.

80. As briefly mentioned in chapter 1, during the 1930s, several thousand Rwandans were relocated from densely populated Rwanda to the sparsely populated Congo as a source of labor. It should also be noted that these policies of conscripted labor would have been familiar in much of colonial Africa. As explained by Dunaway 2010, colonial administrators were determined to drag Africans out of their "uneducated and unproductive idleness to the labour market," where they would be taught to work "under good European supervision," to quote the governor of Kenya in 1920. Dunaway comments drily, "Despite such chest pounding by the colonial powers, only about 1 percent of all African adults had been transformed into wage earners by 1930" (2010, 20).

81. Siebert 2010, 383.

82. See Geary 2003, 44–55, for a discussion of how the Belgian state printed thousands of propaganda photographs of the Belgian Congo in magazines, such as *L'Illustration Congolaise*, a magazine founded in 1924 to raise interest in and promote the colony.

83. See, for example, Sliwinski 2006, 341–342; and Linfield 2010, 49. The name of the daughter was also Boali; the Harrises' lengthy description of their encounter with Nsala, who took the remains of his daughter "to bring and show to the white man, in case he should disbelieve what he said," can be found in Morel 1904, 444–445. I am struck by Nsala's awareness, even in the midst of his shock, that his testimony alone would not generate the desired emotional impact. He also lost his wife and young son.

84. Butler 2004a, 34.

85. Ibid., 21.

86. Ibid.

87. I am borrowing here from Butler, who, in describing the impact of grief, writes, "My narrative falters, as it must" (ibid., 23).
88. Ibid., 33. The term "derealization" might be more accurate than "dehumanization" if one's humanity was never recognized in the first place.
89. International Rescue Committee 2003. For a discussion of the controversy behind the IRC's figure, see T. Turner 2013, 121–123. See also Jina Moore, "New Study Argues War Deaths Are Often Overestimated," *Christian Science Monitor*, January 22, 2010.
90. International Rescue Committee 2003, 14.
91. As early as 2001, the IRC's director was calling the conflict the deadliest since World War II ("Not since World War II," *Washington Post*, August 26, 2001); however, the phrase did not pick up steam in the media until the release of the 2003 report, at which point it caught on like wildfire.
92. See transcript of *Anderson Cooper 360 Degrees* at http://www.cnn.com/TRANSCRIPTS/0610/02/acd.02.html; Žižek (2008, 2) refers to *Time* magazine's story, "The Deadliest War in the World" (June 5, 2006).
93. Wällstrom 2011.
94. Baaz and Stern 2013, 92; the quotation is from Trinh 1989, 82.
95. Autesserre 2012, 215. Here she is quoting Justice Byron R. White.
96. Ibid.
97. Ensler 2013, 41.
98. Spivak 2004, 535–537. I borrow here from Baaz and Stern's use of Spivak's term (2013, 96).
99. Baaz and Stern 2013, 95.
100. Baaz and Stern 2013 provide several examples of this prevailing trend; see, for example, 90–92.
101. Ticktin 2011, 260.
102. The text of this poem can be found at the V-Day 2009 Spotlight Video, available at https://www.youtube.com/watch?v=-JGL9ALaeKE, accessed July 17, 2015.
103. Ensler's bio is provided at http://www.vday.org/about/more-about/eveensler.html#.VbJmHkXSf8E, accessed July 24, 2015.
104. Ensler attracted considerable media attention to the issue with an article in the August 2007 issue of *Glamour*, "Women Left for Dead—and the Man Who Is Saving Them," which described her visit to the DRC earlier that year. See http://www.glamour.com/magazine/2007/08/rape-in-the-congo; this article includes the earliest reference that I have found to "femicide" in the DRC.
105. Although the press presents it otherwise, Douma and Hilhorst report that 1 percent of the operations at Panzi Hospital are for fistulas caused by rape; the vast majority are caused by childbirth (2012, 10). I attended Ensler's "Turning Pain to Power" event at the 92nd Street Y in New York City on February 4, 2009; the auditorium was packed with mostly young, very enthusiastic white women. Mukwege seemed ill at ease with his celebrity status.
106. City of Joy, http://drc.vday.org/about-city-of-joy/program-philosophy-makes-different/, accessed July 24, 2015.
107. City of Joy, http://drc.vday.org/about-city-of-joy/vagina-warrior-program/, accessed July 24, 2015. Ensler explains further to Jeffrey Gettleman, "You build an army of women.... And when you have enough women in power, they take over the government and they make different decisions. You'll see. They'll say 'Uh-uh, we're not taking this any longer,' and they'll

put an end to this rape problem fast" ("Fighting Congo's Ills with Education and an Army of Women," *New York Times*, February 6, 2011).

108. Katharine Viner, "City of Joy: New Hope for Congo's Brutalised Women," *Guardian*, April 8, 2011.

109. As discussed in chapter 2, the championing of arts and theatre therapy is a fundamentally western concept. See http://www.onebillionrising.org/870/eves-update-from-city-of-joy-the-women-will-rise/, accessed August 15, 2017, for more discussion of Ensler's inclusion of theatre in the programming and the exercises that she led, called "Shared Secrets." I acknowledge, though, that Ensler also refers to a class run by "two brilliant local Congolese actors," which suggests that the organization has reached out to local artists.

110. More information can be found at http://www.enoughproject.org/.

111. Prendergast, "Can You Hear Congo Now?," 2.

112. Ibid., 3.

113. Global Witness was also at the forefront of the conflict-minerals movement; see https://www.globalwitness.org/campaigns/conflict-minerals/ for more information.

114. Although the two organizations have rarely collaborated officially, Prendergast assures his supporters that the two campaigns "work on parallel tracks and cooperate closely" (Prendergast and Cheadle 2010, 20). The two organizations worked together in 2009 to develop materials for "Teach-Ins" about the DRC, such as a Powerpoint presentation titled "Congo Teach In: Educate and Activate."

115. *Confronting Rape and Other Forms of Violence against Women in Conflict Zones: Spotlight: DRC and Sudan; Hearing before the Subcommittee on African Affairs and the Subcommittee on International Operations and Organizations, Human Rights, Democracy, and Global Women's Issues of the Committee on Foreign Relations, United States Senate*, May 13, 2009, available at http://www.gpo.gov/fdsys/pkg/CHRG-111shrg53635/html/CHRG-111shrg53635.htm, accessed July 15, 2015. My discussion is also based on a viewing of a video of the hearing, available at http://www.foreign.senate.gov/hearings/confronting-rape-and-other-forms-of-violence-against-women-in-conflict-zones-spotlight-drc-and-sudan, accessed July 20, 2015.

116. These activists were Neimat Ahmadi and Chouchou Namegabe Nabintu.

117. Eve Ensler, comments in *Confronting Rape*. The hearing is discussed in more detail later in this chapter.

118. Prendergast, "Can You Hear Congo Now?," 3–4.

119. Chouliaraki 2013, 6.

120. Robins 2012, 594.

121. Eichstaedt 2011, 5.

122. Baaz and Stern 2013, 102. See also Heaton 2013 for a controversial article about the "over-reporting" of sexual violence in the eastern DRC, as well as Jason Stearns's interview with Heaton, "Interview: Is There Too Much Focus on Sexual Violence in the Congo?," *Congo Siasa* blog, March 8, 2013, available at http://congosiasa.blogspot.com/. See also Douma and Hilhorst 2013.

123. Dragotesc 2011, 139. Emphasis in the original.

124. The neoliberal embrace of the sexually violated woman dovetails with the workings of contemporary global capitalism, as articulated by Cheah: "Contemporary global capitalism . . . functions not by obscuring the voice of the oppressed through psychical mechanisms but rather by recognizing them, by incorporating their interests as subjects of corporeal needs into the very fabric of the global system of accumulation where they can be augmented and cultivated as human capital" (2011, 217).

125. *Confronting Rape*.

126. Graham 2014, 146.

127. Ensler originally used this phrase in her *Glamour* article, "Women Left for Dead—and the Man Who Is Saving Them."

128. That is, miners are perceived as male unless the topic at hand is slave labor, in which case the emphasis shifts to women and children. See, for example, Diane Taylor, "Congo Rape Victims Face Slavery in Gold and Mineral Mines," *Guardian*, September 2, 2011. Overall, though, mining is gendered as male for reasons that can be traced back to Belgian colonialism; see Makori 2015, 2.

129. See Holly Dranginis, "Grand Theft Global: Prosecuting the War Crime of Pillage in the Democratic Republic of the Congo," January 2015, 6, available at http://www.enoughproject.org/blogs/ending-grand-theft-global-scale-prosecuting-war-crime-pillage-0.

130. Kelly 2014.

131. "Show Me the Data," *Texas in Africa* blog, December 10, 2009, available at http://texasinafrica.blogspot.com/2009/12/show-me-data.html, accessed August 22, 2017. See also *Demographic and Health Survey, 2013–2014*, available at http://dhsprogram.com/pubs/pdf/SR218/SR218.e.pdf, which states that overall, 27 percent of women in the DRC have experienced sexual violence, and 16 percent experienced it in the past twelve months; the highest rate was in Kasaï Occidental (24 percent) (18). Stearns's posting, "What Socio-economic Data Tells Us about Sexual Violence, Découpage, and Living Conditions in the Congo," March 27, 2015, available at http://congosiasa.blogspot.com/2015/03/what-socio-economic-data-tells-us-about.html, accessed July 25, 2015, provides a useful discussion of this survey and its significance.

132. Autesserre 2012, 205.

133. Ibid., 213.

134. The debate on the repercussions of Dodd-Frank in the Congo even reached the mainstream press; one example is Christoph Vogel and Ben Radley's op-ed "In Eastern Congo, Economic Colonialism in the Guise of Ethical Consumption?," *Washington Post*, September 10, 2014. See also Sudarsan Raghavan, "How a Well-Intentioned U.S. Law Left Congolese Miners Jobless," *Washington Post*, November 30, 2014. The *Post*'s investigation, which was picked up in several other media forums, called attention to the devastating effect of the legislation on Congolese livelihoods. Although evidence on the damaging effects of what has been termed "Obama's Law" is certainly persuasive, it should also be noted that members of the US Congress were eager to appropriate this evidence in an attempt to weaken Dodd-Frank's regulations on US banking; apparent concern for Congolese livelihoods served as a mask for a conservative political agenda. As this book is going to press, the law is under serious threat by the Trump administration and the Securities and Exchange Commission.

135. Bleasdale's talk, "Capturing Conflict Mineral Trade in DRC," which was delivered on March 8, 2014, is available at https://www.youtube.com/watch?v=jjVkNxT8Zsg, accessed August 15, 2017.

136. Bleasdale 2009. The book has no page numbers; it also includes almost no text aside from the captions and occasional inserts that quote various Congolese about the political, economic, and security situations in which they live.

137. These photographs can be viewed at marcusbleasdale.com; from the homepage, one can click on "Rape of a Nation" and view a slide show of the photographs included in his book.

138. Mongbwalu is located in Ituri Province. See Fahey 2008 for an in-depth discussion of how Mongbwalu's mining industry intersects with its experiences of conflict; it was particularly hard hit by the war in 2002 and 2003.

139. Butler emphasizes that our experiences of grief reveal "the thrall in which our relations with others hold us, in ways that we cannot always recount or explain, in ways that often interrupt the self-conscious account of ourselves we might try to provide, in ways that challenge the very notion of ourselves as autonomous and in control" (2004a, 23). In borrowing her use of the term "thrall" to describe my reaction to this series of photographs, I suggest that we are thrown into a sense of loss in that we cannot know Sakura Lisi and thus cannot access her family's grief.

140. "Congo/Women," at http://congowomen.org/, accessed July 25, 2015. *Congo/Women* was produced by Art Works Projects and the Ellen Stone Belic Institute for the Study of Women and Gender in the Arts and Media, Columbia College, Chicago.

141. http://congowomen.org/why/, accessed July 25, 2015. Jane M. Saks and Leslie Thomas curated the exhibit.

142. Kassie Bracken, "Behind the Scenes: Suffering, Writ Large," *Lens*, October 19, 2009, http://lens.blogs.nytimes.com/2009/10/19/behind-20/?_r=0.

143. http://congowomen.org/why/.

144. Addario's series of photographs that depict a woman's fistula operation, for example, was not included in the exhibit. These photos are available at http://www.lynseyaddario.com/healthcare-maternal-mortality-and-sexual-violence/rape-in-the-democratic-republic-of-congo/drcrape002/, accessed October 30, 2017.

145. Image manual of *Congo/Women*, 6, available at http://congowomen.org/wp-content/uploads/2008/09/Congo-Women-Manual-images.pdf.

146. Ibid., 9.

147. Jeffrey Gettleman, "The Price of Precious," *National Geographic*, October 2013.

148. Ibid.

149. As persuasively argued by Christoph Vogel and Ben Radley, though, these regulations amount to little more than economic colonialism. They maintain that the "bag and tag scheme" is primarily aimed at ensuring access to mineral supplies by the London-based tin industry body, the International Tin Research Institute (ITRI); moreover, "ITRI's employees are mostly busy with levying enormous fees from its local partners and preventing the scheme's competitors in the 'traceability market' from establishing alternative systems." They explain further, "The same industry proposing to seek a clean market for Congolese minerals appears to be completely disinterested in local realities, including minerals' actual 'cleanliness,' as long as the market continues to function. Moreover, almost no corporate stakeholder—despite their nicely publicised corporate social responsibility policies—has visibly engaged in eastern Congo to help Congolese actors comply with regulations, improve labor security, or increase decent livelihoods." See Vogel and Radley, "In Eastern Congo."

150. Cheah 2011, 221.

151. V-Day, http://drc.vday.org/press-room/photo-library/city-of-joy/, accessed July 26, 2015.

152. Image manual, *Congo/Women*, 18.

153. The capitalization of "Raped Woman" is borrowed from Baaz and Stern 2013.

154. Hunt 2008, 241.

155. Ibid.

156. I borrow here from Stamatov 2013, 10.

157. Ferguson 2014, 257.

158. As one Congolese victim has explained, "I do not feel like a man. I do not know whether I will ever have children" (Moses Seruwagi, "Unreported Horrors—Male Rape in the

DRC," *Street News Service*, November 13, 2011). See also Douma and Hilhorst 2012, 21, for a brief discussion of the incompatibility of masculinity and victimhood. In that same report, though, Douma and Hilhorst also mention their finding about false reporting of rapes among women in order to access aid. They note, "Most organisations turn a blind eye to this reality, because they assume that the social stigma associated with rape will deter women from reporting fake cases. None of the Congolese respondents to the research sustains this view, as they maintain that poor women in search of assistance see no other choice" (2012, 10). My point is that social stigma cannot be automatically assumed.

159. See the Refugee Law Project's 2015 report about the Men of Hope Refugee Association in Uganda for more information about its advocacy and assistance for male victims of rape, available at http://www.refugeelawproject.org/files/others/men_of_hope_magazine_may_2015.pdf, accessed August 15, 2017.

160. Bernstine's performance at the reception can be viewed at https://www.youtube.com/watch?v=SsqyhiaacO8, accessed July 26, 2015.

161. Nottage 2009, 68.

162. Ibid., 94. The report, "Women's Bodies as a Battleground: Sexual Violence against Women and Girls during the War in the Democratic Republic of the Congo (1996–2003)," was released in 2005 by Réseau des Femmes pour un Développement Associatif, Réseau des Femmes pour la Défense des Droits et la Paix, and International Alert, available at http://www.international-alert.org/sites/default/files/publications/women%27s-bodies-as-a-english.pdf, accessed August 15, 2017.

163. "Lynn Nottage: Playwright," a pamphlet issued by the US State Department in November 2013, available at http://photos.state.gov/libraries/amgov/133183/english/1311_African_Americans_Lynn_Nottage_English_LO.pdf, accessed August 15, 2017.

164. Quoted in Prendergast 2010, 216. Not surprisingly, the Enough Project actively sought to promote *Ruined*, organizing a staged reading of the play at the Kennedy Center and appearing on a panel discussion after a production at the Arena Stage in Washington, D.C. (http://www.enoughproject.org/blogs/pulitzer-winning-play-brings-plight-women-congo-stage, accessed August 15, 2017).

165. See, for example, "Play on Rape in Congo Wins Pulitzer," Public Radio International, April 21, 2009 (available at https://www.pri.org/stories/2009-04-21/play-rape-congo-wins-pulitzer); "Congo's Civil War Is Rich Seam for Pulitzer Prize–Winning Playwright," *NewsHour with Jim Lehrer*, June 15, 2009 (available at http://www.pbs.org/newshour/bb/africa-jan-june09-nottage_06-15/); and "Rape in Congo—Rights Watch #10," a podcast posted by Human Rights Watch on June 4, 2009 (available at https://www.hrw.org/video-photos/audio/2009/06/11/rape-congo-rights-watch-10). All links were accessed August 15, 2017.

166. Brecht 1966, 111.

167. Ibid., 81.

168. Ibid.

169. Nosheen Iqbal, "Lynn Nottage: A Bar, a Brothel, and Brecht," *Guardian*, April 20, 2010.

170. Nottage 2009, 17.

171. Ibid., 10.

172. Ibid., 13.

173. Ibid., 17.

174. Ben Brantley, "War's Terrors, through a Brothel Window," *New York Times*, February 10, 2009.

175. I saw *Ruined* on February 11, 2009.

176. Mitchell and Snyder 2000, 56. In the production I saw, I do not think that the diminishing limp was intentional on the part of actress Condola Rashad; I simply note that it upheld Mitchell and Snyder's ideas of narrative prosthesis.

177. Ibid.

178. Taussig 1986, 132.

179. Jill Dolan, "Ruined, by Lynn Nottage," *The Feminist Spectator* blog, March 16, 2009, available at http://feministspectator.princeton.edu/2009/03/16/ruined-by-lynn-nottage/, accessed August 15, 2017.

180. Feldman 2004, 165.

181. Fox 2011, 1. As a testament to the complexities of the play, the anthology *A Critical Companion to Lynn Nottage* includes a special section devoted to *Ruined*. See Mobley 2016, Paden 2016, and Terry 2016.

182. Fox 2011, 2.

183. Ibid., 12.

184. Nottage 2009, 14.

185. Ibid., 18.

186. Ibid., 36.

187. Ibid., 57.

188. Smillie 2010, 118.

189. Harari's character also gestures to a colonial past insofar that Lebanese dominated the diamond trade emerged in West Africa in the nineteenth century. Andrew Arsan explains that the Lebanese of West Africa, the largest non-African migrant group in the region, "play a conspicuous, and controversial, role in the economies of West and Equatorial Africa" because of their dominance in economic sectors that range from diamond and cobalt mining to transportation to industrial production (2014, 5). He notes that academic accounts regard them as "eternal 'hyphen[s]' between European and African, white and black, formal and informal" (2014, 7). Harari's character certainly deserves more attention than I am giving him in this chapter; suffice it to say that in the play, Harari seems to function primarily as a surreptitious proxy for the west rather than as an ambiguous figure of hybridity. He exoticizes Josephine through insisting that she dress "traditionally" for him in a classic othering move associated with the west (Nottage 2009, 24, 28); further, his theft of the diamond erases any sense of sympathy that he might have generated among audience members and readers.

190. Nottage 2009, 33.

191. Ibid., 54–55.

192. Ibid., 90.

193. Ibid., 91–92.

194. Ibid., 14.

195. Ibid., 15.

196. Human Rights Watch, "Ituri: Covered in Blood; Ethnically Targeted Violence in Northeastern Congo," July 2003, available at https://www.hrw.org/reports/2003/ituri0703/DRC0703full.pdf, accessed August 15, 2017.

197. James Astill, "UN Troops Wait behind Razor Wire as Congo's Streets Run with Blood," *Guardian*, May 23, 2003.

198. Nottage 2009, 32.

199. Ibid., 77.

200. Ibid., 86.
201. Ibid., 16.
202. Ibid., 11, 12.
203. Ibid., 69.
204. Ibid., 87–88.
205. Ibid., 94.
206. Ibid., 97.
207. Hilgers 2012, 86.
208. Nottage 2009, 69.
209. Ibid., 13.
210. Ibid., 37.
211. Ibid., 54.
212. Ibid., 55.
213. The original German in both scenes is "Ich bin ruiniert" (Brecht 2010, 110, 142).
214. Nottage 2009, 96.
215. Ibid., 102.
216. Ibid.
217. Ibid., 31.
218. Ibid., 45, 48.
219. Ibid., 53.
220. Ibid.
221. The photographs can be viewed at http://www.marketroadfilms.com/projects/photography/ruined/#prettyPhoto, accessed July 27, 2015. The photographs have also been included in the final pages of the published version of the play (Nottage 2009, n.p.).

5

GIFTED BY TRAUMA

The Branding of Postconflict Northern Uganda

> Welcome to beautiful Uganda, the friendliest country in Africa!
> Gifted by nature.
> The land of the source of the Nile
> the land of the mountain gorillas
> the land where the East African savanna meets the West African jungle....
> You are a special group of people to have come here.
> Very, very special.
> You saw past the stories of Idi Amin
> AIDS
> Ebola virus
> the murdered tourists near the Congo border
> the travel advisories from the U.S. state department
> you heard the stories and came anyway
> to see what a beautiful place Uganda can be.[1]

This ironic speech appears in *Forged in Fire*, a solo performance by Okello Kelo Sam, developed in collaboration with Robert Ajwang and myself. Sam alternates among three different characters—the Tour Guide, the Rebel Commander, and himself—to tell the story of his younger brother, Godfrey Omony Sam, who was abducted by the LRA from Pongdwongo Secondary School in Gulu in 1996.[2] In this speech, Sam appears as the sardonic Tour Guide who addresses the audience as tourists traveling to northern Uganda. He bypasses conventional tourist destinations in favor of the "LRA National Park," where he points out a "herd" of abductees "migrating" to Sudan: "Their endurance amazes wildlife biologists!" He also teases the audience with the promise of

Fig. 12. Okello Kelo Sam as the Tour Guide in the 2015 production of *Forged in Fire* at the Voorhees Theatre. Photo by John Huntington.

seeing the "elusive" Joseph Kony: "Keep your camcorders ready at all times. . . . You'll know him by his mane of dreadlocks and his fondness for Ralph Lauren clothing." Throughout the macabre tour, which includes a visit to an IDP camp to visit "the habitat of that peculiar species, the internally displaced," he plays with rhetorical slippage among African wildlife, the LRA, and northern Ugandans, all of which are subjected to western exoticization and fantasy.

The phrase that he uses to describe Uganda, "Gifted by nature," refers to a slogan coined by the UK-based public relations firm Hill & Knowlton for a 2006 campaign that included a series of advertisements on CNN.[3] The earnest phrase was meant to conjure up Uganda's Rwenzori Mountains, Murchison Falls, and bountiful wildlife, bolstered by a "steady stream of commercials featuring lush jungle foliage, silver-backed gorillas in the mist, and rugged river gorges."[4] Tourism in Uganda has long played second fiddle to that of neighboring Kenya and Tanzania, and the CNN advertisements marked an ambitious effort to improve Uganda's visibility and cash in on East Africa's multimillion-dollar tourist industry.[5] In hiring Hill & Knowlton to the tune of £350,000, the state was searching for "a cluster of values that enables a nation to make a promise about a unique and welcomed experience."⁶ In short, Uganda was seeking a brand.

This chapter explores the branding of postconflict Uganda. In *Nation Branding*, Keith Dinnie explains that nation-states have increasingly turned to brands in order to appropriate commercial strategies of visibility and shift their reputation; as he delicately puts it, "Nation branding can help erase misconceptions about a country and allow the country to reposition itself more favourably with regard to targeted audiences."⁷ With "Gifted by Nature," Uganda was seeking not only to reposition itself but also to wholeheartedly reject its unsavory reputation for violence and disease. The subtext of these images of lush forests and beautiful waterfalls could be termed "Gifted by Safety." A newly LRA-free Uganda was negotiating the promotional culture of a neoliberal era through an embrace of generic natural landscapes in which Ugandans themselves were merely incidental.⁸

The expensive endeavor failed. David Pier points out that branding allows for a certain amount of bluffing, since marketing discourse encourages one "to inflate one's image" and "justifies strategies of public masquerade."⁹ In this case, though, the bluff was called. Uganda's attempt at rebranding was openly mocked in a *Foreign Policy* article: "Close your eyes and imagine Uganda. What comes to mind? Images of Idi Amin and his genocidal murders? Or more recent scenes of 'nightcommuting' children swarming rural towns at dusk to avoid impressment into the Lord's Resistance Army?"¹⁰ Within the country, Ugandan journalists have turned "Gifted by Nature" into a catchphrase that mocks the failures of the state: "Gifted by nature but mismanaged by man," "Gifted by nature, betrayed by poor leadership," and "Gifted but poor" are just a few examples of how the phrase circulates in the Ugandan press.¹¹ In our development of the script, Sam gleefully seized the opportunity to mock the "Gifted by Nature" advertising campaign. As the Tour Guide implies, the new brand cannot help but fail in light of Uganda's reputation for state authoritarianism, insurgency violence, and infectious disease. Given that Joseph Kony has become an international household name while Uganda's scenic Rwenzori Mountains and Murchison Falls languish in relative obscurity, one is tempted to substitute the phrase "Gifted by Trauma."

But as the Tour Guide might remind us, this phrase carries its own cachet. Branding aims to generate symbolic capital and, ultimately, material profit. In this regard, the trauma brand has achieved a startling amount of success. The phenomenon of *Kony 2012* exemplifies its potency; Invisible

Children raised $5 million within forty-eight hours after the video's release through its strategic emphasis on the plight of northern Ugandan children coupled with affirmations of the US's ability to stop the suffering through military intervention.[12] Invisible Children cofounder Jason Russell embraced the logic of branding in the creation of the film: "We felt, with branding, it's important to go after the one that everyone can see and recognize," and thus the organization focused on "a simple story with one bad guy and a solution."[13] Ideally, branding locates the sweet spot between uniqueness and universality through a singular identity that also caters to reassuring generic categories.[14] The LRA's notoriety serves as Uganda's competitive edge—its brutality shocks and horrifies the potential western consumer but also affirms stereotypes of African savagery and darkness. Photogenic child victims of this brutality are churned out in droves.

What a traumatized Uganda promotes, though, is not so much Uganda itself. Instead, the lure of child soldiers and night commuters is leveraged to benefit the promotional machinery of celebrity activism and humanitarian organizations.[15] "Africa is sexy and people need to know that," Bono, arguably the celebrity activist par excellence, has declared.[16] My sense is that people—US celebrities in particular—know this all too well and are quick to take advantage. In this equation, those child soldiers and night commuters serve as unpaid laborers who are folded into the "instrumental logics of corporate capitalist culture."[17] Their smiles light up countless documentaries, photographs, and webpages as if they are delighted to have Bearers of Geopolitical Privilege within their midst. US and European celebrities and would-be celebrities have appropriated local expressions of resilience and suffering in northern Uganda with a blitheness that borders on the obscene.

The force of the machine makes its own truth. At the time of this writing, the LRA has not carried out an attack in northern Uganda for more than ten years.[18] The abductees and night commuters are no longer children, and the urban centers of Lira and Gulu have become hubs of economic activity rather than desolate war zones.[19] Despite economic growth and political stability, organizations such as Invisible Children continued to portray northern Uganda as being in perpetual crisis. To call attention to the plight of the night commuters, Invisible Children staged mass rallies as late as 2009, three years after the commuters had ceased to exist and the shelters had closed.[20] Although *Kony 2012* includes a brief acknowledgment that the LRA had left Uganda for the neighboring countries of the Central African Republic, South

Sudan, and the DRC, this piece of information was easily lost in the film's outpouring of graphic footage of Ugandan suffering at the hands of the LRA.[21] Even the flood of criticism that followed the video's release failed to make much of a dent in the rhetoric of crisis.[22] In 2013, at a New York City benefit gala for Hope North, a secondary and vocational school in Uganda discussed later in this chapter, US film and television actress Mary Louise Parker emphasized to the audience that the school was safe because it was located south of the Nile River, which served as a barrier against the LRA.[23] The intensity of the rhetoric exceeds promotional bluffing. In the collective determination to boost brand equity, sign and referent are easily detached.[24]

This chapter examines how Uganda's trauma brand is bolstered, expanded, and contested among celebrity activists, humanitarian organizations, and northern Ugandans. I begin by focusing on A River Blue, a vocational training program in northern Uganda that emphasizes music, dance, and drama (MDD) as a source of empowerment and healing. Although A River Blue has languished on the ground because of a lack of resources, it flourishes in the US cyberculture of self-promotion. I then turn to the example of Hope North, a secondary school and vocational program with an official mission of helping war-affected youth from the northern region. A River Blue and Hope North are both community-based NGOs that emphasize the performing arts; however, in contrast to A River Blue, Hope North has achieved a considerable degree of prominence thanks to the efforts of US celebrities such as Parker and film actor Forest Whitaker. Although these celebrities appropriated Hope North as a medium of self-branding in the context of celebrity activism, their multiple interventions are then reappropriated by the Hope North students. Finally, I address the dynamics of rebranding in the context of memorialization, in which Gifted by Trauma is rejected in favor of Gifted by Dignity.

THE BRANDING OF A RIVER BLUE

> Shelter me
> We need you
> Blood of Africa
> A river blue

This distinctly nonironic passage appears in the song "A River Blue," composed by US folksinger Joseph Arthur to commemorate the launch of an arts festival in northern Uganda with the same name.[25] Arthur came to Uganda in 2006 at the invitation of Chandler Griffin, the founder of Barefoot Workshops, which advocates the use of documentary filmmaking as a tool of social change. As explained on the River Blue website, Griffin and Arthur conceived the idea of visiting an IDP camp in order to "witness for themselves the destruction wrought by nearly two decades of fighting," as well as organize a music, art, and drama festival for the youth.[26] They selected the Alebtong IDP camp based in Lira, a district in northern Uganda that experienced considerable suffering and loss during the final years of the LRA conflict.[27] During the festival, the hundred child participants created about two hundred pieces of artwork and presented choir, dance, and drama performances. Unsurprisingly, the promotional literature of A River Blue heralds the event as a great success: "As hoped, the kids used these various artistic mediums to share their experiences and strength with one another and their community, exploring their pasts as a first step in beginning to look toward the future."[28] Documentary footage includes obligatory shots of smiling, delighted children.[29]

The momentum of the festival culminated in the founding of the Alebtong Vocational Training and Rehabilitation Center program. When local officials donated an unfinished building, according to the website, Barefoot Workshops renovated the building as a rehabilitation and vocational training center. Rehabilitation was to be "realized through counseling and the arts, empowering young people with a means of self-expression, nurturing their creative abilities as a way to heal," while vocational training "provides students with concrete skills that enables [sic] them to sustain themselves and work towards rebuilding their communities."[30] With the establishment of this program, A River Blue seemed to counter the usual narrative of foreign-led artistic initiatives that I introduced in chapter 2. The single event of an arts festival grew into a sustained initiative that provided local youth with the vocational training that continues to be widely seen as a ticket to a sustainable livelihood.[31]

But the success story rings hollow. I originally came to River Blue as part of the 2011 "More Life" program organized by Erik Ehn, who was interested in the program's initiatives in the performing arts.[32] Okweny George Ongom, a forester by training who had taken over as the program director, had impressed Ehn with his deep commitment to using the arts as a means of rehabilitation and cultural healing. When we arrived, Ongom gathered a group of about twenty youths who came to our guest house and sang to welcome us.[33] All these songs were delivered in the style that is characteristic of the Christian tradition of choir singing that is familiar throughout Uganda.[34] The River Blue song—the organization's trademark—was excluded from their welcome.

This omission in itself is not surprising and merely speaks of the ease with which a US folksong with a disturbing narrative of victimization was discarded. What startled me was the lack of buildings and equipment; contrary to what I expected from reviewing the organization's website, Ongom had no facilities to speak of, which is why he brought the youths to our guest house. When I visited Ongom again in 2013, the situation had further deteriorated. In 2011, he had received funding from the Office of the Prime Minister, which subsidized the vocational training of approximately a hundred students; however, in 2013, the government was reeling from a corruption scandal in the prime minister's office, in which about $13 million targeted for rehabilitation and development in northern Uganda had been embezzled.[35] In the aftermath of the scandal, A River Blue lost its funding and was languishing once again. Even Ongom's investment in MDD as a source of cultural healing, which had originally caught Ehn's interest and speaks of a kind of "niche branding" in the northern Ugandan humanitarian world, was failing to sustain long-term interest.

One might explain A River Blue's struggles in light of Uganda's new status as postconflict. Perhaps Griffin and Arthur were simply too late. In the month during which the art festival occurred, the Ugandan press reported that people were leaving the Alebtong IDP camp and returning to the rural areas to take advantage of the LRA's withdrawal.[36] Alternatively, one might chalk up A River Blue's struggle as an example of Lira District's marginalization in narratives of the LRA conflict, which emphasizes Acholiland as the epicenter of suffering despite the considerable violence that the LRA inflicted on the Langi people in the final years of the conflict.[37] Although this emphasis might be justified in light of the duration of the conflict (the LRA began to target Acholiland in the late 1980s, whereas Lira was not seriously affected until 2003), it tends to foster division and resentment among the Langi people, who see the Acholi as receiving a disproportionate amount of aid.[38]

But these explanations do not account for the seeming paradox of A River Blue. The program might be languishing on the ground, but it thrives as a source of self-branding through websites, blogs, interviews, and publications. The ability of A River Blue to live on through the US culture of self-promotion is emblematic of the brand's mysterious force. As Alison Hearn explains in her analysis of promotional culture, "Here what matters most is not 'meaning' per se, or 'truth' or 'reason' . . . but 'winning'—attention, emotional allegiance, and market share."[39] She adds that "promotion entails a re-arrangement of the relation between sign and referent, whereby the sign comes to displace the material object to which it refers, and, in this way, acquires a kind of agency."[40] In using A River Blue as a source of self-branding, the sign runs amuck, and the realities of the organization are evacuated. "It was amazing, it was the best thing that ever happened to me," Joseph Arthur told an NPR interviewer about his experience in northern Uganda, which was highlighted on his website as late as 2013 even though he has not returned to Uganda since the festival in 2006.[41] The song that he composed was no longer a theme song for the organization but instead served as a trademark for Joseph Arthur. "We need you," he sings as the self-proclaimed voice of the children of Lira. The question is, who needs whom?

The forces of self-branding played out vividly during the "More Life" visit to Lira in 2011. At first, it seemed that the demands of empire would be sidestepped. Once the River Blue youths had welcomed us with choir songs, Ongom singled out a few members and explained some of the hardships they had experienced. He mentioned that a few of the male youths had been abducted by the LRA, adding that one had been involved in burning local villages. Contrary to preferred narratives of trauma, Ongom's introduction touched on the complex range of hardships that the youths had experienced regardless of whether they had been abducted. Many of the youths had lost parents, for example, and several of the young women were single mothers or were raising younger siblings. These details resonated with what Chris Dolan has called the "social torture" of northern Uganda, an endemic sense of loss and deprivation that far exceeds the LRA's abductions of children that received so much emphasis in the international media.[42] The youths avoided salacious detail in their individual testimonies. Instead, they described their desire to study agriculture at the university or to buy a sewing machine to help support their brothers and sisters. They refused to cater to the sensationalism of past suffering and instead put forward a pragmatic emphasis on the future.

Their careful, detailed presentations came to naught because members of the group insisted on interpellating these young people as abducted children or child soldiers. Two "More Life" participants, both of whom had cultivated public personas, described their experiences on blogs.[43] I interpret these blogs as technologies of "micro-celebrity," that is, "as a set of practices in which audience is viewed as a fan base; popularity is maintained through ongoing fan management; and self-presentation is carefully constructed to be consumed by others."[44] As Hearn explains, "Celebrity functions not only as [a] cultural resource in and through which individuals construct their identities, but becomes a generalizable model of profitable self-production for all individuals."[45] In order to transform A River Blue into a generalizable model of profitable self-production, the blogs reduced the complexities of the youths' testimonies to generic flatness. According to one blog, "They were abducted. They were made to burn houses with people inside. They were made into slaves for the LRA. Each story is a painful testimony of war."[46] The second participant made a curious attempt to divide the youths into categories even though the tales of trauma overlapped: "Of the 18 children we met, 9 had been abducted by the LRA. 10 had multiple family members killed by the LRA. 9 had held weapons while in the bush. One was a former child soldier. One was a child mother."[47] This diverse group of youths was swept into a collective category of victimhood in a move that betrayed a deep-seated investment in the notion of abduction.

A second intervention also came to naught. During our visit, Ongom sponsored a dance competition in the town of Aloi, offering a prize of 100,000 shillings (about $36) to the winner. Although our visit might have served as the catalyst for the event, the local population seized on and relished the opportunity to demonstrate their considerable prowess in local traditions of music and dance. Hundreds of people gathered for a festival that lasted for several hours. Dozens of groups performed intricate combinations of song and choreography, showcasing their high levels of skill in *ikoce, okeme,* and *otule* dances.[48] "More Life" participant Gerard Stropnicky published a description of the festival in *American Theatre* magazine in which Ugandan playwright and fellow participant Deborah Asiimwe eloquently summarizes the event: "Here memory, resilience, laughter and joy met. The earth, the sweat and the performers' bodies mingled into a story I believe no local or foreign journalist has told about the Acholi and Langi communities. It was sacred."[49] Ongom succinctly describes the festival as "a restoration of our spirit."[50] It marked a testament to cultural creativity that exceeded prosaic notions of theatre for development or arts therapy. We foreigners were merely incidental to a powerful display of nuanced resilience and cultural memory.

But even here, the empire of trauma reared its head. Ongom commented to the group that an LRA weapons cache had been discovered near the clearing where the dance competition occurred. This single piece of information took on a curious life of its own. In the collective journal, a participant pondered the day's experiences: "This land where George is building a new River

Blue Secondary School, this land where thousands gather today (some walked 20 km) to dance, laugh, sing, meet, was also once a killing field. Here the LRA buried a huge cache of weapons."[51] Ehn expanded on the idea of a killing field in a poetic rumination posted on his *Soulographie* blog:

> There was a small group of elderly widows who danced in a microscopic Akoshe troupe—the form is marked by its panoply of tuned drums.... They had not one drum. The lead singer/dancer dropped to her knees after an a capella stretch and played the earth the with full flats of her palms. This is the same dirt under which the LRA hid its weapons; also a massacre site; also the site where the war in the region ended (when the weapons cache was surrendered). She beat the poison out of the earth; she beat the dirt to a dance floor.[52]

I appreciate the intensity of Ehn's prose, but I question these descriptions. The LRA's violence devastated Lira District in the final years of the conflict, but to call the clearing a killing field homogenizes the entire landscape of northern Uganda and diminishes actual massacre sites. On our way to A River Blue, we stopped at the Barlonyo memorial site, where we learned of the horrific killing of more than three hundred civilians in an LRA attack in 2004.[53] Did we somehow confuse Barlonyo with Aloi? The festival offerings were powerful and evocative as performance; why call forth a story of a massacre in order to expound on the people's vitality and spirit? Does it take a killing field to legitimate their strength? Does violence ramp up their net worth?[54]

Ongom persists in his dedication to the arts. When we reconnected in Aloi in 2013, he explained that the vocational training that he offers to the youth of Alebtong District serves as a way to "lure them in" so that he can then expose them to the arts, which he sees as crucial to the community's survival as its "lifeblood." He showed me plans for the development of the program, which included the building of an arts center in order to bolster the visibility of the arts in the district and also strengthen A River Blue's offerings in the performing arts. As I examined these ambitious plans, I thought of the beautiful Lalela Arts Centre gracing the center of the Hope North campus about 150 kilometers away. Hope North and A River Blue share several characteristics: both programs are committed to the arts, attract celebrity attention, and offer educational opportunities to the war-affected youth of northern Uganda. The difference between these two programs in resources and funding, though, is stark. Among the countless NGOs and charity organizations scattered across northern Uganda, Hope North has cultivated a highly successful brand.[55]

Hope North: A Tale of Cobranding and Spinoffs

Hope North emerged from Sam's personal experiences of grief and loss. When he founded Hope North in 1998, he was living in Kampala as a leading musician, dancer, and actor in Ndere Troupe, one of Uganda's leading performing-arts companies. As a means of trying to cope with the abduction of his younger brother, coupled with his sense of helplessness regarding the escalating violence at home in Pajule, Sam bought a piece of land in what is now called Kiryandongo District near the town of Bweyale, south of the Nile River and just off the Gulu–Kampala road.[56] In 1998, he began moving communities from Pajule to this piece of land as a safer alternative to the impoverished, disease-ridden state-ordained IDP camps. The early years of Hope North consisted of a continuous scramble for funding and basic supplies. When I first met him at the 2004 screening of the film *War Child: Abducted* described in chapter 2, he had begun the construction of a school with the assistance of Q94, a Dutch NGO with the mission of helping children displaced by the war.[57]

Today, the Hope North Secondary School and Vocational Program has achieved a considerable degree of fame. The campus is located in a bucolic, peaceful setting that includes a field of neatly cultivated aloe vera plants, labeled a "Hope North demonstration field." Round huts with thatched roofs built in the traditional Luo style dot the campus, the centerpiece of which is the spacious Lalela Arts Centre, filled with a wealth of art supplies. Solar panels provide electricity for computers and the charging of cell phones. One building boasts an internet café; another is called the Olympus Hope Bread bakery. The campus fairly bursts at the seams with interventions and projects.

A surprising number of these projects developed from arts initiatives. In contrast to A River Blue, Sam's emphasis on using music and dance as a means of healing has provided significant leverage and visibility. During the filming of *The Last King of Scotland*, a 2006 film about Idi Amin that was mostly filmed in Uganda, Sam, who played the role of an aid worker in the movie, arranged for Hope North students to perform an Acholi dance in a celebratory scene in which Amin, played by Whitaker, gives a speech.[58] Whitaker's curiosity about the dancers led to a visit to Hope North campus, which marked the beginning of an ongoing relationship that has included Whitaker's donation of computers and textbooks, as well as the contribution of $30,000 to build a dormitory. Another prominent example of an arts intervention is the Lalela Arts Centre, which was built through a dedicated fund-raising effort of Lalela, an organization based in New York City and Cape Town that is dedicated to facilitating arts education for children affected by extreme poverty.[59] Even the field of aloe vera plants owes its existence to an arts intervention. Maarten Bootsma of Theatre Thot Worldwide in Holland began working with a Hope North theatre group called Loyo Loyo in 2011 to develop a play around the issue of sexual violence, titled *Who Is to Blame?*[60] He conceived of the idea of growing aloe vera at Hope North after meeting women in Gulu whose lips had been cut off by the LRA, because the aloe would provide a soothing ointment for their scars. In the instance of Hope North, the success of the MDD niche brand has provided a surprising variety of technological and agricultural spinoffs.

Hope North's success has become increasingly dependent on Sam himself. In light of a rapidly shrinking population of child soldiers in Uganda because of several years of relative stability, it has become increasingly difficult to describe the school as dedicated to "educating and healing the young victims of Uganda's civil war, including orphans and former child soldiers, empowering them to become voices for peace and development."[61] The school's mission has occasionally been rephrased as serving "child soldiers, orphans, and other disadvantaged youth," an expanded category that allows the school to broaden its reach beyond northern Uganda and enroll students from other regions.[62] But in the context of northern Uganda, a successful brand depends on the notion of LRA abduction and child soldiers, and Sam's life history is often marshaled to fulfill that need. In 2005, when we began collaborating on *Forged in Fire*, Sam referred obliquely to his past as a child soldier in the 1980s when he had served with the Uganda National Liberation Army (UNLA), the remnants of Obote's army that had fled north once Museveni's army seized control of Kampala. He preferred, though, to focus on the loss of his brother, and therefore, his own experience as a child soldier did not appear in the script.[63] As Hope North became more prominent, Sam referred to this period in his life more frequently; for example, a video ran for several years on the Hope North website in which Sam described his experiences with the UNLA.[64] The nuances of Uganda's history in the 1980s are, not surprisingly, lost on an insatiable media machine in search of a straightforward story. Sam has occasionally been described as a child soldier abducted by the LRA; that is, his past has been confused with that of his brother.[65] Having a younger brother abducted and killed is apparently not sufficient on empire's scale of African pain, and thus the tale must be embellished.

The holy grail of visibility was achieved at a cost. In part because of Whitaker's interest in Hope North, Cause Effect Agency (formerly known as Silent Five), an organization that facilitates and manages relationships between charity organizations and celebrities, has signed up Hope North as a client.[66] Although Cause Effect Agency perhaps serves as too easy a target since its raison d'être is to promote, simplify, and brand, I want to comment on the use of silence as a tool in its promotional arsenal. Sam has showcased his ability to provide critical and sharp political commentary on Ugandan affairs in multiple forums, from *Forged in Fire*, in which he condemns humanitarian intervention in no uncertain terms, to the radio stations in Kampala, where he frequently airs his political views in call-in shows. In Kampala, Sam is a "big man," as a local *boda* driver, clearly impressed that I knew him, said to me; he uses his position as a well-respected artist, activist, and entrepreneur to question the state. But the publicity machine of Hope North tends to edge out his critical voice and instead showcases his music. His music is compelling and intricate on its own terms, but this emphasis means that political speech is replaced with singing in the Acholi language. Even if his songs contain political commentary, these nuances are lost on a US and European public.[67]

At a star-studded benefit gala for Hope North held in Manhattan in 2013, the electronic music was deafening, but a similar kind of silence could be discerned. Here, the voices of the children at Hope North, the beneficiaries of the event, were not heard.[68] Aside from a video in which they thanked Mary Louise Parker for her support of Hope North, they appeared only through silent videos that contained their images and brief bios. The event culminated in an auction in which Chris Talbott, Cause Effect's founder and a longtime supporter of Hope North, earnestly pleaded with the audience to donate money to cover the costs of a year of tuition and board for one student ($1,500). When the bidding started to peter out, he began lowering the bar. "Two months for $250?" "One month for $125?" Perhaps the end justified the means—the event raised $100,000, according to Cause Effect's blog—but the objectification of the students for an event in which Parker could share her opinion of *Despicable Me 2* and Alec Baldwin's wife could show off how quickly she had "snapped back to her pre-baby figure" was, on a purely subjective note, singularly depressing.[69]

Instead of dwelling on the inevitable compromises that come with fame, a more interesting story emerges from the abundance of interventions that Hope North has attracted.[70] The organizations and individuals facilitating these various interventions fold Hope North into their promotional narratives in a process that the business world might call cobranding, "a wide range of marketing activity involving the use of two (and sometimes more) brands" that come together in a commercial alliance.[71] The concept of cobranding resonates with the dynamics of humanitarian aid, in which the (international) aid organization uses the (grassroots) NGO in its promotional material as a way of demonstrating its effectiveness and scope; meanwhile, the grassroots NGO is assumed to reap the benefits of additional exposure. A kind of cobranding occurred, for example, when the Starkey Hearing Foundation, a prominent US-based charity organization that fits children in developing countries with hearing aids, stopped at Hope North in March 2013 before moving on to Gulu with an assortment of celebrity NFL linebackers in tow.[72] Hope North might have served as an example of Starkey's global reach, but it also garnered a mention in the *Wall Street Journal* as a result of its participation in the campaign.[73]

Before proceeding further, I should acknowledge that the entire humanitarian enterprise has been roundly denounced. Linda Polman, David Rieff, and Alex de Waal are just a few of the more prominent voices who have argued that humanitarian interventions wreak more harm than good.[74] Adam Branch's critique of humanitarian interventions in northern Uganda is particularly germane to this discussion. He concludes in no uncertain terms that humanitarian organizations "directly and destructively enflamed, enabled, and prolonged the war, displacement, and civilian suffering."[75] Aid agencies might have helped feed 1.8 million displaced northern Ugandans, but instead of being praised, they should be censured for their complicity with the Ugandan government since the outpouring of aid made the camps sustainable, if barely habitable.[76] Dolan compares international aid organizations, churches, and NGOs in northern Uganda to "doctors in a torture situation," since they "appear to be there to ease the suffering of victims, but in reality they enable the process to be prolonged by keeping the victim alive for further abuse."[77] More insidiously, the humanitarian complex seeks to inculcate passivity in the general population. In another damning critique, Branch argues that "because relief agencies need the beneficiaries of aid to be incapable of doing anything about their own condition or of articulating their own demands, they help to turn the population into those requisite victims by forging a microlevel disciplinary regime whose effect is to infantilize individuals and render them helpless, thereby allowing the population to be managed through macrolevel regulation."[78] Those who resist or challenge these systems of pacification are categorized as deviant and against peace—and thus in need of even more intervention.[79] Branch focuses on macrolevel interventions carried out by agencies such as the UNHCR and the World Food Programme, but small-scale arts interventions call for a similar critique. Many of the short-term MDD interventions, in which a foreign theatre artist or company swoops down on Gulu or Lira for a brief workshop, exemplify the lack of accountability that he singles out for especially harsh criticism. I return to this critique in the next chapter.

What interests me here, though, is how the students at Hope North work within and manipulate these interventions. Relief agencies may have forged what Branch calls a microlevel disciplinary regime, but the students are quite capable of practicing microlevel resistance in return. They perform helplessness as needed, but they also use the resources provided through the interventions to serve their own purposes and ends. The Lalela Arts Centre, for example, may have been intended as an arts studio and rehearsal space, but it also provides a handy venue for the students' practices of Christian worship, such as nightly prayers and the singing of hymns—cultural expressions about which they tended to be far more enthusiastic than about conventional MDD. Like the example of Joseph Arthur's earnest "A River Blue" song, the students demonstrate considerable agency in discarding or ignoring those interventions that do not speak to their desires and aims. When I first heard about the Starkey Foundation's work at Hope North, the staff had trouble remembering the exact name of the organization, so they called it the "Sitaki Foundation" ("sitaki" translates to "I don't want" in Swahili). The significance of this nickname was clarified when I learned that many of the children who had been outfitted with hearing aids stopped wearing them within a few days because they were perceived as an embarrassment.[80] Although it is difficult to classify this refusal to wear hearing aids as an example of resistance since it also affirms the dominance of ableism, it suggests that the disciplinary regime of humanitarianism contains at least a few gaping holes.

Whitaker's activism at Hope North helps illuminate these dynamics. At first glance, Whitaker stands out as a welcome alternative to the usual parade of celebrity activists.[81] His commitment to Hope North emerged through his genuine curiosity and interest in Ugandan culture through the filming of *The Last King of Scotland*, and his dedication has manifested itself in a multifaceted and sustained manner. In addition to raising money for dormitories and donating computers, he cofounded the International Institute for Peace with Aldo Civico at Rutgers University in 2011 and went on to found his own nonprofit organization, PeaceEarth, in 2012. PeaceEarth aimed "to help societies affected by conflicts and violence transform into safe and productive communities" through a combination of "conflict resolution training, personal empowerment, education and community building."[82] In January 2013, he led PeaceEarth peace-building workshops at Hope North and then traveled to Juba in South Sudan for additional workshops. Granted, celebrity activists are inextricably caught in the machinery of self-promotion and what Lilie Chouliaraki deems, in her critique of celebrity advocacy, a "theatre of pity."[83] More specifically, Whitaker's decision to found his own organization rather than to ally himself with local initiatives is indicative of a self-aggrandizing approach that negates grassroots knowledge and community formations.[84] Still, Whitaker's tireless efforts to "cultivate the next generation of peace and community builders" brings to mind Dan Brockington's insightful comment that "we may need . . . to consider the possibility that some celebrities may wish to free themselves from the hegemonic regimes of which they are part."[85]

The sticking point is that peacemaking itself is implicated in neoliberal sovereignty since it operates in tandem with pacification and self-governance. In a quote that appears in large type in the brochures for both PeaceEarth and the International Institute for Peace, Whitaker states, "We can start by ending the war that sometimes wages inside of us. A war that can manifest itself in violence inside our homes, escalate to violence inside our communities and can lead to civil unrest in our society, which ultimately can explode into war on the world stage."[86] This well-meaning and seemingly nuanced statement unwittingly participates in a regime of societal peacemaking that, as Branch explains, "internalize[s] the causes and effects of violence to the community of victims, attributing it to deviations on the part of groups or individuals."[87] A productive northern Ugandan is a quiescent one. If an Acholi or Langi dares to protest the actions of the state or the NGO system, she risks being labeled a deviant and a troublemaker who refuses to support the regime of reconciliation and peace. Ultimately, organizations such as PeaceEarth replicate "the neoliberal logic underlying participatory development interventions, one of promoting self-management and depoliticization in the name of celebrating resilience and agency."[88] The civil unrest to which Whitaker refers could culminate in collective protests and strikes rather than war.

In these interventions, Whitaker assumes the role of the benevolent, authoritative outsider. This stance perpetuates the assumption that northern Ugandans are "incapable of autonomous action," and thus the impetus for transformation must be instigated from the outside.[89] In a UNESCO video of Whitaker's workshops in South Sudan, an unidentified South Sudanese participant explains that while working in small groups, the participants came up with five solutions "to achieve peace and stability in our regions."[90] But the video never describes what these solutions were; instead, it shifts to a scene in which Whitaker is giving a presentation on the tools of peacemaking to the room of South Sudanese youth and adults, in which he urges them to listen for "verbal cues, " that "one word" that "might cue you in to knowing where you need to direct yourself in order to be able to continue to talk." He also leads them in a meditation exercise, which is another cornerstone of PeaceEarth's philosophy. South Sudanese solutions to systematic violence are replaced with the need for careful listening and relaxation techniques. Given that social workers in the region are commonly trained in basic mediation techniques, it is unclear from the video, or from my conversations with Hope North students and staff, what Whitaker offered to the conversation aside from the weight of his fame.[91]

Whitaker's version of peacemaking did, however, include a tangible benefit. The PeaceEarth website was established as a "dynamic digital platform that gives people the power to learn, engage and act" in order to "foster dialogue among communities, practitioners and scholars; giving people key information about conflict zones, best practices in peace-building and solutions."[92] In order to provide access to this platform, PeaceEarth partnered—that is, cobranded—with the multinational technology company Ericsson, whose representatives arrived at Hope North in December 2012 with a plethora of Sony smartphones and laptops. Each participant received a smartphone along with airtime credit to facilitate access to the PeaceEarth network, where she or he might share peace-building experiences and seek out advice. Although the gifts of the smartphones came with the usual problems of foreign aid—for example, they triggered some jealousy from the staff, who were excluded from Ericsson's generous gesture—they also ensured that the peacemaking rhetoric faded into the background because of excitement over access to technology. In a blog kept by Elaine Weidman-Grunewald, Ericsson's vice president of sustainability and corporate responsibility, the students' enthusiasm is clearly conveyed: "The program runs for three days and we had set aside about two hours of the curriculum each day for ICT. However, the students' enthusiasm was so great that on day one that the [sic] plan went straight out of the window. After the full program, the Ericsson team stayed on and worked with the students for several hours more. Some even stayed on until 1.30 in the morning to get all the connectivity basics established for the students."[93] Although Weidman-Gruenwald's emphasis is, naturally enough, on the dedication of the Ericsson team, it is clear that the students were determined to take full advantage of this unique opportunity. They articulated their preferences for additional training in a context that included several powerful international players from UNESCO, Hollywood, and multinational corporations. They were decidedly not quiescent in making their claim on global technology and access.

The alliance among Whitaker's PeaceEarth, Ericsson, and Hope North might be classified as an example of what Brockington calls the "celebrity-charity-corporate complex," in which corporations in pursuit of the CSR (corporate social responsibility) brand seek out associations with NGOs that have developed links with celebrities in order to become associated with (and subtly endorsed by) those celebrities.[94] In this sense, Hope North serves as little more than a convenient stepping-stone to boost Ericsson's visibility and already substantial hold on the global market through its association with Forest Whitaker and UNESCO. Alternatively, one might perceive the technology as a kind of sugarcoating to lure Ugandan youth into the clutches of the peacemaking disciplinary regime. Indeed, this regime manifested itself when the participants were warned not to use the smartphones to listen to music, which was presumably a frivolous pastime that would detract from the "serious" peacemaking work for which the smartphones were intended.

Again, though, the regime could be ignored. Its lack of coherence makes it easy to do so; PeaceEarth's vaunted internet platform was down for weeks when I was writing the first draft of this chapter.[95] Also, because of a lack of funds, the participants often purchased airtime at their own expense, making it easy to justify using the smartphones as they wished. "The celebrity charity corporate complex" is a daunting phrase that might loom large on a macro-level; however, its articulation on the ground was relatively shaky and readily ignored by its designated subjects.

Whitaker's projects are folded into a profusion of activities that are par for the course at Hope North. The rush of projects and workshops, which range from theatre to fine art to peacemaking to meditation, makes Hope

North a veritable marketplace of interventions in which students assume the role of selective consumers. Granted, the ubiquity of these interventions calls to mind Vinh-Kim Nguyen's argument that workshops do little more than serve as evidence of "program outputs" for charitable organizations and NGOs, whereas the real problem—namely, the lack of material resources—is pushed aside.[96] My point here, though, is that the humanitarian regime falters in the midst of these multiple and overlapping interventions. The frenzy of activities throws a coherent humanitarian or neoliberal agenda into disarray; even the machinery of branding struggles to keep up.

Several arts interventions at Hope North were facilitated by Maarten Bootsma, the energetic and irrepressible founder of Theatre Thot Worldwide, a Netherlands-based theatre company that aims to use theatre to empower Ugandan youth. As he bounds around the country starting theatre companies in Mbale, Gulu, and Mukono and at Hope North, he dispenses material support in exchange for the group's commitment to create and tour plays aimed at social change. For example, as mentioned previously, he worked with the Loyo Loyo theatre company at Hope North to develop a play titled *Who Is to Blame?*, which tells the tale of a girl who is seduced by a boy who abandons her when she finds out that she is pregnant. In exchange for touring the production to villages around Bweyale, Bootsma provided the school with a social worker and a nurse, as well as medical supplies and new doors and windows for the buildings on Hope North's campus. Such actions demonstrate a keen awareness that drama creation and production are labor-intensive processes that demand material support. Whereas the development industry uses generous per diems to ensure that local participants attend its workshops, Maarten provides his theatre companies with sewing machines, pharmaceuticals, and a peanut grinder.[97] Although economists such as Christopher Blattman might point out that cash transfers would probably be more effective in improving the participants' standard of living, Bootsma's awareness of the limitations of theatre projects in resource-poor locations provides a refreshing corrective to the naïveté or arrogance of most foreign arts interventions.[98]

My personal favorite of his projects was the flash mob. During his residency at Hope North in 2013, Bootsma aimed to extend Theatre Thot's activities into the wider student population, beyond the relatively small group of students who were active in Loyo Loyo. To that end, he conceived of the idea of producing a flash mob in Bweyale—that is, having the students stage a seemingly spontaneous performance that would be short and impactful and would quickly disappear. He brought two female choreographers from his theatre company in Holland to teach the students a dance that would be performed at the flash mob. True to his commitment to exchange, he promised to take all the students who participated on a trip to Murchison Falls National Park. Although his use of Dutch company members to choreograph the flash mob overlooks the many talented and skilled choreographers in Kampala, the women developed an effective choreography that was compelling, allowed for improvisational movement, and could be learned by the students regardless of their prior exposure to hip-hop dance.

They also selected a powerful recording that the students embraced. The music they chose for the flash mob was Michael Jackson's "They Don't Care about Us," considered one of Jackson's most controversial and angriest singles.[99] The lyrics consist of a frank call for social justice; I am not sure that the students understood all the lyrics (which were not always clear on the recording), but they clearly understood and delighted in the oft-repeated refrain, "All I wanna say is that / they don't really care about us!"[100] The half-hour rehearsals, held daily in the late afternoon, were filled with a sense of eagerness and excitement as the students practiced the lively and forceful choreography. I suspect that the students would have participated regardless of Bootsma's offer to take them to the Murchison Falls National Park in exchange for performing in the flash mob.[101]

Bootsma expressed disappointment about the flash mob's actual execution, which occurred in the late afternoon of March 6, 2013. He had wanted it to start unobtrusively on the periphery of town and slowly build in the characteristic style of the flash mobs in Europe and the United States. The Bweyale police, however, foiled his plans. For security reasons, they insisted that the dance be performed on the main Gulu–Kampala road that runs through Bweyale; in addition, the sizable police detail served to alert the townspeople well in advance that a special event was on the horizon. As a result, hundreds of Bweyale residents were waiting with anticipation to see what the Hope North students would present. Bootsma might have been disappointed, but the people of Bweyale, which contains a multifaceted population of former refugees from surrounding countries, as well as a diverse mix of northern Ugandans, cheered with gusto, and youthful spectators imitated the choreography and improvised their own movements.[102] Adult staff at Hope North participated alongside the students with a clear sense of enjoyment. I was reminded of the dancing at the World Vision rehabilitation center described in chapter 2, in which the

Gifted by Trauma | 237

Fig. 13. The Hope North flash mob in Bweyale, Uganda, March 2013.

force of mutual enthusiasm caused usual hierarchical structures to be at least temporarily blurred.

The flash mob stands out as one of the most pleasurable moments in my fieldwork, perhaps because it escaped the machinery of branding in which Hope North seemed so thoroughly caught. Although flash mobs were originally created with the idea of escaping branding—they were semispontaneous, highly participatory, and "purposeless" aside from bringing together people in an act of performance—corporations have been quick to seize on their marketing potential.[103] In 2012, for example, a flash mob was performed in Garden City Mall in Kampala, at the end of which a large banner depicting the logo of Airtel, a local cell-phone service, was unfurled.[104] In contrast, the Hope North flash mob returned to the kind of brandlessness in which the flash mob had originally been conceived. Neither Hope North nor Theatre Thot Worldwide referred to the event in their websites, Facebook accounts, or other kinds of publicity; instead, the event fell through the cracks of the branding machine as if it had never occurred. Perhaps the defiant refrain of Jackson's song—"They don't really care about us!"—was simply too close for comfort. One might interpret the song as an indictment of the entire humanitarian enterprise. To my mind, Jackson's harsh condemnation of the social system served as a welcome corrective to Joseph Arthur's paean to passivity and victimization at A River Blue.

At the flash mob, Sunday Komakech, one of the few remaining former child soldiers at Hope North at the time, stood out from his peers in his confident execution of the dance steps. I close this discussion of Hope North with a particular focus on Sunday's ability to pick and choose from the plethora of interventions at Hope North in order to fashion his self-brand, which might be termed Gifted by Coolness. As a participant in PeaceEarth's workshops, Sunday added to his already stylish wardrobe a PeaceEarth backpack and a Sony smartphone. One might argue that by accepting these new accessories, he consented to being branded by Sony and PeaceEarth since he now bore their logos wherever he went. This approach, though, disavows the ease with which he used these markers of a global economy to assert, as James Ferguson put it, "a declaration of comparability, an aspiration to membership and inclusion in the world."[105] The brands of Sony and PeaceEarth paled next to his dynamic and strategic promotion of his modern, hip self.

Accessorizing was just the beginning. He took full advantage of Ericsson's technical training in the PeaceEarth workshops; he was adept at using not only his smartphone but also my laptop computer, demonstrating functions and settings of which I was quite unaware.[106] In following Whitaker's call to create a peacemaking culture among the youth, he founded a peace club in his home area of Pabbo, a former IDP camp that has become a bustling town center.[107] Peace organizations are endemic in northern Uganda and call to mind Branch's point that such clubs often serve as a tool of pacification.[108] Sunday's peace club, though, served an eminently practical purpose. He was able to use his role as a liaison between Hope North and the peace club to provide application forms and guide its members through the application process; most of the membership went on to matriculate at Hope North. Impressed by his intellect and drive, I asked him to accompany me to a memorial ceremony in Atiak as a research assistant. At the ceremony, he posed in front of the memorial for a photo, which he subsequently posted on his Facebook account as an example of his commitment to peacemaking. When we visited the World Vision rehabilitation center in Gulu, which was empty save for about a dozen adult men who had escaped from the LRA or surrendered in the DRC, he enthusiastically extolled the benefits of aloe vera gel to director Susan Alal as a salve for one of the men whose lips had been cut off. He also took full

Fig. 14. Sunday Komakech at the Atiak memorial, April 2013.

advantage of Bootsma's acting workshops and was cast in the lead role in Loyo Loyo's play, *Who Is to Blame?* Like youth across the continent, Sunday was a young man on the move. He freely patched together pieces of knowledge gleaned from his participation in Hope North's many interventions in order to take on a range of leadership roles. In the process, his past as a former child soldier receded before his continually crafted, newly authoritative identity.

Even the Buddhist practice of mindfulness was folded into Sunday's self-brand. In 2007, Ehn brought his "More Life" group to Hope North to participate in theatre workshops with the students. These workshops are discussed in more detail in chapter 6 as an example of activism; for now, though, I mention that the participants included Theo Koffler, who founded her charity organization Mindfulness Without Borders that same year. With Sam's encouragement, she returned to Hope North in 2011 to conduct a mindfulness and meditation workshop, in which Sunday participated. Like the peace interventions that Branch critiques, her organization could be categorized as catering to neoliberal ideology that emphasizes individual responsibility as opposed to that of the state. As she explains on her website, an "'education of the heart' will help foster caring, responsible and accountable global citizens."[109] The international community and the state escape accountability despite their heavy-handed role in the conditions that merit her intervention in the first place. Koffler describes further, "We all have stresses in our life; however, it's the causes and conditions that change as you cross borders. . . . No matter what the history, drama or conflict, we can learn universal skills to help mediate those stresses."[110] Given that the practice of relaxation, breathing, and listening as a solution to the "stress" of a twenty-year civil war could be construed as an especially peculiar intervention, one might dismiss Koffler's mission as an amusing example of the tired old story of misguided humanitarianism.

But from Sunday's perspective, the story takes an intriguing twist. Koffler provided each of the participants in the program with a Mindfulness Without Borders certificate that designated him or her as an Ambassador of Mindfulness. The significance of a certificate presented by a US-based organization in a region of extremely scarce opportunities for formal schooling cannot be overstated: this certificate represented access, opportunity, and authority. The certificate provided Sunday with considerable traction in his home community of Pabbo, where he was welcomed as a mediator in a variety of land and domestic disputes. Sunday's specific techniques were not nearly as important as the possession of the certificate, in which mindfulness was understood as mediation.

He told me with considerable pride about an instance in which he was asked to help mediate a land dispute—"I was the youngest person in the room!" Sunday's ability to assemble these various accoutrements into a polished self-presentation speaks to another kind of brand-in-the-making—Gifted by Dignity.

Memorialization and the Rebranding of Northern Uganda

Memorials dot the landscape of postconflict northern Uganda. Atiak, Barlonyo, and Lukodi are just a few sites of the more spectacular massacres conducted by the Lord's Resistance Army.[111] Local communities have responded to these cataclysmic events by organizing annual ceremonies and constructing memorials made of cement or mud bricks. The structures seem straightforward enough. "HERE LIE THE REMAINS OF 121 INNOCENT UGANDANS," reads the caption engraved on the Barlonyo memorial. "IN LOVING MEMORY OF OUR SONS AND DAUGHTERS MASSACRED IN ATIAK," proclaims the memorial in Atiak. These forthright statements and rectangular structures belie layers of tension between local communities and the Ugandan government. Visitors to the Barlonyo memorial are invariably informed that the engraved number 121 is grossly incorrect, and that at least 300 victims died in the attack. If visitors stay a bit longer, they might also hear about President Museveni's speech at the mass burial a month after the attack, in which he blamed northern Ugandans for their own suffering because of their role in perpetuating state violence under Obote's regime in the 1980s.[112] If they continue to linger, they might hear more about the circumstances of this mass burial, in which UPDF soldiers ordered bodies that had been buried in family compounds in accordance with local custom to be dug up and reburied in the mass grave.[113] It is relatively easy to scratch the surface and reveal long-standing anger and hostility toward the government, which perhaps is an easier target than the LRA itself.

Layers of meaning are seemingly infinite in contexts of direct and structural violence. As previously mentioned, I first visited the Barlonyo memorial with the "More Life" exchange in 2011. Instead of dwelling on the actual massacre, our Barlonyo guide, Quinto Okello, emphasized the reprehensible behavior of the UPDF after the attack, Museveni's unfulfilled promises (which included a vocational school and a bridge) made in 2004, and Barlonyo's ongoing impoverishment despite the emergence of political stability after the LRA's departure from Uganda. The memorial was being used as an impromptu chalkboard by children who had covered the tiles of the vertical structure with mathematical equations. Although this gesture of reappropriation serves as an example of the resourcefulness and pragmatism found throughout Central Africa, it also articulated a subtle demand in a region with extremely scarce opportunities for education beyond the primary level.[114]

The equations had vanished when I visited Barlonyo again in 2013.[115] In a sense, the demand had been answered—the promised vocational school had finally opened about two months earlier, at a cost of about 500 million shillings (US$200,000). The memorial had been refurbished; cracks had been sealed, and shrubbery had been trimmed. Even the construction of the promised bridge was well under way. This time, I was visiting with Ongom from A River Blue, as well as Laurence Ocen, a PhD student from Makerere University whose dissertation topic was memorialization in northern Uganda.[116] Like Ongom, Ocen hailed from Lira, the subregion in which Barlonyo was located. Moses Ogwang, a representative of the Barlonyo Memorial Preservation Association, took considerable pride in pointing out the new school compound and describing the bridge; he also shared the community's plans to build a memorial center that would help visitors learn more about the tragedy that had occurred. Not content with simply describing the bridge project, he invited us to see it for ourselves, and we took a short drive to the Moroto River. The bridge would provide a much-needed link from the poverty-stricken rural area of Barlonyo to the bustling commercial center of Lira Town, allowing access to Lira's markets even during times of flooding. Then came the clincher: it was to be called Kaguta Bridge. "Why Kaguta?" I asked, startled—Kaguta is Museveni's middle name. "To show our gratitude," Ogwang said with a smile; Ongom and Ocen laughed at the joke. Their obvious delight in the irony of naming the bridge after Museveni reminded me that in the context of northern Uganda, pragmatism often trumps revenge. Anger is not forgotten, but it might be deferred.

Memory, though, is steadfast. Ongom drew me away from the bridge. He pointed at the river and explained that this was where his elder brother had drowned while fleeing Acholi soldiers during the 1985 coup of Tito Okello.[117] Ongom's retelling of his brother's death served as a stark reminder that the conflict between the Ugandan government and the LRA is only the most recent manifestation of a multifaceted and harrowing narrative of conflict and violence. Museveni is merely the tip of the northern Ugandan iceberg as a cause of regional suffering, and he, at least, capitulated to popular demand to build a bridge—a bridge that would facilitate the sale of their produce and help them access the economic advantages of a postconflict era; a bridge that might facilitate a crossover to a more dignified life despite the painful memories that ran just beneath.

Memorialization serves as a means for forging a postconflict identity. In 2006, as the LRA withdrew from Uganda and the region started to develop an uneasy identity as postconflict, the rhetoric of memorialization began to flourish. Grassroots attempts to remember and mourn the dead turned into heated terrain as victim associations, government forces, cultural foundations, opposition politicians, NGOs, and tourist agents sought to lay claim to the memorials as a point of access to material resources and visibility. The annual ceremonies have become political theatre on an elaborate scale, featuring casts of grandstanding politicians, members of victim associations in matching T-shirts, representatives of NGOs bearing ostentatious wreaths, and, in one memorable instance, a pregnant goat. In Uganda, South Africa and Rwanda dominate theories and conventions of memorialization; cultural workers in northern Uganda both react against and draw from these traditions and offer startling interventions into the politics and performance of memory. As described in the final pages of this chapter, pregnant goats and bridges serve as tangible manifestations of their reinvention of a global tradition.[118]

Meanwhile, the branding machine nips at their heels. In 2011, Tourism State Minister Agnes Akiror announced a new initiative to develop four LRA sites for tourism.[119] In a frank choice of words, she called the initiative "dark tourism," a term coined to describe "the act of travel to sites associated with death, suffering and the seemingly macabre."[120] Dark tourism is practiced throughout the world, but in northern Uganda, where Rwanda's shadow looms, the concept takes on a competitive edge. Rwanda's vast network of genocide memorials and specifically the Kigali Memorial Centre are often mentioned in the Ugandan press as a model well worth following in order to mine the economic potential of Uganda's violent past.[121] Private organizations, keen to borrow from Rwanda's example, knew better than to wait for the Ministry of Tourism to make a decisive move. In 2012, Uganda Radio Network reported that a Gulu-based tourist agency was charging foreign visitors a hundred dollars to take them to see the memorial in Atiak, not a cent of which was received by the survivors.[122] In 2015, US criminologist Diana Peel founded Changing Horizons, a company that specializes in dark tourism in northern Uganda. Visitors can book the "Child Soldier Tour," the "LRA Historical Tour," the "ICC Indictee Tour," and, for those short on time, the "LRA Weekend Tour."[123] Mass pain can be profitable for those who are quick to take advantage.

I suspect, though, that these operators face a formidable obstacle because the people of northern Uganda are fiercely cognizant of how their pain can be marketed for others' profit. A vivid glimpse of this collective awareness appears in an Al Jazeera video that documents the screening of *Kony 2012* in Lira. The screening, which was sponsored by the Lira-based NGO African Youth Initiative Network (AYINET), was shut down because of the angry response of the spectators, some of whom threw stones at the screen. "It celebrates our suffering," one former LRA abductee insisted.[124] An unidentified spectator at the screening expresses anger against "some kind of NGO [that is] trying to mobilize funds using the atrocities committed in northern Uganda!" Despite an official explanation that AYINET stopped the screenings out of fear of "retraumatizing" the victims, it was startlingly clear that the Lira spectators were simply and defiantly angry about a system that sensationalizes, appropriates, and oversimplifies their past.[125] The determination and anger have not dissipated since *Kony 2012*. In 2015, AYINET coordinated a memorial ceremony at Barlonyo that brought together over thirty-five representatives from war-affected areas across Uganda, including the Acholi subregion, the Lango subregion, Teso, West Nile, the Luwero Triangle, and the western Ugandan districts of Isingiro and Kasese.[126] The Lira representatives used the high-profile event to issue frank warnings against the forces of appropriation. Denis Omara, a survivor of the Barlonyo massacre, requested, "To some people, do not make this kind of arrangement a personal gain. If you have been doing that make a U-turn. Pray for change in your houses."[127] Ogwang, speaking as a representative of the Barlonyo Memorial Association, was more direct: "Never be surprised one time, to hear that the people of Barlonyo have turned against visitors who come with the aim of benefiting from our own blood."[128] Tourist operators, NGOs, and foreign researchers, take heed.

Such determination ensures that the forces of neoliberalism are at least partly subdued. In this section, the discourse of branding fades into the background because it simply cannot account for the dynamics of memorialization, in which the demands of justice, therapy, and spirituality coalesce. The Ministry of Tourism's grand announcement about the four LRA sites, for example, signified a relatively halfhearted attempt to latch on to a carefully conceived collaboration between the state-run Uganda Museum and the Directorate of Norwegian Heritage; the ministry's impact on the project was marginal at best. This collaboration, which began in 2009 and culminated in an exhibition in Kampala in 2013, facilitated a series of interactions among the state and local communities affected by war.¹²⁹ The official mission of the three-year project was "to promote reconciliation and peace through documentation and presentation of memorial places, buildings, and cultural heritage sites of significance to the conflict."¹³⁰ In addition to tangible results, such as refurbished memorials, a documentary film, and an exhibition in Kampala, the project also clarified the ambivalences and dissonances of dark heritage.

The combination of the four sites captures some of the breadth and the complexity of the conflict. Three of the sites—Barlonyo, Lukodi, and Pabbo—were IDP camps and therefore speak to the looming shadow of state and structural violence that exacerbated the violence of the LRA. Barlonyo and Lukodi are perhaps the most conventional choices in terms of dark heritage since both camps experienced two of the most notorious examples of LRA massacres; they also encompass both Langi and Acholi suffering because of their respective locations in Lira and just outside Gulu town.¹³¹ Pabbo, located in Amuru District north of Gulu, was one of the earliest and largest IDP camps in the region, with an estimated population of 60,000 at its peak. Although Pabbo did not experience mass killing per se, it epitomizes the practice of social torture insofar that it was wracked by disease, malnutrition, and massive insecurity.¹³² The fourth site, St. Mary's College at Aboke, is famous as a girls' boarding school where 139 schoolgirls were abducted by the LRA in 1996. Although Aboke is located in Apac District, which is part of the Lango subregion, the abducted girls came from all over northern Uganda. Aboke offers a counternarrative of violence insofar as the school's annual memorial event marks a day of celebration rather than mourning since almost all the abducted girls have returned; therefore, Aboke emphasizes restoration rather than victimhood and pain.¹³³ The geopolitics of the four sites counteract standard narratives of the LRA conflict that emphasize the suffering of the Acholi and marginalize the experiences of other northern ethnic groups, such as the Langi; they also speak to a nuanced continuum of violence rather than singling out the most direct and spectacular. The museum curators sought to provide an array of glimpses into the complexities of the conflict that encompassed geographic and ethnic diversity, as well as multifaceted experiences of war.

Despite the boldness of the concept, ambivalence prevailed in its execution. On the one hand, the Norwegian funding of US$270,000 was put to effective use because it facilitated several months of research and documentation in the site areas. The curators also sought to strengthen alliances among the affected communities through organizing a dance festival at Aboke and opening the exhibition in Kampala; groups and individuals from all four sites participated in these celebratory events.[134] Finally, the Barlonyo mass grave, which was in dire need of repair because of extensive cracking, was cleaned and refurbished; the dormitory at Aboke where the girls had been abducted was also repainted.[135] On the other hand, the two Acholi sites, Lukodi and Pabbo, fell through the cracks of attention and support. During my first visit, the Lukodi memorial structure was overgrown with tall grass and shrubs, and a large section of a plaque listing names of the dead had fallen off. Justin Ocan, a survivor of the Lukodi massacre, pointed out the site where the new memorial will be built and spoke hopefully of receiving funding for its design and construction. Similarly, Orach Otim, a former resident of the Pabbo IDP camp and an informal historian who had assembled an archive of photographs of the camp, spoke eagerly of the day when the museum would construct a memorial center where his collection of photos and other artifacts could be displayed.[136] Back in Kampala, museum curator Nelson Abiti smiled ruefully when I shared these hopes with him—he had his own hopes that new sources of funding would be found so that Pabbo and Lukodi could receive the resources they needed.[137] Even the government's awareness of the sites' potential for tourism, which usually has the effect of moving a sluggish state into action, has not translated into tangible effects.[138]

Scholars of memorialization might point out that ambivalence is par for the course in dark heritage. In *Places of Pain and Shame: Dealing with "Difficult Heritage,"* a book that influenced the Uganda Museum's conception of the memorial project, William Logan and Keir Reeves note that "all places of pain and shame reveal dissonances, since there are always perpetrators and sufferers and their perceptions inevitably differ radically."[139] But ambivalence has a distinctive cadence in Uganda, where the roles of perpetrators and sufferers go hand in hand. In 2015, senior LRA commander Dominic Ongwen was taken into custody in the CAR and transferred to the ICC at The Hague to be tried for war crimes and crimes against humanity.[140] Although the ICC prosecution has singled out his alleged leadership of the massacre in Lukodi and attacks in Pajule, Odek, and Abok, Ongwen is linked to numerous atrocities; he not only participated in but also orchestrated the suffering of thousands of people in Uganda, the DRC, and the CAR.[141] But Ongwen's childhood has become a flash point of legal and moral controversy because the LRA killed his mother and abducted him from his home village in Amuru district at the age of nine.[142] As Erin Baines observes, "Ongwen is the first known person to be charged with the same crimes of which he is also a victim."[143] She asks a series of pointed questions designed to expose the arbitrariness of international justice: "How should individual responsibility be addressed in the context of collective victimization? What agency is available to individuals who are raised within a setting of extreme brutality? How can justice be achieved for Ongwen and for the victims of the crimes he committed?"[144] As several northern Ugandans have pointed out, the Ugandan government should also be on trial since it failed to protect Ongwen in the first place.[145] To return to Logan and Reeves, dissonances are not just revealed but threaten to invalidate the entire process.

The curators at the Uganda Museum demonstrated keen awareness of the tensions that pervaded their project. The brochure includes a quote from Marita Sturken's analysis of the Vietnam War Memorial: "How . . . does a society commemorate a war for which the central narrative is one of division and dissent, a war whose whole history is highly contested and still in the process of being made?"[146] Unlike the examples of Rwanda and South Africa, Uganda has not ushered in a new political order tasked with forging unity and cohesion out of a population of perpetrators, victims, bystanders, and witnesses. The title of the exhibition, *Road to Reconciliation*, echoes the slogan of South Africa's Truth Commission, "Truth: The Road to Reconciliation," but also gives it a Ugandan twist. As Catherine Cole points out, the South African slogan posits a single path to a single destination and thus forecloses alternative routes.[147] Although the Ugandan version also privileges the notion of reconciliation, the actual route is left unstated, as if to acknowledge that the people of northern Uganda are on uncharted terrain.

How to memorialize ambivalence? When the Justice and Reconciliation Project (JRP), a well-organized and prominent NGO based in Gulu, began documenting the role of memorialization in northern Uganda, one of its interviewees provided a glimpse into the depths of Ugandan violence.[148] In Atiak, which experienced one of the most brutal massacres in the history of the LRA conflict, the interviewee expressed his deep ambivalence over memorialization with the striking statement "We can't be sure who killed us and worse still we know that nothing shall come of it."[149] Julian Hopwood, the author of the JRP report, muses on the implication of this quote in light of the fact that "in a war clouded in mystery, the Atiak massacre is one of only a few relatively well-documented incidents."[150] The people of Atiak *do* know who killed them; in particular, it is well known that Vincent Otti, the LRA's second-in-command, who himself came from Atiak, ordered the attack. Hopwood interprets this statement as an example of how the involvement of Otti, one of their own, is "impossible to comprehend or, as in the case of the man quoted above, to even acknowledge."[151]

I would extend the implications of this statement beyond the LRA itself. "We can't be sure who killed us" because when did the killing begin? Ongom's reference to his brother's death in the Moroto River serves as a stark reminder that the extent of the violence far exceeds that of the LRA conflict, encompassing the NRA's pacification of the north, the Bush War, Amin's and Obote's regimes, and the *longue durée* of British colonialism.[152] If accountability is not possible, as the Atiak respondent suggested, then memorialization is futile. Alternative narratives and counternarratives of memory disappear into the quicksand of ambivalence. Instead, the memorials of northern Uganda achieve the startling task of articulating absence. They withhold memory. They withhold grief. They withhold catharsis. The north has reached new heights of ambivalence, culminating in memorials that manage to evade the substance of what is being remembered.

To be clear, memorials are desired. As late as 2013, the people of Abia constructed their own memorial structure to mark a local massacre, which occurred in 2004 just before the one at Barlonyo, and more will probably be built in the years to come.[153] But these memorials are often perceived as a gateway to economic development and reparations rather than a means of giving closure to their grief. Northern Ugandans might be ambivalent regarding definitions of victimhood, but impoverishment and loss throughout the region are undeniable. The emphasis on redress marks not only a reappropriation of memorial discourse but also a rebranding of northern Uganda. The prefix "re" suggests both repetition and withdrawal and thus helps capture the dynamics of the memorial ceremonies.[154] The communities of Atiak, Barlonyo, and Lukodi participate in the branding of northern Uganda, but they alter the terms of the exchange. In an act of withdrawal, they refuse to trade pain for material aid.[155] They reject the neoliberal ideology that underlies much of the humanitarian emphasis on individual accountability and responsibility. Instead, they articulate a distinct, direct, and sustained demand on the Ugandan state. "In Alebtong, on Feb. 4th, 2004 we lost 190 people to the LRA," Odia Ray of Abia told the crowds at the 2015 Barlonyo ceremony. "For these people to come back to life, we want government to restock our region."[156] This statement encapsulates both the straightforwardness of their claim and the intensity of their need. Remembrance and compensation are fused.

My thoughts are based primarily on my observations of the 2013 memorial ceremonies at Atiak and Lukodi.[157] Memorial ceremonies have taken on a fairly standard structure found throughout the north. On the eve of the main ceremony, locals gather at the site of the memorial for a prayer ceremony. After a priest leads the people in prayer, candles are distributed. As Christian hymns are sung (occasionally in English but mostly in Acholi or Langi), participants light their candles through a passing of the flame. Then a final prayer is given. At the candlelight service in Lukodi, a representative of the victim's association reminded us to leave our candles burning on the memorial structure itself so that the victims would know that they are not forgotten.

The following morning, tables and desks are set up in a clearing at some distance from the memorial, typically in the compound of the local primary school. The official ceremony begins once a sizable group of locals and invited guests (primarily NGO representatives and Local Council members) has gathered. At the event in Atiak, several major politicians attended, including Norbert Mao, one of the leading opposition politicians in Uganda, and Hilary Onek, the minister of internal affairs. After a series of prayers, everyone proceeds to the memorial, where designated representatives lay funeral wreaths on it in a formal procession. Participants and observers then return to the clearing for more speeches and prayers; at this point, local choirs and dance groups also perform. The event culminates in a communal meal and the distribution of sodas. In Atiak, several hundred people were served a meal; in Lukodi, the number was closer to 150.

When I attended the event in Atiak, it became clear that this was not an occasion for public mourning.[158] There were no tears, testimonies, or reading of the victims' names. Instead, we listened to hours of speeches , in which the ruling NRM party, represented by the measured Onek, confronted the opposition Democratic Party, represented by the charismatic and fiery Mao. Although two of the male survivors were recognized—they were the first to lay the wreaths at the memorial structure—they never spoke. The female survivors were highly visible at Atiak in their matching white T-shirts (provided courtesy of the JRP); these women took charge of the preparation of the food and the serving of the meal at the end of the ceremony. But even when they took center stage during the actual event and sang to us, they sang in innocuous praise of Museveni's government for bringing an end to the violence. One of the religious leaders acknowledged these women in his speech that followed their performance, mentioning that they had been forced to applaud the LRA once the killing was finished. This comment was the only specific reference to that day during the entire event, which went on for about seven hours.

The following month, I attended the memorial ceremony at Lukodi on May 19. I anticipated that a mood of mourning would be more pronounced at this event given that the massacre occurred in relatively recent memory—in 2004, as opposed to 1995 in the case of Atiak. I was privileged to attend the candlelight ceremony the night before the official ceremony; the singing was beautiful and, to me, moving. The visual image of the stone covered with flickering, melting candles seemed to me a powerful way of remembering the dead without making survivors relive their trauma through the sharing of testimony. Unlike similar memorial events I had attended in neighboring Rwanda, no one wept. No one became angry. They sang, held their burning candles, and prayed.[159]

The Lukodi ceremony was smaller and less elaborate than the Atiak event. Although a few representatives from NGOs such as the JRP attended, it lacked the political grandstanding of Atiak. In this sense, Lukodi perhaps came closer to the international model of how memorialization is supposed to "look." In an analysis of the 2007 memorial ceremony at Atiak, JRP researchers lament its emphasis on politics: "Apart from the laying of the wreaths and the preaching by the religious leaders, there was no other indication that the ceremony was in memory of the massacre which occurred. The organizers need to find a way of cutting down on the politics in the speeches of the politicians, and replace them with testimonies from surviving victims and relatives of those massacred."[160] The JRP would presumably approve of the diminished political presence at Lukodi. What is striking, though, is that Lukodi's absence of politics was not filled with the specifics of memory. Even if the organizers had wished to include testimonies, they would have been in short supply; to the distress of the organizers, many of the families of the victims had chosen not to attend either the candlelight ceremony or the official memorial event. In the absence of politics and memory, the event wrapped up relatively quickly by midafternoon with the obligatory communal meal—which, as Sunday pointed out to me, was considerably smaller than the portions served at Atiak. During the ceremony, the organizers spoke wistfully of Atiak's ceremony as a model of what Lukodi might one day achieve.[161]

To return to the example of Atiak, though, the politics is precisely what interests me. In the midst of the grandstanding and posturing, northern Ugandans are pushing a very specific agenda—a meticulous insistence on a politics of repair. In Cole's discussion of the South African Truth and Reconciliation Commission, she calls attention to Albie Sachs's suggestion that "rather than a 'Truth and Reconciliation Commission,' what South Africa needed was a 'Commission of Truth and *Repair*."[162] Cole expands on this concept: "Repair is a continuous process, at once practical and immediate. If the nation, like a house, is to be habitably maintained, repairs will be ongoing and never ending."[163] The concept of repair mimics the idea of reparation, but with a critical difference: instead of a one-off payment meant to silence further criticism and dialogue, the social fabric of northern Uganda will need mending for decades.

To mend, northern Ugandans need cash. The Atiak ceremony provided several opportunities for audience members to donate money. The most spectacular example occurred when a pregnant goat wearing a sign, "Atiak Massacre Survivors Association Auctioning," was paraded through the audience and auctioned off; the money that was collected through the auction was handed over to the association in a moment of public recognition. The group of politicians sitting in the VIP seats located front and center were called on to drop 20,000 and 50,000 Ugandan shilling notes into an enormous wooden mortar, which they did in the ostentatious East African style of waving the notes over their heads as they slowly made their way to the mortar. Mao and Onek were the main bidders in a showdown of performed generosity. Once the goat was sold to the tune of 600,000 Ugandan shillings (about US$240 in 2013), the mortar and pestle were auctioned off, raising another 400,000 Ugandan shillings (about US$160) for the Atiak Sub-county Peace Committee. Faced with Museveni's refusal to consider financial reparations and the systemic corruption of a government that steals aid earmarked for the north, the people of Atiak appropriate the symbolic capital of memorials and translate it into hard cash.[164] Given that northern Ugandans have endured two decades of social torture, a mere $400 hardly marks a triumphant moment of radical politics. That said, the annual ceremonies provide regular opportunities to empty the pockets of attending politicians and profit from the games and tensions of multiparty democracy. They also serve as public forums in which participants can exert pressure on the government to fulfill its social contract through the provision of educational programs and infrastructure; unfulfilled promises are gleefully and regularly reported in the Ugandan press. To return briefly to the Barlonyo example, the building of the Kaguta Bridge and the vocational school were hardly manifestations of state largesse.

Fig. 15. The annual memorial ceremony in Atiak, April 2013. Norbert Mao, president of the opposition Democratic Party, contributes cash toward the goat auction.

The people pushed for them, using the annual ceremony as a forum to articulate their demands and agitate for state promises to be fulfilled.[165]

Another tantalizing quote appears in the JRP literature: "They should pay us for this torture. They should pay us so we can forget."[166] This quotation, drawn from an interview in West Nile, appears in a report about the politics of economic reparations in northern Uganda.[167] Lest this quotation be construed as a crass exchange of memory for cash, it should be noted that the respondent uses the term *forget*, not forgive. Because of course, they cannot forget. The ludicrousness of the statement underscores its impossibility. The stories of loss are seared into households, extended families, and villages. Deaths and disappearances of loved ones are endemic. A Ugandan proverb states that the teeth may smile. but the heart does not forget.[168] Pay us so we can smile at the ludicrous name of the Kaguta Bridge. Pay us so we can resume the beleaguered project of nation building, which is, of course, dependent on the notion of forgetting. Pay us, or we will take the Ugandan government to court.[169]

Living memorials allow for the fusion of reparation and remembrance. Nelson Abiti, a curator of the Uganda Museum who played a key role in the memorialization project, explained passionately that memorials should be alive, not static, and that they should contribute to capacity building among communities. "They should be *living* memorials," he stated firmly.[170] The concept of living memorials is often traced to Albie Sachs, who, in *The Strange Alchemy of Life and Law*, defines living memorials as material, tangible things that benefit those who experienced loss. His examples of living memorials include "scholarships for the children of those who died, streets renamed, gardens created, and monuments designed—not grandiose 'monumental' monuments but ones as simple as the people themselves and as searing, sharp and evocative as the pain they had suffered."[171] I believe that his first example—scholarships for the children of those who died—comes the closest to what northern Ugandans would categorize as living memorials, meaning those that help them *live*.[172] Such memorials emphasize an imagined future rather than a painful past. The more grandiose the annual ceremony, the more likely it is that this imagined future will be achieved. Through their large-scale politics and meticulous insistence on repair, I anticipate that Barlonyo and Atiak will come to reign as models of living memory in northern Uganda.

In a 2012 news story whose title contained the phrase "Survivors 'Rebrand' Barlonyo," Ugandan journalist Joe Wacha explains that Barlonyo refers to a Lango word meaning "field of wealth."[173] After describing the business and educational initiatives under way in Barlonyo during the postconflict era, he quotes Ogwang, the community leader who showed us the Kaguta Bridge, as saying "that he is optimistic that Barlonyo will someday, live [up to] its name of field of wealth." I am not so sure that Ogwang is as optimistic as he is determined. The headline's use of the term "rebranding" resonates with their collective refusal of Gifted with Trauma. Instead, they insist on their bridge, their technical school, and their ability to improve their standard of living. The new brand in Barlonyo is Gifted by Livelihoods. Pay them, and their teeth will smile. It is less a bluff than a demand.

Notes

1. Quotes from *Forged in Fire* are taken from an unpublished manuscript; excerpts of the play are published in Sam, Ajwang, and Edmondson 2013, 61–66. The play was produced at the Voorhees Theatre in Brooklyn, New York, in May 2015; it was directed by Kevin Free.

2. For a brief account of the Pongdwongo school abduction, in which thirty-nine students were reported to have been abducted in July 1996, see Caroline Lamwaka, "Kony

Holding at Least 19 Students," *New Vision*, October 20, 1997. Sam believes that his brother was shot while trying to escape in 2000.

    3. Kahn 2006, 90.

    4. Ibid.

    5. Brian Mukisa, "Is Uganda Suffering from Brand Deficit?," *Monitor*, September 28, 2007.

    6. Dinnie 2008, 16.

    7. Dinnie 2008, 18–19.

    8. The year of the advertising campaign, 2006, marked the beginning of the postconflict era in northern Uganda.

    9. Pier 2015, 21, 22. Pier usefully expands on the concept of bluffing in the formation of African modernity put forward by Newell 2012.

    10. Kahn 2006, 90.

    11. Enock Musinguzi, "The Beautiful Garden That Can't Feed the Hungry," *Independent*, August 8, 2011; Muniini K. Mulera, "Uganda: Gifted by Nature, Betrayed by Poor Leadership," *Daily Monitor*, June 10, 2013; Benson Ekwe Ocen, "Uganda@50—Gifted but Poor," *Observer*, September 28, 2012.

    12. Ben Child, "Kony 2012: Angelina Jolie Calls for Ugandan Warlord's Arrest," *Guardian*, March 13, 2012.

    13. Liam Casey, Jennifer Pagliaro, and Kate Allen, "Kony 2012: Meet the Group behind the Viral Stop Kony Movement," *Toronto Star*, March 8, 2012. The first quote is Russell's; the second quote is found in the news story itself.

    14. John Comaroff and Jean Comaroff speak to the brand's attempt to stand out from the crowd and also cater to a sense of familiarity: "Those who seek to brand their otherness, to profit from what makes them different, find themselves having to do so in the universally recognizable terms in which difference is represented, merchandised, rendered negotiable by means of the abstract instruments of the market: money, the commodity, commensuration, the calculus of supply and demand, price, branding" (2009, 24).

    15. Scholarship on celebrity humanitarianism is a rapidly burgeoning field; see, for example, Brockington 2014a, 2014b; Chouliaraki 2013; Kapoor 2013; Richey 2016; and Richey and Ponte 2011. My analysis in this chapter was especially influenced by Brockington 2014a and 2014b and Richey 2016 (see, in particular, Budabin's and Brockington's contributions to this volume).

    16. David Carr, "Citizen Bono Brings Africa to Idle Rich," *New York Times*, March 5, 2007.

    17. Hearn 2008, 200.

    18. The last LRA attacks in Uganda took place in 2006. From 2006 to 2008, Riek Machar of South Sudan moderated the Juba peace talks between the government and the LRA. Although the talks ultimately failed, the LRA withdrew from northern Uganda during this time, and the region achieved a sense of stability. Residents of the IDP camps in Lira subregion were quick to take advantage of the cessation of hostilities; a 2007 United Nations High Commissioner for Refugees (UNHCR) report estimated that about 92 percent of the IDPs in the Lango subregion had returned home (UNHCR briefing notes, "Closure of Camps Starts in Northern Uganda as IDPs Return Home," September 11, 2007, available at http://www.unhcr.org/46e66ea52.html). Even though residents of the Acholi subregion (which roughly includes Gulu, Pader, and Kitgum Districts) were more cautious, most of them had also returned home by 2010. See Patience Aber and Al-Mahdi Ssenkabirwa, "IDPs Refuse to Return Home as

Camps Close Down in North," *Monitor*, July 1, 2008; and Chris Ocowun, "76,000 Stranded in Former IDP Camps," *New Vision*, August 10, 2010, for more information about the closing of the camps; see also Whyte et al. 2014. It is customary to problematize the term "postconflict" because it tends to neglect the continuation of other forms of violence, both subtle and overt, that persist even after the guns are silenced. But as discussed in the introduction, empire has often forestalled the efforts of northern Uganda to claim the category of postconflict, thus negating local efforts to sustain a hard-won semblance of stability. In light of this tension, I use the label "postconflict" for northern Uganda despite my awareness that the zones of conflict and postconflict are regularly blurred.

19. Visible markers of a growing stability include the establishment of a Uchumi supermarket in 2011 and a new marketplace in Lira Town in 2013.

20. Video footage of a belated rally in support of the (nonexistent) night commuters, held in April 2009 at the University of Texas at Austin, can be viewed at http://link.brightcove.com/services/player/bcpid1418565568?bctid=21094344001, accessed August 10, 2016.

21. *Kony 2012*, March 5, 2012, available at http://www.youtube.com/watch?v=Y4MnpzG5Sqc, accessed August 18, 2016.

22. See Edmondson 2012 for a discussion of the criticism leveled at *Kony 2012*.

23. I attended this event, which was held on September 18, 2013, at the City Winery in Manhattan.

24. I do think, though, that the fierceness of the criticism aimed at *Kony 2012* has ultimately shifted the rhetoric of crisis; when I was working on the final version of this chapter in 2016, it was rare to come across an assertion that northern Uganda was still at war. Perhaps crisis does have a shelf life.

25. The song can be heard at http://www.ariverblue.org/music/music.html, accessed January 26, 2015.

26. A River Blue, "The Story," http://www.ariverblue.org/story/story.html, accessed October 10, 2014.

27. Ibid. It is unclear why they selected this camp, given that 251 camps existed across eleven districts in 2005 (William Spindler, "UNHCR Closes Chapter on Uganda's Internally Displaced People," Briefing Notes, January 6, 2012, http://www.unhcr.org/en-us/news/briefing/2012/1/4f06e2a79/unhcr-closes-chapter-ugandas-internally-displaced-people.html). According to the River Blue website, they worked with Daniel Adams and Shane Gilbert from the Ugandan NGO Jangu Tuzine (Come, Let's Dance!) to help prepare for the festival before their arrival; they also credit George Mawa, director of the Obangatek Orphanage, as "a key figure in the production and management of festival activities." Obangatek Orphanage is no longer in existence.

28. A River Blue, "The Story."

29. Barefoot Productions, "A River Blue Arts Festival w/ Joseph Arthur," 2010, available at http://vimeo.com/10200435, accessed October 13, 2014.

30. A River Blue, "The Story."

31. Generally speaking, northern Ugandans are deeply invested in vocational training as the ticket to a better life despite indications that these programs are not cost effective; see Blattman and Ralston 2015.

32. The program began in Kigali on July 26 and ended in Kampala on August 17. Our visit to Uganda included visiting the Barlonyo memorial site of the LRA war in northern Uganda, A River Blue (described below), and an indigenous Jewish community in Mbale in eastern Uganda. The participants, who numbered about twenty in Rwanda, had decreased to

about ten for our visit to Uganda and included several Ugandans, as well as participants from the United States, South Africa, and Tanzania.

33. This visit occurred in the Oloo village on August 11, 2011.

34. Choir singing, also called *kwaya*, is a vibrant musical tradition throughout East Africa. Ethnomusicologist Gregory Barz has written extensively about this tradition in the Tanzanian context (2004); for discussions of Ugandan choir singing, see also Ssempijja 2012.

35. See "Uganda: Public Services under Threat" 2013 for a discussion of the 2012 corruption scandal in the Office of the Prime Minister.

36. Denis Ocwich, "Uganda: Lack of Shelter," *New Vision*, August 29, 2006.

37. See, for example, Invisible Children, "History of the War: 1986 to Now," http://invisiblechildren.com/about/history/, accessed October 15, 2014, which mentions only the Acholi. Major books about the LRA conflict also focus primarily on the impact on the Acholi; as an exception to this broad rule, see Justice and Reconciliation Project 2012a for a discussion of the war's impact in the Teso subregion.

38. See Refugee Law Project 2004, 34–37, for a discussion of the spread of the violence beyond the Acholi subregion in 2003, which also reached Teso. Hostility between Acholi and Langi do not stem only from the politics of visibility and aid but can also be traced to the 1985 coup against Obote; see chapter 1 for more information. Note that this chapter emphasizes Acholi and Langi at the expense of the suffering of other northern Ugandan groups, such as the Teso and West Nilers. It also tends to bypass tensions within these ethnic groups; the people of Pader and Kitgum, for example, often held Gulu responsible for their suffering at the hands of the LRA (Hopwood 2011, 14).

39. Hearn 2010, 204.

40. Ibid.

41. "Joseph Arthur in Studio on World Café," *NPR*, October 18, 2006, available at http://www.npr.org/templates/story/story.php?storyId=6291189, accessed August 15, 2017. Granted that Arthur, a critically acclaimed musician who approached his work in Uganda with thoughtfulness and care, is simply participating in the widely accepted practice of celebrity activism, it is perhaps unfair to single him out for criticism. See Brockington 2014a for a thorough analysis of how celebrities are produced by and implicated in a system of inequality. He points out that "if there are economic and political relationships at work—trade rules, economic policies, taxation regimes—that are more directly responsible for more inequality than celebrity, then celebrity is not the most important thing to be worried about" (2014a, 168). What interests me here is the disparity between A River Blue on the ground, so to speak, and A River Blue as a thriving source of self-promotion. As late as 2013, Arthur's experience in northern Uganda was showcased on the homepage of his website, josepharthur.com; in 2014, the River Blue song was linked to the homepage at http://www.josepharthur.com/av/. When I checked the website again in 2016, any reference to either the song or the organization had been removed.

42. C. Dolan 2009, 1. See also Blattman and Annan 2010a and 2010b for a detailed analysis of the impact of abduction and child soldiering on Ugandan children.

43. One blog was kept by Tselane Tambo, daughter of the antiapartheid activist Oliver Tambo and herself a celebrity in South Africa; the other blog was kept by Emily Kassie, who, at the time, was a student at Brown University who had already begun to accumulate a relatively impressive record of film credits, including an appearance in the Universal Pictures 2010 film *Scott Pilgrim vs. the World*. Since then, she has become a successful documentary filmmaker and journalist, as detailed on her website emilykassie.com, accessed August 22, 2017. Both blogs contain earnest, sincere attempts to come to terms with the stark poverty of north-

ern Uganda; Tambo's blog in particular contains insightful comments on what she considers the group's insensitivity to the economic needs of A River Blue. My point is that both blogs flatten the heterogeneity of the youths, perhaps in a well-meaning attempt to drive home the point of their desperation. Also, the examples of Tambo and Kassie clarify that the fetishization of child soldiers crosses the boundaries of race, nationality, and age, though perhaps not those of economic privilege.

44. Marwick and Boyd 2011, 140.

45. Hearn 2008, 208.

46. Tselane Tambo, "Uganda Diary Leaving Kampala," *Nocturnal Ramblings of a Mind Unplugged* (blog), August 24, 2011, http://tt13.wordpress.com/2011/08/24/uganda-diary-contd/. The website was still accessible as of August 15, 2017.

47. Emily Kassie, "Day 18," *Em in Rwanda & Uganda* (blog), August 13, 2011, http://emilykassie.blogspot.com/2011/08/day-18.html. The website was still accessible as of August 15, 2017.

48. *Okeme* and *otule* dances are named after the musical instrument that is especially prominent in each dance; *okeme* is the Langi word for the thumb piano, and *otule* means flute. The *ikoce* is a men's dance characterized by vigorous leaping. See Cooke 1999 for a useful discussion of music and dance performance traditions in Lira District as they appeared in the late 1990s.

49. Stropnicky 2012. Asiimwe is the author of the play *Forgotten World*, which is discussed in the introduction. See Stropnicky 2016 for a discussion of a follow-up project with A River Blue, called "Langi Voices."

50. Stropnicky 2012.

51. The collective journal can be accessed online at https://images.indiegogo.com/medias/130705/files/429684.doc, accessed August 15, 2017. More can be said here—the Oloo primary school, which we also visited, was somehow (mis)interpreted as "LRA headquarters"—but this would belabor the point.

52. Erik Ehn, "dance more," *Soulographie: Our Genocides* (blog), August 16, 2011, http://www.soulographie.org/dance-more/, accessed October 30, 2017. I think that he means *otule* instead of *akoshe*.

53. Our visit to Barlonyo, which will be discussed in more detail later in the chapter, occurred on August 11.

54. I wrote to Ehn about my concerns about how the visit to A River Blue was being represented in the collective journal, which prompted him to post a lively rumination on his blog. soulographie.org, in which he draws on Philip Gourevitch's critique of humanitarianism and Giorgio Agamben's theories of witnessing. On the one hand, he sees child soldiers as "extreme cases that illuminate the norm"; that is, the brutality helps one understand all of humanity. On the other hand, he acknowledges how child soldiers can skew our understanding of the larger geopolitical contexts: "For example—we see a trauma, a violation—a child soldier. Our eye focuses, we are entranced, we act with something close to total dedication. Then we also see that the concentration of resources disturbs the ecology of the region; we're drawing food away from widows, medicine away from whole towns; we see that people are falsifying records in order to seem more like child soldiers; in extreme cases, we see regions permitting disaster so as to be more attractive to aid. In seeing all this, we can leave that first child soldier at a point of origin in the biography of our knowledge—the soldier can seem smaller and smaller—we can feel betrayed by the soldier, abandoned, cheated of our own virtue (Erik Ehn, "here and here," *Soulographie: Our Genocides* [blog], September 11, 2011, http://www.soulographie.org/here-and-here/, accessed October 30, 2017). This kind of dialogue speaks to the potential of the "More Life" program, which will be addressed in much more detail in chapter 6.

55. As of 2017, Ongom's passion and persistence have continued to ensure the survival of A River Blue. A US-based Christian NGO called Together We Can currently serves as a donor; see "A River Blue Update," April 5, 2017, at http://togetherwecaninc.org/river-blue-update/, accessed August 22, 2017.

56. Pajule is located in what is now called Pader. Before 2000, when Pader District was created, Pajule was located in Kitgum District. A sense of the escalating violence in Kitgum in the late 1990s can be found in Anna Borzello, "Rebels Attack in Kitgum District of Uganda," *Agence France-Presse*, July 22, 1997.

57. Steven Candia, "Dutch NGO to Build Settlement for IDPs," *New Vision*, May 3, 2004.

58. *The Last King of Scotland* was produced by Fox Searchlight and directed by Kevin Macdonald; Whitaker won the Academy Award for Best Actor in 2007 for his portrayal of Amin. The Hope North dancers appear during an Amin rally to reinforce the celebratory atmosphere; the scene is meant to showcase Amin's popularity upon coming to power.

59. See the Lalela website, lalelaproject.org. Unlike some of the arts interventions that I critique in chapter 2, Lalela seeks sustainable arts interventions; for example, it provided funding for one of the Hope North faculty members to receive additional arts training in South Africa in 2013 as a follow-up to the establishment of the Lalela Arts Centre.

60. Some of this information can be found on the Theatre Thot website, http://www.thot-worldwide.com/nl/waar-werkt-thot, accessed July 16, 2014. I also had several conversations with Bootsma during his visits to Uganda in February and March 2013.

61. Hope North Uganda, "About Hope North and Okello Sam," http://www.hopenorth.org/about-hope-north-and-okello-sam/, accessed August 11, 2016.

62. This phrase, which began cropping up in 2009, no longer appears in the official promotional literature of Hope North and dates to an earlier version of the Hope North website in 2012.

63. This period of Uganda's history is touched on in chapter 1; see also Behrend 1999 for more information about the political climate in Uganda in the mid-1980s. Sam demonstrates a similar reticence about his past in an article about his life and activism in the anthology *Men of the Global South* (Beadle 2006, 196); also, in a documentary made about Sam and Hope North, *The Thing That Happened* (Walton Films, 2011), Sam speaks only of his brother's abduction and does not mention his personal history as a child soldier.

64. "Hope North—Okello Sam Talks about His Abduction as a Child," September 5, 2008, available at https://www.youtube.com/watch?v=d0AwfNvP7v0, accessed August 15, 2017. As of 2017, the video is no longer available on the Hope North website, which has become considerably more streamlined and polished than in previous years.

65. See, for example, the nonprofit organization Gen Next's description of Sam at http://www.gen-next.org/programs/upcoming-programs/okello, September 27, 2012, accessed July 17, 2014; and Mark Colvin's report, "US vs Terror Group in Central Africa," *Australian Broadcasting Corporation (ABC)*, October 25, 2011, http://www.abc.net.au/pm/content/2011/s3347763.htm, accessed January 7, 2015.

66. Brockington 2014b, 96, refers to Cause Effect Agency as an example of the growth of such companies that specialize in facilitating relationships between celebrities and charities.

67. When he spoke at the Hope North gala in 2013, for example, Sam explained that he preferred to play music rather than give a speech. Examples of Sam's music can be found at https://www.reverbnation.com/samkelookellosmiziziensemble, accessed August 22, 2017; he currently performs with Mzizi Ensemble, which he founded in 2013.

68. Sam tried to arrange for some of these students to attend the gala; at his request, I wrote to the US embassy visa officer in hopes of facilitating arrangements but to no avail.

69. Case Effect Agency, "Hope North's Inaugural Gala Honoring Mary-Louise Parker Raises over $100,000," *What's Good Blog*, September 19, 2013, http://causeeffectagency.com/blog/hope-norths-inaugural-gala-honoring-mary-louise-parker-raises-over-100000/; Carly Sitzer, "Mary-Louise Parker Admits the Movie That Makes Her Cry at Hope North Gala," *In Touch Weekly*, September 19, 2013; Cassie Carpenter, "Alec and Hilaria Baldwin Leave Baby Carmen at Home as They Suit Up for Date Night at Charity Gala in New York," *Mail Online*, September 19, 2013. It is only fair to add, though, that the evening ended on a high note when Sam took the stage to play music with Rufus Wainwright and Sahr Ngaujah. Clips of the evening can be viewed on the Hope North Facebook page at https://www.facebook.com/hopenorthuganda/videos/708900079146712/?video_source=pages_finch_thumbnail_video, accessed August 22, 2017.

70. It should be noted that visibility and fame do not necessarily translate into success. During 2012 and 2013, when I visited Hope North several times, the school struggled to maintain a paid staff, keep the latrines in order, and manage the well.

71. Blackett and Russell 1999, 1.

72. See starkeyhearingfoundation.org for more information. Its slogan is "So the world may hear."

73. Starkey's 2013 visit to Uganda was reported in *Entertainment Close-Up*, *Health and Medicine Week*, *Health and Beauty Close Up*, and the *Wall Street Journal*; much of this coverage repeated the information that Starkey had provided in a press release. See, for example, "Thousands Receive Free Hearing Aids in Uganda," *Wall Street Journal*, April 10, 2013.

74. Polman 2010; Rieff 2002; Waal 1997. The literature here is extensive; I am quoting only a few of the more prominent authors who are often mentioned in the mainstream press. See also Fassin 2007a, 2007b, 2010, 2011a; and Pandolfi 2003, 2008, 2010.

75. Branch 2011, 4.

76. Ibid., 90–118.

77. C. Dolan 2009, 1–2, also cited in Branch 2011, 97.

78. Branch 2011, 102.

79. See Lenz 2017, 130–131, for a discussion of the gendered repercussions of the "rehabilitation" of former female LRA combatants.

80. To the Starkey Foundation's credit, though, it launched a program in 2015 in which it trained local activists, including Sunday Komakech, to learn to recognize hearing-impaired people in their home communities; this program seems promising in that it borrows from local energies instead of imposing foreign expertise.

81. On the one hand, these activities could be understood as examples of self-branding or cobranding in terms of boosting his visibility; for example, Whitaker was named a UNESCO goodwill ambassador for peace and reconciliation in 2011, and his Facebook profile image (as of July 2014) displayed him playing a calabash at Hope North. On the other hand, Whitaker seems uninterested in using his peacemaking and charitable activities in Uganda as a source of publicity. When he came to Hope North in December 2013, these workshops were closed to outsiders and received very little publicity. At the gala event that I attended in 2013, he was conspicuously absent even though he was listed as one of the hosts.

82. These quotes are taken from a PeaceEarth brochure, which I downloaded from the www.peaceearth.org website in August 2013. As explained later in the chapter, this website is no longer in operation.

83. Chouliaraki 2011, 16.

84. See Budabin 2016, 139, for a similar critique of Ben Affleck's founding of his Eastern Congo Initiative.

85. Erin Carlyle, "Role of a Lifetime," *Forbes*, December 24, 2012; Brockington 2014b, 104. See also Brockington 2014a, 160–162, and Brockington 2016.

86. The International Institute for Peace brochure, "Building Peace, Building Communities," is available at www.unesco.org/fileadmin/MULTIMEDIA/HQ/BSP/images/IIP%20Brochure.pdf, accessed November 5, 2017.

87. Branch 2011, 120.

88. Ibid., 131.

89. Ibid., 120.

90. "Youth Peacemaker Network—A Joint Project of Forest Whitaker, UNESCO & Ericsson in South Sudan," available at https://www.youtube.com/watch?v=8mJzPnvNf2o, accessed August 18, 2016.

91. Clearly, Whitaker made a concerted effort to include well-trained experts in peace building and conflict mediation in his project; for example, his team included conflict-resolution expert Brian Williams, who has worked in Sierra Leone, Burundi, the Democratic Republic of the Congo, Uganda, Tanzania, Swaziland, Lesotho, and South Africa. Given the vagueness of the students' recollections of the peace-building workshops, though, the impact is unclear. Because of Whitaker's desire for privacy, as mentioned in n81, I was unable to attend the workshop myself.

92. Forest Whitaker, "Another Step towards Global Peace," *Huffington Post*, September 24, 2012.

93. Weidman-Grunewald made this comment on December 12, 2012, on the *Technology for Good Blog*, available at www.ericsson.com/thecompany/sustainability_corporateresponsibility/technology-for-good-blog/2012/12/12/a-hunger-for-ict/, accessed November 5, 2017.

94. Brockington 2014b, 88.

95. I checked fairly regularly starting in September 2013, only to be met with the message that the website was unavailable; this was replaced by a message in July 2014 that a "new website" was "launching soon." The new program is called the Whitaker Peace & Development Initiative (see wpdi.org, accessed August 16, 2016). Copyright issues had emerged over the name "Peace Earth," prompting a renaming of his organization.

96. Nguyen 2010, 41.

97. Information on the various initiatives and exchanges can be found at http://www.thot-worldwide.com/nl/oeganda-afrika, accessed August 22, 2017.

98. Blattman, Fiala, and Martinez 2014; see also a discussion about cash transfers as an alternative to traditional humanitarian assistance in his *New York Times* op-ed, "Let Them Eat Cash," June 30, 2014. See also Ndaliko 2016 for an excellent critique of arts interventions by NGOs that favor "grandiose visions of inspiration and global interconnection without allowing mundane material realities, such as the need for artists to eat, the cost of production equipment, or institutional politics, to enter the picture" (188).

99. The song, which was included on Jackson's 1996 *HIStory* album, includes these lyrics: "Tell me what has become of my rights / Am I invisible because you ignore me? / Your proclamation promised me free liberty, now / I'm tired of bein' the victim of shame." As Brian Rossiter writes in a compelling analysis of the song, which he contextualizes in Jackson's articulation of black nationalism, "None [of the singles on *HIStory*] subscribes to an African-American

group identity, or to the feeling of being a powerless and victimized member of a social minority, as rigorously as 'They Don't Care About Us'" (2012, 208); he also describes the song as expressing an "aura of rage" (203). Rossiter's article includes a nuanced discussion of the anti-Semitic bent of the song, which includes the highly controversial lyrics "Jew me" and "kike me" (209–210). (These words did not appear on the version that was used for the Hope North flash mob.)

100. As Sunday Komakech explained to me, "[The song] entered into people's hearts" (conversation in Kampala, August 2015).

101. Bootsma fulfilled this promise on the morning of the day of the scheduled flash mob; two chartered buses took well over a hundred Hope North faculty and staff to see the elephants, lions, and zebras that many of them had heard of but few had actually seen. The excitement was palpable.

102. "Bweyale—A Refugee Haven," *New Vision*, September 5, 2011.

103. Grant and Boon 2013, 191.

104. The flash mob occurred on March 23, 2012, and can be viewed at http://www.youtube.com/watch?v=TtWkWdAp37w, accessed August 18, 2016.

105. Ferguson 2006, 17.

106. Granted, youths typically have an advantage over their elders when it comes to technology regardless of nationality. My point is that even though his exposure to formal computer training was limited to these scattered workshops, he was still able to display a level of confidence analogous to that of, say, my US-raised teenaged daughter.

107. As will be discussed in the final section of this chapter, Pabbo was also designated as a memorial site.

108. Branch 2011, 130.

109. Mindfulness Without Borders, "Theory of Change," http://mindfulnesswithoutborders.org/theory-of-change, accessed July 18, 2014.

110. Courtney Lawrence, "Crossing the Borders to Peace," *Dalai Lama Center* (blog), August 29, 2013, http://dalailamacenter.org/blog-post/crossing-borders-peace.

111. Other well-known massacres include the Mucwini subcounty in Kitgum District (July 23–24, 2002), the Omot subcounty in Pader District (October 23, 2002), and Abia in Lira District (February 4, 2004); state-sponsored massacres in the region include those in the Mukura subcounty in Teso (July 11, 1989) and Burcoro Village in Gulu (April 18, 1991). A particularly violent LRA attack occurred in 1997 in the Palabek subcounty in Kitgum, which left an estimated two hundred to three hundred dead. See Justice and Reconciliation Project 2012b for a discussion of the LRA attack at Palabek, as well as the history of harsh UPDF violence that preceded it. As discussed in chapters 1 and 2, this list of massacres in northern Uganda does not begin to capture the extent of the violence. Although the scale of the attacks waxed and waned over two decades of conflict in response to various military offensives and peace talks, LRA attacks, abductions, and ambushes were ubiquitous throughout the northern region and affected the Acholi, Langi, Madi, and Teso. As mentioned in previous chapters, massacres were hardly confined to Ugandan soil. After receiving support from the Sudanese government in 1994, the LRA committed massive violence in southern Sudan; in 2002, for example, the LRA attacked the town of Katire in the Imatong Mountains, killing an estimated 350 villagers (Human Rights Watch, "LRA in Northern Uganda and Southern Sudan, 2002," October 29, 2002, available at https://www.hrw.org/legacy/press/2002/10/uganda1029-bck.htm). Once the LRA left northern Uganda after the failed Juba peace talks (2006–2008), it continued its

string of mass killings, as in the Christmas and Makombo massacres committed in the Haut-Uele Province in the northeastern DRC in 2008 and 2009. I have not come across references to memorialization of LRA massacres committed outside Uganda.

112. Museveni's speech is briefly discussed in chapter 1.

113. These details, all of which were shared with me during my two visits to Barlonyo, are also discussed in the JRP report on the Barlonyo massacre (Justice and Reconciliation Project 2009), as well as Proctor 2013. In 2003, as the LRA increasingly targeted the Lango subregion, the UPDF based a small army detachment at Barlonyo, and an estimated five thousand people relocated there for protection, forming an IDP camp. In January 2004, the UPDF soldiers were sent to fight the LRA in Teso District and were replaced by forty-seven local militia fighters (Local Defense Units and Amuka), who were poorly trained and frequently unpaid. On the day of the attack, February 21, 2004, defense was minimal. The LRA is believed to have attacked Barlonyo as revenge for its losses in the UPDF attacks in Teso. LRA commander Okot Odhiambo led the mission with the order to "kill every living thing."

114. The mathematical equations could also suggest a recasting of mass graves. Like many East and Central Africans, northern Ugandans customarily bury their loved ones on the family compound; in light of the UPDF's brutal insistence on digging up the bodies of the Barlonyo victims, it is quite possible that the mass grave does not signify sacred space as much as it represents state violence.

115. This visit occurred on April 23, 2013.

116. Ocen defended his PhD dissertation, "Reading Monuments: Politics and Poetics of Memory in Post-war Northern Uganda," at the Makerere Institute of Social Research in early 2017.

117. As discussed in chapter 1, General Tito Okello, an Acholi, carried out a coup against Obote, a Langi, in 1985; Ongom's brother was a victim of the violence that immediately followed the coup.

118. See Williams 2007 for a discussion of the "global rush to memorialize atrocities."

119. Mike Ssegawa, "Government Gazettes Four IDP Camps for Tourism," *Daily Monitor*, June 21, 2011.

120. Stone 2006, 146; see also Sharpley 2009, 10. The term "dark tourism" was coined by John Lennon and Malcolm Foley; see, for example, Lennon and Foley 2000.

121. See, for example, "Emulate Rwanda in Tourism Promotion," *Daily Monitor*, June 13, 2013; James Tumusiime, "A Fortune Can Be Made out of Misfortune," *Observer*, March 23, 2012; and David Mugabe, "Idi Amin Tourism Trail to Be Created," *New Vision*, March 31, 2014. Also, as part of the Uganda Museum memorial project discussed later in this chapter, curators and community leaders at the memorial sites traveled to Rwanda to see memorials in Kigali and Butare. The impact of this visit can be discerned in Proctor 2013, which mentions that the Barlonyo leadership had been "beguiled" by the Rwandan example of mass graves (19).

122. "Atiak Massacre Site Turned into Tourist Attraction," *Uganda Radio Network*, July 30, 2012.

123. See "Changing Horizons" at changinghorizons.org, accessed August 18, 2016.

124. The video, which was posted on March 14, 2012, is available at http://www.aljazeera.com/news/africa/2012/03/201231432421227462.html, accessed August 18, 2016. The spectator's last name is Odong; the first name is not intelligible on the video.

125. NTV Uganda broadcast, "Screening Angers Lira Locals," March 14, 2012, available at www.youtube.com/watch?v=PJYisE8vjv4. See Rosebell Kagumire and David Smith, "Kony 2012 Video Screening Met with Anger in Northern Uganda," *Guardian*, March 14, 2012, for a more nuanced explanation of why the screenings ended.

126. See AYINET, "A Report on the Barlonyo Memorial Service Held on the 21st Feb 2015," available at www.africanyouthinitiative.org/assets/barlonyo-memorial-service-report.pdf, accessed August 18, 2016. Isingiro was a battleground between Tanzanian forces and Amin's troops in 1978; Kasese experienced attacks by the Allied Democratic Forces (ADF) starting in 1996. The impact of the Bush War in Luwero, in central Uganda, is discussed in chapter 1.

127. AYINET, "Report on the Barlonyo Memorial Service," 3–4.

128. Ibid., 5. It is striking that these outspoken speeches were all delivered by Lira residents. That said, I heard similar sentiments regularly expressed by Acholi, especially former LRA combatants, in less public settings.

129. The Uganda Museum is a state-funded institution, and thus the curators could be seen as a kinder, gentler version of the UPDF, armed with spackling tools and video cameras rather than guns. My sense is that the communities regarded the curators and visiting Norwegians warily, and that considerable time and effort were expended in gaining a sense of trust. It should be noted that Nelson Abiti, one of the leading curators, is from West Nile and had a personal investment in the project as a northern Ugandan. The state's oversight of the project was perhaps most clearly perceived in the Kampala exhibit, which presented a master narrative of the conflict that excluded the role of the NRA/UPDF in exacerbating the violence. As Elen-Marie Meggison Tandberg explains, "The pervasive scepticism between the central government and Acholi communities in northern Uganda meant that the [Norwegian Directorate] and [Uganda Museum] were concerned that the political nature of the projects would make the exhibition too controversial in the eyes of the central government" (2014, 107–108), and thus they were careful to emphasize the projects over the context in the exhibit. A similar approach can be discerned in a documentary about the project that the curators produced, *Northern Uganda: Featuring Efforts at Peace & Reconciliation* (Uganda Museum 2012), which steers clear of any critical reference to the role of the Ugandan government and its troops in the conflict.

130. Uganda National Museum brochure, "Road to Reconciliation." For a helpful overview and analysis of this project, see Tandberg 2014, 73–89. Tandberg provides a thorough account of how the Norwegian Directorate came to be involved in the project, as well as the parameters of the collaboration between the museum and the directorate. She also describes how the project team gathered information from the affected communities through site visits and carried out the renovations at the four sites. The project culminated in an exhibition in Kampala in 2013. See also Giblin 2014 and Bamuturaki Musinguzi, "Revisiting a Bloody 20-Year War through Monuments, Key Sites," *East African*, March 22, 2013.

131. Lukodi is located about seventeen kilometers north of Gulu town. Although Lukodi had experienced several smaller-scale LRA attacks in prior years, the massacre occurred on May 19, 2004. At the time of the attack, a small army detachment that consisted mostly of Local Defence Unit members was located in the center of the Lukodi IDP camp; it was overwhelmed by the estimated one hundred LRA fighters, and an estimated sixty people were killed. The camp was a prime target for raiding because it had just received a distribution of aid supplies, such as food and cooking equipment, from the organization Caritas. Also, as was the case with Atiak and Barlonyo, the LRA believed that Lukodi should be "punished" because the inhabitants were believed to be sharing information on the LRA's whereabouts with the UPDF. About a year after the massacre, an organization called Child Voice International assisted the community with the building of a memorial that listed individual names of forty-five victims. See Justice and Reconciliation Project 2011.

132. The camps were subjected to LRA raids despite the rhetoric of state protection; in June 2003, for example, the LRA killed thirteen people in the Pabbo camp during a raid. Mergelsberg summarizes the situation at Pabbo during the conflict: "Supposedly protected by the government army, they felt threatened by soldiers of both sides as well as the disastrous living conditions," which included extreme crowding and an alarming lack of sanitation (2014, 66). See Branch 2013 and Whyte et al. 2014 for more nuanced discussions of the IDP camps than are typically found in the literature on the LRA conflict.

133. Most of the Lango subregion was not seriously affected until 2003, but Apac was an exception because it was located just south of Gulu and Pader. (St. Mary's is now located in Kole District, which was created in 2010.) The story of the Aboke girls is among the more famous narratives in the LRA conflict. Sister Rachele Fassera, the deputy headmistress of St. Mary's College Secondary School in Aboke, followed the rebels the night they were abducted, October 10, 1996, and insisted that they return the girls. The rebels returned all but thirty, many of whom were given as "wives" to Kony and other top commanders. Of the thirty girls, four (Judith Enang, Jesca Anguu, Brenda Ato, and Luiza Namahele) died in captivity; one girl, Miriam Akello, is still missing. The remaining twenty-five girls have returned home. To describe the memorial ceremony as conveying a celebratory quality is not meant, of course, to diminish the pain and anguish of the family and friends of Akello and the four deceased girls; I am sharing here what I learned during a visit to the Aboke school on April 25, 2013. Another Aboke student, Susan Apio, was abducted from the school in 1989, in the very early years of the LRA, and was eventually killed. The names of the five deceased girls are listed on an extraordinary memorial at the Aboke school, which includes references to the Atiak massacre, as well as the notorious ADF attack on June 8, 1998, at the Kichwamba Technical College near the city of Fort Portal in western Uganda, in which an estimated eighty students died. The memorial's attempt to contextualize the Aboke attack in a larger landscape of Ugandan violence resonates with the concept of anagnorisis, or recognition, that I discuss in chapter 1.

134. The Aboke festival was held on October 6, 2012. The exhibition had an opening celebration on February 28, 2013, that gathered key representatives from the different sites; Orach Otim, for example, presented an original poem about Pabbo at the event.

135. Although the refurbishment of the mass grave might seem like an obvious gesture of respect for the dead and the survivors alike, the people of Barlonyo undoubtedly perceived it as a highly political gesture. Keith Proctor's research in Barlonyo revealed that many community members believe that the bodies should be exhumed for individual reburial since mass burial is an affront to cultural and religious practices; it offends the dead. The leadership of Barlonyo, however, opposes exhumation; Proctor quotes Ogwang as expressing concern over retraumatizing the community and the complications of identifying the remains. The museum's actions would be perceived as an affirmation of the leadership's wishes (2013, 16–18).

136. My conversations with Ocan and Otim occurred during a visit to Gulu District on January 26 and 27, 2013. Pabbo was officially closed in 2010; however, in part because of its prime location on the road connecting Gulu to South Sudan, it has become a bustling town center (Mergelsberg 2012). In the section of Pabbo that has been designated as the memorial site, displaced people continue to live as squatters in a uniquely Ugandan version of what Albie Sachs has termed "living memorials," discussed later in this chapter.

137. This exchange occurred at the Uganda Museum, Kampala, March 15, 2013.

138. I should clarify that this is not meant to depict the state's intervention in a positive light; my point is simply to underscore the ambivalence surrounding memorialization.

139. Logan and Reeves 2009, 3.

140. The circumstances of Ongwen's arrest are murky. It is unclear whether he surrendered or was captured by Séléka rebels in the Central African Republic. The rebels demanded the $5 million reward promised by the US military for information leading to his capture; it is uncertain whether they received this reward, given that the US military was loath to be perceived as working alongside a rebel army that was notorious for its human rights abuses on CAR soil. These brief references to the ICC cannot, of course, do justice to the complexity of its politics and its impact on the region. The court is implicated, for example, in the derailing of the Juba peace talks. See Nouwen 2013 for an in-depth discussion of ICC politics related to northern Uganda and Darfur.

141. On October 10, 2003, the LRA attacked the Pajule trading center; an estimated sixty people were killed, and another five hundred were abducted. The Odek IDP camp was attacked on April 29, 2004; an estimated ninety-three people were killed, and seventy-one were abducted. On June 8, 2004, at Abok, the LRA killed an estimated twenty-five people and abducted twenty-six. Although the ICC's charges center on the Lukodi massacre and these three attacks, Ongwen has also been linked to numerous atrocities, including the Christmas massacre and the Makombo massacre in the DRC in 2008 and 2009. A *New Vision* article indicates that he also might have led the attack on the Aboke school in 1996; see Taddeo Bwambale, "Why Ongwen Is Facing Trial at The Hague," *New Vision*, February 2, 2015. A central question in the Ongwen controversy is how to contextualize his actions as a child victim of abduction without negating his moral agency.

142. Ongwen's age at the time of his abduction in 1988 is murky; his defense claims that he was nine years old and was abducted on his way to primary school, but in his first ICC court appearance, he said that he was fourteen. See "LRA Commander Dominic Ongwen Appears before ICC in The Hague," *BBC News*, January 26, 2015.

143. Baines 2009, 163.

144. Ibid., 163–164.

145. This sentiment is frequently mentioned in press coverage; see, for example, Lizabeth Paulat, "Uganda Split over Ongwen's Confirmation Charges," *VOA*, January 21, 2016. In general, Ongwen's arrest has prompted sustained calls for restorative justice and forgiveness. Acholi leaders, for example, have advocated that Ongwen receive the national amnesty passed in 2000 granted to all rebel combatants who surrendered. (The Amnesty Act has a complex legacy and has been inconsistently applied by the Ugandan government; see Nouwen 2013, 206–227, for more information on the Amnesty Act.) They have also called for Ongwen to be subjected to Mato Oput, a traditional Acholi cleansing ritual that is often referenced as a method of transitional justice in northern Uganda. See, for example, Michela Wrong's excellent analysis of the Ongwen case, "Making a Murderer in Uganda," *Foreign Policy*, January 20, 2016. Although I am deeply sympathetic to these calls for restorative rather than retributive justice, it should be noted that the Acholi leaders calling for amnesty are invariably adult men who enjoy a relatively privileged position in their communities. A greater diversity of voices is likely to add alternative perspectives; the conclusion of Wrong's article provides a glimpse of such a perspective.

146. The brochure of this exhibit was downloaded at http://www.riksantikvaren.no/filestore/Ugandaexhibition_small.pdf, accessed October 1, 2013. Unfortunately, as of August 17, 2016, the brochure was no longer available. The quote, which is not cited in the brochure, is also prominently displayed in the JRP report on memorialization (Hopwood 2011, 15). The original reference is Sturken 1991, 118.

147. Cole 2010, 136.

148. Erin Baines and Michael Otim cofounded the JRP in 2005 as a means of counteracting the ICC's and Human Rights Watch's emphasis on top-down systems of retributive justice with research and documentation of local solutions for sustainable peace (Baines 2009, 166–167).

149. Hopwood 2011, 14. The massacre at Atiak, which occurred on April 20, 1995, was one of the earliest large-scale massacres in the conflict. In revenge for perceived collaboration with the Ugandan army, the LRA shot a group of about three hundred men and boys en masse. It ranks among the most famous massacres in Uganda; in speaking to my southern Ugandan colleagues at Makerere University in Kampala, I learned that they all had heard of Atiak, but few knew the names of Barlonyo or Lukodi. See Justice and Reconciliation Project 2007 for more information on the Atiak massacre.

150. Hopwood 2011, 14.

151. Ibid.

152. See Chapter 1 for an overview of these events. For more information on the intersection of British colonial policy and contemporary ethnic divisions in Uganda, see Omara-Otunnu 1987; Kasozi 1994; and Kisekka-Ntale 2007.

153. The memorial structure, which includes the names of sixty-five victims, was built by the Office of the Prime Minister and is located at Abia Survivors' Vocational Institute near the Abia Trading Centre. My thanks to Laurence Ocen for this information. See also Laurence Ocen, "Laurence Ocen on Memory and Loss in Northern Uganda," November 27, 2015, at the Makerere Institute of Social Research website, available at https://misr.mak.ac.ug/news/laurence-ocen-memory-and-loss-northern-uganda, accessed August 18, 2016, for a fascinating introduction to his research on memorialization in northern Uganda.

154. As described in the *Oxford English Dictionary*, the prefix "re" encompasses a wide range of meanings, including "back from a point reached" and "back to or towards the starting point," which suggests a kind of starting anew. The entry adds that "in many cases the idea of force is present . . . hence arises the sense of resistance." This latter part of the definition is suggestive of an active withdrawal.

155. This is not to suggest that northern Ugandans are unaware of the possibility that these memorials might attract tourist dollars (see Giblin 2014, 508), but simply that they refuse to engage in the usual transaction of exchanging testimonies and tears for cash.

156. AYINET, "Report on the Barlonyo Memorial Service," 4. The official estimate is that fifty-two people died in the attack; Ray's statistic of 190 calls to mind Ocen's warning about death statistics: "The figures represent only dead bodies found on the scenes of massacre. The figures do not consider those who fled and perished in the bushes, or those who died of war effects, a long time after the fateful events. These figures also do not consider those that must have developed fatal complications arising from war trauma" (2015, 25). Ocen also contextualizes Ray's reference to restocking with his explanation that the term, which refers to replenishing numbers of cattle, is a concept particularly connected with Teso and Lango (12).

157. I visited all four of the memorial sites targeted by the Uganda Museum: Barlonyo, Aboke, Lukodi, and Pabbo. As discussed later in this chapter, I also attended the memorial ceremonies at Atiak and Lukodi. I had planned to attend the 2013 memorial event at Barlonyo, but for reasons that are pertinent to this analysis, I was discouraged from attending and informed that the memorial prayers would be private that year because of a lack of funding. I attended the memorial ceremonies in Atiak and Lukodi with Sunday Komakech; I visited Lira and Nakaseke in the company of Laurence Ocen. I am grateful to Komakech and Ocen for their

intellectual companionship during these sensitive site visits; Ocen was particularly helpful in clarifying tensions between the Langi and the Acholi.

158. Ugandans might point out that this is not surprising given that grief is considered a deeply private matter. When I mentioned to Nelson Abiti that I was surprised by the lack of emotion at the ceremonies, particularly in contrast to the public expressions of grief associated with Rwandan memorialization of the genocide, he commented that "Rwandans like to overgrieve," suggesting that Ugandan stoicism serves as a mark of pride. Given that the monuments in Lukodi and Atiak are memorial stones rather than mass graves, one might also argue that their symbolic significance exceeds any sense of emotional attachment; when they are mass graves, as in Barlonyo, the decision was ordained and executed by the state.

159. See Hopwood 2011, 13–18, for a thoughtful discussion of the "fault lines" between traditionalist and Christian understandings of mourning the dead, as well as how these fault lines might manifest differently among Langi and Acholi populations.

160. Justice and Reconciliation Project 2007, 15.

161. The Lukodi community leaders received their wish on May 19, 2016. Because of Lukodi's rush to prominence as a result of Ongwen's hearing at the ICC earlier that year, VIPs descended on the memorial ceremony in droves. As described on the International Justice Monitor website, "for the first time ever," Rwot David Onen Acana II, the Acholi paramount chief, attended, as well as representatives of the ICC from the Office of the Prosecutor and the Victims' Participation and Reparations Section. Other attendees included ICC victims' representatives Francisco Cox, Joseph Akwenyu Manoba, and Jane Anywar Adong. See "Support for ICC Trial of Ongwen Is Shown at Commemoration of the Lukodi Massacre," May 24, 2016, available at www.ijmonitor.org, accessed August 19, 2016; note that this report demonstrates a pro-ICC bias. Earlier that year, in January, the ICC hearing was screened live in Lukodi; see "Live from The Hague: The Confirmation of Charges Hearing in Lukodi, Northern Uganda," January 22, 2016, www.ijmonitor.org, accessed August 19, 2016. The impact of Lukodi's burst of fame calls for further research and analysis. I noticed, for example, in a video posted by NTV Uganda on January 17, 2015, that Lukodi now boasts a small memorial center that includes a narrative of the atrocity dating back to Idi Amin; I am curious whether the funding for this center came from the ICC, which has been lobbying hard in Lukodi to win support and counteract widespread criticism that its pursuit of justice serves only to exacerbate violence. For footage of the memorial center, see "10 Years On but the Wounds of Gulu's Lokudi Massacre Are Still Fresh," available at https://www.youtube.com/watch?v=Clf8_MTKYOo, accessed August 18, 2016.

162. Cole 2010, 136, emphasis in the original.

163. Ibid.

164. See Otwili and Schulz 2012 and McClain and Ngari 2011 for more complete discussions of reparation politics in Uganda.

165. Barlonyo is not unique in this regard; see Hopwood 2011 for a discussion of how these memorial ceremonies function more broadly in northern Uganda. It should also be noted that these efforts were hardly limited to the annual ceremony. In November 2011, for example, Works State Minister John Byabagambi received what the *Monitor* called a "rude welcome" from about 150 Barlonyo women who loudly cried and wailed upon his arrival (Emmanuel Opio, "Women Welcome Ministers with Sobs," *Daily Monitor*, November 3, 2011). See also Patrick Okino, "Former IDPs Want Govt to Fulfill Pledges," *New Vision*, December 29,

2009. The annual ceremonies, though, occupy prime importance given that they are often covered in the Ugandan press.

166. McClain and Ngari 2011, 3.

167. The West Nile subregion, the birthplace of Idi Amin, certainly suffered the impact of the LRA conflict, but less so than the Acholi, Lango, and Teso subregions. It is possible that the respondent was referring to the economic blight that descended over West Nile once Amin was deposed, given that successive regimes have indirectly punished the area through sustained neglect.

168. This phrase is an Ankole proverb that was popularized through Andrew Rice's book *The Teeth May Smile but the Heart Does Not Forget: Murder and Memory in Uganda* (New York: Metropolitan Books, 2009), which recounts the story of Duncan Laki's search for justice for the murder of his father, Eliphaz Laki, committed during Amin's regime. Using a southern Ugandan proverb in the context of northern Uganda might be a questionable choice, but I believe that the idea of "forgetting" resonates across the north/south divide. On April 25, 2013, Ocen and I visited a memorial of war victims of Museveni's Bush War against Obote's forces in the early 1980s. The famous "skulls of Luwero," the remains of victims of the war, which were originally displayed along the roadside, were collected for burial in a specially built tomb in Nakaseke in 1995. The filth, broken glass, and rusted-out lock at the site spoke of sustained neglect; insects infested the skulls. In light of what I saw in Luwero, I cannot help but wonder whether forgetting is endemic.

169. See Moses Ogwang's statement in AYINET, "Report on the Barlonyo Memorial Service," 5.

170. In 2005, Albie Sachs called for embodied and performed versions of memorialization that are "conveyed through words and images, songs, and gestures" (quoted in Ronan 2007, 27; see also Cole 2010, 135). During my visits to the memorials, I heard tantalizing references to dance and drama groups that had formed around the Pabbo and Barlonyo memorials (see also Tandberg 2014, 78, 85). The Uganda Museum's documentary on the memorialization project includes substantial footage of community-based dance groups, intermingled with a few clips of drama groups performing scenes of LRA violence (Uganda Museum 2012). More research needs to be done to ascertain whether these groups speak to Sachs's original conception of living memorials, or whether the performances serve mainly to draw further attention to the "real" memorials.

171. Sachs 2009, 77.

172. Keith Proctor found that the discourse of living memorials also circulated in Barlonyo, which perhaps suggests the discursive impact of the Uganda Museum project (2013, 18).

173. Joe Wacha, "Trading Center Replaces IDP Camp as Survivors 'Rebrand' Barlonyo," *Uganda Radio Network*, February 29, 2012.

6

CONFESSIONS OF A FAILED THEATRE ACTIVIST

When I traveled to Gulu, Uganda, in the summer of 2004, I proudly bore an invitation to facilitate theatre workshops at the World Vision rehabilitation center for former child soldiers. In the heart of this war zone, I probably should not have been surprised to meet another US theatre artist who was as eager as I was to contribute her skills. She had arranged for private workshops at the Gulu Save the Children Organization (GUSCO), another rehabilitation center in Gulu, which she invited me to observe.[1] She led a group of about fifteen teenaged girls in a series of conventional acting exercises, working with them to use their bodies as a tool of expression. She was wearing a loose, flowing skirt, and as she demonstrated the movement exercises, all of us in the room caught regular glimpses of her underwear. As members of a culture in which modest dress is a social norm, the girls reacted with outbursts of giggling and whispering among themselves. These outbursts continued despite the obvious annoyance of the facilitator, who repeatedly requested but failed to capture their undivided attention. I immediately activated the machinery of othering, distancing myself from her behavior with self-assurances that I was more cognizant of cultural expectations than she was. Although I am reasonably certain that the residents of Gulu did not see my underwear, the image of white woman as ludicrous spectacle haunted my own fumbling attempts to contribute to the practice of activist theatre.[2]

Metaphorically speaking, numerous foreign theatre artists have undoubtedly flashed their underwear. As the LRA withdrew and overt episodes of regional violence declined, performers descended in droves. In 2007, Clowns Without Borders (CWB) in Ireland, which travels the world, "offer[ing] laughter to relieve the suffering of all persons, especially children, who live in areas of crisis," gave public performances and workshops in Gulu, Arua, and Pader.[3] Its tour generated a sarcastic blog post from political scientist Christopher Blattman, "You Know It's No Longer a War Zone . . . ," in which he used CWB as evidence of how Gulu had become a "circus" of various aid interventions now that the subregion had stabilized.[4] In 2009, he went a step further and nominated CWB as "the worst NGO on the planet," which prompted a wave of criticism among his readers, many of whom pointed out that CWB was no more "ridiculous" than, say, the International Monetary Fund, and the clowns, at least, made kids laugh.[5]

Well, sure. All of us westerners stumbling around northern Uganda undoubtedly make kids laugh. Certainly the former female combatants at GUSCO were entertained. But I am more inclined to use these examples to think through the implications of theatre activism in East and Central Africa. Both projects can be chalked up as manifestations of the "white savior industrial complex" eloquently described by Teju Cole. As Cole explains, Africa provides especially fertile terrain for the production of white saviors: "It is a liberated space in which the usual rules do not apply: a nobody from America or Europe can go to Africa and become a godlike savior or, at the very least, have his or her emotional needs satisfied."[6] In her work on international humanitarian agencies in Somalia and Kenya, Jennifer Hyndman offers another useful phrase, the "colonialism of compassion," as a reminder of how compassion in the guise of humanitarianism shores up the existing order through dividing the world between Northern benefactors and Southern victims.[7] Similarly, Alain Badiou emphasizes the hegemonic imperative that pervades humanitarian projects, even those that cast themselves in the seemingly more radical framework of human rights, insofar that both discourses depend on a split between "a passive, pathetic [pathétique], or reflexive subject—he who suffers" and "the active, determining subject of judgment—he who, in identifying suffering, knows that it must be stopped by all available means."[8] From these perspectives, theatre activism that depends on a separation between helper and helped is hardly transformative but instead props up tired notions of intact subject versus fragmented victim with all the socioeconomic hierarchies that this binary entails.

Theatre artists, increasingly deemed inconsequential in late capitalist contexts, are perhaps especially vulnerable to the siren call of the savior industry. In a neoliberal moment that demands that art be useful and productive, theatre activists carve out a niche brand that casts the seemingly useless practice of theatre and performance in the framework of social transformation. In a complex intertwining of self-branding and entrepreneurship, they seek direct access to suffering bodies that inhabit this corner of the global South. As they swoop in to rescue their victims from a theatre-less landscape,[9] the headiness of this enterprise obscures the possibility that noble intentions pave the road to ethical violations of subjects. As Cole reminds us, if they fail to save the world, they can experience an emotional satisfaction that reassures them of their own goodness. After describing a performance in Arua, a member of CWB characterizes it as "a greatly satisfying day that was finely topped off by the company of Mama Salome, who by telling us her life story, made three clowns cry."[10] Cole might say, bully for them.

As the giggling young women and girls in my opening anecdote indicate, this version of activism is routinely resisted or at least mocked. But instead of exploring the ways in which ideological rugs are pulled from beneath western feet, I focus on theorizing alternative frameworks of theatre activism that exceed the potentially colonialist model that beckons with such ideological and affective force. This chapter takes a different approach than the rest of this book insofar that it seeks to offer a kind of road map to western theatre activists who seek to sidestep the pitfalls of empire. Although an obvious answer to this dilemma is to stay home, it is also obvious that neoliberal pressures are more easily negotiated than opposed. Artists will always be heading to traumatized or semitraumatized areas in hopes of making a difference, gathering source material for the writing of plays, or endowing their work with greater authenticity in the guise of "fieldwork." If affective labor is a hallmark of empire, how might it be cast in the service of the East and Central African multitudes? How might we send in the clowns differently? In pursuing these questions, I rely primarily on my experiences in a cultural exchange trip in Uganda and Rwanda in 2007, although the clowns reappear toward the end.

Compassionate Colonialism

Numerous theatre activists and scholars have interrogated the limits of the interventionist model. In an introduction to a *TDR* special issue devoted to social theatre, James Thompson and Richard Schechner emphasize the idea of mutual transformation: "It ought to become a performance that can transform the practitioners, the participants, and the public's existing knowledge and experience. It ought not to just map onto or sit authoritatively above."[11]

Sonja Arsham Kuftinec expands on the idea of transformation, noting that "theatrical encounters . . . highlight productive ruptures—moments of 'truths colliding' that undo the stability of what we think we know of ourselves and others."[12] Such encounters "offer the opportunities to examine our assumptions, to reconstitute the world beyond in-group and out-group, beyond a nationalized (and naturalized) 'us' and 'them.'"[13] These reflections indicate acute discomfort with the colonialist and imperialist implications of authoritative models and seek to overturn or at least unsettle them through an emphasis on theatre exchange as a means of producing new forms of knowledge.[14]

But even when we march into these international contexts armed with ideas of mutual transformation and collaboration, we might still overlook the distinct possibility that our presence is not wanted or is simply tolerated out of the hope that more tangible benefits will be forthcoming. In *Theatre of Good Intentions*, Dani Snyder-Young asks hard questions about the appropriateness of theatre interventions in the first place. She "implores artists to ask, as they contemplate a project's goals, whether theatre is indeed the intervention needed to make the change for which they fight."[15] In specific circumstances—not all—our eagerness to use the performing arts as a forum for the exploration of trauma might be entirely misplaced. Good intentions too easily serve as a mask for arrogance.

I turn to experiences in northern Uganda to clarify my discomfort. In 2007, three years after my first encounter with the civil war in northern Uganda, I visited Hope North, the vocational and secondary school for war-affected youth discussed in chapter 5.[16] The terms of this visit were considerably different from my previous attempt to integrate research and activism in 2004. This time, I was a participant in the "More Life" cultural exchange program organized by Erik Ehn, of which Hope North was the final segment.[17] Okello Kelo Sam, the founder and director of Hope North, who makes several appearances in chapter 5, had invited us; he was keen to encourage artistic activity at Hope North and welcomed the opportunity to have us work with the schoolchildren in theatre workshops.[18] The situation boded well for an artistic interaction that would, in Kuftinec's terms, "reconstitute the world beyond in-group and out-group."[19] The first night, the dances that the Hope North children performed for us around the bonfire grew into a communal performance in which we participated. The workshops held the following day adhered to a relatively hierarchical structure as the "More Life" participants led workshops in playwriting, poetry, and hip-hop.[20] That evening, though, Sam unsettled our positions of authority when he assigned us specific tasks to contribute to the evening meal, such as chopping wood, killing and butchering a goat, or fetching water; Hope North staff and students stepped in as our instructors because of the obvious lack of skill of the US participants. He also organized a soccer match between the "More Life" participants and the Hope North students, which Hope North easily won. These activities helped ensure that the potential for mutual transformation was once again intact.

The next day, the ideal of co-creation was actively sought. Ugandan playwright and "More Life" participant Deborah Asiimwe moderated a discussion about the challenges that the Hope North students faced. Under Asiimwe's guidance, Hope North students raised a few issues that concerned them at the school, chief of which was a lack of time to study for their exams that were scheduled for the following week. We then divided into three groups, one of which was categorized as optimistic that solutions to these problems could be found, and two of which were more ambivalent. Each group was charged to develop a performance that addressed the problems that the students confronted at Hope North.

This technique is not, of course, a radical approach to theatre creation; instead, it relies on standard notions of theatre-for-development, in which theatre is used to target specific problems within the community. What ensued, however, was a tribute to the creative capacity of the Hope North students as they seized this opportunity to target us, the "More Life" participants, as the problem. Our chosen group leader, a Hope North student named Owen, assigned us roles in a play that singled out visitors to Hope North as a primary part of the problem—the point being that entertaining the visitors and providing them with food and water interrupted their study time. The enthusiasm for this production was palpable among the collaborators. We gleefully created scenes in which the Hope North students were forced to carry massive amounts of water for the shower and flush toilet that were in the VIP hut (where I and some of the other older members of "More Life" were staying), and we also parodied the exhausted students forcing themselves to dance at the evening bonfire. We, the "More Life" participants, were directly confronted with the information that all these activities had consumed valuable study time for the exams that were scheduled for the very next week. I felt as if I was participating in a textbook example of how theatre can produce unique knowledge and break down hierarchies. I confess: it was exhilarating.

Then we broke for lunch. Visitors and students ate separately, and the ever-present hierarchical structure descended yet again. When we reassembled, we were asked to hear an announcement. Owen stood with a clenched jaw as another participant explained that the play was "too difficult" for the group to present well. Instead, the group should quickly assemble another play about AIDS or the war in the north.

We were due to present our play in about twenty minutes.

Silence ensued. "It would be easier to develop a new play about AIDS or the war in the north than to present the play we developed this morning?" I asked. Oh yes, we were assured. It would take only "some minutes" to create such a play. More silence followed. Then, Owen's spokesperson said in an undertone, "The play is too frank." Too close, too uncomfortable, too fraught. Never mind that I believe that Sam, as a fellow artist, would have supported the students' collective expression of indignation. The stakes of artistic representation in 2007, when the status of postconflict was just beginning to be achieved, were too high. A safe space for free artistic expression could be as elusive as peace itself. Ehn hastened to explain that the actual performance was not important and that we could simply use the time to get better acquainted. His suggestion, however, was brushed aside, and Owen dictated to one of the young female students a speech he would read in lieu of our performance. His speech consisted of a generic tale of how he came to Hope North, how grateful he is to Hope North, and how wonderful it is that international visitors come to see its success. A satirical representation of life at Hope North gave way to promotional material.

The experience was undoubtedly rich. We, the visitors, learned that *we* were the problem, and, given the reflexive nature of many of the "More Life" participants in 2007, I believe that many of us took this lesson deeply to heart. I participated in numerous heated conversations afterward about how we might have altered our approach at Hope North, or if we should have visited in the first place. I began to understand theatre activism as a kind of ethnographic encounter that cultivates a more nuanced and complex way of understanding the world rather than attempting to change it.[21] Kuftinec calls attention to this overlap, noting that "like critical ethnography, . . . ethical activism needs to wrestle with the politics of when to do less and listen more."[22] I push this observation further and suggest that in resource-poor or otherwise sensitive contexts, activism should yield to ethnography in an acknowledgment that it can be more useful as a means of generating new forms of knowledge than as energetic actions to bring about social change. Perhaps, in the fraught circumstances of northern Uganda, one should simply listen and not try to "do" anything at all.

That said, ethnography is packed to the brim with doing. The framework of ethnography calls to mind the model of co-performance, which has long been hailed in performance studies for its transgressive potential. Margaret Drewal theorizes performative ethnography as a means of "breaking down the boundaries between self and other, subject and object, subjectivity and objectivity; and engaging in a more dialogical relationship with our subjects of study."[23] She specifically advocates participation in African performance in order to attain this methodological ideal, an approach that Dwight Conquergood describes in a broader context as co-performance and, with D. Soyini Madison, as co-performative witnessing.[24] Instead of observing and recording the actions of others, the antihegemonic ethnographer of performance seeks "to be inside the breath and pulse of cultural performance as a feeling, sensing, being, and doing witness."[25] As much as I have been inspired and guided by these ideas, beginning with my first fieldwork experience in Tanzania in 1993, I am also aware that co-performance can be appropriated to serve one's epistemological advantage. As explained in chapter 2, the workshops that I conducted at the World Vision rehabilitation center in Gulu yielded a pivotal understanding of the stakes of representation and narrative in northern Uganda. But I also recall my sense of eagerness as I sought to secure the opportunity to conduct those workshops. The experience of working *with* the children as opposed to simply observing them would mean that I had fulfilled the gold standard of ethnographic research, in which performative ethnography and co-performance serve as a crucial step to dismantling the subject/object dichotomy that the conventional model of ethnography upholds. Johannes Fabian suggests that performative ethnography, "the kind where the ethnographer does not call the tune but plays along," might correlate to a historical moment in which Western societies no longer exercise direct control over the colonial other.[26] The act of "playing along" can then be fetishized as a sign of academic authority. Knowledge about the other remains paramount as a method of control; the techniques of obtaining that knowledge have simply become more covert.

To state that the experience was rich begs a crucial qualification: it was rich for *me*. Even as this complicated interaction played out, I was already envisioning how I would write about it. The moment in which Owen recited a humanitarian paean to Hope North helped crystallize my understanding of an empire of trauma as a force that colonizes the creative impulse itself. But what were the implications to Owen and the other students?[27] Kant's second formulation of the categorical imperative warns against treating people as a means rather than as an end in themselves. Thinking of these encounters as a source of ethnographic knowledge skims over the larger implications and could be interpreted as a violation of this imperative, a fundamental tenet of human rights.[28]

I cannot shake my investment in the coevalness of creativity and critical knowledge and my hope that knowledge can be folded into a praxis of anticolonial compassion. In the next section, I explore Lévinas's concept of radical passivity as an alternative starting point. Theatre artists will always be found in far-flung corners of the globe attempting to make a difference—what might be the end result of these encounters beyond the production of (western) knowledge? A temporal disjuncture occurs at this point in the chapter. In order to elaborate on the idea of radical passivity, I turn to our experiences in Rwanda that preceded our travel to Hope North in Uganda. During the last two weeks of July 2007, the "More Life" group visited genocide memorial sites, listened to survivor testimony, and attended a series of presentations by state officials on reconstruction. These events were primarily coordinated by the Kigali-based NGO Interdisciplinary Genocide Studies Center (IGSC), which Ehn's partner in the Rwandan program, Jean-Pierre Karegeye, cofounded and directed.[29] The focus in Rwanda was on witnessing rather than artistic activity, and therefore, our experiences during these two weeks serve as a counterpoint to our experiences in Hope North. Despite my reservations about certain aspects of the Rwanda program, I believe that it marked a radical intervention into conventional understandings of activism that reinscribe the other as victim.

Radical Passivity

The Rwandan program was predicated on a concept of theatre activism that exceeds conventional understandings of activism as interventionist. In a 2007 *American Theatre* article about the "More Life" exchange, Ehn articulates this vision in the rhetoric of witnessing: "The essential action of the artist, the audience, is to see, to experience, to witness (and deriving from witness—to give testimony), to trust.... Seeing can be a moral act: We consent to take in, we draw our attention to focus, we turn our heads and open our eyes—we change our own place to put ourselves squarely in the presence of a unique event."[30] He adds, "In seeing in this way, by deliberately committing to a new perspective, we allow ourselves to be shaped by the event—to be created by it."[31] It is telling that these passages make up almost the entirety of a section subtitled "Arts=Activism." Rather than seeking to promote healing and reconciliation through theatre, the mission of "More Life" is to carve out a site of witnessing for the transformation of ourselves. And this, Ehn suggests, is a version of activism.

His formulation could be read as an invitation to navel-gazing and inertia. What is the point of sending US theatre artists halfway across the world only to put the focus on their own journeys of self-transformation? But in the context of conflict and postconflict zones in Central Africa, it marks a strategic point of departure. Ehn and Karegeye's approach was particularly attuned to the limitations of our group. The majority of the US participants barely spoke French, let alone Kinyarwanda or Swahili, and thus depended primarily on the Rwandan interpreters in the group in their interactions with survivors. In addition, much of their knowledge of the genocide was drawn from trade books by US authors, such as Philip Gourevitch's *We Wish to Inform You That Tomorrow We Will Be Killed with Our Families* and the single chapter devoted to the genocide in Samantha Power's *"A Problem from Hell": America in the Age of Genocide*.[32] Given this background of ignorance, the desire to "do something" needed to be thoroughly interrogated and ideally forestalled.

But it should be noted that witnessing also contains land mines. The witness can easily fall into the category of a voyeur who, in Ehn's words, "feels sexy because they've had an encounter with death and haven't died."[33] Ehn is acutely aware of the dangers of "witnessing by proxy," a phrase he uses to describe the position of outsiders who seek to learn and understand about the Rwandan genocide.[34] In an attempt to develop an ethical response to atrocity that evades the pitfalls of appropriation and titillation, he articulates a version of witnessing that embraced complexity, vulnerability, and precarity. Ehn urged us to work on staying present during our meetings with survivors and visits to genocide sites, warning that "to be overwhelmed with emotion is a way of protecting ourselves."[35] Excessive emotion could easily rush into the stillness as a means of distancing ourselves from the other for whom we are a witness. Staying present was an ultimately more challenging task insofar that it unsettled our activist, compassionate bent to do something and instead asked us simply to dwell on the discomfort of testimony. When one participant eagerly shared intimate details of the testimony of a survivor whom she had encountered on an excursion of her own, Ehn spoke with uncharacteristic sharpness that "a testimony is like a secret."[36] Again, we were asked to simply dwell in the space of testimony and not to try to discharge its horror by explaining it to others, an act that would position us as authorities on Rwandan experience. When another participant spoke admiringly of the courage and bravery of the survivors in sharing their testimonies, Chantal Kalisa, a Rwandan scholar of Francophone literature and an advisory member of the IGSC, reminded us that "this doesn't mean they'll be able to get out of bed in the morning."[37] We must dwell not only on the discomfort of the tale but also on our awareness of the cost of the telling.

Emmanuel Lévinas's concept of passivity helps clarify the potential of activism as inaction. In a theory of selfhood that systematically and thoroughly undermines the agency and sovereignty of the subject, Lévinas positions the self as radically passive in the encounter with the other.[38] This encounter with the other calls forth a primal, precognitive ethical relationship in which the self is inseparable from an infinite responsibility for the other. To speak of responsibility in the Lévinasian sense refuses the usual dichotomy of self-as-beneficiary and other-as-victim. Instead, he defines the self as its responsibility for the other; thus, infinite responsibility is intertwined with infinite vulnerability. His insistence on the vulnerability of the subject is often conveyed through terms such as "hostage" and "victim" to describe subjecthood.[39] "Subjectivity is being hostage," Lévinas states.[40] More expansively, he writes, "The oneself cannot form itself; it is already formed with an absolute passivity. In this sense, it is the victim of a persecution that paralyses any assumption that could awaken in it, so that it would posit itself *for* itself."[41] This infinite responsibility cannot uphold the self's desire for superiority but instead erodes the singularity of the ego.

The Lévinasian stakes are raised when the US theatre-activist-self encounters the Rwandan survivor-other. Thomas Carl Wall's reading of Lévinas suggests that an encounter with those who have exceeded "localizable contexts" and have become "radically dis-placed" is filled with the potential to script new kinds of relations between self and other: "When this happens, all proper relations to the other are suspended and there is, before anything else, a fascination."[42] He goes on to argue that this fascination is not one that sensationalizes but one that stuns an experience "to which there is no proper response."[43] The potential of this encounter relates to the theoretical minefield of Lévinasian ethics, of which Wall's conceptualization is well worth quoting at length:

> The call of the Other will never cease to place an incoherent demand in the soul of the subject to which no response is adequate.... Every response to the other, every restoration to the general, will betray the demand. But at the same time, each betrayal will be a new relation with the other and thus ethics will mime or "confirm" to mimesis, to the improper "itself." There will be no reaching ethics, no teaching it, no instituting it. There will be instead the slow emptying out of any determinate relation whatsoever, and this emptying out will articulate by exhaustion and exclusion the singular "itself."[44]

The singular "itself" is the abyss, and perhaps it is a glimpse of the abyss that I think should be the cornerstone of any attempt to understand genocide. Only then, perhaps, would it be appropriate to act on our desire to "do something"—if we still feel equal to the task.

So perhaps we should, in our encounters with survivors and others affected by sustained crimes against humanity, strive to accept the lack of a proper response. In a thoughtful application of Lévinasian thought to ethnographic practice, Peter Benson and Kevin Lewis O'Neill suggests that a Lévinasian ethnography would emphasize "the active maintenance of an elected affinity to being marked by the other's knowledge and experience."[45] Similarly, the would-be activist could actively seek out this elected affinity and adopt the notion of radical passivity as "a cautionary brake to headlong (Western) activist manifest destiny."[46] Radical passivity could avoid the neocolonialist and imperialist connotations of cross-cultural exchange and clear a space for the articulation of the counter-agendas of those for whom we are a witness. In his essay "Neighbors and Other Monsters: A Plea for Ethical Violence," Slavoj Žižek writes, "To recognize the Other is thus not primarily or ultimately to recognize the other in a certain well-defined capacity... but to recognize you in the abyss of your very impenetrability and opacity. This mutual recognition of limitation thus opens up a space of sociality that is the solidarity of the vulnerable."[47] Radical passivity clears a path to Žižek's solidarity of the vulnerable and an anticolonial compassion, in which an inchoate desire to help founders on the recognition that the distress and pain that one desires to alleviate cannot be contained. Žižek's unflinching gaze into what he calls "the unfathomable abyss of radical Otherness, of a monstrous Thing that cannot be gentrified" exposes the domesticating force of multicultural rhetoric and its respect for difference and confronts the "monstrous dimension of subjectivity" in the face of which all of us are vulnerable.[48]

Did we catch glimpses of the abyss through practicing radical passivity? Did we inhabit the space of vulnerability? When I reflect on those extraordinary weeks in Rwanda, I fail to locate a vivid example—an anecdote—that captures the potential of this approach. Although our experiences at Hope North were complex and ambiguous, a narrative could still be discerned in which "the literary is knotted to the real," as Jane Gallop describes the process of anecdotalizing theory.[49] Gallop believes that "an emphasis on the moment" is crucial to the project of dismantling the dichotomy of example and theory,[50] and certainly this chapter has been filled with moments of deep significance: the moment when the theatre activist inadvertently flashed her underwear, the moment when Owen cast me as the intrusive foreigner, the moment when the students at Hope North refused to move forward with our play—these are keystones that have been deeply influential in my thinking. But they are also moments that are relatively digestible and can be neatly situated in my pursuit of the ethics of theatre activism. These moments transpired through attempts to intervene rather than witness and thus perhaps lend themselves more easily to a linear narrative of cause and effect.

In contrast, what I offer from the Rwandan experience is more ambiguous. The following discussion depends primarily on moments when I was confounded and exhausted by contradiction and paradox. Only rarely were we able to lose ourselves in a specific experience and sink into the luxury of emotion uninterrupted by present-day Rwandan realities. More frequently, we were jolted out of our reveries through competing forces for our attention and the volatility of a postgenocide society. I offer a few of my vivid memories as representative examples of how the impossibility of what we saw and heard triggered a kind of "emptying out," as Wall put it, and a surrender to radical passivity.[51] These are perhaps the kind of moments that Gallop has in mind when she writes that "it is precisely this ability to interrupt and divert a project conceived in theory which makes incident a force with which theory must reckon."[52] These are moments that interrupt and divert the momentum of intervention.

Murambi. Toward the end of the first week of the program, we visited Murambi Technical School, where several thousand Rwandans were slaughtered after being lured to the complex by the promise of safety.[53] The remains of dozens of bodies, regularly dusted with preservative chemicals, are displayed on wooden pallets in a series of small classrooms. The bodies are achingly vulnerable; it is easy to find yourself alone with them in one of the many rooms. Local children who were playing along the edges of the memorial site sought to make us laugh with their antics. I came out of one classroom and encountered a smiling young boy who held out his hands and asked for *faranga* (francs). I have no idea what my emotional state was at that moment, but I do know that it was abruptly broken as I confronted the world of a child who plays alongside bodies permanently stiffened "in the postures of annihilation."[54] How humorous the sobbing *bazungu* must have appeared.[55] Our postures of mourning were abruptly exposed, and I expect that we elicited much laughter.

Sovu. We visited the Benedictine convent in Sovu, a small town near Butare (Huye) in southern Rwanda, where two nuns, Sisters Maria Kizito and Gertrude, actively assisted in the killing of several thousand Rwandan Tutsi.[56] Ehn's play *Maria Kizito* had been inspired by the actions of the two nuns and their subsequent trial in Belgium for crimes against humanity; he was particularly shocked by Maria Kizito's act of supplying the militia with gasoline for the burning of about five hundred Tutsi in the convent's garage.[57] We gathered in a circle on the convent's well-manicured lawn, complete with a volleyball net and gazebos, where we were told that much of the slaughter occurred while the nuns watched from the terrace and served tea to the militias during their breaks.[58] But before we could feel sexy about this experience of death that would leave us only with grass stains, a young man began screaming at us through the gates. He screamed in Swahili about the murders, about the children who were killed, and the names of people involved. Disagreements broke out within the group about his sanity and his identity as one of the survivors of Sovu, a bystander, or a murderer.[59] The thread of Ehn's narrative about Sovu was lost as, instead, we were forced to grapple with the living legacy of the massacres.

Gahanga. We visited the village of Gahanga, located in the outskirts of Kigali, to listen to survivor testimony and visit the small memorial site. As local children jockeyed for our attention, we listened to a survivor's testimony as he took us on a tour of the school compound: here was where they began to kill the women and children, here was where we tried to fight them off with sticks and stones, here was the room where we hid with the livestock (later removed so the animals would not be harmed), and here is the garbage pit that we transformed into a mass grave because it was already paved with cement.[60]

Meanwhile, we could overhear a raucous soccer match, and we had to step around the millet that was drying in front of the mass grave. The survivor then took us to the local Catholic church where the bodies had been kept, "a kind of store of bodies," until the stacks reached the ceiling. We sat in this church, which continues to serve as a house of worship, and dwelled in our discomfort. There was nothing else to do. At the end of our visit to Gahanga, we gathered in the open-air shelter that served as the local *gacaca* building. Itamar Stern, a CalArts student who had participated in the "More Life" program for the two previous years, spoke passionately about relinquishing the need "to connect the dots" and allowing the soccer game, the church, the millet, and the testimony to exist simultaneously—allowing the labor of everyday life in Rwanda to exist alongside markers of carnage and fear.

The gaps and interruptions that characterized our days in Rwanda disallowed our attempts to reconcile contradiction, explain away paradoxes, and comprehend mass death. Instead, confusion was our master. Žižek might concur: "The first ethical gesture is thus to abandon the position of absolute self-positing subjectivity and to acknowledge one's exposure/thrownness, being overwhelmed by Other(ness)."[61] We were regularly thrown and overwhelmed. We were held hostage to the abyss.

Our hegemonic selves did not take kindly to this approach. Resistance manifested itself in multiple ways. Many of my fellow participants repeatedly and fervently expressed a desire to "do something" to help—a desire that some managed to act on through conducting various workshops in Theatre of the Oppressed (TO) and meditation techniques, giving money to survivors, or doing volunteer work for women's organizations in Kigali.[62] Simply dismissing these activities as misguided adopts a patronizing stance toward the local Rwandans who participated in these workshops as (unradically) passive recipients instead of as active subjects who are capable of rejecting, accepting, or transforming the skills as they deem appropriate (see chapter 5). I also do not doubt that, in certain cases, the skills being offered were eagerly welcomed, as when Brent Blair, a noted TO practitioner and an especially thoughtful "More Life" participant, offered a workshop to an organization of student survivors at the National University of Rwanda who seemed keen to learn Boalian techniques.[63] But the reliance on westerners who are anxious to share their skills to respond to the harsh injustices of the world order must also be contextualized: why us and why not a Rwandan theatre artist? TO techniques have a long history at the Centre of the Arts at the university.[64] Why was Blair asked to give a workshop instead of a staff member at the Centre of the Arts? Why was I asked to give workshops at the World Vision rehabilitation center in Gulu instead of one of the members of Gulu Theatre Artists, a local theatre collective?[65] How do these interventions uphold the westerner's authoritative stance as the purveyor of skills?

I conceive of radical passivity as a sustained point of departure that might allow for alternative kinds of engagement. In a summary of the 2007 trip, Ehn echoes these sentiments: "The trip to Rwanda/Uganda wants to be contemplative at core, with space for listening, and ethical guidance around issues of accepting testimony and entering into colloquy with trauma. The trip is at its best when there is internal and external quiet, when we take time; the dancing and singing come out of a sweeter place when they are responsive to their counterparts."[66] This rich passage emphasizes the idea of radical passivity as a starting point, but it also leaves room for praxis—the dancing and singing—once one has dwelled within the space of witnessing. As discussed in the next section, though, even our dancing and singing had unexpected repercussions. Our offerings might have been sweetly made, but they were soundly rejected.

Precarious Hospitality

The theme of hospitality runs throughout Ehn's rhetoric. In his opening remarks for the 2007 Arts in the One World conference, he offered an understanding of hospitality as a kind of panacea for cultural differences: "I believe the theater of the future will not be framed by style or technique, but by ethics ... specifically, the theater of hospitality. Hospitality may be defined as a mitigation of estrangement. This is the world's next great phase, lest, as we communicate more swiftly, we go at each other more than grow with. Remaining strange (local), but not estranged. The lion is still a lion, the lamb a lamb, but they lay down together."[67] Ehn's relatively modest definition of hospitality as "a mitigation of estrangement" gives way to a utopian vision in which differences between the lion's and the lamb's sociopolitical statuses are erased. Elsewhere, though, Ehn provides a nuanced conception of hospitality that underscores the precariousness of the artist's position. Artists are seekers of hospitality rather than its providers: "Artists who celebrate the ecological concept of hospitality run the risk of thinking they're inside the house welcoming the others into it, 'Welcome the stranger, come into my house of art,' when they have to understand that in their own weakness, in their own strangeness, artists make a gift of their need and serve by being welcomed."[68] By taking the risk of hospitality, we also assume the risk of rejection. Ehn adds, "It's what I fail to bring to a community, in a way, that is my gift to the community, where my emptiness in the face of the community, my dependence on the community is what I can bring as an artist."[69] In contrast to colonialist notions of activism that inscribe the western outsider as "the active, determining subject of judgment" (to return to Badiou), Ehn offers up a compelling image of the artist as a suppliant rather than a benefactor.[70]

In light of Ehn's ideas, it seemed fitting that our own encounters with hospitality clarified our vulnerability and the fragility of our relationship with our hosts. For the 2007 program, Ehn and Karegeye planned to include two public performances by the participants. One performance was to consist of various interpretations of violence (not necessarily related to Rwanda) presented by individual participants during our visit to the National University of Rwanda in Butare. The second performance was designed as a collective interpretation of our Rwandan experiences, to be presented in Kigali at the end of our visit. In preparation for the Butare performance, several participants rehearsed poems, dramatic readings, and songs during our first week. This performance could be understood as a well-intentioned attempt to share our concept of artistic creation, to serve as the spectacle, to perform for the Rwandan gaze.

The reality was that our weakness and our strangeness exploded in our faces. These intentions played out in the auditorium at the National University as scheduled, and we served up a smorgasbord of performance pieces that testified to the heterogeneity of the group.[71] Offerings included an improvisational dance piece by Kathy Carbone, a dance instructor and the performing-arts librarian at CalArts; hip-hop by Los Angeles–based Native American artist Sista Hailstorm (assisted by Vanessa Penaloza, a Los Angeles–based Chicana community activist and poet); a monologue written by the US playwright and "More Life" participant Lynn Nottage and performed by Asiimwe (the Ugandan playwright who facilitated our workshop at Hope North); a Swahili popular song about poverty by Tanzanian participant Robert Ajwang; and an abstract puppetry piece by students John Kern and Catherine Strecker. Aside from the crowd's enthusiastic response to the hip-hop and the Swahili music, the overwhelming and extremely vocal reaction from the Rwandan audience was either amusement, catcalls to the younger female performers, or overt boredom. A sizable number of the spectators simply left. The gift of our need was rejected. Rest assured, none of us felt sexy.

I am perhaps alone in interpreting this event as a positive experience. Plans for the second performance in Kigali were abruptly discarded after the debacle at Butare, which was barely mentioned again. But it was during this performance that our feelings of discomfort and vulnerability were the most acute. To return to an earlier point, the risk of rejection is one that we must embrace given the distinct possibility that our presence is not wanted. We can waltz into Central Africa filled with Lévinasian/Derridean notions of how the intercultural encounter might pave the way for a dismantling of thresholds, but we might also be sent packing. "Is not hospitality an interruption of the self?"[72] Derrida asks. In light of what happened in Rwanda, I would also ask, does not the denial of hospitality produce an interruption of the (privileged) self? In his reading of Lévinas, Derrida concludes that hospitality and ethics are inextricable, that hospitality is "the whole and the principle of ethics."[73] Another principle is to question the grounds on which hospitality is offered.

I am not suggesting that public humiliation is a stepping-stone toward an ethics of vulnerability. Nevertheless, I do think that methods of dehegemonizing should be actively sought as a means of shedding some of the messianic vestiges of theatre activism. Such moments constitute a radical intervention into conventional frameworks of activism that reinscribe the other as victim. Although Žižek's solidarity of the vulnerable was not achieved, this position of vulnerability led us closer to the abyss. The multiple intra- and intercultural tensions, anxieties, and discomforts that we experienced were points of departure for learning to understand that the abyss does not exist only within the other but also pervades and occupies ourselves.

Return of the Clowns

Although I find the concept of radical passivity compelling, I am aware that it is hardly an anticolonial panacea. Theatre activism that seeks to maintain a passive—even abject—position in regard to the other begins to smack of masochism.[74] Ideally, the path of radical passivity would serve not as a recipe for inertia but as a blueprint for new models of theatre activism, models that take the less sexy but more meaningful route of coalition building with fellow theatre artists.[75] In this section, I borrow from ideas of fidelity to conceptualize subsequent action.

I draw my understanding of fidelity from Alain Badiou, who refuses the Lévinasian emphasis on the other and instead asserts that ethical subjectivity is formed through fidelity to an event. As Simon Critchley put it, "The subject commits itself ethically in terms of a demand that is received from the situation."[76] Critchley's use of the phrase "a demand that is received from the situation" places the subject in a passive position in regard to the situation and thus resonates with the Lévinasian approach. Once the demand is received, however, the ethical subject cannot evade it and must commit itself to the process of truth. Truth is an immanent break that "tak[es] the *sustained* form of a *faithful* process."[77] One must "persevere in the interruption,"[78] a rich phrase that refuses the isolated moment of epiphany in favor of continual, ceaseless activism. Badiou's nuanced and provocative concept of truth as a process, as labor, as persistent and sustained inquiry, is rife with potential for theatre activists.

In a Badiouian turn of phrase, Ehn writes, "One persists through this line of inquiry, this application of art to the task of witnessing to genocide, questioning continually."[79] Certainly Ehn's commitment to Rwanda, sparked by the initial event of writing *Maria Kizito*, could be interpreted as an example of fidelity.[80] *Maria Kizito* serves as the singular event that expanded into a sustained, multifaceted engagement with postgenocide Rwanda. His collaboration with Karegeye not only generated the annual visit to Rwanda each summer but also annual Arts in the One World conferences devoted to the intersection of the arts and genocide. Their efforts culminated in the formation of the IGSC in Kigali, which supports research on genocide in an effort "to understand various mechanisms and structures of violence, with the goal of preventing genocide and mass violence."[81] Through his collaborations with Karegeye, Ehn practiced fidelity in his rigorous examination of what it means to be human in a genocidal world.

But what kinds of truths are being understood? After insisting on the process of continual questioning, Ehn offers two "practical" pieces of advice: (1) to travel and (2) to be *with* (his emphasis).[82] When does the act of "being with" begin to interfere with critical awareness? How do you ensure that you are traveling in such a way that you are *with* a variety of witnesses, each of whom can offer a crucial vantage point? Even as I was being unsettled and overwhelmed during those weeks in Rwanda, I was noticing that our experience of witnessing and learning about the genocide was a relatively airtight package that aligned itself closely with the current Rwandan official narrative about the events of 1994. As a representative example, Ehn and Karegeye followed state rhetoric and called the events that occurred in 1994 "the Tutsi genocide" instead of "the Rwandan genocide of 1994." This semantic shift erases the thousands of "Hutu moderates" who were killed alongside the targeted Tutsi.[83]

It also sidesteps the controversy surrounding the thousands of Hutu civilians who were killed in the former Zaire and in Rwanda.[84] Criticisms of state policies never entered into the conversation; nothing that we heard or saw diverged from the dominant understanding of President Paul Kagame and the Rwandan Patriotic Front as the bulwarks of democracy and reconciliation.[85] In *Remnants of Auschwitz*, Giorgio Agamben writes, "At a certain point, it became clear that testimony contained at its core an essential lacuna; in other words, the survivors bore witness to something it is impossible to bear witness to."[86] Although Agamben uses the term "lacuna" to refer to the incomprehensibility of suffering, in this context, it takes the form of a forceful silence. David Newbury warns of "the cultural veil that filters all intercultural encounters, not least in a period of post-genocide Rwanda where emotions remain raw and political legitimacy remains fragile."[87] In the instance of "More Life," the veil not only filtered but also actively concealed nuanced understandings of Rwandan histories and politics. It is easy for me, as an outsider, to take a cue from Badiou and suggest that fidelity to the truth should exceed partisan narratives. But I am reminded of Owen at Hope North, who could not speak his truth because of fear of the consequences. Perhaps the stakes are too high at this historical moment in postgenocide Rwanda for the lacuna to be exposed, interrogated, and filled. Others may disagree.[88]

How to proceed? In contexts where the pursuit of fidelity runs the risk of seeming insensitive, rude, or dangerous, how might a theatre activist–cum–ethnographer proceed? How is one to detach activism from its humanitarian baggage? One possibility is to recast theatre activism as cross-cultural or intercultural theatre, which emphasizes the process of shared creativity as openness.[89] The pursuit of a shared imagination instead of a militant notion of truth facilitates intersubjectivity and fluidity. Rustom Bharucha notes that if the future of intercultural theatre is "to be posited in tangible terms, and not just as an empty fantasy, we will have to open ourselves to those realities that resist being imagined easily . . . realities that would seem to annihilate the imagination—poverty, hunger, homelessness, ethnic cleansing."[90] Such openness might enable theatre practitioners "to transcend the conceit of [their] existing complacencies by igniting new possibilities of being human."[91] I am not convinced that western theatre practitioners are complacent—I think that it is their anxiety that is triggering these interventions in the first place—but I find it noteworthy that the majority of his examples of realities that would seem to annihilate the imagination emphasize structural violence over episodic or direct violence. In order to imagine new possibilities of being human, artists should forestall the sensationalist impulse that attracts them to the plight of former child soldiers and genocide survivors instead of the everyday violence of extreme poverty and marginalization. Lofty rhetoric might then translate to a grounded praxis.

Back to the clowns, who sought to make grounded and collaborative offerings of their own. This section returns to Clowns Without Borders as a cautionary tale of the elusiveness of alliance. In 2009, the Spanish chapter of CWB visited the eastern DRC on a tour of the refugee camps. Political scientist Laura Seay, a specialist in the DRC and author of the popular blog *Texas in Africa*, writes that she "nearly choked" when she heard the news.[92] She reluctantly acknowledges that the children in the camps could use the entertainment but then notes that "there's a fantastic acrobatic troop in Goma that could've done the same thing without the need to finance a massive 25-day tour of the seven camps."[93] At the very least, CWB might have used its international cachet to collaborate with local circus and acrobatic troupes in an act coalition building instead of keeping the humanitarian limelight to itself.

When the Irish chapter of CWB headed to Rwanda in 2012, criticisms of the group had clearly registered. The report of this visit, during which it performed for refugee camps along the western border, as well as for schools in Kigali, acknowledges "some of the concerns we would wrestle with and others level at CWB," such as "Why send clowns to Africa? Is it worth the expense? Is it deserving of state funding? Is it a worthwhile demand on UN staff? Traumatised and hungry children's needs are greater than a visit from clowns."[94] As a means of responding to this criticism, CWB emphasizes its collaboration with six members of the Gisenyi Acrobats, a professional acrobatics troupe based in the western town of Gisenyi on the shores of Lake Kivu. Although both Irish and Rwandan acrobats collaborated on particular stunts, such as a popular stunt called the human caterpillar, the Gisenyi Acrobats performed separately as the final act in the shows they put on at the camps.[95] This schedule suggests that the Irish clowns served as a kind of warm-up for the "real" performance of the Gisenyi Acrobats, a well-established group whose gravity-defying stunts were not only captivating but also familiar to Rwandan audiences since acrobatics is a popular performance tradition across the region.[96] In other words, the exotic gave way to the known, and the Irish clowns played second fiddle to their Rwandan counterparts in a dehegemonizing move.

Fig. 16. The Gisenyi Acrobats in Kigali, August 2015.

Earlier that same year, the Gisenyi Acrobats collaborated with the Swedish branch of CWB, which has used some of its resources for the benefit of the Rwandan group; for example, the Swedish CWB developed a promotional video and brought several members to Sweden on a tour.[97] The Swedish branch also sponsored a two-year collaboration between the Gisenyi Acrobats and an acrobatics group based on Goma and thus provided funding to facilitate artistic collaboration between two countries that are often perceived as political enemies.[98] Perhaps these gestures could be perceived as an intervention in Teju Cole's industrial complex.

Jonathan Irakiza, the head of Gisenyi Acrobats, though, would disagree with this rosy interpretation. In August 2015, I attended a performance of the group that was hosted at a private home in Kigali, which included a creative mix of daredevil feats, magic tricks, and, yes, clowning.[99] Irakiza was quick to correct my interpretation that the clowning sketches had been inspired by their collaboration with CWB, stressing that they were influenced by numerous collaborations, as well as their study of You Tube videos. He emphasized that CWB was just one organization within a larger network that his group had cultivated in the region and overseas. He went on to speak critically about the group's collaboration with CWB, which had broken down because of disagreements over financial arrangements and other expectations. CWB might have put considerable weight on its positive interactions with the Gisenyi Acrobats, but clearly the feeling was not mutual.[100]

I attended the performance along with Simon Rwema, a leading actor and assistant director of the Kigali-based Mashirika Performing Arts and Media Company, which, like the Gisenyi Acrobats, has also engaged in several collaborative experiences with western artists. Our conversation generated a lively discussion of the ethics of international collaboration in which both Rwema and Irakiza demonstrated a keen awareness of how their work is appropriated for the purposes of promotion and branding. "What doesn't work," Rwema stated emphatically, "is when they say they want to promote our work but instead they promote their work using *our* work." Irakiza agreed, adding that potential collaborators should seek "not [to favor] themselves but [see] what's favorable to both." The context of the conversation indicated that CWB had not met this standard.

So how should clowns go to Africa? In our promotion-saturated present, appropriation is inevitable. But what choices might geoprivileged collaborators make differently if they are aware of how their efforts at outreach are often perceived? How might they channel material resources to East and Central African artists in a way that puts those artists' need to pursue a livelihood at the center of the equation? Ehn presents a characteristically evocative way to theorize artistic collaborations that emphasizes process as opposed to the production of text: "All the text we are pumping out nowadays is nothing without textile: the series of knots and overlays that combine to give expansive networks their strength."[101] How might the pursuit of radical collaboration put less emphasis on the generation of texts and more on the development of texture? How might these collaborations not only generate income and publicity but also expand regional and transnational networks? How might these collaborations spin out in ways that build coalitional strength?

With all the caveats and qualifications I can muster, these musings boil down to the following road map for the not-so-heroic theatre activist: (1) to commit to a stance of radical passivity; (2) if a demand emerges through that stance, to respond to that demand with fidelity; and (3) to pursue shared creativity through the generation of texture. My hope is that this stance will facilitate a sense of humility and critical awareness and a means of confronting the endemic neoliberalism in which we work and live. Finally, we should cultivate awareness that failure will permeate the process. "Failure is inevitable," Critchley warns, "for we can never hope to fulfill the radicality of the ethical demand."[102] In this sense, then, all activists are failed activists, and we should embrace the potential of those failures as we lurch toward a mutually vulnerable world—ideally, one with much laughter.

Notes

1. This workshop took place on July 10, 2004.

2. James Thompson and Richard Schechner acknowledge the "diverse and bewildering nomenclature" of theatre activism: "applied theatre (UK and Australia), community-based theatre (USA), theatre for development (certain Asian and African countries), or popular theatre" (2004, 11). They adopt the term "social theatre" from their Italian colleagues as an umbrella form for a wide range of performance forms, loosely categorized as theatre for (1) healing, (2) action, (3) community, and (4) transforming experience into art (2004, 15). They also use the term "social theatre worker" or "social theatre practitioner" as a more encompassing term than "theatre activist." My preference for the term "theatre activist," though, is linked to my larger project in this chapter of expanding the conventional definition of activism as associated with interventionism and "energetic action" (*Oxford English Dictionary*).

3. This quote can be found in CWB's mission statement at www.cwbireland.com/about-us/mission-statement/, accessed September 25, 2014. CWB was originally founded in Barcelona in

1993 and now includes branches in nine countries. As discussed in the conclusion of this chapter, the Irish branch of CWB also visited Rwanda in 2012, whereas the Spanish CWB (Payasos sin Fronteras) visited Goma in 2009.

4. Chris Blattman, "You Know It's No Longer a War Zone...," December 4, 2007, http://chrisblattman.com/2007/12/04/you-know-its-no-longer-a-war-zone/, accessed September 25, 2014.

5. Both the original blog post and comments can be found at http://chrisblattman.com/2009/03/30/the-worst-ngo-on-the-planet/, accessed September 25, 2014.

6. Teju Cole, "The White-Savior Industrial Complex," *Atlantic*, March 21, 2012, 3.

7. Hyndman 2000, 44.

8. Badiou 2001, 9.

9. See Thompson and Schechner 2004, 13, for a spirited critique of the notion of "theatreless" cultures.

10. The CWB report, "Uganda '07," can be found at www.cwbireland.com/gallery/uganda-07/, accessed October 2, 2014.

11. Thompson and Schechner 2004, 13.

12. Kuftinec 2009, xiv.

13. Ibid., 2.

14. See Salverson 1996 and 2001.

15. Snyder-Young 2013, 17.

16. I discuss Hope North in considerable detail in chapter 5. During the time of our visit in August 2007, security in northern Uganda had improved considerably because of the slow progress of peace talks between the Ugandan government and the LRA, and locals had begun to visit their farms during the day to work their fields before returning to the protection camps at night.

17. "More Life" is an umbrella term referring to a host of initiatives related to Rwanda spearheaded by Ehn and Karegeye; however, I am using it here to refer to the cultural exchange in Rwanda and Uganda as I experienced it in July and August 2007. The Rwandan portion of the program began on July 14 and ended on July 30. The group then continued to Uganda for another week. Our diverse group, which numbered about fifty at the height of the Rwandan program, included undergraduate and graduate theatre students in the United States (mostly from the California Institute of the Arts and the University of Southern California), US theatre artists and scholars, independent artists from Uganda and Rwanda, a Tanzanian dancer and musician, and a Canadian visual artist. See Ehn's reflections on the 2007 program, "More Life: Reflections on Rwanda, Uganda, and Bosnia," posted on http://www.themagdalenaproject.org/phpBB2/viewtopic.php?p=739, accessed on September 4, 2008. About eighteen members continued on to Uganda.

18. We arrived at Hope North from Kampala on August 2 and returned to Kampala on August 5.

19. Kuftinec 2009, xiv.

20. Ehn taught a playwriting workshop; Sista Hailstorm, a Native American hip-hop artist who was based in Los Angeles, taught a hip-hop workshop; and Vicki Grise, who was an MFA playwriting student at the California Institute of the Arts and has since become a nationally recognized playwright, taught a poetry workshop.

21. Of course, ethnography cannot be so easily separated from activism, as Nancy Scheper-Hughes (1995) notes in her call for a more engaged anthropology.

22. Kuftinec 2009, 4.

23. Drewal 1991, 33.

24. Conquergood 1991, 188; Madison 2007. See also V. Turner 1975, 28–29. Conquergood's quest for an ethical methodology of performance also yielded concepts such as dialogic performance; see Conquergood 2013 for an overview of his shifting theoretical paradigms.

25. Madison 2007, 829.

26. Fabian 1990, 19.

27. In 2013, I sought to track Owen's whereabouts. I learned that he did not finish his studies at Hope North; the staff believed that he lived in Kitgum.

28. See Benhabib et al. 2006 for a discussion of Kant's categorical imperative as it intersects with human rights.

29. As of 2017, the IGSC was on temporary hiatus.

30. Ehn 2007b, 36.

31. Ibid.

32. Gourevitch 1998; Power 2003.

33. These remarks were made on July 16 at the Kigali Genocide Memorial Centre.

34. Ehn 2007b, 72. Ehn's concept of "witness by proxy" differs from Primo Levi's use of the term for survivors of the Shoah. In *The Drowned and the Saved*, Levi insists that the only "true" witness is a dead witness (1986, 83), and even survivors such as himself "speak in their stead, by proxy" because, by virtue of their survival, they did not experience the extent of the horror (84).

35. Ehn made this remark on July 18, 2007.

36. These remarks were made during a morning gathering at Hotel Tech in Kigali on July 27.

37. Kalisa made these remarks at the end of our visit to Gahanga on July 17.

38. The phrase "radical passivity" does not come directly from Lévinas; as translated by Alphonso Lingis, he uses terms and phrases such as "passivity . . . more passive than every passivity" (1987, 146), "an extreme passivity" (1981, 109), and a "hyperbolic passivity" (1981, 49) to describe the self's receptivity to the other. My use of "radical passivity" is influenced by Wall 1999.

39. Benson and O'Neill 2007, 33–34.

40. Lévinas 1981, 127.

41. Ibid., 104. Emphasis in the original.

42. Wall 1999, 53.

43. Ibid., 54.

44. Ibid., 56.

45. Benson and O'Neill 2007, 45. Their construction of a Lévinasian ethnography was also influenced by Veena Das's "love of anthropology," which she briefly and tantalizingly discusses in the conclusion of her article "Wittgenstein and Anthropology" (1998).

46. John Fletcher used this phrase in reference to the concept of radical passivity in an e-mail communication with me (February 22, 2008).

47. Žižek 2005, 138–139.

48. Ibid., 143, 162.

49. Gallop 2002, 3.

50. Ibid.

51. Wall 1999, 56.

52. Ibid., 15.

53. Statistics of the dead at Murambi vary widely, from 5,000 to 50,000 (Des Forges 1999, 15–16). Murambi is the largest memorial site in Rwanda after the Kigali Memorial Centre; see Eltringham 2014 for an excellent overview of the ethical and political controversies that surround the Murambi site and its display of unburied remains.

54. Ehn 2007b, 72.

55. *Bazungu* is a Kinyarwandan word for "foreigner," usually with connotations of being European or European American.

56. As explained in Des Forges 1999, the extermination of Tutsi was postponed for about two weeks in Butare Prefecture, as the area was known in 1994. In addition to serving as the location of the national university, Butare had the highest percentage of Tutsi in the country, 17 percent. "As intellectual center of the nation and focus of a region where Hutu and Tutsi long lived together, Butare had a reputation for tolerance and moderation" (526). Its prefect, Jean-Baptiste Habyalimana (or Habyarimana), was the only Tutsi prefect in Rwanda at the time at which the genocide commenced. But on April 17, the government summarily removed him from power, and extremists gained control. Thousands of Rwandan Tutsi in Sovu gathered at the convent's health center, pleading for protection from the nuns. The majority of those seeking shelter at the convent were killed in a massacre that began on the morning of April 22. The remainder were finished off by early May. See African Rights 2000 for survivor testimony. See also Des Forges 1995, 810–812; and Rettig 2011.

57. See Edmondson 2009a for more information on *Maria Kizito*.

58. This visit occurred on July 21. I recall that this explanation was quickly absorbed and repeated among us; however, further research suggests that the actual killing was excluded from the convent grounds; thousands were killed at the garage and health center outside the convent's gates (see African Rights 2000). This detail might seem like a technicality, but I am reminded of how the "More Life" group in 2011 interpreted the River Blue dance festival grounds as a "killing field," as discussed in the previous chapter. The land must always be blood soaked. See Rettig 2011, 207n3, for an analysis of the identity of the Sovu militias.

59. No one voiced the possibility that he might have been a Hutu survivor of RPF atrocities, such as the Kibeho massacre of 1995. See Rettig 2011, 197.

60. More information about Gahanga during the genocide can be found at http://genocidearchiverwanda.org.rw/index.php/Gahanga_Memorial, accessed November 4, 2017.

61. Žižek 2005, 138.

62. Theatre of the Oppressed can be loosely defined as a highly participatory methodology of theatre practice that aims to liberate marginalized and oppressed people through a series of embodied, interactive exercises that seek to analyze and deconstruct structures of power. See Boal 1985.

63. See Blair and Fletcher 2010 for an account of their Theatre of the Oppressed work in Rwanda.

64. See Kalisa 2006, 517–518, for a discussion of how Koulsy Lamko from Chad introduced Theatre of the Oppressed techniques to the university's Center of the Arts.

65. An immediate answer to this question, of course, is that the visiting theatre artist is usually willing to do these workshops for free, in exchange for the experience of authenticity and depth, whereas local artists would need transportation money, meals, and payment for their services.

66. Ehn, "More Life."

67. Ehn offered these comments in his opening address to the annual Arts in the One World Conference at the California Institute of the Arts in Valencia, January 24, 2008.

68. "Peace by Artful Means," Australian Broadcasting Corporation, broadcast on September 17, 2006. Transcript available at http://www.abc.net.au/rn/encounter/stories/2006/1739042.htm, accessed September 25, 2007.

69. Ibid.

70. Badiou 2001, 9. Jacques Derrida has famously theorized at length the aporia that permeates the concept of hospitality, which usually operates within limits and affirms sovereignty; see Derrida and Dufourmantelle 2000.

71. The performances took place on July 20, 2007.

72. Derrida 1999, 51.

73. Ibid., 50.

74. Simon Critchley alludes to the masochistic potential of Lévinas's demand for infinite responsibility to the face, noting that his "conception of the ethical subject runs the risk of chronically overloading—indeed masochistically persecuting—the self with responsibility" (2007, 11). See also Kucich 2006 for a discussion of how colonialism and masochism were intertwined.

75. It should be noted that Ehn worked with Rwandan and Ugandan theatre artists to develop the Centre X Centre theatre and dance festival in the summer of 2011, which it was my deep pleasure to attend. The festival in Kigali, which was co-organized by Hope Azeda, Carole Karemera, and Ehn, burst with the creative energy of Congolese, Tanzanian, Ugandan, Burundian, and Kenyan artists, many of whom were able to attend the festival thanks to a grant from the US organization Theatre Communications Group. This project speaks to the potential afforded by an emphasis on coalition building beyond and within the Great Lakes region. The energy of Centre X Centre continues through the annual Ubumuntu Arts Festival at the Kigali Genocide Memorial, which Azeda founded in 2015; the festival serves as a magnet for bold and daring theatre and dance throughout the region and beyond.

76. Critchley 2007, 42.

77. Badiou 2001, 45. Emphasis in the original.

78. Ibid., 47.

79. Ehn 2007b, 73.

80. Ehn 2007a.

81. IGSC website, http://www.igscrwanda.net/en/index.php/, accessed on September 10, 2008.

82. Ehn 2007b, 73.

83. See Eltringham 2004, 69–79, for a useful deconstruction of the phrase "Hutu moderates."

84. These controversies are discussed in chapter 1 and chapter 3.

85. The following statement of Hintjens particularly resonates with the portrait of Rwanda that was painted in the course of the "More Life" program: "For a long time, the RPF was able to cultivate an image, especially in the anglophone world, of a brave, overpopulated little country, battling its genocidal legacies, trying to grapple with lawless killers across the border, whilst fighting backwardness and poverty at home" (2008, 11). It should be noted that as a Rwandan-based organization, the IGSC was expected to uphold state rhetoric; it did so with enthusiasm.

86. Agamben 2002, 13.

87. D. Newbury 2011, xxvii.

88. Several scholars of Rwanda would suggest (or even insist) that the silencing of alternative narratives has generated simmering resentment that could lead to future mass violence (see, for example, Hintjens 2008; Pottier 2002; and Reyntjens 2004).

89. Granted, the idea of intercultural theatre is laden with its own theoretical baggage because it is frequently linked with notions of cultural appropriation, of which the most notorious example is Peter Brook's 1985 production of *The Mahabharata*, which Rustom Bharucha

accused of appropriating Southwest Asian performance traditions and mythologies in an orientalist move. See Bharucha 1988 for a spirited critique of Brook's 1985 production. But in an overview of cross-cultural performance, Jacqueline Lo and Helen Gilbert emphasize the complexity of the process: "While there is a general desire to maintain equitable power relations between partners, the aim is not to produce a harmonious experience of theatre-making but rather to explore the fullness of cultural exchange in all its contradictions and convergences for all parties" (Lo and Gilbert 2002, 39). Their analysis resonates with Anna Tsing's oft-cited concept of friction, "the awkward, unequal, unstable, and creative qualities of interconnection across difference," which "reminds us that heterogeneous and unequal encounters can lead to new arrangements of culture and power" (2005, 4, 5).

90. Bharucha 2000, 161.

91. Ibid., 162.

92. Laura Seay, "Weekend This and That," *Texas in Africa* (blog), March 28, 2009, http://texasinafrica.blogspot.com/2009/03/weekend-this-that_28.html, accessed October 2, 2014. The news item to which she refers is "Clowns Bring Smiles to DR Congo," *BBC News*, March 27, 2009.

93. Seay, "Weekend This and That."

94. The report can be found at www.cwbireland.com/gallery/rwanda-12/, accessed October 2, 2014. The group was clearly responding to criticism on multiple fronts. The Rwandan visit, which received €5,000 in government arts funding, attracted considerable ire among opposition politicians in Ireland; see Senan Molony, "€5k to Send Clowns to Rwanda ... It's No Joke," *Irish Daily Mail*, November 3, 2012.

95. Jonathan Irikiza confirmed this impression during our conversation in Kigali on August 15, 2015.

96. Acrobatics is, for example, extremely popular in neighboring Tanzania, and I recognized many of the stunts from my fieldwork on the Swahili coast in 1996 and 1997.

97. Information on the Gisenyi Acrobats' further interaction with CWB in Sweden can be found at http://gisenyiacrobats.blogspot.com/p/news.html, accessed October 2, 2014. (Interestingly, their collaboration with CWB Ireland is not mentioned.) The promotional video can be viewed at www.youtube.com/watch?v=gJ9yG7lq1H4, accessed on October 2, 2014.

98. Obviously, much more could be said about the Goma/Gisenyi collaboration, given that this is a fascinating example of a collaboration between Rwandan and Congolese performing artists. Despite the length of the project, Clowns Without Borders does not make reference to it on its promotional materials available on the web; I learned about it only through Irakiza's description of it during our conversation. Irakiza posted a short video of this collaboration in 2013, available at https://www.youtube.com/watch?v=e-3-DRVmAeE, accessed September 14, 2015.

99. The performance occurred on August 15, 2015, in the Kigali suburb of Gikondo. It was hosted by an expatriate who wished to support the organization by helping it cultivate an audience in Kigali.

100. It should be noted that a rival group, Future Vision Acrobats, had splintered off from Gisenyi Acrobats; the founder, Elisee Niyonsenga (formerly the president of Gisenyi Acrobats) has described the collaboration with CWB in highly positive terms (David Toovey, "Flying without Wings," *Inzozi*, June–August 2015).

101. "Peace and Trauma, Part II," in the online journal *HowlRound*, March 27, 2011, available at http://howlround.com/peace-and-trauma-part-ii, accessed October 2, 2014.

102. Critchley 2007, 55.

AFTERWORD

Faustin Linyekula and the Labors of Hope

In October 2011, I had the opportunity to ask Faustin Linyekula, world-renowned dancer and choreographer from the eastern DRC, what he thought of *Ruined*.[1] As readers may recall, this play by Lynn Nottage, which explores the ramifications of war and sexual violence in the Ituri rain forest, not only won the Pulitzer Prize for Drama in 2009 but also became one of the most produced plays in the United States. The US-centric assumptions that prompted my question were exposed when Linyekula responded that he had not heard of it. His lack of familiarity might be attributed to the gap between the disciplines of theatre and contemporary dance, the cultural distance between the Anglophone and Francophone art worlds, and, of course, the constraints of US insularity. It speaks of the dominance of humanitarian logic in which a US playwright is more apt to reach out to an international NGO to conduct research than to a fellow Congolese artist in the interests of mutual collaboration. A combination of disciplinary and geopolitical distance ensured that an intercultural encounter between Nottage and Linyekula, both of whom work at the intersection of art, activism, and the DRC, did not occur.

Linyekula knows intimately the repercussions of war. In 2006, he and his company Studios Kabako moved from Kinshasa to Kisangani, the capital of the former Orientale Province. Kisangani had become known as the City of Martyrs because of the fierce fighting between Ugandan and Rwandan troops in three separate battles in 1999 and 2000; thousands of Congolese died in the crossfire.[2] Surrounded by war stories, Linyekula and members of Studios Kabako seek to acknowledge but also to exceed parameters of violence. Through the creation of stunning productions in which video, contemporary dance, theatre, and popular music coalesce, the company redefines Kisangani as a source of creative power. Linyekula states on the Studios Kabako website, "There are people crazy enough to believe obstinately in the celebration of beauty, despite the somersaults of history, wars, revolutions, regimes. To hope that the derisory nature of art can face up to the enormity of the hideousness of life. To dare dream that the independence of thought, free will, and personal initiative can push against this heap of ruins—'Oh country! My beautiful people!'—we inherited."[3] They have pushed against narratives of ruination through the establishment of two cultural centers in a bid "to activate the circulation of ideas, people, and energies through the urban body."[4] They seek to transform the City of Martyrs into the city of dreams.

The title *Ruined* was a slap in the face. "Who is this playwright to say that we're *ruined*?" Linyekula demanded, looking askance at my copy of the play. Although I have previously discussed Nottage's work as a nuanced refusal of humanitarian narratives and colonial legacies, Linyekula's passionate response to the play's title gives me pause. As Achille Mbembe might point out, the title affirms well-worn imperial tropes that consign the continent to an eternal present of devastation and oblivion.[5] The multivocality of Linyekula and Studios Kabako throws the linearity and singular logic of *Ruined* into sharp relief. In the same year in which *Ruined* won the Pulitzer, Studios Kabako premiered *more more more . . . future*, the title of which stands in opposition to *Ruined*. "You have a right to the future!" sings performer Patient Mafutala Useni, a phrase that grounds the optimism of hope in the operations of justice.[6] In a production that explodes with the electricity of Congolese *ndombolo* music, ruination is defiantly reconfigured as futurity.

Instead of multivocality and futurity, I have written of empire. As a result, this book has excluded several extraordinary works of theatre and dance. Lucy Judith Adong, Deborah Asiimwe, Hope Azeda, and Odile Gakire Katese join the ranks of Linyekula and Studios Kabako as artists who broaden the critical and artistic horizons of Central African performance. Adong's *Silent Voices*, which is set in postconflict northern Uganda, comes immediately to mind as an incisive critique of master narratives of the LRA war. The play includes a stylized representation of *tek gungu*, a notorious practice of male rape employed by government soldiers to subjugate Acholi civilians, and thus refigures "silent voices" as victims of the Ugandan state rather than the LRA. Instead of calling for peace, which is recognized as a means of silencing dissent, the play insists on the economic justice of reparations.[7] A gentler but no less powerful approach is explored by Katese through *The Book of Life*, an ambitious performance project for which she collected anonymous letters from Rwandans writing to those they lost or killed during the genocide; one letter was read on the radio for the one hundred days commemorating the genocide. The anonymity of the letters allowed for a capacious expression of loss.[8] In Butare in 2015, I had the pleasure of watching a rehearsal of *The Book of Life*, in which her company of female performers presented an excerpt of a play developed from some of the letters. Even though I did not understand the Kinyarwanda in which they spoke, I was electrified by the intensity of the female performers' direct address and the cadences of the script's overlapping dialogue; their passion served as a keen reminder that death and suffering exceed and blur the parameters of ethnicity. Adong's and Katese's projects are just two examples that call for another book, one that will showcase texts and productions that evade and refuse the demands of state and empire, a book that will be all the more meaningful to write as a response to the forces that seek to constrain radical creativity and critical thought.

In lieu of this future book, I offer this afterword, in which I explore Linyekula's 2011 solo piece *Le Cargo* as a labor of hope. Invocations of hope all too often serve as a kind of sugarcoating or a theoretical salve that makes mass pain and terror in "other" populations seem palatable and thus minimizes questions of accountability. The proverbial ray of hope illuminates an otherwise bleak landscape of global inequities and evacuates the traction of emancipatory politics.[9] Hope becomes an imperial tool. How is one to refute tales of ruination without falling into the clichés of resilience and the triumph of the human spirit? As an alternative, *Le Cargo* articulates hope as labor, that is, as a prolonged effort to keep a dehumanizing world order at bay.[10] As conveyed in Linyekula's artistic imagination, hope is hardly sugarcoating—it is, rather, extraordinarily hard work. Pushing against the ruins calls for disciplined acts of dreaming with "the feet kept firmly on the ground."[11]

Describing Linyekula's work only in the context of trauma and war diminishes the complexities of his politics, which emphasize structural and economic violence in order to counteract the colonialist territorialization of ethnicity. Instead of using the NGO-speak of blood minerals and femicide, he invokes his friend Kabako, for whom the company is named. Kabako died in 1994 from an epidemic of bubonic plague near the Ugandan border and was buried in an unmarked grave. The year 1994 looms large in this book: it was not only the year of the Rwandan genocide, which contributed to the intensification of violence in the eastern DRC, but also the time when the Sudanese government began supporting the LRA and thus unleashed fresh waves of violence in northern Uganda and in what is now called South Sudan. Linyekula's homage to his friend serves as a reminder that 1994 was also marked by the deaths of several hundred Zairians from plague, victims of Mobutu's eradication of social services rather than of genocide and war. Linyekula takes on Kabako's identity in the opening lines of *Le Cargo*: "I am Kabako, my name is Kabako, again Kabako, always Kabako, Kabako is my name."[12] Here Linyekula summons the spirits of invisible deaths to which empire pays no heed. His work abounds in what Slavoj Žižek's calls "sideways" glances at violence, many of which undoubtedly escape my attention.[13] I hope to catch a few.

A Sideways Glance at *Le Cargo*

> What difference does it make for the people of the Congo that I go around the world telling stories of their joys and miseries? Telling over and over again the same stories of suffering niggers, dying niggers, what difference does it make, what difference would it make, if I told you that again, we are in another crisis, another war? Crisis, war, crisis, war, crisis, war, crisis, war, what difference does it make? There is at least one thing that seems to be clear, which is that telling the stories makes a difference for me, the storyteller, because every time I tell one of them . . . I get paid.[14]

Linyekula speaks these lines into a microphone, sitting on a carved wooden stool. The dancer celebrated around the world for his physical virtuosity is motionless. He promises the audience that "tonight I'm not here to tell any stories . . . I'm simply here to dance," but his promise gives way to a choreography of stillness, disrupted only by the restlessness of his hands that refuse to be colonized and subdued by the flow of speech. From his vantage point of stillness, he wonders whether he has ever "really danced" but then chides himself: "That would be a very romanticized idea of dance. Dance as an entity that would be outside geography, outside politics, outside this space that we constantly have to negotiate between the living and the dead." *Le Cargo* is, in part, an exploration of the impossibility of dance and drama as modes of storytelling. The term "cargo," which refers to goods or merchandise and thus gestures to the processes of commodification, signifies the narrative baggage that weighs down his embodiment of what it means to be Congolese.

Perhaps Linyekula is reluctant to dance. What difference does it make? The multivocality of his creative expression will inevitably be reduced to

Fig. 17. *Le Cargo* by Faustin Linyekula. Photo by Agathe Poupeney.

humanitarian catchphrases. He dances, and it becomes a story of resilience. He delivers a monologue, and it becomes a testimony of either victimization or heroism. Whether he presents stories of joy or miseries, all serve as reifications of ruination. Crisis, war, crisis, war, crisis, war... he will spare us the details. He is aware that we do not care about the breakdown of the Ugandan/Rwandan alliance that caused such devastation in Kisangani or even the tens of thousands of Rwandan refugees who sought refuge in Obilo, the village that serves as the primary setting for *Le Cargo*.[15] With biting humor, Linyekula reminds us of the financial transactions that keep the machinery of Trauma, Inc. in motion: "I get paid." The line serves as a jolting reminder that despite the intimacy of his tone, we are not his confidants; we are simply customers sitting in the dark, eager to be seduced. His shocking vocabulary further underscores the racism that permeates the transactions of the empire.

The story he tells in *Le Cargo* is deceptively simple. As he explains during his choreography of stillness, he decides to return to Obilo, the village where he lived as a child, in order to experience the dances that he remembers from his childhood. He speaks with special longing of the "dances of the night" from which he and the other children were excluded. Returning to the village, Linyekula explains, will "renew [his] trade" as a dancer and storyteller. His thoughts of Obilo usher in a rush of memories, among which his father singing in the parish church as the choirmaster is especially vivid. "It is with him that I learned how to sing," Linyekula confides before breaking into a haunting Swahili hymn, "Bwana Utusikilize" (Father, listen to us). Slowly, we in the audience hear the sounds of Obilo over the speakers; the chattering of villagers and a crying baby overlap with his storytelling. It is as if the hymn called forth their voices. As the sounds of the village increase in volume, Linyekula's stillness yields to a dance in which the restless energy of his hands infuses the rest of his limbs and his torso; we catch a glimpse of the coiled energy within his slender frame as scattered strains of an electric guitar are heard.[16] He then elaborates on the challenges of traveling the eighty-two kilometers from Kisangani to Obilo via the train that takes four to five days to cut through the dense undergrowth of the forest. Abruptly, however, he resolves the difficulty when he simply hops on his father's motorbike, arriving in Obilo after only a couple of hours. After an absence of twenty-eight years, after decades of crisis and war, the moment of homecoming is achieved with a sense of relative ease. The hard work is still to come.

This seeming simplicity belies *Le Cargo*'s infinite layers. Linyekula enters the stage holding a carved wooden stool in one arm and Achille Mbembe's

Sortir de la grande nuit: Essai sur l'Afrique décolonisée in the other.[17] Mbembe's *Sortir* serves as an extended meditation on Frantz Fanon's clarion call in *The Wretched of the Earth* to "shake off the great mantle of night" of colonialism and "reach for the light" of a radical kind of independence that rejects the European model of nationhood.[18] Mbembe argues that fifty years after independence, the legacy of colonialism holds fast; independence failed to become an event because of continued investment in colonial systems and mentalities.[19] Initially, *Le Cargo* lends support to Mbembe's ideas. Once the initial thrill of homecoming subsides, Linyekula learns that the dances of his childhood no longer exist: "Because with the war and the crisis, people need miracles. That's when all these new religions preaching miracles came in." The new religions deemed the traditional dances demonic, "exactly," Linyekula observes sardonically, "what European missionaries had done in the late nineteenth century." Hanabouton, the greatest percussionist of the village, had given up drumming in favor of preaching; Linyekula explains that the church forbade him even to touch the drums. The legacies of colonialism continue to cast their long shadow over the vibrancy of the traditions that kept Linyekula awake at night as a child, listening, imagining vivid pictures in his mind. Mbembe's explanation of colonialism's looming presence serves as an explanatory framework for the effacement of tradition. Even when Linyekula tosses the book aside during his opening monologue, claiming that those answers are not *his* answers, he returns to *Sortir* later in the piece, carefully leafing through the pages, suggesting that its theories still hold traction.

But if we understand the great mantle of night as a metaphor for colonialism, what are we to make of Linyekula's yearning for the dances of the night, beckoning with mystery and excitement? Is *Le Cargo* in part a reclamation of the night, a rejection of Belgian colonialism as a defining moment of Congolese history? Is it reconfigured as the richness of Congolese culture rather than an era of brutality and exploitation? As Linyekula's story continues to unfold, we learn how easily the dances are reawakened. For the sum of 30,000 Congolese francs, less than $30, Linyekula purchases palm wine and other local alcohol to help launch the festivities. As with the lack of public transportation, the problem of the drummer is easily solved: a younger drummer from a neighboring village seventeen kilometers away is hired for the occasion. The younger generation continues to learn and absorb the rhythms of the dances from Linyekula's childhood, and thus the power of the new religions is hardly totalizing. In response to Linyekula's invitation, the women "dressed in their best," and the dances obligingly burst forth. Colonialism rapidly recedes as an explanatory framework; it is revealed as weak, unable to withstand the cash that Linyekula has at his disposal. As a recording of the drumming in Obilo is heard through the speakers, the coiled potential of his earlier choreography unfolds into a vigorous dance that integrates contemporary and traditional movements to the point that the terms become meaningless. Shadows loom on the wall behind him as if the ancestors have joined in the celebration.

The cultural resilience of the Congolese is presented as firmly intact. Even Hanabouton is not immune to its strength. Excitement builds when he comes closer to the musicians; he even sits beside them as his resistance continues to falter. "Take the drums!" the villagers call in encouragement. "Take them, take them, take them!" The music rises in intensity, pointing the way to a climactic moment in which he would succumb to the forces of indigenous culture and play his heart out. This kind of apex would adhere to a narrative thread that circulates throughout this book, in which dance is framed as a cultural resource that eludes the tentacles of empire. Whether I am describing a flash mob in Bweyale, *otule* in Lira, or *lararakara* in Gulu, hierarchical structures weaken, and a temporary utopian performative is invariably achieved.[20] One might argue that the evocative, abstract realm of physical expression confounds the tyranny of institutional ideologies ranging from Pentecostalism to humanitarianism. A more cynical perspective, though, might suggest that dance functions as my sugarcoating device. To depict the form as an entity detached from geography and politics is, as Linyekula might put it, very romanticized.

Linyekula knows better than to cater to empire's demands. Wary of the dangers of sugarcoating, he refuses to give the audience a rousing narrative finish. We do not learn whether Hanabouton touches the drums. Instead, the recording of the drumming slowly fades away; Linyekula slumps over the stool as if drained. To revive his strength, he launches into the Swahili hymn that he sang earlier in the piece while sharing details of his childhood in Obilo. Is this transition from "traditional" music to a Christian hymn meant as a reminder of the strength of Christian theology that overwhelms the intensity of the dance? But the moment is too haunting for such a cut-and-dried interpretation. The hymn speaks too powerfully of Linyekula's father, Valentin Linyekula Ngoy, whose presence permeates *Le Cargo*.[21] Each of Linyekula's references to his father, who passed away after his visit to Obilo, aches with yearning. The shift from vigorous drumming to evocative hymn speaks of the potency of familial love rather than the forces of cultural hegemony. The hymn itself—"Father, listen to us"—is a plea to be heard. Might Linyekula be speaking to his father, using the music to negotiate the space between the living and the dead? Toward the end of *Le Cargo*, the hymn is heard a third time as a recording of Linyekula's singing plays. This time, Linyekula sings along with the recording as if he is temporarily united with his father, singing with him as a small boy in church. The cargo of Christian imperialism is worn down by the forces of remembrance and love.

I have previously referred to Žižek's concept of a sideways glance at violence as a way of refusing the mesmerizing impact of direct, or what he calls subjective, violence; instead, we should cultivate looking "awry" in order to understand the objective and systemic violence that serves as the all-too-crucial but often invisible context.[22] *Le Cargo* can be understood as a strategic sideways glance—one that leads the audience not to alternative understandings of violence but instead to a revelation of the richness of Congolese lives. Linyekula lures us with references to crisis, war, crisis, war, and we sign up for the ride, only to find ourselves in an extended homage to his loved ones. When he sardonically comments on getting paid for his stories of joys and miseries, he also ruminates on how our admission fees translate into material benefits for his family in the DRC. As he explains, they allow him to pay the school fees of his brothers and sisters and to help his aged grandmother, Atosha.[23] We might not care about the specificities of Congolese history and politics, but we might remember his grandmother and her fragility. We might remember the devoted father teaching his young son to sing. We are enticed into a sideways, and thus multifaceted, understanding of his world.

Linyekula takes care to remind us, though, that the bounds of our knowledge are limited—we are, after all, only customers in this world. After he tells the story of Hanabouton, he sets up his laptop to face the audience and launches a slide show of photographs of his family and friends in the village. The tiny screen taunts us to try to see them, and we obligingly crane our necks and squint, only to be reminded that we can never see them fully, that our understanding of their complex humanity is inevitably obscured no matter how we direct our gaze. Sideways, direct, or awry—it does not matter since we lack the experience and the imagination to cope with their beauty. We are excluded, like Linyekula as a child sent away from the dances of the night. Whereas Linyekula lay in bed at night, his mind brimming with pictures based on the snatches of overheard music, we can only continue to squint and, perhaps, surrender to failure.

Linyekula experiences his own failure. He never sees the dances of the night; the reason for his visit to Obilo comes to naught. Rather than framing this failure as a moment of defeat, Linyekula shrugs it off as if to acknowledge the myth of a utopian past. In *Sortir*, Mbembe urges a politics of disenclosure in order to realize a true liberation that eluded the continent with the ending of formal colonization.[24] Disenclosure would facilitate the circulations of worlds rather than the iteration of tired myths of precolonial glory and colonial pain. In refusing the romanticization of tradition, Linyekula enacts a radical move of disenclosure and embraces the world in all its complexity. The music of the electric guitar, the chattering of villagers in Obilo, the thundering drums, and the Christian hymn coalesce in a soundscape that stretches the parameters of Congolese identity. A circle is literally formed on stage through an arrangement of footlights as if to evoke the communal, inclusive world he remembers from his childhood. Characteristically, though, Linyekula conveys a sense of distrust and skepticism; he moves uneasily in and out of the circle before finally unplugging each footlight, plunging the stage into darkness. In this moment, the darkness does not signify a traumatic past but rather the possibility and mystery of the future. In the great mantle of the night, narratives of crisis, war, crisis, war are silenced. The only light comes from the computer screen. It serves as a new kind of fire around which Congolese communities, scattered through ever-widening regional and transnational circles, gather.

Speaking of the future means that hope has reared its persistent head. In his book *So Much Wasted*, Patrick Anderson asks, "Why is it that so many books end spiritedly, but almost in spite of themselves, with notes on hope? . . . Could it be that hope's implied optimism is too arrogant to bear the weight or plumb the depths of its own unconscious premonition of a terrible, terror-filled future? Could it be that what hope names is in part a promise of failure?"[25] Linyekula's final dance fuses the politics of hope and the aesthetics of failure; as the recording of his Obilo story plays in the background, his movement takes on a frenzied quality, as if he is struggling against the cargo of imperialism and the baggage of narrative. At one point, he is pulled to the ground in a horizontal position; he persists in dancing even though the weight of gravity constrains his limbs. He might be caught in a Möbius strip of storytelling, but its circularity is transformed into a glimpse of the infinite.[26] Perhaps our collective gaze is what prevents him from fully taking flight.

The world will continue to generate waves of unspeakable and nonspeakable violence about which untold numbers of academics will attempt to theorize and write ethically. Ending on a hopeful note might seem arrogant, as Anderson suggests, given the weight of its incipient failure. But it would also be arrogant of me to dismiss Linyekula's cautious articulation of hope in which a night of colonialist trauma is reconfigured as possibility and futurity. I do not want Linyekula to look at the cover of this book as he looked at my copy of *Ruined*. And so I seek to look differently. To look sideways is to catch a glimpse of the infinite. To look sideways is to try to return Linyekula's act of love. It is also, inevitably, to fail.

Notes

1. I organized his residency at Dartmouth College, which took place from October 22 to October 24, 2011, and included a dance workshop, a public talk, and a classroom visit.
2. Linyekula left the former Zaire in 1993 and lived in exile in Kenya and the United Kingdom before relocating to Kinshasa in 2001. See Dupray 2013 and A. Scott 2010 for accounts of Linyekula's biography. See also Stearns 2011 for more information regarding Kisangani as a staging ground of the conflict that began in 1996; his discussion of battles between Ugandan and Rwandan troops can be found on pages 235–248. Currently, Kisangani is located in the recently established Tshopo Province.
3. See the home page of Studios Kabako, available at http://www.kabako.org/, accessed September 30, 2016. I borrowed some of this translation, such as "somersaults of history," from Jewsiewicki 2016.
4. Program notes for *more more more . . . future*, available online at https://www.redcat.org/sites/redcat.org/files/event/linked-files/2012-07/10.05.11_Linyekula_0.pdf, accessed October 4, 2016.
5. See Mbembe 2016 for a critique of these Hegelian tropes.
6. This description is based on my viewing of the production at the Kitchen in New York City on October 15, 2011.
7. The play, which was translated into Luo as *Dwon Ma Peke*, toured Gulu, Kitgum, and Lira in 2015. See http://www.silentvoicesuganda.org/judy-adong for more information; my thanks to Adong for providing me with the manuscript of the play.
8. See moving excerpts of these letters in Jina Moore's description of this project, "In the 'Book of Life,' Rwandans Write Letters to the Dead," April 7, 2014, http://www.buzzfeed.com/jinamoore/in-the-book-of-life-rwandans-write-letters-to-the-dead, accessed November 4, 2017. I observed a rehearsal in Butare on August 17, 2015.
9. See Edmondson 2007 for more discussion of the "sugarcoating of hope."
10. Here I am thinking of Alain Badiou's statement that "hope indicates the real of fidelity in the ordeal of its exercise, here and now" (2003, 95).
11. Program notes for *more more more . . . future*.
12. This opening line in *Le Cargo* is a simplified version of what appears as the opening statement on the company's home page: "I am Kabako, Kabako is who I am, still Kabako, always Kabako, and it's when there is Kabako that Kabako becomes Kabako." This passage is a

quotation from Bernard Dadié's 1979 play *Mhoi-Ceul* (Me alone). The servant character Kabako, who speaks these opening lines of the play, is described by Linyekula as "someone who sees inside, and who sees outside.... It is a position that speaks to me as an artist, as a citizen" ("Faustin Linyekula × Christine Y. Kim," *Studio*, Summer/Fall 2015, 39, available at https://www.studiomuseum.org/sites/default/files/36075_singles_lo_res.pdf). Linyekula also explains that Kabako became his friend's nickname when he played this role in the late 1980s. The name Studios Kabako thus straddles the company's political visions and personal legacies. See http://www.kabako.org/, accessed October 4, 2016.

13. Žižek 2008.

14. All quotations from *Le Cargo* are transcribed from a video recording made during a performance in Portland, Oregon, in September 2012. My sincere thanks to Virginie Dupray for her generosity; she not only shared the recording but she also reviewed a draft of this afterword and corrected my quotations of the text. I saw the production at the Clarice Smith Performing Arts Center in College Park, Maryland, on November 21, 2014; many thanks to Catherine Cole for organizing an excursion to see *Le Cargo* during the 2014 ASTR conference.

15. See Umutesi 2004, 171–179, for an eyewitness account of Obilo's role in the desperate march of the Rwandan refugees fleeing Kabila's forces in 1997 (see chapter 1 for a discussion of Kabila's AFDL and the First Congo War, as well as the United Nations' implication of the RPF in the widespread killing of the Rwandan refugees). The village in which Linyekula was born, Ubundu, is also mentioned several times in Umutesi's account. See also Stearns 2011, 134–135.

16. The guitar music was composed and played by Linyekula's frequent collaborator, Flamme Kapaya, who was also a performer in *more more more . . . future*.

17. In the production that I saw in 2014, I recall Linyekula holding only the Mbembe book; however, in the video footage, he is holding three books, the titles of which I could not decipher. In her review of *Le Cargo*, Lital Khaikin identifies one of the books as a collection of early twentieth-century photographs of Central Africa taken by Casimir Zagourski ("Between Rhythm and Silence: 'Le Cargo' by Faustin Linyekula," *Herd Magazine*, February 11, 2015, available at http://www.herdmag.ca/tag/casimir-zagourski/).

18. Fanon 2007 [1961], 235.

19. Mbembe 2010, 58.

20. The reference to a utopian performative comes from J. Dolan 2005.

21. Linyekula shared the information of his father's passing in the audience talkback after the show in College Park; in a sense, though, he had already communicated this through the sense of loss that pervaded the performance.

22. Žižek 2008, 1–3.

23. His grandmother passed away in March 2016 (e-mail communication from Virginie Dupray, October 2016).

24. Mbembe 2010, 55–92. See also Karera 2013 for a useful discussion of Mbembe's theories of disenclosure.

25. Anderson 2010, 150.

26. I am thinking here of Mbembe's idea of art as "an attempt to capture the forces of the infinite; an attempt to put the infinite in sensible form, but a forming that consists in constantly doing, undoing, and redoing; assembling, disassembling, and reassembling," an idea that he calls "typically 'African'" (2016, 95).

References

Adelman, Howard, and Astri Suhrke. 1996. *Early Warning and Conflict Management: Study 2 of the International Response to Conflict and Genocide; Lessons from the Rwanda Experience*. Copenhagen: Steering Committee of the Joint Evaluation of Emergency Assistance to Rwanda.

African Rights. 1995. *Rwanda: Death, Despair and Defiance*. 2nd ed. London: African Rights.

———. 2000. *Obstruction of Justice: The Nuns of Sovu in Belgium*. London: African Rights.

Agamben, Giorgio. 2002. *Remnants of Auschwitz: The Witness and the Archive*. Translated by Daniel Heller-Roazen. New York: Zone Books.

———. 2005. *State of Exception*. Translated by Kevin Attell. Chicago: University of Chicago Press.

Ahmed, Sara. 2004. *The Cultural Politics of Emotion*. New York: Routledge.

Anderson, Patrick. 2010. *So Much Wasted: Hunger, Performance, and the Morbidity of Resistance*. Durham, NC: Duke University Press.

Anderson, Patrick, and Jisha Menon. 2009. Introduction to *Violence Performed: Local Roots and Global Routes of Conflict*, edited by Patrick Anderson and Jisha Menon, 1–14. Basingstoke: Palgrave Macmillan.

A'ness, Francine. 2004. "Resisting Amnesia: Yuyachkani, Performance, and the Postwar Reconstruction of Peru." *Theatre Journal* 56 (3): 395–414.

Annan, Jeannie, Christopher Blattman, Dyan Mazurana, and Khristopher Carlson. 2011. "Civil War, Reintegration, and Gender in Northern Uganda." *Journal of Conflict Resolution* 55 (6): 877–908.

Ansoms, An, and Donatella Rostagno. 2012. "Rwanda's Vision 2020 Halfway Through: What the Eye Does Not See." *Review of African Political Economy* 39 (133): 427–450.

An Answer to Mark Twain. 1907. Anonymous pamphlet. Brussels.

Appadurai, Arjun. 1996. *Modernity at Large: Cultural Dimensions of Globalization.* Minneapolis: University of Minnesota Press.

Appiah, Kwame. 1992. *In My Father's House: Africa in the Philosophy of Culture.* Oxford: Oxford University Press.

Argenti-Pillen, Alex. 2003. *Masking Terror: How Women Contain Violence in Southern Sri Lanka.* Philadelphia: University of Pennsylvania Press.

Aristotle. 1931. *The Poetics.* Translated by Ingram Bywater. Oxford: Clarendon Press.

Arsan, Andrew. 2014. *Interlopers of Empire: The Lebanese Diaspora in Colonial French West Africa.* Oxford: Oxford University Press.

Atkinson, Ronald R. 1994. *The Roots of Ethnicity: The Origins of the Acholi of Uganda before 1800.* Philadelphia: University of Pennsylvania Press.

Autesserre, Séverine. 2010. *The Trouble with the Congo: Local Violence and the Failure of International Peacebuilding.* New York: Cambridge University Press.

———. 2012. "Dangerous Tales: Dominant Narratives on the Congo and Their Unintended Consequences." *African Affairs* 11 (443): 202–222.

Baaz, Maria Eriksson, and Maria Stern. 2013. *Sexual Violence as a Weapon of War? Perceptions, Prescriptions, Problems in the Congo and Beyond.* London: Zed Books.

Badiou, Alain. 2001. *Ethics: An Essay on the Understanding of Evil.* Translated by Peter Hallward. London: Verso.

———. 2003. *Saint Paul: The Foundation of Universalism.* Translated by Ray Brassier. Stanford, CA: Stanford University Press.

Baines, Erin K. 2009. "Complex Political Perpetrators: Reflections on Dominic Ongwen." *Journal of Modern African Studies* 47 (2): 163–191.

Banham, Martin, Errol Hill, and George Woodyard, eds. 1994. *The Cambridge Guide to African and Caribbean Theatre.* Cambridge: Cambridge University Press.

Barber, Karin. 1997. "Views of the Field: Introduction." In *Readings in African Popular Culture*, edited by Karin Barber, 1–12. Bloomington: Indiana University Press.

———. 2000. *The Generation of Plays: Yoruba Popular Life in Theatre.* Bloomington: Indiana University Press.

Barnette, Michael N. 2011. *An Empire of Humanity: A History of Humanitarianism.* Ithaca: Cornell University Press.

Barz, Gregory. 2004. *Music in East Africa: Experiencing Music, Expressing Culture.* New York: Oxford University Press.

Beadle, Dixie. 2006. "Okello Kelo Sam: Artist and Activist." In *Men of the Global South: A Reader*, edited by Adam Jones, 195–199. London: Zed Books.

Behrend, Heike. 1999. *Alice Lakwena and the Holy Spirits: War in Northern Uganda, 1986–1997.* Translated by Mitch Cohen. Oxford: James Currey.

Benhabib, Seyla, with Jeremy Waldron, Bonnie Honig, and Will Kymlicka. 2006. *Another Cosmopolitanism: Hospitality, Sovereignty, and Democratic Iterations.* Edited by Robert Post. Oxford: Oxford University Press.

Benjamin, Walter. 1977. *The Origin of German Tragic Drama.* Translated by John Osbourne. New York: Verso.

Benson, Peter, and Kevin Lewis O'Neill. 2007. "Facing Risk: Levinas, Ethnography, and Ethics." *Anthropology of Consciousness* 18 (2): 29–55.

Berlant, Lauren. 2008. *The Female Complaint: The Unfinished Business of Sentimentality in American Culture.* Durham, NC: Duke University Press.

———. 2011. *Cruel Optimism.* Durham, NC: Duke University Press.

Berlant, Lauren, and Lee Edelman. 2013. *Sex, or the Unbearable.* Durham, NC: Duke University Press.

Beswick, Danielle. 2010. "Peacekeeping, Regime Security and 'African Solutions to African Problems': Exploring Motivations for Rwanda's Involvement in Darfur." *Third World Quarterly* 31 (5): 739–754.

———. 2011. "Democracy, Identity and the Politics of Exclusion in Post-genocide Rwanda: The Case of the Batwa." *Democratization* 18 (2): 490–511.

Bewes, Timothy. 2011. *The Event of Postcolonial Shame.* Princeton, NJ: Princeton University Press.

Bharucha, Rustom. 1988. "Peter Brook's 'Mahabharata': A View from India." *Economic and Political Weekly* 23 (32): 1642–1647.

———. 2000. *The Politics of Cultural Practice: Thinking through Theatre in an Age of Globalization.* Hanover, NH: University Press of New England.

Blackett, Tom, and Nick Russell. 1999. "What Is Co-branding?" In *Co-branding: The Science of Alliance,* edited by Tom Blackett and Bob Boad, 1–20. Basingstoke: Palgrave Macmillan.

Blair, Brent, and Angus Fletcher. 2010. "'We Cry on the Inside': Image Theatre and Rwanda's Culture of Silence." *Theatre Topics* 20 (1): 23–31.

Blattman, Christopher, and Jeannie Annan. 2010a. "The Consequences of Child Soldiering." *Review of Economics and Statistics* 42 (4): 882–898.

———. 2010b. "On the Nature and Causes of LRA Abduction: What the Abductees Say." In *The Lord's Resistance Army: Myth and Reality,* edited by Tim Allen and Koen Vlassenroot, 132–155. London: Zed Books.

Blattman, Christopher, Nathan Fiala, and Sebastian Martinez. 2014. "Generating Skilled Self-Employment in Developing Countries: Experimental Evidence from Uganda." *Quarterly Journal of Economics* 129 (2): 697–752.

Blattman, Christopher, and Laura Ralston. 2015. "Generating Employment in Poor and Fragile States: Evidence from Labor Market and Entrepreneurship Programs." Working paper. https://www.povertyactionlab.org/sites/default/files/publications/Blattman_Employment%20Lit%20Review.pdf.

Bleasdale, Marcus. 2003. *One Hundred Years of Darkness*. London: Pirogue.

———. 2009. *The Rape of a Nation*. Amsterdam: Mets and Schilt.

Boal, Augusto. 1985. *Theatre of the Oppressed*. Translated by Charles A. McBride and Maria-Odilia Leal McBride. New York: Theatre Communications Group.

Bob, Clifford. 2005. *The Marketing of Rebellion: Insurgents, Media, and International Activism*. Cambridge: Cambridge University Press.

Bogdan, Robert, with Martin Elks and James Knoll. 2012. *Picturing Disability: Beggar, Freak, Citizen, and Other Photographic Rhetoric*. Syracuse, NY: Syracuse University Press.

Boitani, Piero. 2013. "Something Divine in Recognition." In *Recognition and Modes of Knowledge: Anagnorisis from Antiquity to Contemporary Theory*, edited by Teresa G. Russo, 1–32. Edmonton: University of Alberta Press.

Bornstein, Erica, and Peter Redfield. 2011. *Forces of Compassion: Humanitarianism between Ethics and Politics*. Santa Fe: School for Advanced Research Press.

Bracke, Sarah. 2008. "Conjugating the Modern/Religious, Conceptualizing Female Religious Agency: Contours of a 'Post-secular' Conjuncture." *Theory, Culture and Society* 25 (51): 51–67.

Branch, Adam. 2011. *Displacing Human Rights: War and Intervention in Northern Uganda*. Oxford: Oxford University Press.

———. 2013. "Gulu in War . . . and Peace? The Town as Camp in Northern Uganda." *Urban Studies* 50 (15): 3152–3167.

Brecht, Bertolt. 1966. *Mother Courage and Her Children: A Chronicle of the Thirty Years' War*. Translated by Eric Bentley. New York: Grove.

———. 2010. *Mother Courage and Her Children; Mutter Courage und ihre Kinder*. [Parallel texts.] Translated by Tony Kushner. London: Methuen Drama.

Breed, Ananda. 2014. *Performing the Nation: Genocide, Justice, Reconciliation*. London: Seagull Books.

Breitinger, Eckhard. 1994. *Theatre for Development*. Bayreuth: University of Bayreuth.

Brockington, Dan. 2014a. *Celebrity Advocacy and International Development*. Abingdon, Oxon: Routledge.

———. 2014b. "The Production and Construction of Celebrity Advocacy in International Development." *Third World Quarterly* 35 (1): 88–108.

———. 2016. "The Politics of Celebrity Humanitarianism." In *Celebrity Humanitarianism and North-South Relations*, edited by Lisa Ann Richey, 210–218. Abingdon, Oxon: Routledge.

Brown, Wendy. 1995. *States of Injury: Power and Freedom in Late Modernity*. Princeton, NJ: Princeton University Press.

Budabin, Alexandra Cosima. 2016. "Ben Affleck Goes to Washington: Celebrity Advocacy, Access and Influence." In *Celebrity Humanitarianism and North-South Relations*, edited by Lisa Ann Richey, 131–148. Abingdon, Oxon: Routledge.

Buckley-Zistel, Susanne. 2006. "Remembering to Forget: Chosen Amnesia as a Strategy for Local Coexistence in Post-Genocide Rwanda," *Africa* 76 (2): 131–150.

———. 2008. *Conflict Transformation and Social Change in Uganda: Remembering After Violence*. Houndmills: Palgrave Macmillan.

Burnet, Jennie E. 2005. "Genocide Lives in Us: Amplified Silence and the Politics of Memory in Rwanda." PhD diss., University of North Carolina at Chapel Hill.

———. 2012. *Genocide Lives in Us: Women, Memory, and Silence in Rwanda*. Madison: University of Wisconsin Press.

Büscher, Karen, and Koen Vlassenroot. 2010. "Humanitarian Presence and Urban Development: New Opportunities and Contrasts in Goma, DRC." *Disasters* 34: S256–S273.

Butler, Judith. 1997. *The Psychic Life of Power: Theories in Subjection*. Stanford, CA: Stanford University Press.

———. 2004a. *Precarious Life: The Powers of Mourning and Violence*. London: Verso.

———. 2004b. *Undoing Gender*. New York: Routledge.

Butler, Judith, and Gayatri Chakravorty Spivak. 2007. *Who Sings the Nation State? Language, Politics, Belonging*. London: Seagull Books.

Carlson, Marla. 2003. "Antigone's Bodies: Performing Torture." *Modern Drama* 46 (3): 381–403.

Carney, J. J. 2014. *Rwanda before the Genocide: Catholic Politics and Ethnic Discourse in the Late Colonial Era*. New York: Oxford University Press.

Casement, Roger. 2003. *The Eyes of Another Race: Roger Casement's Congo Report and 1903 Diary*. Edited by Séamas Ó Síocháin and Michael O'Sullivan. Dublin: University College Dublin Press.

Cheah, Pheng. 2011. "Female Subjects of Globalization." In *Genre et postcolonialismes: Dialogues transcontinentaux*, edited by Anne Berger and Eleni Varikas, 215–228. Paris: Éditions des Archives Contemporaines.

Chouliaraki, Lilie. 2013. *The Ironic Spectator: Solidarity in the Age of Post-humanitarianism*. Cambridge: Polity Press.

Chow, Rey. 2010. "Postcolonial Visibilities: Questions Inspired by Deleuze's Method." In *Deleuze and the Postcolonial*, edited by Simone Bignall and Paul Patton, 62–76. Edinburgh: Edinburgh University Press.

Chrétien, Jean-Pierre. 2003. *Great Lakes of Africa: Two Thousand Years of History*. Translated by Scott Straus. New York: Zone Books.

Clark, Phil. 2005. Review of *Hotel Rwanda*, Lions Gate Entertainment. *Dissent* 52 (2): 121.

Cole, Catherine. 2010. *Performing South Africa's Truth Commission: Stages of Transition*. Bloomington: Indiana University Press.

Comaroff, Jean, and John L. Comaroff. 2011. *Theory from the South; or, How Euro-America Is Evolving toward Africa*. Boulder, CO: Paradigm.

Comaroff, John L., and Jean Comaroff. 2008. "Law and Disorder in the Postcolony: An Introduction." In *Law and Disorder in the Postcolony*, edited by Jean Comaroff and John L. Comaroff, 1–56. Chicago: University of Chicago Press.

———. 2009. *Ethnicity, Inc.* Chicago: University of Chicago Press.

The Congo: A Report of the Commission of Enquiry Appointed by the Congo Free State, A Translation. 1906. New York: G.P. Putnam's Sons.

Congo Reform Association. 1905. *Evidence Laid before the Congo Commission of Inquiry*. Liverpool: John Richardson and Sons.

———. 1906a. *The Camera and the Congo Crime*. London: Congo Reform Association.

———. 1906b. *The Indictment against the Congo Government: Report of the King's Commission of Inquiry and the Testimony Which Compelled It*. Boston: Congo Reform Association.

Conquergood, Dwight. 1991. "Rethinking Ethnography: Towards a Critical Cultural Politics." *Communication Monographs* 58: 179–194.

———. 2013. *Cultural Struggles: Performance, Ethnography, Praxis*. Edited by E. Patrick Johnson. Ann Arbor: University of Michigan Press.

Conrad, Joseph. 1963 [1899]. *The Heart of Darkness*. Edited by Robert Kimbrough. New York: W. W. Norton.

Cooke, Peter. 1999. "Fieldwork in Lango, Northern Uganda, Feb–Mar 1997." *African Music* 7 (4): 66–72.

Coulter, Chris. 2009. *Bush Wives and Girl Soldiers: Women's Lives through War and Peace in Sierra Leone*. Ithaca, NY: Cornell University Press.

Crisafulli, Patricia, and Andrea Redmond. 2012. *Rwanda, Inc.: How a Devastated Nation Became an Economic Model for the Developing World*. New York: Palgrave Macmillan.

Critchley, Simon. 2007. *Infinitely Demanding: Ethics of Commitment, Politics of Resistance*. London: Verso.

Cruvellier, Thierry. 2010. *Court of Remorse: Inside the International Criminal Tribunal for Rwanda*. Madison: University of Wisconsin Press.

Das, Veena. 1998. "Wittgenstein and Anthropology." *Annual Review of Anthropology* 27: 171–195.

de Certeau, Michel de. 1984. *The Practice of Everyday Life*. Berkeley: University of California Press.

———. 1988. *The Writing of History*. Translated by Tom Conley. New York: Columbia University Press.

de Lame, Danielle. 2005. *A Hill among a Thousand: Transformations and Ruptures in Rural Rwanda*. Translated by Helen Arnold. Madison: University of Wisconsin Press.

de Winton, Francis. 1886. "The Congo Free State." In *Proceedings of the Royal Geographic Society and Monthly Record of Geography*, 609–624. London: Edward Stanford.

Debord, Guy. 1995 [1967]. *The Society of the Spectacle*. Translated by Donald Nicholson-Smith. New York: Zone Books.

Decker, Alicia C. 2014. *In Idi Amin's Shadow: Women, Gender, and Militarism in Uganda*. Athens: Ohio University Press.

Deleuze, Gilles, and Félix Guattari. 1987. *A Thousand Plateaus*. Translated by Brian Massumi. Minneapolis: University of Minnesota Press.

Department for International Development (DfID). 2004. "Rwanda: Country Assistance Plan, 2003–2006." London. Available at http://webarchive.nationalarchives.gov.uk/20050705174534/http://www.dfid.gov.uk/pubs/files/caprwanda.pdf.

Derrida, Jacques. 1999. *Adieu to Emmanuel Levinas*. Translated by Pascale-Anne Brault and Michael Naas. Stanford, CA: Stanford University Press.

———. 2009. *The Beast and the Sovereign*. Vol. 1. Translated by Geoffrey Bennington. Chicago: University of Chicago Press.

Derrida, Jacques, and Anne Dufourmantelle. 2000. *Of Hospitality: Anne Dufourmantelle Invites Jacques Derrida to Respond*. Stanford, CA: Stanford University Press.

Des Forges, Alison. 1999. *"Leave None to Tell the Story": Genocide in Rwanda*. New York: Human Rights Watch. http://www.hrw.org/reports/pdfs/r/rwanda/rwanda993.pdf.

———. 2011. *Defeat Is the Only Bad News: Rwanda under Musinga, 1896–1931*. Edited by David Newbury. Madison: University of Wisconsin Press.

Desrosiers, Marie-Eve. 2014. "Rethinking Political Rhetoric and Authority during Rwanda's First and Second Republics." *Africa* 84 (2): 199–225.

Diamond, Elin. 1997. *Unmaking Mimesis: Essays on Feminism and Theater*. New York: Taylor and Francis.

Dinnie, Keith. 2008. *Nation Branding*. Oxford: Butterworth-Heinemann.

Dolan, Chris. 2009. *Social Torture: The Case of Northern Uganda, 1986–2000*. New York: Berghahn Books.

Dolan, Jill. 2005. *Utopia in Performance: Finding Hope at the Theater*. Ann Arbor: University of Michigan Press.

Doom, Ruddy, and Koen Vlassenroot. 1999. "Kony's Message: A New Koine? The Lord's Resistance Army in Northern Uganda." *African Affairs* 98 (390): 5–36.

Douma, Nynke, and Dorothea Hilhorst. 2012. *Fond de Commerce? Sexual Violence Assistance in the Democratic Republic of Congo*. Wageningen: Wageningen University.

Doyle, Arthur Conan. 1909. *The Crime of the Congo*. New York: Doubleday.

Dragotesc, Andra-Mirona. 2011. "Imagined(?) Identities: The Victim and the Villain in Awareness Raising Re-presentations of Wartime Violence against Women." *Studia Europaea* 56 (2): 125–144.

Drewal, Margaret T. 1991. "The State of Research on Performance in Africa." *African Studies Review* 34 (3): 1–65.

Drumbl, Mark A. 2009. Review of *International Justice in Rwanda and the Balkans: Virtual Trials and the Struggle for State Cooperation*, by Victor Peskin. *Criminal Law Forum* 20 (4): 495–502.

Dunaway, Wilma A. 2010. "Nonwaged Peasants in the Modern World-System: African Households as Dialectical Units of Capitalist Exploitation and Indigenous Resistance, 1890-1930." *The Journal of Philosophical Economics* 4 (1): 19–57.

Dunn, Kevin C. 2003. *Imagining the Congo: The International Relations of Identity*. New York: Palgrave Macmillan.

———. 2004. "Africa's Ambiguous Relation to Empire and *Empire*." In *Empire's New Clothes*, edited by Paul Passavant and Jodi Dean, 143–162. New York: Routledge.

Dupray, Virginie. 2013. "Kisangani: A Chronicle of Return." Translated by Allen F. Roberts. *African Arts* 46 (1): 30–35.

Duschinsky, Robbie, Monica Greco, and Judith Solomon. 2015. "Wait Up! Attachment and Sovereign Power." *International Journal of Politics, Culture, and Society* 28 (3): 223–242.

Edmondson, Laura. 2007. "Of Sugarcoating and Hope." *TDR* 51 (2): 7–10.

———. 2009a. "Genocide Unbound: Erik Ehn, Rwanda, and an Aesthetics of Discomfort." *Theatre Journal* 61 (1): 65–83.

———. 2009b. "The Poetics of Displacement and the Politics of Genocide in Three Plays about Rwanda." In *Violence Performed: Local Roots and Global Routes of Conflict*, edited by Patrick Anderson and Jisha Menon, 54–78. Basingstoke: Palgrave Macmillan.

———. 2012. "Uganda Is Too Sexy: Reflections on *Kony 2012*." *TDR: The Drama Review* 56 (3): 10–17.

Ehn, Erik. 2007a. *Maria Kizito*. In *The Theatre of Genocide: Four Plays about Mass Murder in Rwanda, Bosnia, Cambodia, and Armenia*, edited by Robert Skloot, 178–220. Madison: University of Wisconsin Press.

———. 2007b. "A Space for Truth: Meditations on Theatre—and the Rwandan Genocide." *American Theatre* 24 (3): 34ff.

Ehrenreich, Barbara. 2009. *Bright-Sided: How the Relentless Promotion of Positive Thinking Has Undermined America*. New York: Metropolitan Books.

Eichstaedt, Peter. 2011. *Consuming the Congo: War and Conflict Minerals in the World's Deadliest Place*. Chicago: Chicago Review Press.

Eltringham, Nigel. 2004. *Accounting for Horror: Post-genocide Debates in Rwanda*. London: Pluto.

———. 2014. "Bodies of Evidence: Remembering the Rwandan Genocide at Murambi." In *Remembering Genocide*, edited by Nigel Eltringham and Pam Maclean, 200–219. London: Routledge.

Emizet, Kisangani N. F. 2000. "The Massacre of Refugees in Congo: A Case of UN Peacekeeping Failure and International Law." *Journal of Modern African Studies* 38 (2): 163–202.

Ensler, Eve. 2013. *In the Body of the World: A Memoir*. New York: Metropolitan Books.

Etherington, Norman A. 2010. Introduction to *Grappling with the Beast: Indigenous Southern African Responses to Colonialism, 1840–1930*, edited by Peter Limb, Norman Etherington, and Peter Midgley, 1–12. Leiden: Brill.

Fabian, Johannes. 1990. *Power and Performance: Ethnographic Explorations through Proverbial Wisdom and Theatre in Shaba, Zaire*. Madison: University of Wisconsin Press.

Fahey, Dan. 2008. "*Le Fleuve d'Or*: The Production and Trade of Gold from Mongbwalu, DRC." In *L'Afrique des Grands Lacs, Annuaire 2007–2008*, edited by Stefaan Marysse, Filip Reyntjens, and Stef Vandeginste, 357–384. Paris: L'Harmattan.

Fanon, Frantz. 2007. *The Wretched of the Earth*. Translated by Richard Philcox. New York: Grove.

Farmer, Paul E., Cameron T. Nutt, Claire M. Wagner, Claude Sekabaraga, Tej Nuthulaganti, Jonathan L. Weigel, Didi Bertrand Farmer, Antoinette Habinshuti, Soline Dusabeyesu Mugeni, Jean-Claude Karasi, and Peter C. Drobac. 2013. "Reduced Premature Mortality in Rwanda: Lessons from Success." *BMJ* 346: f65.

Fassin, Didier. 2007a. "Humanitarianism: A Nongovernmental Government." In *Nongovernmental Politics*, edited by Michel Fehrer, 149–160. New York: Zone Books.

———. 2007a. "Humanitarianism as a Politics of Life." *Public Culture* 19 (3): 499–520.

———. 2010. "Heart of Humaneness: The Moral Economy of Humanitarian Intervention." In *Contemporary States of Emergency: The Politics of Military and Humanitarian Interventions*, edited by Didier Fassin and Mariella Pandolfi, 269–293. New York: Zone Books.

———. 2011. *Humanitarian Reason: A Moral History of the Present*. Berkeley: University of California Press.

Fassin, Didier, and Richard Rechtman. 2009. *The Empire of Trauma: An Inquiry into the Condition of Victimhood*. Translated by Rachel Gomme. Princeton, NJ: Princeton University Press.

Feldman, Allen. 2000. "Violence and Vision: The Prosthetics and Aesthetics of Terror." In *Violence and Subjectivity*, edited by Veena Das, Arthur Kleinman, Mamphela Ramphele, and Pamela Reynolds, 46–78. Berkeley: University of California Press.

———. 2004. "Memory Theaters, Virtual Witnessing, and the Trauma-Aesthetic." *Biography* 27 (1): 163–202.

Felman, Shoshana, and Dori Laub. 1992. *Testimony: Crises of Witnessing in Literature, Psychoanalysis, and History*. New York: Routledge.

Ferguson, James. 2006. *Global Shadows: Africa in the Neoliberal World Order*. Durham, NC: Duke University Press.

———. 2014. "From Antipolitics to Post-neoliberalism: A Conversation with James Ferguson." Interview by Nils Gilman and Miriam Ticktin. *Humanity* 5 (2): 247–259.

Festa, Lynn. 2006. *Sentimental Figures of Empire in Eighteenth-Century Britain and France*. Baltimore: Johns Hopkins University Press.

Finnström, Sverker. 2008. *Living with Bad Surroundings: War, History, and Everyday Moments in Northern Uganda*. Durham, NC: Duke University Press.

———. 2010. "An African Hell of Colonial Imagination? The Lord's Resistance Army/Movement in Uganda, Another Story." In *The Lord's Resistance Army: Myth and Reality*, edited by Tim Allen and Koen Vlassenroot, 74–89. London: Zed Books.

Fletcher, John. 2013. *Preaching to Convert: Evangelical Outreach and Performance Activism in a Secular Age*. Ann Arbor: University of Michigan Press.

Fox, Ann. 2011. "Battles on the Body: Disability, Interpreting Dramatic Literature, and the Case of Lynn Nottage's *Ruined*." *Journal of Literary and Cultural Disability Studies* 5 (1): 1–15.

Frank, Marion. 1995. *AIDS-Education through Theatre: Case Studies from Uganda*. Bayreuth: Bayreuth African Studies.

Gallie, W. B. 1955–1956. "Essentially Contested Concepts." *Proceedings of the Aristotelian Society* 56: 167–198.

Gallop, Jane. 2002. *Anecdotal Theory*. Durham, NC: Duke University Press.

Gartrell, Beverly. 1983. "British Administrators, Colonial Chiefs, and the Comfort of Tradition: An Example from Uganda." *African Studies Review* 26 (1): 1–24.

Geary, Christraud M., with an essay by Krzysztof Pluskota. 2003. *In and out of Focus: Images from Central Africa, 1885–1960*. London: Philip Wilson.

Giblin, John Daniel. 2014. "Post-conflict Heritage: Symbolic Healing and Cultural Renewal." *International Journal of Heritage Studies* 20 (5): 500–518.

Gilmore, Leigh. 2010. "American Neoconfessional: Memoir, Self-Help and Redemption on Oprah's Couch." *Biography* 33 (4): 657–679.

Girling, F. K. 1960. *The Acholi of Uganda*. London: Her Majesty's Stationery Office.

Glassman, Jonathon. 1995. *Feasts and Riot: Revelry, Rebellion, and Popular Consciousness on the Swahili Coast, 1856–1888*. Portsmouth, NH: Heinemann.

Gómez-Peña, Guillermo. 1996. *The New World Border: Prophecies, Poems, and Loqueras for the End of the Century*. San Francisco: City Lights.

Goodfellow, Tom. 2013. "The Institutionalisation of 'Noise' and 'Silence' in Urban Politics: Riots and Compliance in Uganda and Rwanda." *Oxford Development Studies* 41 (4): 436–454.

Goodfellow, Tom, and Alyson Smith. 2013. "From Urban Catastrophe to 'Model' City? Politics, Security and Development in Post-conflict Kigali." *Urban Studies* 50 (15): 3185–3202.

Gourevitch, Philip. 1998. *We Wish to Inform You That Tomorrow We Will Be Killed with Our Families: Stories from Rwanda*. New York: Farrar, Straus and Giroux.

Graham, Aubrey. 2014. "One Hundred Years of Suffering? 'Humanitarian Crisis Photography' and Self-Representation in the Democratic Republic of the Congo." *Social Dynamics* 40 (1): 140–163.

Grant, Kevin. 2005. *A Civilised Savagery: Britain and the New Slaveries in Africa, 1884–1926*. New York: Routledge.

———. 2015. "The Limits of Exposure: Atrocity Photographs in the Congo Reform Campaign." In *Humanitarian Photography: A History*, edited by Heide Fehrenbach and David Rodogno, 64–88. New York: Cambridge University Press.

Grant, Philip, and Edward Boon. 2013. "When the Persuasion Attempt Fails: An Examination of Consumers' Perception of Branded Flash Mobs." *Journal of Public Affairs* 13 (2): 190–201.

Gundel, Joakim. 2003. "Assisting Structures of Violence? Humanitarian Assistance in the Somali Conflict." In *Shadow Globalization, Ethnic Conflicts and New Wars: A Political Economy of Intra-state War*, edited by Dietrich Jung, 163–183. London: Routledge.

Guriev, Sergei, and Daniel Treisman. 2015. "How Modern Dictators Survive: An Informational Theory of the New Authoritarianism." National Bureau of Economic Research Working Paper no. 21136. ww.nber.org.

Hall, Katori. 2015. *Our Lady of Kibeho*. *American Theatre* 32 (2): 65ff.

Hankivsky, Olena, and Rita Kaur Dhamoon. 2013. "Which Genocide Matters the Most? An Intersectionality Analysis of the Canadian Museum of Human Rights." *Canadian Journal of Political Science* 46 (4): 899–920.

Hanson, Holly. 2009. "Mapping Conflict: Heterarchy and Accountability in the Ancient Capital of Buganda." *Journal of African History* 50 (2): 179–202.

Hardt, Michael, and Antonio Negri. 2000. *Empire*. Cambridge, MA: Harvard University Press.

———. 2001. "Adventures of the Multitude: Responses of the Authors." *Rethinking Marxism: A Journal of Economics, Culture and Society* 13 (3/4): 236–243.

———. 2004. *Multitude: War and Democracy in the Age of Empire*. New York: Penguin.

———. 2009. *Commonwealth*. Cambridge, MA: Harvard University Press.

Harms, Robert. 1975. "The End of Red Rubber: A Reassessment." *Journal of African History* 16 (1): 73–88.

Harris, Alice. 1908. *Enslaved Womanhood of the Congo: An Appeal to British Women*. London: Congo Reform Association.

Harris, John. 1908. *Essential Facts on the Congo Question*. London: Edward Hughes.

Harrow, Kenneth W. 2005. "'*Un train peut en casher un autre*': Narrating the Rwandan Genocide and Hotel Rwanda." *Research in African Literatures* 36 (4): 223–232.

Hartman, Saidiya V. 1997. *Scenes of Subjection: Terror, Slavery, and Self-Making in Nineteenth-Century America.* New York: Oxford University Press.

Hayman, Rachel. 2010. "Abandoned Orphan, Wayward Child: The United Kingdom and Belgium in Rwanda since 1994." *Journal of Eastern African Studies* 4 (2): 341–360.

Hearn, Alison. 2008. "'Meat, Mask, Burden': Probing the Contours of the Branded 'Self.'" *Journal of Consumer Culture* 8 (2): 197–217.

———. 2010. "'Through the Looking Glass': The Promotional University 2.0." In *Blowing Up the Brand: Critical Perspectives on Promotional Culture*, edited by Melissa Aronczyk and Devon Powers, 195–218. New York: Peter Lang.

Heaton, Laura. 2013. "What Happened in Luvungi?" *Foreign Policy* 199: 32–36, 10.

Heidegger, Martin. 1995 [1983]. *The Fundamental Concepts of Metaphysics: World Finitude, Solitude.* Translated by William McNeill and Nicholas Walker. Bloomington: Indiana University Press.

Herbst, Jeffrey and Greg Mills. 2013. "The Invisible State." *Foreign Policy* 201: 78–80.

Hermkens, Anna-Karina, Willy Jansen, and Catrien Notermans. 2009. *Moved by Mary: The Power of Pilgrimage in the Modern World.* Farnham, Surrey: Ashgate.

Hesford, Wendy. 2011. *Spectacular Rhetorics: Human Rights Visions, Recognitions, Feminisms.* Durham, NC: Duke University Press.

Hilgers, Mathieu. 2012. "The Historicity of the Neoliberal State." *Social Anthropology* 20 (1): 80–94.

Hintjens, Helen M. 2008. "Post-genocide Identity Politics in Rwanda." *Ethnicities* 8 (5): 5–41.

Hinton, Alexander Laban. 2002. "The Dark Side of Modernity: Toward an Anthropology of Genocide." In *Annihilating Difference: The Anthropology of Genocide*, edited by Alexander Laban Hinton. 1–40. Berkeley: University of California Press.

Hinton, Devon E., and Alexander L. Hinton, eds. 2015. *Genocide and Mass Violence: Memory, Symptom, and Recovery.* New York: Cambridge University Press.

Hirsch, Marianne. 2008. "The Generation of Postmemory." *Poetics Today* 29 (1): 103–128.

Hochschild, Adam. 1999. *King Leopold's Ghost: A Story of Greed, Terror, and Heroism in Colonial Africa.* New York: Houghton Mifflin.

Hoffman, Danny. 2004. "The Civilian Target in Sierra Leone and Liberia: Political Power, Military Strategy, and Humanitarian Intervention." *African Affairs* 103 (411): 211–226.

———. 2011. *The War Machines: Young Men and Violence in Sierra Leone and Liberia.* Durham, NC: Duke University Press.

Hopwood, Julian. 2011."We Can't Be Sure Who Killed Us": Memory and Memorialization in Post-Conflict Northern Uganda.* Gulu: Justice and Reconciliation Project. http://justiceandreconciliation.com/2011/02/we-cant-be-sure-who-killed-us-memory-and-memorialization-in-post-conflict-northern-uganda/.

Huggan, Graham. 2001. *The Postcolonial Exotic: Marketing the Margins.* London: Routledge.

Huggins, Chris. 2009. "Agricultural Policies and Local Grievances in Rural Rwanda." *Peace Review: A Journal of Social Justice* 21 (3): 296–303.

Human Rights Watch/Africa and Human Rights Watch Children's Rights Project. 1997. "The Scars of Death: Children Abducted by the Lord's Resistance Army in Uganda." New York and Washington, DC. http://www.hrw.org/sites/default/files/reports/uganda979.pdf.

Hunt, Nancy Rose. 2008. "An Acoustic Register, Tenacious Images, and Congolese Scenes of Rape and Repetition." *Cultural Anthropology* 23: 220–253.

———. 2016. *A Nervous State: Violence, Remedies, and Reverie in Colonial Congo.* Durham, NC: Duke University Press.

Hyndman, Jennifer. 2000. *Managing Displacement: Refugees and the Politics of Humanitarianism.* Minneapolis: University of Minnesota Press.

Ibreck, Rachel. 2012. "A Time of Mourning: The Politics of Commemorating the Tutsi Genocide in Rwanda." In *Public Memory, Public Media and the Politics of Justice*, edited by Philip Lee and Pradip Ninan Thomas, 98–120. New York: Palgrave Macmillan.

Ilibagiza, Immaculée. 2009. *If Only We Had Listened.* San Francisco: Ignatius Press.

Ilibagiza, Immaculée, and Sean Bloomfield. 2011. *If Only We Had Listened.* DVD. Directed by Sean Bloomfield and produced by Immaculée Ilibagiza and Sean Bloomfield.

Ilibagiza, Immaculée, with Steve Erwin. 2006. *Left to Tell: Discovering God amidst the Rwandan Holocaust.* Carlsbad, CA: Hay House.

———. 2008a. *Led by Faith: Rising from the Ashes of the Rwandan Genocide.* Carlsbad, CA: Hay House.

———. 2008b. *Our Lady of Kibeho: Mary Speaks to the World from the Heart of Africa.* Carlsbad, CA: Hay House.

———. 2011. *The Boy Who Met Jesus: Segatashya of Kibeho.* Carlsbad, CA: Hay House.

———. 2013. *The Rosary: The Prayer That Saved My Life.* Carlsbad, CA: Hay House.

Ingelaere, Bert. 2016. *Inside Rwanda's Gacaca Courts: Seeking Justice after Genocide.* Madison: University of Wisconsin Press.

International Rescue Committee. 2003. *Mortality in the Democratic Republic of Congo: A Nationwide Survey.* New York: International Rescue Committee.

Jackson, Lisa F., and Bernard Buleri Kalume. 2007. *The Greatest Silence: Rape in the Congo.* New York: Women Make Movies.

Jackson, Paul B. 2009. "'Negotiating with Ghosts': Religion, Conflict and Peace in Northern Uganda." *Round Table: The Commonwealth Journal of International Affairs* 98 (402): 319–332.

Jackson, Stephen. 2006. "Sons of Which Soil? The Language and Politics of Autochthony in Eastern D.R. Congo." *African Studies Review* 49 (2): 95–123.

Jacobsen, Óli. 2014. *Daniel J. Danielsen and the Congo: Missionary Campaigns and Atrocity Photographs.* Troon, Ayrshire: Brethren Archivists and Historians Network.

James, Erica Caple. 2004. "The Political Economy of 'Trauma' in Haiti in the Democratic Era of Insecurity." *Culture, Medicine and Psychiatry* 28: 127–149.

———. 2009. "Neomodern Insecurity in Haiti and the Politics of Asylum." *Culture, Medicine and Psychiatry* 33: 153–159.

———. 2010. "Ruptures, Rights, and Repair: The Political Economy of Trauma in Haiti." *Social Science and Medicine* 70 (1): 106–113.

Jewsiewicki, Bogumil. 2016. "Leaving Ruins: Explorations of Present Pasts by Sammy Baloji, Freddy Tsimba, and Steve Bandoma." *African Arts* 49 (1): 6–25.

Justice and Reconciliation Project. 2007. *Remembering the Atiak Massacre, April 20, 1995.* JRP Field Note 4. Gulu: Justice and Reconciliation Project. http://justiceandreconciliation.com/2007/04/remembering-the-atiak-massacre-april-20th-1995-fn-iv/.

———. 2009. *Kill Every Living Thing: The Barlonyo Massacre.* Justice and Reconciliation Project (JRP) Field Note 9. Gulu: Justice and Reconciliation Project. http://justiceandreconciliation.com/2009/02/kill-every-living-thing-the-barlonyo-massacre-fn-ix/.

———. 2011. *The Lukodi Massacre, 19 May 2004.* JRP Field Note 13. Gulu: Justice and Reconciliation Project. http://justiceandreconciliation.com/wp-content/uploads/2011/04/JRP_FNXIII_Lukodi-Massacre.pdf

———. 2012a. *The Day They Came: Recounting the LRA's Invasion of Teso Sub-region through Obalanga Sub-county in 2003.* JRP Field Note 14. Gulu: Justice and Reconciliation Project. http://justiceandreconciliation.com/2012/09/the-day-they-came-recounting-the-lras-invasion-of-teso-sub-region-through-obalanga-sub-county-in-2003-fn-xiv-2/.

———. 2012b. *When a Gunman Speaks, You Listen: Victims' Experiences and Memories of Conflict in Palabek Sub-County, Lamwo District.* JRP Field Note 15. Gulu: Justice and Reconciliation Project. http://justiceandreconciliation.com/wp-content/uploads/2012/09/When-a-Gunman-Speaks_Final_August-20121.pdf.

Kaahwa, Jessica Atwooki. 2001. "Theatre and Human Rights in Uganda." PhD diss., University of Maryland.

Kagame, Paul. 2009. "The Backbone of a New Rwanda." In *In the River They Swim*, edited by Michael Fairbanks, Marcela Escobari-Rose, Malik Fal, and Elizabeth Hooper, 11–14. West Conshohocken, PA: Templeton.

Kahn, Jeremy. 2006. "A Brand-New Approach." *Foreign Policy* 157: 88–93.

Kaldor, Mary. 1999. *New and Old Wars: Organized Violence in a Global Era.* Cambridge: Polity Press.

———. 2013. "In Defence of New Wars." *Stability: International Journal of Security and Development,* 2(1): 1–16.

Kalisa, Chantal. 2006. "Theatre and the Rwandan Genocide." *Peace Review* 18 (4): 515–521.

Kanyeihamba, George W. 1988. "Power that Rode Naked through Uganda under the Muzzle of a Gun." In *Uganda Now: Between Decay and Development,* edited by Holger Bernt Hansen and Michael Twaddle, 70–82. London: James Currey.

Kapoor, Ilan. 2013. *Celebrity Humanitarianism: The Ideology of Global Charity.* London: Routledge.

Karera, Axelle. 2013. "Writing Africa into the World and Writing the World from Africa: Mbembe's Politics of Dis-enclosure." *Critical Philosophy of Race* 1 (2): 228–241.

Kasozi, Abdu Basajjabaka Kawalya. 1994. *The Social Origins of Violence in Uganda, 1964–1985.* Montreal: McGill-Queen's University Press.

Kasule, Sam. 2013. *Resistance and Politics in Contemporary East African Theatre: Trends in Ugandan Theatre Since 1960.* London: Adonis and Abbey Publishers.

Kelly, Jocelyn T. D. 2014. "'This Mine Has Become Our Farmland': Critical Perspectives on the Coevolution of Artisanal Mining and Conflict in the Democratic Republic of the Congo." *Resources Policy* 40: 100–108.

Kisekka-Ntale, Fredrick. 2007. "Roots of the Conflict in Northern Uganda." *International Journal of Politics and Economics Studies* 32 (4): 421–452.

Klaic, Dragan. 2003. "Zones of Disturbance: Staging Exile and War for Young Audiences." *Modern Drama* 46 (1): 22–34.

Klein, Naomi. 2000. *No Logo: Taking Aim at the Brand Bullies.* Toronto: Vintage Canada.

———. 2007. *The Shock Doctrine: The Rise of Disaster Capitalism.* New York: Metropolitan Books.

Krause, Monika. 2014. *The Good Project: Humanitarian Relief NGOs and the Fragmentation of Reason.* Chicago: University of Chicago Press.

Kucich, John. 2006. *Imperial Masochism: British Fiction, Fantasy, and Social Class.* Princeton, NJ: Princeton University Press.

Kuftinec, Sonja Arsham. 2009. *Theatre, Facilitation, and Nation Formation in the Balkans and Middle East.* New York: Palgrave Macmillan.

Lamphear, John. 1976. *The Traditional History of the Jie of Uganda.* Oxford: Clarendon Press.

Laqueur, Thomas W. 2009. "Mourning, Pity, and the Work of Narrative in the Making of 'Humanity.'" In *Humanitarianism and Suffering: The Mobilization of Empathy,* edited by Richard Ashby Wilson and Richard D. Brown, 31–57. Cambridge: Cambridge University Press.

Le Huenen, Roland. 2013. Preface to *Recognition and Modes of Knowledge: Anagnorisis from Antiquity to Contemporary Theory,* edited by Teresa G. Russo, ix–x. Edmonton: University of Alberta Press.

Lemarchand, René. 1964. *Political Awakening in the Belgian Congo*. Berkeley: University of California Press.

———. 1998. "Genocide in the Great Lakes: Which Genocide? Whose Genocide?" *African Studies Review* 41 (1): 3–16.

———. 2002. "Review Article: A History of Genocide in Rwanda." *Journal of African History* 43: 307–311.

———. 2009. *The Dynamics of Violence in Central Africa*. Philadelphia: University of Pennsylvania Press.

———. 2013. "Reflections on the Recent Historiography of Eastern Congo." *Journal of African History* 54 (3): 417–437.

Lennon, John, and Malcolm Foley. 2000. *Dark Tourism: The Attraction of Death and Disaster*. London: Continuum.

Lenz, Jessica. 2004. "Armed with Resilience: A Study Addressing the Issues of Reintegration and Resiliency of Formerly Abducted Girl Child Soldiers in Northern Uganda and Their Potential Role as Peace Builders." MSc dissertation, Oxford Brookes University.

———. 2017. "Armed with Resilience: Tapping into the Experiences and Survival Skills of Formerly Abducted Girl Child Soldiers in Northern Uganda." In *Children Affected by Armed Conflict: Theory, Method, and Practice*, edited by Bree Akesson and Myriam Denov, 112–138. New York: Columbia University Press.

Levi, Primo. 1986. *The Drowned and the Saved*. Translated by Raymond Rosenthal. New York: Summit Books.

Lévinas, Emmanuel. 1981. *Otherwise than Being; or, Beyond Essence*. Translated by Alphonso Lingis. The Hague: Martinus Nijhoff.

———. 1987. *Collected Philosophical Papers*. Translated by Alphonso Lingis. The Hague: Martinus Nijhoff.

Leys, Ruth. 2007. *From Guilt to Shame: Auschwitz and After*. Princeton, NJ: Princeton University Press.

Lindemann, Stefan. 2011. "The Ethnic Politics of Coup Avoidance: Evidence from Zambia and Uganda." *Africa Spectrum* 46 (2): 3–42.

Linfield, Susie. 2010. *The Cruel Radiance: Photography and Political Violence*. Chicago: University of Chicago Press.

Lionnet, Françoise, and Shu-mei Shih. 2005. "Introduction: Thinking through the Minor, Transnationally." In *Minor Transnationalism*, edited by Françoise Lionnet and Shu-mei Shih, 1–23. Durham, NC: Duke University Press.

Lo, Jacqueline, and Helen Gilbert. 2002. "Toward a Topography of Cross-Cultural Theatre Praxis." *TDR* 46 (3): 31–53.

Logan, William, and Keir Reeves. 2009. "Introduction: Remembering Places of Pain and Shame." In *Places of Pain and Shame: Dealing with "Difficult Heritage,"* edited by William Logan and Keir Reeves, 1–14. Abingdon, Oxon: Routledge.

Lombard, Louisa. 2012. "Raiding Sovereignty in Central African Borderlands." PhD diss., Duke University.

Longman, Timothy. 2010. *Christianity and Genocide in Rwanda*. Cambridge: Cambridge University Press.

Louis, William Roger. 1968. "Morel and the Congo Reform Association, 1904–1913." In *E. D. Morel's History of the Congo Reform Movement*, edited by William Roger Louis and Jean Stengers, 171–220. Oxford: Clarendon Press.

Low, Donald Anthony. 1971. *Buganda in Modern History*. Berkeley: University of California Press.

———. 1988. "The Dislocated Polity." In *Uganda Now: Between Decay and Development*, edited by Holger Bernt Hansen and Michael Twaddle, 36–53. London: James Currey.

———. 2009. *Fabrication of Empire: The British and the Uganda Kingdoms, 1890–1902*. Cambridge: Cambridge University Press.

Madison, D. Soyini. 2007. "Co-performative Witnessing." *Cultural Studies* 21 (6): 826–831.

Maindron, Gabriel. 1984. *Des apparitions à Kibeho: Annonce de Marie au cœur de l'Afrique*. Paris: O.E.I.L.

Makori, Timothy Mwageka. 2015. "When the Future Is in Reverse: Temporality in the Aftermath of Industrialism in Democratic Republic of Congo." Paper presented at CODESRIA conference in Dakar, June 8–12. http://www.codesria.org/spip.php?article2343

Malkki, Liisa H. 1995. *Purity and Exile: Violence, Memory, and National Cosmology among Hutu Refugees in Tanzania*. Chicago: University of Chicago Press.

Mamdani, Mahmood. 2001. *When Victims Become Killers: Colonialism, Nativism, and the Genocide in Rwanda*. Princeton, NJ: Princeton University Press.

Marcus, George E. 1998. *Ethnography through Thick and Thin*. Princeton, NJ: Princeton University Press.

Marwick, Alice, and Danah Boyd. 2011. "To See and Be Seen: Celebrity Practice on Twitter." *Convergence* 17 (2): 139–158.

Marx, Karl. 1976 [1867]. *Capital: A Critique of Political Economy*. Vol. 1. Translated by Ben Fowkes. Harmondsworth: Penguin. Originally published as *Das Kapital: Kritik der politischen Ökonomie* (Hamburg: Otto Meisner).

Matter, E. Ann. 2001. "Apparitions of the Virgin Mary in the Late Twentieth Century: Apocalyptic, Representation, Politics." *Religion* 31 (2): 125–153.

Maurer, Bill. 2003. "On Divine Markets and the Problem of Justice: Empire as Theodicy." In *Empire's New Clothes*, edited by Paul Passavant and Jodi Dean, 57–52. New York: Routledge.

Mbembe, Achille. 2001. *On the Postcolony*. Berkeley: University of California Press.

———. 2003. "Necropolitics." *Public Culture* 15 (1): 11–40.

———. 2010. *Sortir de la grande nuit: Essai sur l'Afrique décolonisée*. Paris: La Découverte.

———. 2016. "Africa in the New Century." *Massachusetts Review* 57 (1): 91–104.

Mbowa, Rose. 1998. "Theatre for Development: Empowering Ugandans to Transform Their Condition." In *Developing Uganda*, edited by Holger Bernt Hansen and Michael Twaddle, 261–270. Oxford: James Currey.

McClain, Lindsay, and Allen Ngari. 2011. "Pay Us So We Can Forget: Reparations for Victims and Affected Communities in Northern Uganda." JRP-IJR Policy Brief 2. Gulu: Justice and Reconciliation Project. http://justiceandreconciliation.com/2011/09/pay-us-so-we-can-forget-reparations-for-victims-and-affected-communities-in-northern-uganda-policy-brief-no-2/.

McMillan, Nesam. 2008. "'Our' Shame: International Responsibility for the Rwandan Genocide." *Australian Feminist Law Journal* 28: 3–28.

———. 2010. "Regret, Remorse and the Work of Remembrance: Official Responses to the Rwandan Genocide." *Social and Legal Studies* 19 (1): 85–105.

Médard, Henri, and Shane Doyle, eds. 2007. *Slavery in the Great Lakes of Africa*. Oxford: James Currey.

Mergelsberg, Ben. 2012. "The Displaced Family: Moral Imaginations and Social Control in Pabbo, Northern Uganda." *Journal of Eastern African Studies* 6 (1): 64–80.

Misago, Augustin. 1991. *Les apparitions de Kibeho du Rwanda*. Kinshasa: Facultés Catholiques de Kinshasa.

Mitchell, David T., and Sharon L. Snyder. 2000. *Narrative Prosthesis: Disability and the Dependencies of Discourse*. Ann Arbor: University of Michigan Press.

Mitchell, Nathan D. 2009. *The Mystery of the Rosary: Marian Devotion and the Reinvention of Catholicism*. New York: New York University Press.

Mlama, Penina Muhando. 1991. *Culture and Development in Africa: The Popular Theatre Approach*. Sweden: Nordiska Afrikainstitutet.

Mobley, Jennifer-Scott. 2016. "Melodrama, Sensation, and Activism in *Ruined*." In *A Critical Companion to Lynn Nottage*, edited by Jocelyn L. Buckner, 129–144. London: Routledge.

Morel, Edmund D. 1902. *Affairs of West Africa*. London: William Heinemann.

———. 1903. *The Development of Tropical Africa by the White Races: Two Divergent Policies*. Liverpool: John Richardson and Sons.

———. 1904. *King Leopold's Rule in Africa*. London: William Heinemann.

———. 1907a. *The Crisis in the Campaign against Congo Misrule*. Liverpool: John Richardson and Sons.

———. 1907b. *The Tragedy in the Congo: An Appeal to Parliament*. Liverpool: John Richardson and Sons.

———. 1908. *A Memorial on Native Rights in the Land and Its Fruits in the Congo Territories Annexed by Belgium (Subject to International Recognition)*. London: Congo Reform Association.

Moses, A. Dirk. 2012. "The Canadian Museum for Human Rights: The 'Uniqueness of the Holocaust' and the Question of Genocide." *Journal of Genocide Research* 14 (2): 215–238.

Mulekwa, Charles. 2012. "Performing the Legacy of War in Uganda." PhD diss., Brown University.

Munt, Sally R. 2008. *Queer Attachments: The Cultural Politics of Shame*. Burlington, VT: Ashgate.

Mutibwa, Phares Mukasa. 1992. *Uganda since Independence: A Story of Unfulfilled Hopes*. Trenton, NJ: Africa World Press.

Mutua, Makau. 2001. "Savages, Victims, and Saviors: The Metaphor of Human Rights." *Harvard International Law Journal* 42 (1): 201–245.

Mwangi, Evan. 2007. "Sex, Music, and the City in a Globalized East Africa." *PMLA* 122 (1): 321–324.

Ndaliko, Chérie Rivers. 2016. *Necessary Noise: Art, Music, and Charitable Imperialism in the East of Congo*. New York City: Oxford University Press.

Newbury, Catharine. 1988. *The Cohesion of Oppression: Clientship and Ethnicity in Rwanda, 1860–1960*. New York: Columbia University Press.

———. 1998. "Ethnicity and the Politics of History in Rwanda." *Africa Today* 45 (1): 7–24.

———. 2011. "High Modernism at the Ground Level: The *Imidugudu* Policy in Rwanda." In *Remaking Rwanda: State Building and Human Rights after Mass Violence*, edited by Scott Straus and Lars Waldorf, 223–239. Madison: University of Wisconsin Press.

Newbury, David. 1991. *Kings and Clans: Ijwi Island and the Lake Kivu Rift, 1780–1840*. Madison: University of Wisconsin Press.

———. 1996. "Convergent Catastrophes in Central Africa." *Review of African Political Economy* 23 (70): 573–576.

———. 1997. "Irredentist Rwanda: Ethnic and Territorial Frontiers in Central Africa." *Africa Today* 44 (2): 211–222.

———. 2005. "Returning Refugees: Four Historical Patterns of 'Coming Home' to Rwanda." *Comparative Studies in Society and History* 47 (2): 252–285.

———. 2009. *The Land beyond the Mists: Essays on Identity and Authority in Precolonial Congo and Rwanda*. Athens: Ohio University Press.

———. 2011. "The Historian as Human Rights Activist." In *Remaking Rwanda: State Building and Human Rights after Mass Violence*, edited by Scott Straus and Lars Waldorf, xxvii–xxxix. Madison: University of Wisconsin Press.

———. 2012. "Canonical Conventions in Rwanda: Four Myths of Recent Historiography in Central Africa." *History in Africa* 39: 41–76.

Newell, Sasha. 2012. *The Modernity Bluff: Crime, Consumption, and Citizenship in Côte d'Ivoire*. Chicago: University of Chicago Press.

Nguyen, Vinh-Kim. 2010. *The Republic of Therapy*. Durham, NC: Duke University Press.

Nietzsche, Friedrich. 1969. *On the Genealogy of Morals*. Translated by W. Kaufmann and P. J. Hollingdale. New York: Vintage.

Nordstrom, Carolyn. 1997. *A Different Kind of War Story*. Philadelphia: University of Pennsylvania Press.

Nottage, Lynn. 2009. *Ruined*. New York: Theatre Communications Group.

Nouwen, Sarah M. H. 2013. *Complementarity in the Line of Fire: The Catalysing Effect of the International Criminal Court in Uganda and Sudan*. Cambridge: Cambridge University Press.

Ntangaare, Mercy Mirembe, and Eckhard Breitinger. 1999. "Ugandan Drama in English." In *Uganda: The Cultural Landscape*, edited by Eckhard Breitinger, 247–272. Bayreuth: University of Bayreuth.

Ocen, Lawrence. 2015. "Justice and Peace after War: Conceptual Difficulties in the Discourses of Transition and Reform in Post-War Societies." Working Paper no. 26, Makerere Institute of Social Research. Available at https://misr.mak.ac.ug/publications/.

O'Halloran, Kevin. 2010. *Pure Massacre: Aussie Soldiers Reflect on the Rwandan Genocide*. Newport, New South Wales: Blue Sky Publishing.

Olesen, Thomas. 2012. "Global Injustice Memories: The 1994 Rwanda Genocide." *International Political Sociology* 6 (4): 373–389.

Omara-Otunnu, Amii. 1987. *Politics and the Military in Uganda, 1890–1985*. London: Macmillan.

Ong, Aihwa. 2007. "Neoliberalism as a Mobile Technology." *Transactions of the Institute of British Geographers* 32 (1): 3–8.

Opiyo, Lindsay McClain, and Tricia Redeker Hepner. 2013. "Youth in Transition: The Arts and Cultural Resonance in Post-conflict Northern Uganda." In *Political Conflict and Peace Building in the African Great Lakes Region*, edited by Kenneth Omeje and Tricia Redeker Hepner, 179–196. Bloomington: Indiana University Press.

Orford, Anne. 2003. *Reading Humanitarian Intervention: Human Rights and the Use of Force in International Law*. Cambridge: Cambridge University Press.

Otunnu, Ogenga. 1999a. "An Historical Analysis of the Invasion by the Rwanda Patriotic Army (RPA)." In *The Path of a Genocide: The Rwanda Crisis from Uganda to Zaire*, edited by Howard Adelman and Astri Suhrke, 31–50. New Brunswick, NJ: Transaction.

———. 1999b. "Rwandese Refugees and Immigrants in Uganda." In *The Path of a Genocide: The Rwanda Crisis from Uganda to Zaire*, edited by Howard Adelman and Astri Suhrke, 3–30. New Brunswick, NJ: Transaction.

Otunnu, Olara A. 2006. "The Secret Genocide." *Foreign Policy* 155: 44–46.

Otwili, Evelyn Akullo, and Philipp Schulz. 2012. *Paying Back What Belongs to Us: Victims' Groups in Northern Uganda and their Quest for Reparation*. JRP Field Note 16. Gulu: Justice and Reconciliation Project. http://justiceandreconciliation.com/wp-content/uploads/2014/04/Victims-groups-in-Northern-Uganda.pdf.

Paden, Jeff. 2016. "Renegotiating Realism: Hybridity of Form and Political Potentiality in *Ruined*." In *A Critical Companion to Lynn Nottage*, edited by Jocelyn L. Buckner, 145–160. London: Routledge.

Pandolfi, Mariella. 2003. "Contract of Mutual (In)Difference: Governance and the Humanitarian Apparatus in Contemporary Albania and Kosovo." *Indiana Journal of Global Legal Studies* 10 (1): 369–381.

———. 2008. "Laboratory of Intervention: The Humanitarian Governance of the Postcommunist Balkan Territories." In *Postcolonial Disorders*, edited by Mary-Jo DelVecchio Good, Sandra T. Hyde, and Byron J. Good, 157–188. Berkeley: University of California Press.

———. 2010. "From Paradox to Paradigm: The Permanent State of Emergency in the Balkans." In *Contemporary States of Emergency: The Politics of Military and Humanitarian Interventions*, edited by Didier Fassin and Mariella Pandolfi, 153–172. New York: Zone Books.

Patraka, Vivian M. 1999. *Spectacular Suffering: Theatre, Fascism, and the Holocaust*. Bloomington: Indiana University Press.

Pavlakis, Dean. 2010. "The Development of British Overseas Humanitarianism and the Congo Reform Campaign." *Journal of Colonialism and Colonial History* 11 (1).

———. 2016. *British Humanitarianism and the Congo Reform Movement, 1896–1913*. London: Routledge.

Peffer, John. 2008. "Snap of the Whip/Crossroads of Shame: Flogging, Photography, and the Representation of Atrocity in the Congo Reform Campaign." *Visual Anthropology Review* 24: 55–77.

Perry, Nicholas, and Loreto Echeverría. 1988. *Under the Heel of Mary*. London: Routledge.

Peskin, Victor. 2011. "Victor's Justice Revisited: Rwandan Patriotic Front Crimes and the Prosecutorial Endgame at the ICTR." In *Remaking Rwanda: State Building and Human Rights after Mass Violence*, edited by Scott Straus and Lars Waldorf, 173–183. Madison: University of Wisconsin Press.

Peterman, Amber, Tia Palermo, and Caryn Bredenkamp. 2011. "Estimates and Determinants of Sexual Violence against Women in the Democratic Republic of Congo." *American Journal of Public Health* 101 (6): 1060–1067.

Pham, Phuong, Patrick Vinck, and Eric Stover. 2007. *Abducted: The Lord's Resistance Army and Forced Conscription in Northern Uganda*. Berkeley: Human Rights

Center (UC Berkeley) and Payson Center for International Development (Tulane University).

Pickard, Terry. 2008. *Combat Medic: An Australian's Eyewitness Account of the Kibeho Massacre*. Newport, NSW: Big Sky.

Pier, David. 2015. *Ugandan Music in the Marketing Era: The Branded Arena*. New York: Palgrave Macmillan.

Piot, Charles. 1999. *Remotely Global: Village Modernity in West Africa*. Chicago: University of Chicago Press.

———. 2010. *Nostalgia for the Future: West Africa after the Cold War*. Chicago: University of Chicago Press.

Polman, Linda. 2010. *The Crisis Caravan: What's Wrong with Humanitarian Aid*. New York: Metropolitan Books.

Pottier, Johan. 2002. *Re-imagining Rwanda: Conflict, Survival and Disinformation in the Late Twentieth Century*. Cambridge: Cambridge University Press.

———. 2010a. "Representations of Ethnicity in the Search for Peace: Ituri, Democratic Republic of Congo." *African Affairs* 109 (434): 23–50.

———. 2010b. Review of *Combat Medic: An Australian's Eyewitness Account of the Kibeho Massacre*, by Terry Pickard. *African Studies Review* 53 (1): 189–190.

Povinelli, Elizabeth A. 1998. "The State of Shame: Australian Multiculturalism and the Crisis of Indigenous Citizenship." *Critical Inquiry* 24 (2): 575–610.

Power, Samantha. 2003. *"A Problem from Hell": America and the Age of Genocide*. New York: HarperCollins.

Prendergast, John, with Don Cheadle. 2010. *The Enough Moment: Fighting to End Africa's Worst Human Rights Crimes*. New York: Three Rivers.

Proctor, Keith. 2013. *"They Were Just Thrown Away, and Now the World Is Spoiled": Mass Killing and Cultural Rites in Barlonyo*. Somerville, MA: Feinstein International Center.

Prunier, Gérard. 1995. *The Rwandan Crisis, 1959–1994: History of a Genocide*. Kampala: Fountain.

———. 1998. "The Rwandan Patriotic Front." In *African Guerrillas*, edited by Christopher Clapham, 119–133. Bloomington: Indiana University Press.

———. 2009. *Africa's World War: Congo, the Rwandan Genocide, and the Making of a Continental Catastrophe*. Oxford: Oxford University Press.

Puga, Ana Elena, and Víctor M. Espinosa. "Staging Migrant Suffering: Melodrama in Latin American and Latino Activism." Unpublished manuscript.

Rae, Paul. 2009. *Theatre & Human Rights*. Basingstoke: Palgrave Macmillan.

Reed, Wm. Cyrus. 1996. "Exile, Reform, and the Rise of the Rwandan Patriotic Front." *Journal of Modern African Studies* 34 (3): 479–501.

Refugee Law Project. 2004. "Behind the Violence: Causes, Consequences and the Search for Solutions to the War in Northern Uganda." Refugee Law Project Working Paper no. 11, Kampala, Uganda. http://pdf.usaid.gov/pdf_docs/pnacx535.pdf.

Reporters Sans Frontières. 2002. *Rwanda—Annual Report 2002*. Paris: Reporters Sans Frontières. http://en.rsf.org/rwanda-rwanda-annual-report-2002-30-04-2002,01834.html.

Rettig, Max. 2011. "The Sovu Trials: The Impact of Genocide Justice on One Community." In *Remaking Rwanda: State Building and Human Rights after Mass Violence*, edited by Scott Straus and Lars Waldorf, 194–209. Madison: University of Wisconsin Press.

Reydams, Luc. 2016. "NGO Justice: African Rights as Pseudo-Prosecutor of the Rwandan Genocide." *Human Rights Quarterly* 38 (3): 547–588.

Reyntjens, Filip. 1996. "Rwanda: Genocide and Beyond." *Journal of Refugee Studies* 9 (3): 240–251.

———. 1997. "Estimation de nombre de personnes tuées au Rwanda en 1994." In *L'Afrique des grands lacs: Annuaire 1996/1997*, edited by Stefaan Marysse and Filip Reyntjens, 179–186. Paris: L'Harmattan.

———. 2004. "Rwanda, Ten Years On: From Genocide to Dictatorship." *African Affairs* 103 (411): 177–210.

———. 2009. *The Great African War: Congo and Regional Geopolitics, 1996–2006*. Cambridge: Cambridge University Press.

———. 2013. *Political Governance in Post-genocide Rwanda*. Cambridge: Cambridge University Press.

———. 2015. "Briefing: The Struggle over the Truth—Rwanda and the BBC." *African Affairs* 114 (457): 637–648.

Richey, Lisa Ann, ed. 2016. *Celebrity Humanitarianism and North-South Relations*. Abingdon, Oxon: Routledge.

Richey, Lisa Ann, and Stefano Ponte. 2011. *Brand Aid: Shopping Well to Save the World*. Minneapolis: University of Minnesota Press.

Rieff, David. 2002. *A Bed for the Night: Humanitarianism in Crisis*. New York: Simon and Schuster.

Rittner, Carol, John K. Roth, and Wendy Whitworth, eds. 2004. *Genocide in Rwanda: Complicity of the Churches?* St. Paul: Paragon House.

Roberts, A. D. 1962. "The Sub-imperialism of the Baganda." *Journal of African History* 3 (3): 435–450.

Robins, J. E. 2012. "Slave Cocoa and Red Rubber: E. D. Morel and the Problem of Ethical Consumption." *Comparative Studies in Society and History* 54 (3): 592–611.

Rodríguez, Dylan. 2015. "Inhabiting the Impasse: Racial/Racial-Colonial Power, Genocide Poetics, and the Logic of Evisceration." *Social Text* 33 (3): 19–44.

Rombouts, Heidy. 2004. *Victim Organisations and the Politics of Reparation: A Case-Study on Rwanda*. Holmes Beach, FL: Intersentia.

Ronan, Kate. 2007. "Memory, Place and Nation-Building: Remembering in the 'New' South Africa." Brattleboro: SIT Digital Collections. http://digitalcollections.sit.edu/cgi/viewcontent.cgi?article=1124&context=isp_collection.

Rossiter, Brian. 2012. "'They Don't Care about Us': Michael Jackson's Black Nationalism." *Popular Music and Society* 35 (2): 203–222.

Rothberg, Michael. 2009. *Multidirectional Memory: Remembering the Holocaust in the Age of Decolonization*. Stanford, CA: Stanford University Press.

"Rwanda: Genocide Anniversary." 2014. *Africa Research Bulletin: Political, Social and Cultural Series* 51 (4): 20112B–20114A.

Rwanda's Untold Story. 2014. Directed by John Conroy and produced by Jane Corbin. BBC Two.

Sachs, Albie. 2009. *The Strange Alchemy of Life and Law*. Oxford: Oxford University Press.

Salverson, Julie. 1996. "Performing Emergency: Witnessing, Popular Theatre, and the Lie of the Literal." *Theatre Topics* 6 (2): 181–191.

———. 2001. "Change on Whose Terms? Testimony and an Erotics of Injury." *Theater* 31 (3): 119–125.

Sam, Okello Kelo, Robert O. Ajwang, and Laura Edmondson. 2008. "Forged in Fire." Manuscript.

———. 2013. "Play Extract: Forged in Fire." In *Refugee Performance: Practical Encounters*, edited by Michael Balfour, 61–66. Bristol: Intellect Books.

Sartre, Jean-Paul. 2003. *Being and Nothingness: An Essay on Phenomenological Ontology*. London: Routledge.

Saur, Léon. 2004. "From Kibeho to Medjugorje: The Catholic Church and Ethnonationalist Movements and Regimes." In *Genocide in Rwanda: Complicity of the Churches?*, edited by Carol Rittner, John K. Roth, and Wendy Whitworth, 211–227. St. Paul: Paragon House.

Scarry, Elaine. 1985. *The Body in Pain: The Making and Unmaking of the World*. Oxford University Press.

Scheper-Hughes, Nancy. 1995. "The Primacy of the Ethical," *Current Anthropology* 36 (3): 409–420.

Schomerus, Mareike. 2012. "'They Forget What They Came For': Uganda's Army in Sudan." *Journal of Eastern African Studies* 6 (1): 124–153.

Scott, Ariel Osterweis. 2010. "Performing Acupuncture on a Necropolitical Body: Choreographer Faustin Linyekula's Studios Kabako in Kisangani, Democratic Republic of Congo." *Dance Research Journal*, 42 (2): 11–27.

Scott, James C. 1990. *Domination and the Arts of Resistance: Hidden Transcripts*. New Haven, CT: Yale University Press.

Seremba, George Bwanika. 2008. "Robert Serumaga and the Golden Age of Uganda's Theatre: Solipsism, Activism, Innovation (1968–1978)." PhD diss., Trinity College Dublin.

Sharpley, Richard. 2009. "Shedding Light on Dark Tourism: An Introduction." In *The Darker Side of Travel: The Theory and Practice of Dark Tourism*, edited by Richard Sharpley and Philip R. Stone, 3–22. Bristol: Channel View.

Sherbo, Arthur. 1957. *English Sentimental Drama*. East Lansing: Michigan State University Press.

Siebert, Julia. 2010. "More Continuity than Change? New Forms of Unfree Labor in the Belgian Congo, 1908–1930." In *Humanitarian Intervention and Changing Labor Relations: The Long-Term Consequences of the Abolition of the Slave Trade*, edited by Marcel van der Linden, 369–386. Leiden: Brill.

Síocháin, Séamas Ó, and Michael O'Sullivan. 2003. Introduction to *The Eyes of Another Race: Roger Casement's Congo Report and 1903 Diary*, edited by Síocháin and O'Sullivan, 1–44. Dublin: University College Dublin Press.

Skrbiš, Zlatko. 2005. "The Apparitions of the Virgin Mary of Medjugorje: The Convergence of Croatian Nationalism and Her Apparitions." *Nations and Nationalism* 11 (3): 443–461.

Slaughter, Joseph R. 2007. *Human Rights, Inc: The World Novel, Narrative Form, and International Law*. New York: Fordham University Press.

Sliwinski, Sharon. 2006. "The Childhood of Human Rights: The Kodak on the Congo." *Journal of Visual Culture* 5 (3): 333–363.

Smillie, Ian. 2010. *Blood on the Stone: Greed, Corruption and War in the Global Diamond Trade*. London: Anthem.

Smith, Stephen D. 2009. *Never Again! Yet Again! A Personal Struggle with the Holocaust and Genocide*. Jerusalem: Geffen.

Snyder-Young, Dani. 2013. *Theatre of Good Intentions*. Basingstoke: Palgrave Macmillan.

Sodaro, Amy. 2011. "Politics of the Past: Remembering the Rwandan Genocide at the Kigali Memorial Centre." In *Curating Difficult Knowledge: Violent Pasts in Public Places*, edited by Erica Lehrer, Cynthia E. Milton, and Monica Eileen Patterson, 72–88. Basingstoke: Palgrave Macmillan.

Sontag, Susan. 2003. *Regarding the Pain of Others*. New York: Farrar, Straus, and Giroux.

Southall, Aidan. 1988. "The Recent Political Economy of Uganda." In *Uganda Now: Between Decay and Development*, edited by Holger Bernt Hansen and Michael Twaddle, 54–69. London: James Currey.

Spivak, Gayatri. 2004. "Righting Wrongs." *South Atlantic Quarterly* 103 (2/3): 523–581.

Sriram, Chandra Lekha, and Amy Ross. 2007. "Geographies of Crime and Justice: Contemporary Transitional Justice and the Creation of 'Zones of Impunity.'" *International Journal of Transitional Justice* 1 (1): 45–65.

Ssempijja, Nicolas. 2012. "Glocalising Catholicism in Uganda through Musical Performance: Case Study of the Kampala Archdiocesan Schools' Musical Festivals." In *Ethnomusicology in East Africa: Perspectives from Uganda*, edited by Sylvia A. Nannyonga-Tamusuza and Thomas Solomon, 132–140. Kampala: Fountain Books.

Stamatov, Peter. 2013. *The Origins of Global Humanitarianism: Religion, Empires, and Advocacy*. New York: Cambridge University Press.

Starr, Frederick. 1907. *The Truth about the Congo: The "Chicago Tribune" Articles*. Chicago: Forbes.

Stearns, Jason K. 2011. *Dancing in the Glory of Monsters: The Collapse of the Congo and the Great War of Africa*. New York: PublicAffairs.

———. 2012a. *From CNDP to M23: The Evolution of an Armed Movement in Eastern Congo*. London: Rift Valley Institute.

———. 2012b. *North Kivu: The Background to Conflict in North Kivu Province of Eastern Congo*. London: Rift Valley Institute.

———. 2013. "Helping Congo Help itself: What it Will Take to End Africa's Worst War?" *Foreign Affairs* 92 (5): 99–112.

Stearns, Jason K., and Christoph Vogel. 2015. *Landscape of Armed Groups in the Eastern Congo*. Congo Research Group. New York: Center on International Cooperation.

Steinhart, Edward I. 1978. *Conflict and Collaboration: The Kingdoms of Western Uganda, 1890–1907*. Princeton, NJ: Princeton University Press.

Stone, Philip R. 2006. "A Dark Tourism Spectrum: Towards a Typology of Death and Macabre Related Tourist Sites, Attractions and Exhibitions." *Tourism* 54 (2): 145–160.

Straus, Scott. 2006. *The Order of Genocide: Race, Power, and War in Rwanda*. Ithaca, NY: Cornell University Press.

Stroeken, Koen. 2013. "War at Large: Miner Magic and the Carrion System." In *Virtual War and Magical Death: Technologies and Imaginaries for Technology and Killing*, edited by Neil L. Whitehead and Sverker Finnström, 234–250. Durham, NC: Duke University Press.

Stropnicky, Gerard. 2012. "The Earth Is My Drum." *American Theatre* 29 (2): 34.

———. 2016. "Healing Arts." *American Theatre* 33 (3): 56–59.

Sturken, Marita. 1991. "The Wall, the Screen, and the Image: The Vietnam Veterans Memorial." *Representations* 35: 118–142.

Stys, Patrycja. 2012. "Revisiting Rwanda." *Journal of Modern African Studies* 50 (4): 707–720.

Sundaram, Anjan. 2016. *Bad News: Last Journalists in a Dictatorship*. New York: Doubleday.

Tandberg, Elen-Marie Meggison. 2014. "A Cultural Based Approach to Development? Norwegian Public and Foreign Policy and the Role of Cultural Development in

Bids to Promote Socio-political Stability and Sustainable Development in Northern Uganda." Master's thesis, Norwegian University of Life Sciences.

Taussig, Michael. 1986. *Shamanism, Colonialism, and the Wild Man: A Study in Terror and Healing.* Chicago: University of Chicago Press.

———. 1999. *Defacement: Public Secrecy and the Labor of the Negative.* Stanford, CA: Stanford University Press.

Taylor, Alexander. 2015. "Rwanda's *Gacaca* Trials: Toward a New Nationalism or Business as Usual?" In *Genocide and Mass Violence: Memory, Symptom, and Recovery,* edited by Devon E. Hinton and Alexander L. Hinton, 301–320. New York: Cambridge University Press.

Taylor, Edgar C. 2013. "Claiming Kabale: Racial Thought and Urban Governance in Uganda." *Journal of Eastern African Studies* 7 (1): 143–163.

ter Haar, Gerrie. 2003. "A Wondrous God: Miracles in Contemporary Africa." *African Affairs* 102 (408): 409–428.

Terry, Esther J. 2016. "Land Rights and Womb Rights: Forging Difficult Diasporic Kinships in *Ruined.*" In *A Critical Companion to Lynn Nottage,* edited by Jocelyn L. Buckner, 161–178. London: Routledge.

The Thing That Happened. 2011. Directed by Andrew Walton. New York: Walton Films.

Thompson, James. 2009. *Performance Affects: Applied Theatre and the End of Effect.* Basingstoke: Palgrave Macmillan.

———. 2014. *Humanitarian Performance: From Disaster Tragedies to Spectacles of War.* London: Seagull Books.

Thompson, James, and Richard Schechner. 2004. "Why 'Social Theatre'?" *TDR* 48 (3): 11–16.

Thompson, T. Jack. 2012. *Light on Darkness? Missionary Photography of Africa in the Nineteenth and Early Twentieth Centuries.* Grand Rapids, MI: William B. Eerdmans.

Thomson, Susan. 2011. "Re-education for Reconciliation: Participant Observations on Ingando." In *Remaking Rwanda: State Building and Human Rights after Mass Violence,* edited by Scott Straus and Lars Waldorf, 331–339. Madison: University of Wisconsin Press.

———. 2013. *Whispering Truth to Power: Everyday Resistance to Reconciliation in Postgenocide Rwanda.* Madison: University of Wisconsin Press.

Ticktin, Miriam. 2011. "The Gendered Human of Humanitarianism: Medicalising and Politicising Sexual Violence." *Gender and History* 23 (2): 250–265.

Titeca, Kristof, and Theophile Costeur. 2015. "An LRA for Everyone: How Different Actors Frame the Lord's Resistance Army." *African Affairs* 114 (454): 92–114.

Tosh, John. 1978. *Clan Leaders and Colonial Chiefs in Lango: The Political History of an East African Stateless Society, c. 1800–1939.* Oxford: Clarendon Press.

Trinh, T. Minh-ha. 1989. *Woman, Native, Other: Writing Postcoloniality and Feminism*. Bloomington: Indiana University Press.

Tsing, Anna L. 2005. *Friction: An Ethnography of Global Connection*s. Princeton, NJ: Princeton University Press.

Turner, Thomas. 2013. *Congo*. Cambridge, UK: Polity Press.

Turner, Victor. 1975. *Revelation and Divination in Ndembu Ritual*. Ithaca, NY: Cornell University Press.

Twain, Mark. 1905. *King Leopold's Soliloquy: A Defense of His Congo Rule*. Boston: F. R. Warren.

Twomey, Christina. 2014. "The Incorruptible Kodak: Photography, Human Rights and the Congo Campaign." In *The Violence of the Image: Photography and International Conflict*, edited by Liam Kennedy and Caitlin Patrick, 9–33. London: I. B. Tauris.

———. 2015. "Framing Atrocity: Photography and Humanitarianism." In *Photography: A History*, edited by Heide Fehrenbach and David Rodogno, 47–63. New York: Cambridge University Press.

Uganda Museum. 2012. "Northern Uganda: Featuring Efforts at Peace & Reconciliation." DVD.

"Uganda: Public Services under Threat." 2013. *Africa Research Bulletin* 49 (12): 19803A–19804A.

Umutesi, Marie Béatrice. 2004. *Surviving the Slaughter: The Ordeal of a Rwandan Refugee in Zaire*. Translated by Julie Emerson. Madison: University of Wisconsin Press.

United States Department of State. 2013. *Human Rights Reports—Rwanda*. Washington, DC: United States Department of State. http://allafrica.com/stories/201304231135.html.

Uvin, Peter. 1998. *Aiding Violence: The Development Enterprise in Rwanda*. West Hartford, CT: Kumarian.

———. 2001. "Difficult Choices in the New Post-Conflict Agenda: The International Community in Rwanda after the Genocide." *Third World Quarterly* 22 (2): 177–189.

Vansina, Jan. 2004. *Antecedents to Modern Rwanda: The Nyiginya Kingdom*. Madison: University of Wisconsin Press.

———. 2010. *Being Colonized: The Kuba Experience in Rural Congo, 1880–1960*. Madison: University of Wisconsin Press.

Vásquez, Manuel A., and Marie F. Marquardt. 2000. "Globalizing the Rainbow Madonna: Old Time Religion in the Present Age." *Theory, Culture and Society* 17 (4): 119–143.

Verpoorten, Marijke. 2005. "The Death Toll of the Rwandan Genocide: A Detailed Analysis for Gikongoro Province." *Population* 60 (4): 331–367.

Vlassenroet, Koen. 2013. *South Kivu: Identity, Power, and Territory in Eastern Congo.* London: Rift Valley Institute.

Vincent, Joan. 1982. *Teso in Transformation: The Political Economy of Peasant and Class in Eastern Africa.* Berkeley: University of California Press.

Vinci, Anthony. 2005. "The Strategic Use of Fear by the Lord's Resistance Army." *Small Wars and Insurgencies* 16 (3): 360–381.

von Fremd, Sarah. 1995. "Political Power and Urban Popular Theatre in Uganda." PhD diss., Northwestern University.

Waal, Alex de. 1997. *Famine Crimes: Politics and the Disaster Relief Industry in Africa.* Oxford: James Currey.

Wack, Henry Wellington. 1905. *The Story of the Congo Free State: Social, Political, and Economic Aspects of the Belgian System of Government in Central Africa.* New York: G. P. Putnam's Sons.

Wainaina, Binyavanga. 2005. "How to Write About Africa." *Granta* 92: 91–95.

Waldorf, Lars. 2009. "*Revisiting Hotel Rwanda*: Genocide Ideology, Reconciliation, and Rescuers." *Journal of Genocide Research* 11 (1): 101–125.

Wall, Thomas Carl. 1999. *Radical Passivity: Levinas, Blanchot, and Agamben.* Albany: State University of New York Press.

Wällstrom, Margot. 2011. "Ending Sexual Violence: From Recognition to Action." *New Routes* 16 (2): 49–52.

Watson, Catherine. 1991. *Exile from Rwanda: Background to an Invasion.* Edited by Virginia Hamilton. Washington, DC: U.S. Committee for Refugees.

Werbner, Richard. 2002. "Introduction: Postcolonial Subjectivities: The Personal, the Political and the Moral." In *Postcolonial Subjectivities in Africa*, edited by Werbner, 1–21. London: Zed Books.

Whyte, Susan Reynolds, Sulayman Babiiha, Rebecca Mukyala, and Lotte Meinert. 2014. "Urbanisation by Subtraction: The Afterlife of Camps in Northern Uganda." *Journal of Modern African Studies* 52 (4): 597–622.

Wilén, Nina. 2012. "A Hybrid Peace through Locally Owned and Externally Financed SSR-DDR in Rwanda?" *Third World Quarterly* 33 (7): 1323–1336.

Williams, Paul. 2007. *Memorial Museums: The Global Rush to Commemorate Atrocities.* Oxford: Berg.

Wilson, Richard Ashby, and Richard D. Brown. 2009. Introduction to *Humanitarianism and Suffering: The Mobilization of Empathy*, edited by Richard Ashby Wilson and Richard D. Brown, 1–30. Cambridge: Cambridge University Press.

Žižek, Slavoj. 2005. "Neighbors and Other Monsters: A Plea for Ethical Violence." In *The Neighbor: Three Inquiries in Political Theology*, edited by Slavoj Žižek, Eric L. Santner, and Kenneth Reinhard, 134–190. Chicago: University of Chicago Press.

———. 2008. *Violence: Six Sideways Reflections*. New York: Picador.

Zorbas, Eugenia. 2011."Aid Dependence and Policy Independence: Explaining the Rwandan Paradox." In *Remaking Rwanda: State Building and Human Rights after Mass Violence*, edited by Scott Straus and Lars Waldorf, 103–117. Madison: University of Wisconsin Press.

Index

Page numbers in italics refer to illustrations

abduction, 15, 50, 57, 77n145, 82, 105n31, 217–18; of children, 2, 71n92, 79–80, 84–86, *85*, 93, 102n5, 109n80, 109n84, 109n86, 110n88, 220–21, 224, 225, 228, 253n2, 265n141–42; community acceptance of returning abductees, 108n71, 109n74, 109n79; estimates of, 5, 28n17, 103n6. *See also* Aboke; child soldiers; forced marriage; *Kony 2012*; *War Child: Abducted*
Abia massacre memorial, 248, 261n111, 266n153
Abiti, Nelson, 246, 252–53, 263n129, 267n158
Abok, Lord's Resistance Army attack on, 246, 265n141
Aboke: abduction of schoolgirls in, 106n50, 245–46, 264nn133–34, 265n141. *See also* forced marriage; rape
Acholi, 67n35, 70n77, 77n150, 232, 263nn128–29, 265n145, 267n161; dance, 81, 86, 87, 89, 93, 97–102, 227; Idi Amin regime killing of, 48, 59, 70n75; as internally displaced people, 80, 245, 254n18; language, use of, 89, 105n42, 249; Lord's Resistance Army attacks on, 104n20, 223, 261n111; Museveni regime killing of, 40–51; in Obote's army, 47, 48, 71n81; and Okello coup against Obote, 256n38, 262n117; rape of Acholi men, 50, 298; norms of expression, 105n32; resistance to colonial rule, 42, 68nn37–38. *See also* Aboke; Amin, Idi; Barlonyo massacre; Lukodi massacre; Obote, Milton; Pabbo IDP camp

Adong, Lucy Judith, 17, 33n82, 307n7; *Silent Voices*, 107n55, 298
African Youth Initiative Network (AYINET), 64, 244
Agamben, Giorgio, 37, 287
Alebtong IDP camp (Lira District, Uganda), 222, 223, 248
Alebtong Vocational Training and Rehabilitation Center. *See under* A River Blue
Alliance of Democratic Forces for the Liberation of Congo–Zaire (AFDL), 54–55, 56, 75n134
Allied Democratic Forces (ADF), 76n137, 263n126, 264n133
Altman, Robert E., 91, 107n53, 107n58; *War Child: Abducted*, 91–92, 227
Amin, Idi, 48, 59, 70nn74–75, 70n75, 268n167; film depictions of, 227, 258n58
Amnesty International, 116, 167
anagnorisis, 37, 39, 58–64, 78n174, 264n133
Anderson, Patrick, 38, 306, 307
Anglo-Belgian India Rubber Company (ABIR), 43, 168, 176, 205n39, 207–208n69
Angola, 75n127, 83, 208n79
Ankole-Hima, 48, 70n73
Annan, Jeannie, 14, 28n17, 103n6, 108n71
Annan, Kofi, 117
Anti-Slavery International, 171, 204n32, 205n37, 207n69
Aristotle, 37, 39, 63, 65n10

339

340 | Index

Armed Forces for the Democratic Republic of the Congo (FARDC), 56–57, 76n140
Armed with Resilience: A Photographic Dialogue with Girls Affected by the Conflict in Northern Uganda. See Lenz, Jessica
Armstrong, Rev. W. D., 204n26
Arthur, Joseph, 221–22, 223, 224, 256n41
Arusha trials. *See* International Criminal Tribunal for Rwanda
Asiimwe, Deborah, 18, 33n82, 225, 273, 284, 298; *Forgotten World*, 1–3, 2, 9, 18, 25–26, 26n1, 27n2
Atkinson, Ronald, 42, 67n36
Atiak massacre, 247–48, 266n149; memorial, 239, 241, 243, 267n158; politics of, 249–50, 250–52, 252
Autesserre, Séverine, 47, 68n46, 74n119, 178, 184
Azeda, Hope, 18, 33n82, 295n75, 298; *Rwanda My Hope*, 17

Baaz, Maria Ericksson, 178, 182–83
Badiou, Alain, 24, 270, 285, 286, 307n10
Baganda, 42, 47, 59, 66n23. *See also* Buganda; Ganda.
Baines, Erin, 246–47, 266n148. *See also* Justice and Reconciliation Project
Ban, Ki-Moon, 111, 127
Banyamulenge, 66–67n26, 69–70n69, 76n139, 56, 57
Banyarwanda, 40, 47, 68n46, 69–70n69, 71n84, 74n119, 75nn131–32
Barefoot Workshops, 221–22
Barlonyo massacre, 77n150, 95–96, 109n77, 245, 248, 262n113, 266n156; African Youth Initiative Network memorial, 244, 263n128; mass grave, 246, 262n114, 262n121, 264n135, 267n158; memorial, 71n81, 78n173, 226, 241–42, 251–52, 253, 266n157, 267n165, 268n170, 268n172
Barlonyo Memorial Preservation Association, 242, 244
Belgian Congo, 43–44, 67n30, 167, 175, 196, 208n82. *See also* Congo Free State
Berlant, Lauren, 27n11, 113, 114, 146n20
Bernstine, Quincy Tyler, 190, *198*
Bharucha, Rustom, 287, 295–96n89
Biddle, Pippa, 30–31n59
Bizimungu, Pasteur, 133–34
Blair, Brent, 282–83
Blattman, Christopher, 14, 28n17, 103n6, 126n71, 109n84, 235, 270

Bleasdale, Marcus, 162, *186*, 188, 190, 211n136; *Congo/Women*, 186–87, 189; *The Rape of a Nation*, 185–86, *186*, 211n136. *See also* Enough Project
blood minerals. *See* mining
Boali, photographs of in Congo Reform Association literature, 170, *171*, 202, 205n39, 205–206n44, 206n45
Boitani, Piero, 63–64
Bono, 7, 220
Book of Life, The (Katese), 32n74, 299
Bootsma, Maarten, 228, 235–36, 261n101; *Who Is to Blame?*, 228, 235, 240
Boutros-Ghali, Boutros, 115–16, *117*, 147–48n30
Branch, Adam, 21, 49, 50, 230–31, 232, 238
Brecht, Bertolt, 106n44; *Mother Courage*, 192–93, 200, 201
Breed, Ananda, 114, 147n24
Brockington, Dan, 232, 234, 256n41, 258n66
Brown, Wendy, 60–61, 113
Buganda kingdom, 39, 42, 66n21, 66n23. *See also* Baganda; Ganda
Bunia, DRC, 74n122, 197
Burnet, Jennie, 72n102, 133, 135–36, 147n22, 154n121, 155n133, 156n140, 156–57n148, 157n155
Burundi, 41, 67n29, 69nn57–58, 73n105, 75n128; civil war in, 27–28n16, 52; massacre of Hutu in, 45, 46, 64, 65n12; Tutsi diaspora to, 45, 46
Bush War, 48–49, 59, 64, 268n168. *See also* Museveni, Yoweri; Obote, Milton
Butler, Judith, 113–14, 146n20, 176–77, 209n87, 212n139

Casement, Roger, 167, 203n14, 204n26. *See also* Morel, Dean
Catholic Church, 66n23, 131, *135*, *136*, 151n70, 154n114, 157n155; complicity in the genocide, 132, 133–34, 156n148; and the Kibeho apparitions, 129–32, 154n118, 154n121, 155n123. *See also* Misago, Augustin (Bishop); Mukabutera, Julienne (Sister Maria Kizito); Mukangango, Consolata (Sister Gertrude)
Cause Effect Agency, 229, 258n66
celebrity activism, 7, 14–15, 180, 220, 221, 224–25, 229, 232, 256n41, 258n66; and the celebrity-charity-corporate complex, 234. *See also A River Blue*; Arthur, Joseph; Hope North; Starkey Hearing Foundation; Whitaker, Forest

Index | 341

Central African Republic, 27n16, 180; Lord's Resistance Army in, 17, 57, 62, 77n145, 220, 246, 265n140
Cheah, Pheng, 188, 210n124
child soldiers, 96, 107n52, 238; and the empire of trauma, 3-4, 7, 15, 220, 224-25, 228, 243, 256-57n43, 257n54, 288; playwrights' depictions of, 1-2, 17. *See also* abductees; Adong, Lucy Judith; Asiimwe, Deborah; Dahms, Darin; Ehn, Erik; Gulu Save the Children Organisation; Mulekwa, Charles; Sam, Okello Kelo; Weiss, Soenke; World Vision Children of War Rehabilitation Centre
Children as Peacebuilders, 93, 108n63, 108nn67-68
Chow, Rey, 5, 169
Chrétien, Jean-Pierre, 41, 67n30, 68n43
Christmas massacres, DRC, 57, 76n143, 261-62n111, 265n141
Clinton, Bill, 117-18, 148n44, 149nn45-46
Clowns Without Borders, 269-70, 271, 288-91, 289, 291-92n3, 296n94, 296nn98-100
Cole, Catherine, 247, 251
Cole, Teju, 4, 28-29n35, 105n38, 270, 271. *See also* white savior industrial complex
Comaroff, Jean, 6, 254n14
Comaroff, John, 6, 254n14
compassionate colonialism, 270, 271-76. *See also* Cole, Teju; humanitarianism; white savior industrial complex
conflict minerals. *See* mining
Congo. *See* Belgian Congo; Congo Free State; Democratic Republic of the Congo
Congo Commission of Inquiry (1905), 170, 205n39, 206nn44-45
Congo Balolo Mission (CBM), 167-68, 203n21
Congo Free State, 12, 23, 42-44, 58, 164-77, 165, 178-79, 203n17, 207n59, 207n66, 207n68, 207-208n69; amputation and mutilation as punishment in, 161, 169-70; forced labor in, 67n30, 162, 164, 166, 171-72, 173, 175; campaign against, *see* Congo Reform Association. *See also* Belgian Congo; Harris, Alice; Harris, John; Morel, Edmund Dean
Congo Reform Association, 162, 163, 167-75, 203nn16-17; publications of, 204n26, 204n28, 205nn38-39, 205-206n44, 206nn45-46, 208n76; "The Congo Atrocities: A Lecture," 170, 173, 174, 205n39, 205n44; use of Riley Brothers Ltd., "Lantern Lecture on the Congo Atrocities" slides, 204n28. *See also* Harris, Alice; Harris, John; Morel, Edmund Dean
Congo/Women, 186-87, 189-90, 191, 212nn139-41, 212n144
Conquergood, Dwight, 275, 293n24
Conrad, Joseph, 162, 166
Corbin, Jane, 139, 140. See also *Rwanda's Untold Story*
Critchley, Simon, 285-86, 291, 295n74

Dahms, Darin, 17, 33n77
Dallaire, Roméo, 36, 52, 53, 73n106, 111, 118
dance, 32n74, 110n88, 257n48, 258n58, 284; Acholi, 81, 86, 87, 89, 93, 97-102, 225-26, 227; Langi, 225, 257n48; at memorials, 245-46, 249, 268n170. *See also* Azeda, Hope; Linyekula, Faustin; Nottage, Lynn; A River Blue; Sam, Okello Kelo; Theatre Thot Worldwide
Danielsen, Daniel J., 203n19, 204n26
de Certeau, Michel, 81, 82, 108n62
Democratic Forces for the Liberation of Rwanda (FDLR), 56, 76nn138-39
Democratic Republic of the Congo (DRC), 34n87; Banyamulenge in South Kivu, 56, 57, 66-67n26, 69-70n69, 76n139; breakup of, 28n32; citizenship of, 75n132; founding of, 54-55; inequality in, 29n47. *See also* Belgian Congo; Congo Free State; First Congo War; Second Congo War
derealization, concept of, 177, 209n88
Derrida, Jacques, 285, 295n70
Des Forges, Alison, 52, 53-54, 73n115, 77n161, 132, 146nn13-14, 156n142, 294n56
Dodd-Frank Wall Street Reform and Consumer Protection Act, 181, 184, 211n134
Dolan, Chris, 103n6, 224, 230
Drewal, Margaret, 22, 275
drumming, 98, 109n87, 304
Dunn, Kevin, 12, 207n59
Dyer, Wayne, 123, 124

Egeland, Jan, 79, 102n1, 102n3
Ehn, Erik, 33n82, 223, 226, 257n52-54, 292n20, 293nn34-35, 294n67, 295n75; *dogsbody*, 17, 33n77; *Maria Kizito*, 17, 18, 32n74, 281, 283-84, 286, 291; *More Life*, 24, 31n67, 222, 240, 257n54, 272-74, 276-78, 292nn17-18. See also Hope North
empire, concept of, 30n52, 32n71

Enough Project, 57, 162, 163, 164, 180–82, 184–85, 186, 191, 210n114; partnership with *Congo/Women*, 186–87; promotion of *Ruined* (Nottage), 213n164. *See also* Bleasdale, Marcus; Prendergast, John
Ensler, Eve, 5, 161–62, 164, 178–80, 181–83, 183–84, 209n107, 210n109; article in *Glamour*, 209n104, 211n127; and City of Joy, 180, 182, 183, 189; and V-Day, 179, 161, 179, 181–82, 183, 189, 191
Epondo, photographs of in Congo Reform Association literature, 169, 205n37, 206n47
Ericsson (company), 233–24, 238
ethnography, 274–75, 279, 292n21, 293n45
exceptionalism, narrative of, 15, 37–39, 61, 63. *See also* anagnorisis

Fassin, Didier, 6, 9, 13
Feldman, Allen, 92, 106n44, 194
femicide. *See* Ensler, Eve
Ferguson, James, 10, 27n15, 190, 238
Festa, Lynn, 8, 61, 74n122
First Congo War, 54–55, 74n122
forced labor: colonial, 66n26, 67n30, 67n32, 68n37; precolonial, 41, 54. *See also* Congo Free State; mining
forced marriage, 72n95, 99, 102n5, 109n86, 110n88, 264n133. *See also* rape
Forces Armeés Rwandaises (FAR), 54, 55, 73n114
Forged in Fire. See under Sam, Okello Kelo
Forgotten World. See under Asiimwe, Deborah
Foucault, Michel, 113–14, 153n95
Fox, Ann, 194–95

gacaca justice system, 36, 54
Gahanga, 281–82
Ganda, 42, 47, 66n21, 66n23, 67n29, 67n36. *See also* Baganda; Buganda
genocide credit, 23, 111–17, 134, 140–41, 145n5, 145n8, 145n10, 146nn13–14, 146–47n21, 150n62
Gerber, Tony, 201–202
Gertrude, Sister. *See* Mukangango, Consolata
Gettleman, Jeffrey, 188, 209n107
Gisenyi Acrobats, 288–90, 289, 296nn98–100
Gourevitch, Philip, 124, 139, 147n25, 155n134, 277
Grant, Kevin, 203n20, 204n28, 206n45
Griffin, Chandler, 221–22, 223
Groupov, 19, 32n74; *Rwanda 94*
Guinness, Grattan, 167–68, 171, 203n21
Gulu, Uganda, 4–5, 220, 254n18, 256n38, 261n111, 270; abduction of children from, 71n92, 79–80, 217; Acholi legend about the origins of, 81–82. *See also* Gulu Save the Children Organisation (GUSCO); Gulu Walk; World Vision Children of War Rehabilitation Centre
Gulu Save the Children Organisation (GUSCO), 85, 100, 102n5, 105n43, 110n90, 269
Gulu Walk, 79, 102n4
Guriev, Sergei, 19–20

Habyarimana, Juvenal, 46, 68–69n51, 155n123; assassination of, 36, 52, 73n107, 139
Hall, Katori, 17, 18; *Our Lady of Kibeho*, 32n74, 115, 141–44, *143*, 160nn192–93
Hamitic hypothesis, 40–41, 44, 53, 59, 67n29, 70n73, 78n164
Hardt, Michael, 10–13, 16, 19, 30n52, 32n71, 33n85, 83, 163
Harris, Alice, 168–69, 203n25, 204n28, 204n33, 205n36, 206n45, 206n51; *Enslaved Womanhood of the Congo: An Appeal to British Women*, 174, 206n51; photo of Nsala, 175–77, *176*, 208n83. *See also* Congo Reform Association
Harris, John, 168, 206nn44–45, 207n66, 208n83. *See also* Congo Reform Association
Harrow, Kenneth W., 37, 63
Haviv, Ron, 187, 190
Hearn, Alison, 223–24, 224–25
Heidegger, Martin, 16, 32n70
Hema, conflict with Lendu, 78n164, 197
Het Waterhuis, *The Aboke Girls*, 106–107n50
HIV/AIDS, 151n67, 179; performances about, 87–88, 217
Hoffman, Danny, 83, 104n24
Holocaust, the, 58, 67n34, 107n59. *See also* Shoah, the
Holy Spirit Movement, 49–50
Hope North, 14, 15, 221, 226–41, 258n58, 258nn62–64, 259n70, 261n101, 272n74, 280, 287; flash mob, 235–38, *237*; Lalela Arts Centre, 226, 227–28, 231, 258n59. *See also* Sam, Okello Kelo; Whitaker, Forest
Hopwood, Julian, 247–48. *See also* Justice and Reconciliation Project
hospitality, concept of, 283–85, 295n70
humanitarian aid, 6, 59, 83, 105n27, 105n30, 122, 213n158, 223, 230, 263n131. *See also* Ensler, Eve; genocide credit; Nottage, Lynn; white savior industrial complex
Human Rights Watch, 61, 77n161, 197, 266n148

Hunt, Nancy Rose, 164, 168, 169, 171, 189
Hutu: Burundian, 46, 52; Congolese, 55, 74n119; genocides by, 65nn11–12, 73n106, 73n108, 73n115; genocides of, 65nn11–12, 286–87; and Hamitic hypothesis, 40–41, 44, 53, 59, 67n29, 70n73, 78n164
Hutu Power, 51, 52
Hyndman, Jennifer, 8, 270

Ilibagiza, Immaculée, 24, 53, 114–15, 137–39, 144, 152n83, 153n95, 153n99, 154n111; *The Boy Who Met Jesus: Segatashya of Kibeho*, 158n63; *If Only We Had Listened* (book), 138, 158n168; *If Only We Had Listened* (documentary), 138–39, 155n127, 155n133, 158n160; *Led by Faith: Rising from the Ashes of the Rwandan Genocide*, 124, 127, 138, 153n97; *Left to Tell: How I Found God amidst the Rwandan Holocaust*, 23, 114, 123–24, 125–26, 127; and Marian apparitions of Kibeho, 129–32; *Our Lady of Kibeho: Mary Speaks to the World from the Heart of Africa*, 128, 131–32, 137–38, 154n121, 155n122, 155n127, 158n165, 158n167; and the politics of love, 123–29, *129*; *The Rosary: The Prayer That Saved My Life*, 128
Impongi, photographs of in Congo Reform Association literature, 169–70, 173, 205n39, 205–206n44
Interahamwe, 52, 55, 133
Interdisciplinary Genocide Studies Center, 18, 276, 278, 286, 293n29, 295n85
internally displaced people (IDP), 105n27, 222, 223, 227, 230, 245; attacks on IDP camps, 104n20, 254–55n18, 265n141; northern Ugandans, 51, 59, 80, 255n27; plays' depictions of, 87, 88, 93, 218. *See also* Barlonyo massacre; Kibeho; Lukodi massacre; Pabbo IDP camp
International Criminal Court (ICC), 62, 76n141, 246, 265nn140–42, 266n148, 267n161
International Criminal Tribunal for Rwanda, 115, 147n25
International Institute for Peace. *See under* Whitaker, Forest
International Rescue Committee (IRC), 177–78, 209n91
Invisible Children, 3–4, 13, 57, 102–103n5; *Invisible Children: Rough Cut*, 3, 79, 102n4; *Kony 2012*, 4, 13, 28–29n35, 219–20, 220–21
Invisible Children: Rough Cut. *See under* Invisible Children

Irakiza, Jonathan, 290, 296n98. *See also* Gisenyi Acrobats
Isekausu (Isekansu), photographs of in Congo Reform Association literature, 169, 205n39
Isingiro, 244, 263n126

Jackson, Michael, "They Don't Care about Us," track for Theatre Thot Worldwide flash mob, 236, 237–38, 260–61n99, 261n100
Jacobsen, Óli, 204n26, 206n47
James, Erica Caple, 12–13, 30n56
Jolie, Angelina, 7, 180
journalism: repression of, 11, 29n46
Justice and Reconciliation Project, 71n81, 247, 249, 250, 252, 266n148

Kabila, Joseph, 19, 34n87, 55, 56, 59, 74n122
Kabila, Laurent-Désiré, 19, 54–55, 162, 308n15
Kagame, Jeannette, 114
Kagame, Paul, 11, 19, 20, 34n87, 40, 46, 138; alliance with Museveni, 49, 50, 58–59, 74n122, 75n129; documentary film depictions of, 139–40; genocide commemoration speech, 112, 145n8; and the politics of shame, 112, 114, 115–22, 147n25, 150n60; and Rick Warren, 120–22, *121*, 127, 128, 151nn66–68, 151n70; and Rwandan Patriotic Front, 50, 72n99; speeches of, 149n54, 150n60
Kakwa, 68n38
Kaldor, Mary, 82, 104n17
Kalisa, Chantal, 278, 293n37
Kamagaju, Agnes, 130, 155n127, 155n133
Karegeye, Jean-Pierre, 18, 31n67, 276, 277, 284, 286. *See also* Ehn, Erik: *More Life*
Kasozi, Abdu, 48, 70n75
Katese, Odile Gakire, 298; *The Book of Life*, 32n74, 299; *Ngwino Ubeho (Come and Be Alive)*, 32n74
Kayibanda, Grégoire, 45, 46
Kayiranga, Jean-François, 155n136
Kibeho: Assumption Day celebration, 157n153; church, 155n134; IDP camp in, 132, 156n138, 157n157; 1994 genocide, 135, *136*; 1995 genocide, 136–37, 156nn139–40, 157n150, 157n157; Marian apparitions of, 129–34, 135
Kibuye, 123, 132, 152n86, 153n87
Kigali Memorial Centre, 35–36, 37, 40, 53, 58, 61, 64–65n1, 243
Kivu, 44, 54, 55, 56, 68n46, 69n69, 75n131, 76n139; North Kivu, massacres in, 74n119, 76n141

Komakech, Sunday, 238–41, 239, 259n80, 261n100, 261n106
Kony, Joseph, 28–29n35, 77n146, 82, 97, 104n20, 218, 264n133; International Criminal Court investigation of, 62; and origins of Lord's Resistance Army, 49, 50, 71n92; spiritual powers of, 80. *See also* Invisible Children: *Kony 2012*; Lord's Resistance Army
Kony 2012. *See under* Invisible Children
Kuftinec, Sonja Arsham, 272, 274

Lakwena, Alice, 49–50
Lalela Arts Centre, 226, 227–28, 231, 258n59
Langi, 42, 68n38, 70n77, 77n150, 232, 256n38, 262n117; dance, 225, 257n48; killing of, by Idi Amin regime, 48, 59, 70n75; Lord's Resistance Army attacks on, 105n31, 223, 245, 261n111; in Obote's army and civil service, 47, 71n81. *See also* Amin, Idi; Barlonyo massacre; Lukodi massacre; Obote, Milton; Pabbo IDP camp
Last King of Scotland, The (film), 227, 231, 258n58
Le Cargo (Linyekula), 299, 300–307, *301*, 307–308n12, 308n14, 308nn16–17
Lemarchand, René, 16, 38, 46, 47, 51, 55, 56, 65n12, 69n57, 70n71
Lendu, conflict with Hema, 78n164, 197
Lenz, Jessica, 87, 96–97, 105n37, 108n71, 109n79–80, 109n84, 110n88
Leopold (King), 12, 23, 42–43, 66n19, 161, 164–67, *165*, 172, 182, 203n16, 203n20, 207n59; as depicted by Mark Twain in *King Leopold's Soliloquy*, 168, 171, 208n74; relinquishes control over Congo Free State to Belgian parliament, 43, 162, 163, 167, 175. *See also* Congo Free State
Levi, Primo, 293n34
Lévinas, Emmanuel, 24, 278–79, 285–86, 293n38, 295n74
Leys, Ruth (*From Guilt to Shame*), 116–17
Linden, Sonja, 17, 32n74
Linyekula, Faustin, 64, 297, 298, 307n2, 308n15, 308n21, 308n23; *Le Cargo*, 299, 300–307, *301*, 307–308n12, 308n14, 308nn16–17; *more more more ... future*, 298, 308n16; Studios Kabako, 297–98
living memorials, 253, 264n136, 268n170, 268n172
Lokota, photographs of in Congo Reform Association literature, 169, 205n37, 205n39, 206n47
Lomboto, photographs of in Congo Reform Association literature, 169, 205n39
Longman, Timothy, 131, 156n148
Lord's Resistance Army (LRA), 14, 23, 68n38, 77n146, 83, 103n12, 104n20, 223, 225–26, 254–55n18, 292n16; amnesty to former LRA combatants, 94; documentary film representations of, 3–4, 13, 27n13, 28–29n35, 79, 91, 102n4, 219–20, 220–21; massacres by, 57–58, 64, 71n81, 76n143, 241–53, 252, 261n111, 262n113–14, 263n131, 264nn132–33, 266n149, 266n156, 267n158; number of combatants, 77n145; origins and aims of, 49, 50–51, 59, 71n92, 104nn24–25, 256n38; performance about, 99–100, 298–99; playwrights' representations of, 1, 2, 17–18, 25, 27n2, 90–91, 94, 103n13, 253n1, 298; and rape, 72n95, 98–99; Sudanese support for, 72n93, 107n52, 261n111, 300. *See also* abductions; Barlonyo massacre; child soldiers; forced marriage; Kony, Joseph; Museveni, Yoweri
Loyo Loyo theatre company. *See* Who Is to Blame?
Lukodi massacre, 246–47, 263n131, 265n141; memorial, 241, 245, 249, 250, 267n158, 267n161
Lumumba, Patrice, 69n69, 162
Luwero Triangle. *See under* Uganda

Madi, 68n38, 261n111
Makeli, Dominique, 133, 138, 156n143
Makombo massacre, 57, 76n143, 261–62n111, 265n141
Mam, Somaly, 30–31n59
Mamdani, Mahmood, 49, 51, 60, 67n29, 74n120
Mao, Norbert, 249, 251, 252
Maria Kizito, Sister. *See* Mukabutera, Julienne
Maria Kizito (play). *See under* Ehn, Erik
Mbembe, Achille, 29n35, 30n56, 298; *Sortir de la grande nuit: Essai sur l'Afrique décolonisée*, 302–303, 306, 308n26
McMillan, Nesam, 116, 117
MDD (music, dance, and drama), 18, 86, 94, 97–98, 221, 223, 228, 231
Médecins Sans Frontières, 83
Menon, Jisha, 38
migration, 66–67n26. *See also* internally displaced people; refugees
Mindfulness Without Borders, 240, 261n109
mining, 23, 75n128, 162, 163, 164, 177, 183–84, 212n149, 214n189, 299; and gender, 211n128

Misago, Augustin (Bishop), 155n128, 158n165; and the Kibeho apparitions, 131, 134, 158n163, 158n167; complicity in the genocide, 133–34, 138, 156n145, 156–57n148, 157n150
Mobutu Sese Seko, 47, 54–55, 56, 69n69, 74n119, 74n123, 162, 300
More Life program. *See under* Ehn, Erik
Morel, Edmund Dean, 167–68, 171–75, 203nn16–17, 205n44, 206n49, 207n53; *Affairs of West Africa*, 173–74, 207n67; *King Leopold's Rule in Africa*, 172, 173, 207n59; *The Tragedy of the Congo*, 172; *West African Mail*, 171. *See also* Harris, Alice; Harris, John
more more more . . . future (Linyekula), 298, 308n16
Mozambique, 27n16, 82, 83, 84, 104n19
M23 rebellion, 17, 57, 75n134, 75n137, 76n141–42, 140, 146n16; Rwandan support of, 113
Mukabutera, Julienne (Sister Maria Kizito), 155n136, 281, 294n56, 294n58. *See also* Ehn, Erik: *Maria Kizito*
Mukamazimpaka, Anathalie, 130, 133, 137; depiction of in Katori Hall, *Our Lady of Kibeho*, 142–43, *143*
Mukamurenzi, Stéphanie, 130, 137–38, 155n133
Mukangango, Consolata (Sister Gertrude), 155n136, 281, 294n56, 294n58. *See also* Ehn, Erik: *Maria Kizito*
Mukangango, Marie-Claire, 130, 137, 138, 155n133, 158n158; depiction of in Katori Hall, *Our Lady of Kibeho*, 142–43, *143*
Mukwege, Denis, 179–80, 209n105
Mulekwa, Charles, 18, 33n82; *Time of Fire*, 17, 33n77
Mumereke, Alphonsine, 130, 131; depiction of in Katori Hall, *Our Lady of Kibeho*, 142–43, *143*
Munyeshyaka, Wenceslas, 155n136
Murambi massacre, 52, 136, 157n156, 280–81, 293n53
Museveni, Yoweri, 11, 19, 34n87, 55, 71n81, 72n100, 241, 242–43, 249, 251; alliance with Kagame, 58–59, 74n122, 75n129; and the National Resistance Movement, 48–51, 71n91, 228; playwrights' depictions of, 107n55; relations with the United States, 58, 103n12. *See also* Lord's Resistance Army
Mutesa, Edward, 47

National Congress for the Defense of the People (CNDP), 75n134, 116

National Resistance Movement/Army (NRM/A), 48–50, 59, 71n79, 249; atrocities committed by, 49, 50, 59; 71n91; renamed Uganda People's Defence Force (UPDF), 50–51, 80, 85. *See also* Bush War; Museveni, Yoweri
National University of Rwanda, 123, 282, 284
Ndadaye, Melchior, 52
Ndaliko, Chérie Rivers, 29n40, 30n52, 260n98
negationism and genocide denial, discourse of, 61–62, 141, 152n83
Negri, Antonio, 10–13, 16, 19, 30n52, 32n71, 33n85, 83, 163
Newbury, Catharine, 29–30n47, 41, 67n32
Newbury, David, 44, 66n19, 66n22, 66–67n26, 69n55, 69n58, 287; idea of "convergent catastrophes," 17, 32n73, 56
Ngwino Ubeho (Come and Be Alive) (Katese), 32n74
Nietzsche, Friedrich, 60
Nkunda, Laurent, 76n141, 116
Nkurikiye, Eduoard, 155n136
Nkurunziza, Pierre, 27n16
non-governmental organizations, 5, 7, 9, 12, 81, 87, 89, 230; and cultural and arts-based interventions, 105n30, 235, 260n98; and memorials, 243, 244, 249, 250, 255n27; and the Rwandan genocide, 52, 147n30. *See also* A River Blue; Children as Peacebuilders; Clowns Without Borders; Ensler, Eve; Hope North; Interdisciplinary Genocide Studies Center; Invisible Children; Justice and Reconciliation Project; UNICEF; World Food Programme; World Vision
Nordstrom, Carolyn, 4, 82, 84, 88–89, 101–102, 104n19, 106n44, 164
Nottage, Lynn, 18, 284; *Ruined*, 17, 18–19, 33n79, 62, 78n164, 190–202, *198*, 214n181, 214n189, 215n221, 297, 298
Nyiginya dynasty, 40, 66n23, 67n26
Nyiramukiza, Valentine, 130, 131–32, 137, 138, 155n127

Obote, Milton, 47–49, 59, 70n74–76, 92, 107n56; Okello coup against, 48–49, 59, 70n77, 256n38, 262n117
Ocen, Laurence, 242, 262n116, 266n156
Ocen, Victor, 64. *See also* African Youth Initiative Network (AYINET)
Odek IDP camp, Lord's Resistance Army attack on, 104n20, 246, 265n141
Ogwang, Moses, 242, 244, 253, 264n135

Okello, Tito, coup against Obote, 48–49, 59, 70n77, 256n38, 262n117
Olara-Okello, Bazilio, coup against Obote, 48, 70n77
Onek, Hilary, 249, 251
Ong, Aihwa, 30n52
Ongom, Okweny George, 222–23, 224, 225–26, 242, 248, 258n55, 262n117
Ongwen, Dominic, 246–47, 265nn140–42, 265n145, 267n161
Operation Turquoise, 53–54, 123–24, 126, 153n87
Otim, Michael, 266n148. *See also* Justice and Reconciliation Project
Otim, Orach, 246, 264n134
Otti, Vincent, 247–48
Our Lady of Kibeho: Mary Speaks to the World from the Heart of Africa (book). *See under* Ilibagiza, Immaculée
Our Lady of Kibeho (Hall), 32n74, 115, 141–44, *143*, 160nn192–93

Pabbo IDP camp, 238, 245, 246; memorial site, 261n107, 264n136, 268n170; Lord's Resistance Army raids on, 264n132
Pajule, Lord's Resistance Army attack on, 246, 258n56, 265n141
Pandolfi, Mariella, 7, 28n25
Parker, Mary Louise, 221, 229
Party of the Movement for Hutu Emancipation (PARMEHUTU), 68–69n51
Pavlakis, Dean, 203n16, 204nn27–28
PeaceEarth. *See under* Whitaker, Forest
peacekeepers, 57, 75n137, 197; MONUSCO, 76n140; UNAMIR, 36, 52–53, 57, 73n112, 73n115
photography. *See* Bleasdale, Marcus; *Congo/Women*; Gerber, Tony; Harris, Alice; Harris, John; Lenz, Jessica
Pier, David, 219
Pongdwongo school abduction, 217, 253n2
Ponte, Stefano, 7, 8
Pottier, Johan, 115, 133, 148n31
Power, Samantha, 35, 65n4, 124, 277
Prendergast, John, 162, 180–82, 190, 191, 210n114. *See also* Enough Project
Prodigal Son parable, 94–95, 96, 108nn70–71, 109n74
Prunier, Gérard, 16, 45, 50, 72n99, 145n5, 156n139

radical passivity, 276–83, 285, 293n38
Radio Télévision Libre des Mille Collines (RTLM), 53, 73n110, 156n142

Radley, Ben, 211n134, 212n149
Rally for Congolese Democracy (RCD), 55, 56, 74n126, 75n129
rape, 50, 51, 72n95, 76n141, 98–99, 164; of men, 50, 190, 212–13n158, 298; in narratives of suffering and the empire of trauma, 5, 6, 9, 12, 15, 23, 47, 163, 164, 174, 178–85, 189, 209n105, 210n124; playwrights' representations of, 125, 126, 142, 161, 192–202, 213n164, 298; and statistics of sexual violence, 5, 28n17, 211n131. *See also* Ensler, Eve; forced marriage; Nottage, Lynn: *Ruined*
Rashad, Condola, *198*, 214
Rechtman, Richard, 6, 9
refugees, 55, 65n11, 66–67n26, 69n60, 74n120, 124; genocidaires hiding among, 16, 54, 117, 147n25. *See also* Banyarwanda
Reporters Without Borders, 133, 156n143
Reyntjens, Filip, 23, 27n16, 65n11, 74n120, 74n122, 116; concept of "genocide credit," 111, 112, 113, 141, 145n5, 150n62
Richey, Lisa Ann, 7, 8
River Blue, A, 189, 221–26, 255n27, 255n32, 256n41, 257n43, 257n54, 258n55; Alebtong Vocational Training and Rehabilitation Center, 222–23, 255nn31–32
Road to Reconciliation. *See* Uganda Museum memorial project
Rodríguez, Dylan, 38–39
Rogers, J. T. (*The Overwhelming*), 17, 32n74
Ross, Amy, 62–63
Rothberg, Michael, 59, 107n59
rubber, 208n79, 203n17, 207nn66–69; "red rubber," 43, 161, 162, 163, 164–77, *165*, *176*
Ruined (Nottage), 17, 18–19, 33n79, 62, 78n164, 190–202, *198*, 214n181, 214n189, 215n221, 297, 298
Rwabugiri, Kigeri, 41, 68n50
Rwanda, 34n87; aid to, 145n10, 146nn14–16, 146n21; Belgian rule of, 67n30; genocide, statistics of, 5, 28n17, 65n11; inequality in, 29n47. *See also* Banyarwanda; Kibeho massacre; Rwandan Patriotic Front
Rwanda Information Office (ORINFOR), 154–55n121
Rwandan Patriotic Front (RPF), 61, 73n114, 74n119; alliance with Museveni, 59; atrocities, 51–52, 55, 63, 65n11, 72n102, 74n118, 74n125, 115, 132–33, 140; disinformation campaign, 145n6; and genocide credit, 111, 112, 113, 116, 141, 148n31, 150n62, 295n85; invasion of

northern Rwanda, 36, 51, 56; origins of, 36, 50, 51, 72nn98–99; and Rwandan refugees, 47–48, 54, 72n100, 308n15; signing of Arusha Accords, 52; and UNAMIR, 73n115. *See also* Banyarwanda; Hall, Katori, *Our Lady of Kibeho*; Ilibagiza, Immaculée; Kagame, Paul; United Nations Assistance Mission for Rwanda (UNAMIR)
Rwanda's Untold Story, 115, 139–41, 158n172
Rwema, Bisengimana, 47, 69n67
Rwigyema, Fred, 50, 72n99

Sachs, Albie, 251, 253, 268n170
Salima, Vestine, 130
Sam, Godfrey Omony, 217, 254n2
Sam, Okello Kelo, 14, 17, 18, 33n82, 81, 254n2, 258n63; *Forged in Fire*, 103n13, 104n15, 217–18, *218*, 228, 229, 253n1; and Hope North, 227–28, 240, 258n67, 259nn68–69, 272–73; involvement in Robert Altman film *War Child: Abducted*, 92, 107nn56–58
Savimbi, Jonas, 2
Schechner, Richard, 271, 291n2
Seay, Laura, 184, 288
Second Congo War, 55–56, 74n122, 75n127, 75n129
Segatashya, Emmanuel, 154n115, 155n133, 158n163, 130
Shoah, the, 59, 73n105, 293n34. *See also* Holocaust, the
Sierra Leone, 2, 83
Silent Voices (Adong), 107n55, 298
Sista Hailstorm, 284, 292n20
Somalia, 83, 180
South Africa, 75n127, 260n91; Truth and Reconciliation Commission, 247, 251
South Sudan, 27n13, 50, 57, 72n93, 96, 99, 107n52, 181, 233; Lord's Resistance Army camps in, 109n84, 110n88, 300; Lord's Resistance Army massacres in, 261n111
Sovu, 281, 294n56, 294n58. *See also* Ehn, Erik: *Maria Kizito*
Speelman, Liesbeth, 86, 93
Spivak, Gayatri Chakravorty, 33n83, 178
Sriram, Chandra Lekha, 62–63
Stam, Allan, 140–41. *See also* negationism and genocide denial, discourse of
Stanley, Henry Morton, 172, 174
Starkey Hearing Foundation, 230, 231, 259nn72–73, 259n80
Stearns, Jason, 28n32, 55, 68n46, 74n120, 75n137, 76nn139–40, 112, 146n16, 164

Stern, Maria, 178, 182–83
Straus, Scott, 25, 44–45, 73n108
Sudan, 28n16, 75n127, 83, 233; government support for Lord's Resistance Army, 50, 72n93, 107n52, 261n111, 300; Lord's Resistance Army in, 50, 62, 96, 99, 109n84, 110n88, 220–21; sexual violence in, 181, 192, 210n116
Sword, Leslie Lewis, *Miracle in Rwanda*, 127

Tandberg, Elen-Marie Meggison, 263nn129–30
Tanzania, 4, 16, 28n16, 75n127, 296n96; indigenous theatre in, 108–109n72; military involvement in Uganda, 48, 263n126; refugees in, 45, 69n60, 70n74, 74n120
Taussig, Michael, 20, 26, 86, 90, 106n44, 194
ter Haar, Gerrie, 131, 137
terror-warfare, 80, 81, 82–83, 84, 103n12, 106n44
Teso, 67n35, 68n38, 261n111, 262n113, 266n156
theatre activism, 24, 108n69, 291n2, 292n21; and compassionate colonialism, 271–76; and precarious hospitality, 283–91; and radical passivity, 276–83, 285, 293n38
Theatre of the Oppressed, 282–83
Theatre Thot Worldwide, 228; flash mob, 235–38, *237*
Thompson, James, 14, 271, 291n2
Titeca, Kristof, 57, 77n146
tourism, 157n153, 218–19, 266n155; "dark tourism," 243–46, 262n120
Treisman, Daniel, 19–20
Tsing, Anna, 296n89
Tutsi; Burundian, 124; Congolese, 47, 56, 58, 74n119, 75n134, 75n137; genocides by, 65n12; genocides of, 6, 65nn11–12, 73n106, 73n108, 73n115; and Hamitic hypothesis, 40–41, 44, 53, 59, 67n29, 70n73, 78n164
Twa, 36, 40, 41, 53, 74n118; genocides of, 65n11
Twagiramungu, Faustin, 148n3, 158n172
Twain, Mark, *King Leopold's Soliloquy*, 168, 170, 171, 208n74

Uganda, 33n86, 34n87; Acholi resistance to British rule of, 68n37; British rule of, 67n30; Bush War, 48, 59, 64; Luwero Triangle, 48, 59, 71n79, 71n81, 268n168; postconflict stability, 255nn18–19, 255n24; poverty in, 30n47. *See also* Kony, Joseph; Lord's Resistance Army; Obote, Milton; National Resistance Movement/Army; Uganda National Liberation Army; Uganda People's Democratic Army

Uganda Museum memorial project, 244–45, 246, 247, 252–53, 262n121, 263nn129–30, 268n170
Uganda National Liberation Army, 48–49, 228; massacres by, 48. *See also* Obote, Milton
Uganda People's Democratic Army, 49, 50. *See also* Kony, Joseph
Uganda People's Defence Force. *See under* National Resistance Movement/Army
Umutesi, Marie Béatrice (*Surviving the Slaughter: The Ordeal of a Rwandan Refugee in Zaire*), 55, 63–64, 308n15
UN Group of Experts, 57, 121
UNICEF, 83–84, 89
United Nations, 61; criticism of Rwanda, 116; failure to intervene during the genocide, 116, 153n97. *See also* Dallaire, Roméo; peacekeepers; United Nations Assistance Mission for Rwanda (UNAMIR); United Nations Organization Stabilization Mission in the Democratic Republic of the Congo
United Nations Assistance Mission for Rwanda (UNAMIR), 36, 52, 53, 57, 73n112, 73n115, 111
United Nations Educational, Scientific and Cultural Organization (UNESCO), 233, 234, 259n81
United Nations High Commissioner for Refugees (UNHCR), 231, 254n18
United Nations Organization Stabilization Mission in the Democratic Republic of the Congo (MONUC, later MONUSCO), 76n140
Uvin, Peter, 45, 145n5

Vansina, Jan, 41, 43, 67n34
V-Day, 179, 161, 179, 181–82, 183, 189, 191, 210n114. *See also* Ensler, Eve
Verhofstadt, Guy, 117, 148n42
Vogel, Cristoph, 75n137, 211n134, 212n149

Wall, Thomas Carl, 278–79, 280
War Child: Abducted (film), 91–92, 227

Warren, Rick, 120–22, *121*, 127, 128, 151nn66–68, 151n70; *The Purpose-Driven Life*, 120
Weidman-Grunewald, Elaine, 233–34
Weiss, Soenke (*Butterflies of Uganda*), 17, 33n77
West Nile, 48, 59, 268n167
Whitaker, Forest, 221, 229, 259n81; International Institute for Peace, 232; *The Last King of Scotland*, 227, 231, 258n58; PeaceEarth, 232, 233, 234, 238, 260n91, 260n95
white savior industrial complex, 4, 21, 88, 105n38, 270–72, 290. *See also* celebrity activism; Cole, Teju; compassionate colonialism; Ensler, Eve; humanitarian aid; Prendergast, John; Warren, Rick
Who Is to Blame? (Bootsma), 228, 235, 240
World Food Programme, 83, 89, 231
World Vision, 23, 80, 83
World Vision Children of War Rehabilitation Centre, Gulu, Uganda, 79–80, 81, 83–84, 96–100, 102n5, 103n8, 103n12; children's paintings displayed at, 79, 84–85, 101, 103n7, 110n92; director Susan Alal, 103n7, 238; music, dance and drama (MDD) at, 85–89, 93, 94–95; operating budget of, 104–5n27

Yoka, photographs of in Congo Reform Association literature, 169, 205n37

Zaire, 17, 47, 56, 74n119; Alliance of Democratic Forces for the Liberation of Congo-Zaire (AFDL), 54–55, 56, 75n134; Hutu genocidaires in, 16, 53, 54; Hutu refugees in, 53, 54, 55, 124, 153n97; renamed Democratic Republic of the Congo, 55; RPF war crimes in, 54. *See also* Democratic Republic of the Congo
Žižek, Slavoj, 8–9, 20–21, 177, 279–80, 282, 285, 305
Zorbas, Eugenia, 112, 115, 145n10, 146n21

LAURA EDMONDSON is Associate Professor in the Department of Theater at Dartmouth College, where she is also affiliated with African and African American Studies. She is author of *Performance and Politics in Tanzania: The Nation on Stage* (Indiana University Press, 2007).